Working the Past

Working the Past

Narrative and Institutional Memory

Charlotte Linde

OXFORD
UNIVERSITY PRESS

2009

OXFORD
UNIVERSITY PRESS

Oxford University Press, Inc., publishes works that further
Oxford University's objective of excellence
in research, scholarship, and education.

Oxford   New York
Auckland   Cape Town   Dar es Salaam   Hong Kong   Karachi
Kuala Lumpur   Madrid   Melbourne   Mexico City   Nairobi
New Delhi   Shanghai   Taipei   Toronto

With offices in
Argentina   Austria   Brazil   Chile   Czech Republic   France   Greece
Guatemala   Hungary   Italy   Japan   Poland   Portugal   Singapore
South Korea   Switzerland   Thailand   Turkey   Ukraine   Vietnam

Published by Oxford University Press, Inc.
198 Madison Avenue, New York, New York 10016

www.oup.com

Oxford is a registered trademark of Oxford University Press

Library of Congress Cataloging-in-Publication Data
Linde, Charlotte.
Working the past : narrative and institutional memory / Charlotte Linde.
   p.   cm.
Includes bibliographical references and index.
ISBN 978-0-19-514028-6; 978-0-19-514029-3 (pbk.)
1. Communication in organizations—Case studies.   2. Corporate culture—Case studies.   3. Corporate
image—Case studies.   4. Knowledge management—Case studies.   I. Title.
HD30.3.L545 2009
658.4'038—dc22   2008009680

9 8 7 6 5 4 3 2 1
Printed in the United States of America
on acid-free paper

In loving memory:

Alfred Linde: 1912–1991

Ruth Mandel Linde: 1915–2001

Nancy Linde: 1949–2001

ACKNOWLEDGMENTS

It is a pleasure as well as an obligation, in a work on memory, to remember all those who have helped me through the long period of exploration, analysis, and writing.

My primary debt is to MidWest Insurance for commissioning the study from which this work springs, and to all the members of MidWest Insurance whose generosity with their time and enthusiasm for explaining their company have made this work surprising, exciting, and delightful. I hope that I have to some small extent repaid them by producing a portrait of insurance sales and sales agents that conveys the respect I have come to have for them.

I would like to thank Christopher Darrouzet, who was my invaluable colleague and comanager, throughout the entire life of the MidWest project. I am also grateful to my other collaborators on the fieldwork of the project: Libby Bishop, Renee Chin, David Fearon, Maurene Flory, Joe Harding, Nancy Lawrence, Judit Moschkovich, Charline Poirier, and Cheryl Lynn Sullivan.

The analysis would have been impossible without comments, suggestions, and criticisms from my colleagues Susan Anderson, Michael Bamberg, Geoffrey Bowker, Bill Clancey, Penny Eckert, Linda Georgianna, Shelley Goldman, Meg Graham, James Greeno, Jo-anne Kleifgen, Elizabeth Krainer, Ray McDermott, Norma Mendoza-Denton, Sigrid Mueller, Ida Obermann, Livia Polanyi, Leigh Star, Etienne Wenger, Geoffrey White, and Ruth Wodak. I owe a lifetime debt to William Labov for introducing me to the study of narrative.

My friend Robin Kornman was my intellectual companion and conversation partner through almost all of this project; he died less than a year before its completion.

In the text, I have cited his work on the theory of epic and the Tibetan national epic, but his influence pervades the entire study.

Libby Bishop and Naomi Quinn kindly provided thoughtful comments on the entire manuscript, which were invaluable in helping me to move from a heap of chapters to an actual book.

The Institute for Research on Learning, and later, the NASA Ames Research Center, provided an intellectual home for me. Both have offered me the opportunity to pursue my questions where they led me and have provided colleagues in many disciplines who asked questions and suggested directions that I would never have thought of alone.

As always, I am grateful to my husband, Brent Powers, for his unfailing enthusiasm, support, and love.

CONTENTS

1 Introduction: How Institutions Remember   3

2 Data for the Study: The MidWest Insurance Company   15

3 Occasions for Institutional Remembering   44

4 Retold Tales: Repeated Narratives as a Resource
for Institutional Remembering   72

5 Multiple Versions of MidWest's History   89

6 Three Versions of One Story: A Comparison   123

7 Paradigmatic Narratives: Exemplary Narratives of Everyman   141

8 Narrative and Intertextuality: Telling One's Own Story
within a Textual Community   167

9 Noisy Silences: Stories Not Told   196

10 Working the Past: Identity and Memory   221

Notes   225

References   227

Index   235

Working the Past

Introduction

How Institutions Remember

What this book is about

I want to tell you a story about how institutions work their pasts: specifically how institutions and their members use narrative to remember. And in remembering, how they work and rework, present and represent the past for the purposes of the present and the projection of a future. Individuals and groups may have a variety of purposes for recalling and representing the past. These include using the past to establish legitimacy of authority, to claim ownership, to claim political or intellectual priority, to establish stability, to indicate the working out of divine purpose in history, to compare the past with the present to show that things are getting either better or worse. All of these are ways of working the past: invoking and retelling parts of the past for present purposes. In the case study that forms the center of this book, a large insurance company works its past in order to construct a stable narrative of identity, that is, to show that who We are and how We are is consistent with how We have always been.

And why should you care? As careful studies of narrative have shown us, the basic challenge for any storyteller is to avoid the challenge "So what?" (Labov 1972). Perhaps I could scheherazade you into listening, using sheer charm of narration. A narrative challenge indeed, for a story whose protagonist is an insurance company, but possible. Yet there are good reasons why the use of narratives in institutions is important to understand beyond the single story told here.

Narration is one very important way that institutions construct their presentation of who they are and what they have done in the past, and they use these pasts in the present as an attempt to shape their future. Narrative works to establish identity, that is, to answer the question "Who are We?" Narrative is also the link between the way an institution represents its past, and the ways its members use, alter, or contest that past, in order to understand the institution as a whole as well as their own place within or apart from that institution.

Therefore, this book concentrates on the ways in which institutions use narrative in their practices of remembering. There is a range of resources for remembering that institutions use, some of them semiotic or symbolic and others not. Even within the range of semiotic memory resources, narrative is central to transmission of the past. That is, a memorial statue or an annual commemorative ceremony are two of the many symbolic representations of the past (discussed in greater detail in chapter 3).

However, a memorial statue, for example, functions at its fullest only if individuals know and tell the stories about who the man on the horse is and why we should care about him now. And these stories will only be told if there are appropriate occasions for their telling. This work thus looks at the story stock of an institution as well as the occasions for telling and the ways in which the members of an institution tell the stories in this stock of stories. It examines the relations between the stories in an institution, the ways the narrator of a story refers to, and is shaped by, previous tellings. It also looks at how people tell their own stories within an institution, to reveal the small links and minute traces between individual stories and stories of the institution that indicate how people are inducted into institutional membership and, as part of this, learn to shape their stories to harmonize with the events and values of the main institutional narratives.

Let me begin with a metastory about why I care about these issues and what my prejudices in it might be. I came to the question of narrative in institutional memory through my earlier studies of how individuals tell their life stories (Linde 1993). That work is a piece of discourse analysis, focused on how individuals narrate their lives in such a way as to make them coherent, using a variety of cultural resources as well as their own creativity to create a socially appropriate degree of coherence in their narratives. Although this study was concerned with individual life stories, it necessarily moved to the examination of the social resources available to speakers: principles of what types of relations between events count as coherence, and tacit norms of how much coherence is necessary for an appropriate life story.

In the course of doing the analysis, to my surprise, I came upon the question of the ways in which an individual's life story is not the property of that individual alone, but also belongs to others who have shared the events narrated—or were placed to have opinions about them. As I described it:

> Coherence is not an absolute property of texts, but rather is created by speaker and addressee. This creation is not a light matter; it is in fact a social obligation which must be fulfilled in order for the participants to appear as competent members of their culture. In the case of narratives which form part of the life and story, this demand amounts to an obligation to provide coherence, usually in the form of a chain of causality, which is neither too thick nor too thin. If, in the estimation of a given addressee, this obligation is not met, the speaker is liable to be subject to criticism or correction from the addressee. Such examples are rather rare, since we are excellent at the task of constructing coherence, and normally accomplish it without

difficulty and unnoticeably. One example which I observed of a complaint by a hearer came in a conversation between two people who had been friends for at least twenty years. One of the friends corrected the other's account of how his life had gone, complaining that it sounded too fatalistic. To his surprise, he found that his friend indeed did think that his life course was destined. In this case, the correction was attempted and failed because the participants were operating, unknowingly, with different beliefs about the world, and so could not agree on what adequate coherence would be.

Another example was a situation in which I was corrected by a friend for producing a story that he judged as too accidental because I did not create coherences, which he knew I could have drawn. I was attempting to give him an account of how I became involved with Buddhist meditation. The story I told was that I met someone who invited me to a Buddhist institute where he was teaching for the summer, and since I wanted to spend time with him and had no other plans for the summer, I went. There I began meditating, and that was how I got started. My addressee was a close friend of twelve years standing; he thus had both the opportunity and the right to have his own account of my life. He refused to accept my account as I gave it, reminding me that I had always been interested in such matters, citing a number of books on mysticism that I had lent him years ago as evidence that my account could not be completely correct in the form I had given. That is, my failure to include a coherence that we both knew that I could have constructed was an error, subject to social correction. (Linde 1993, 16–17)

This process of social correction of the coherence furnished by an individual is an extremely important aspect of narrative as a socially constructed, rather than an individually constructed, phenomenon. However, I was not able to examine it in detail during my examination of the individual life story, since that work was based on data taken from individual interviews. Interview data is not an appropriate site for the discovery of such examples, since the situation of the interview is defined as one in which the person being interviewed is asked to narrate and reflect on the story of his or her life as the sole expert. Indeed, one reason why people often consent to such interviews, and enjoy the experience, is that for once they are not subject to the normal conversational problem of obtaining the floor and justifying their occupation of it with an account of their lives. Rather, the situation is one in which their life is defined as the topic for interaction, unchallenged as to factuality, relevance, or interest. In contrast, one would need to find a type of interaction in which people regularly correct one another's narratives in order to study this phenomenon, and I still have not found an appropriate research site in which one could find such examples. (Possible situations include high school reunions, family holiday dinners, and wakes. All of these pose challenges for the researcher.)

However, by broadening the question, the issue becomes the fact that an individual's life story is not their possession alone, but rather belongs to those people who have a particular relation to the narrator: they have shared the events, or they have some expertise or authority about the kind of events that happen in the situation being narrated. This issue of the nonindividual aspects of the individual life story led me to wonder about the life story of groups: do groups have the equivalent of a life story? If so, what is it, how is it told, who tells it, and what is it used for? I thus began my search for a research site in which to pursue these questions.

I now need to tell some of my own professional life story to explain how I found appropriate places to study these questions. During most of the period when I was writing my book on individual life stories, I ran my own research and consulting firm, working primarily on issues of small group communications in commercial aviation crews during aviation accidents, in research funded by NASA. Toward the end of this period, in 1989, I became a researcher at the Institute for Research on Learning (IRL). IRL was founded in 1987 and continued through 2000. It was founded through a grant from the Xerox Foundation, as a spin-off from the Xerox Palo Alto Research Corporation. It was a nonprofit research organization that looked at learning in a wide variety of settings, including schools, workplaces, and informal settings, using collaborative, multidisciplinary teams. Research questions were based in real-world problems and settings defined in collaboration with the institutions who hired IRL.

I bring in this description of IRL for two reasons. One is that because my previous work experience had been partially in universities, but primarily as a freelance researcher, IRL was the first institution that I worked in as a full, long-term, adult participant, as opposed to a student or visiting faculty member. It was thus the site of my learning how to be an employee of an institution, and a number of the examples in this book will be taken from my opportunity to observe this institution. The second reason is that at IRL I worked primarily on workplace projects undertaken with corporate sponsors. I thus had the opportunity to do ethnographic research in a number of corporate settings and to hear in detail about the experiences of my colleagues' research in other workplace and school settings.

Data for this book

The primary source of data for this book is a three-year ethnographic study of a major insurance company; it was carried out with a team of colleagues at the Institute for Research on Learning, which is described in detail in the next chapter. When the possibility of this collaboration was first raised, I volunteered to lead it because I guessed that an insurance company would necessarily be a site rich in memory and memory practices. This turned out to be true in ways that I could not have imagined.

I also use a variety of my own observations and those of my colleagues at a range of other U.S. corporations, and I incorporate accounts from the literature. Additionally, I use a study of Waldorf Education, an alternative educational system founded in Germany in 1919, studied by my student and colleague Ida Obermann, since this study uses my institutional memory framework as a tool to understand its eighty-year history (Oberman 1998; 2008).

Because I am discussing the function of narrative in group memory and induction into a group memory, it is important to note that all of these are institutions in which membership is relatively voluntary: business organizations and an alternative schooling movement. This contrasts with types of membership and identity that are not chosen by the individual (or the individual's family). Examples of these kinds of involuntary membership include ascriptive memberships like race or gender, or the membership of being born into a particular nation, a particular class, or a particular religion. Obviously, coming to work for MidWest Insurance is not entirely voluntary (if "voluntary" in this sense is an applicable concept here at all), since it is part of the entire capitalist structure of labor exchange. Further, many agents and employees have kin working for the company now, or who previously worked for MidWest, so there is easy access to the company, as well as family belief in the company. Mid-West regional headquarters are deliberately situated in towns or small cities, where they are often the largest employer or the employer of choice in the town. However, choosing to work as a sales agent at MidWest is as close to voluntary as the labor market affords. Agents are located all over the United States, not limited to the single-employer company towns of the headquarters offices. Further, almost all of the agents recruited were already working when they were recruited and thus did have some choice of job: MidWest did not represent their only option.

The issue of choice is important for this study because matters of choice form a likely topic for narration. There is a social obligation for choices to be justified, particularly as consequential a choice as one's employment. Further, as I have already shown (Linde 1993), choice of employment forms a major part of the construction of personal identity for U.S. middle-class speakers, and thus is a recurring topic for narrative. Also, since one's employment can be changed, allegiance to current employment cannot be taken for granted, since it is always open for reconsideration. Thus membership created by employment is a fertile topic for stories. And allegiance to an institution is easily and gracefully demonstrated by narrative practices.

Additionally, the type of membership and induction into group stories discussed here refers to adults. Children's induction into membership is the highly complex, central question of socialization. I am here discussing something much simpler: the issue of secondary socialization (Berger and Luckmann 1967). Secondary socialization refers not to how a child learns to be a member of a particular family, gender, religion, etc., but to how an adult learns to become a member of a secondary group within the larger culture (such as an insurance company) and to take on that company's past and present as relevant to their own identity.

What is an institution and can it remember?

It is time to examine the way the term "institution" is used in this study. I use the term "institution" rather than "organization," although both terms are used, in different fields, for the phenomena examined here. Institution and organization are terms which have different meanings in different disciplines, as well as overlapping meanings in ordinary use. Institution is the broader category: it includes both formal and informal groupings of people and established and recognizable practices. Thus, institution may describe a corporation, the practice of medicine, or marriage. Organization is a subtype of institution which includes formal and legal structures. A corporation is both an institution and an organization; the practice of medicine is not an organization, but a hospital or the American Medical Association is.

The first reason for the choice is that institution, in common use, is a broader term than organization, and this book surveys work on formal organizations, such as an insurance company, as well as studies of what are normally called institutions such as an educational system and the family. I therefore use the term institution to represent

any social group that has a continued existence over time, whatever its degree of rei-
fication or formal status may be. Thus, an institution may be a nation, a corporation,
the practice of medicine, a family, a gang, a regular Tuesday night poker game, or the
class of 1995. Additionally, the term "institutional memory" is in wide use and covers much of the territory I will be surveying. While "organizational memory" is also
used, it is considerably less common and found mainly in the field of business studies.
Therefore, I use "institution" and "institutional memory" as cover terms.

In the discussion so far, I have made a key assumption that must be examined:
do institutions actually remember? Certainly within institutions, representations of
the past are manifested in the present and carried forward into the future. But is it
correct to say that it is the institutions that remember, or is it the people within them
who do the remembering? This is a question that is important to clarify, since the
phrase "institutional memory" is widely used, both in scholarly circles and in institutions concerned about their own institutional memory. For scholars, getting this right
is a matter of getting the levels and the entities right: not mistaking a metaphor for a
description. (For example, if institutions remember, what are their neurons? How far
do we want to take this figure of speech?) For institutions, the concern is whether the
desired parts of the past are being appropriately retained or discarded.

For more than a decade there has been a great deal of attention to this question, which has been variously called institutional memory, collective memory, social
memory, places of memory, etc. This is a huge area of research: a review of the literature would itself require at least a book. Discussions of the topic span a great number
of established academic fields as well as interdisciplinary areas of concern: anthropology, cognitive science, computer science, folklore, history, linguistics, literary
analysis, management studies, and sociology, to name only a few. There are also
important studies of memory that fall between disciplines. For example, Holocaust
studies are focused not by discipline but by events: the attempt by the Nazis to erase
the memory of what was done, which led to a concerted attempt to remember as a
moral protest and as a way of ensuring that "never again" could such a thing happen.
Similarly, a group of investigations, sometimes called subaltern studies, investigate
the efforts of powerful groups to obliterate the past of conquered groups over which
they rule.

The best way to use these varied studies for the purposes of this book is to ask of
each area of investigation what its central question is. What aspect of the use of the
past in the present is it attempting to understand? This will allow us to distinguish
these many areas of research from the central question of this book, which is the
ways in which institutions use narrative to remember.

History: Whose past?

Let us begin with history, a good place to consider the study of the past. Naively,
one might think of history as the field that is in charge of preserving, organizing,
and presenting the memory of the past. But if this is true, the central question is,
whose past? By now, it is entirely obvious that history is not and cannot be neutral
or purely factual. Rather, it is an account presented by somebody, to somebody, for
some purpose. The past is always preserved for some use. It is proverbial that history

is written by the victors. Traditionally, the victors were defined by nationality: the Romans survived to write their history, while the Carthaginians were narrated (or slandered) by the Romans.

More recently (that is, considerably after the Carthaginian wars), historians have become aware that even within a nation of victors, there are those who do not have a voice, at least not a written voice, in the historical conversation. This is one of the motivating factors behind an interest in oral history: bringing into the written discourse of history the voices of those who are usually ignored or treated as merely the faceless masses.

In an influential work on oral tradition as history, Vansina (1985) specifies that the sources of oral history are contemporary eyewitness accounts of events and situations. He thus distinguishes oral history from folklore or anthropology, which collect traditions, tales, songs "which have passed from mouth to mouth beyond the lifetime of the informant" (13). But given the source, the materials are still subject to the work of historian: analysis of evidence, cross-checking of sources, etc. Vansina's work focused on African history in areas without an indigenous written tradition. This is a classic form of giving voice to the voiceless in the written conversation of history. Another important line of oral history focuses on working-class history in developed nations. (For examples of this form of historical investigation, see Hobsbawm (1985) for a discussion of the working class and underclass in England, and Portelli (1990) for an investigation of oral and written accounts of a worker's death during an industrial strike.) Feminist history and subaltern studies are two additional lines of research that attempt to give a voice to the voiceless. All of these movements within history raise the question: whose voice is heard? Rather than being the impartial voice of the marble Muse of history, any historical account must be understood as being the history of someone, for someone, for some purpose.

Social science: How do social structures
reproduce themselves?

Many of the social sciences, including anthropology and sociology, are concerned with topics that include the collective understanding and representation of the past. For anthropology and sociology, this may be summarized as the question of social reproduction: how do social and cultural structures, practices, habits of mind and heart, remain stable over time? Earlier social scientists took cultures or particular social structures as topics to be described, taking as a given their continuity. In contrast, more recent approaches have focused on continuity as a phenomenon to be explained, asking what must happen, what work is constantly and invisibly performed, for these structures to continue and to be understood as being "the same"? Continuity is thus seen as an accomplishment, rather than a given. One might understand this continuity as the social equivalent of "my grandfather's ax." The handle has been replaced once, and the blade has been replaced three times, but it is certainly still my grandfather's ax, and I cherish it as such. But clearly, it has taken work to keep my grandfather's ax functioning.

As we look at MidWest Insurance and its use of narrative, we will see a constant effort to represent the company as remaining the same under different conditions. As the company faced a variety of economic and social pressures, management worked hard to define changes that were taking place as happening within continuity. They worked the past to make an important claim: "We have to change inessential aspects of how we do business in order to remain true to our real self, the real self that goes back 75 years to the founder and the founding." A great deal of work went into arguing about whether changes were indeed superficial or whether they fundamentally altered the character of MidWest, whether the company was remaining true to its roots or dangerously losing its true nature. Interestingly, both management and its critics took it as a given that the historical character of MidWest should be preserved; they only argued about whether a particular change served to preserve or destroy this much-valued character. No one argued that the company should radically change its nature. (It should be noted that this agreement on the importance of continuity itself was not a given in the 1990s when the fieldwork was taking place. Much corporate rhetoric at that time promoted the need for continuous reinvention, warning about continuity as the dead hand of the past.)

Business and management studies: How to keep the knowledge while losing the people

Within business and management studies, the question of the past and its preservation is both a concern—and also a business opportunity. As U.S. businesses continue the more than a decade of downsizing that we have seen since the early 1990s, and as the cohort of the baby boomer generation begins to reach retirement age, there is a concern about losing knowledge central to the operation of the business. And of course, immediately following any business concern come experts selling solutions for preserving institutional memory as the human carriers of it leave. The statement frequently used to arouse fear about institutional memory is "People are walking out the door and taking their knowledge with them." The claimed solution is usually to attempt to extract knowledge from people and put it in databases: the doomed dream of the knowledge vacuum cleaner (DeLong 2004).

Although there is a great deal of fear about memory loss in business circles, there is also an equal and opposite fear that memory reproduces practices that were better forgotten and that too much memory is as much of a problem as too much forgetting. Institutions may remember all too well: it is believed that reproduction of the past is easy, while change is difficult, even if the past is no longer an adequate guide for the present. Hence, businesses desire both institutional memory but also institutional forgetting in order to be rid of the dead hand of the past. Forgetting is not the major concern of this book, but it is certainly a great issue of concern within institutions that explicitly examine the question of retaining or losing past knowledge.

Do institutions remember?

Thus far, I have spoken loosely as if institutions do remember. But whether institutions actually remember has been the subject of a fair amount of debate. In an influential review article on organizational memory, Walsh and Ungson (1991) show the range of opinions about the ontological status of memory by collectivities:

> Even though these definitions [of memory] pertain mainly to individuals, some researchers have suggested that memory can reside in supraindividual collectivities as well. For example, Loftus (1976) argued that memory functions 'as some kind of repository in which facts (information) may be retained over some period of time...memory is possessed not only by humans but by a great number of things as well.
>
> The extension of these concepts to the organizational level, however, is fraught with ambiguity. Researchers disagree on the specific form of organizational memory and on what level it might reside in the organization. Opinions range from Argyris and Schon (1978,11), who argued that organization memory is only a metaphor (i.e., "organizations do not literally remember"), to Sandelans and Stablein (1987, 136), who raised the possibility that "organizations are mental entities capable of thought." Other opinions that fall some place between these rather divergent perspectives are unclear as to whether information is stored and processed by individuals who comprise the organization (Kiesler and Sproull 1982; O'Reilly 1983; Sims and Gioia 1986; Ungson, Braunstein, and Hall 1981), by the organization itself (Galbraith 1977), or by the dominant coalition or upper echelon as a reflection of the organization. (Hambrick and Mason 1984, 58–59)

For the purposes of this study, there is no problem in sidestepping the question of whether institutions actually remember, or whether they do something that looks metaphorically like remembering. Institutions certainly make efforts to preserve aspects of their past, to find and retrieve some of these representations of the past, and to use them in the present to influence the future. Let us call it memory for now, perhaps with implicit air quotes: the how of "institutional remembering" is more interesting to me than the what.

As many authors have suggested, I too assume for the purposes of this investigation that there exists a spectrum of modes of remembering within institutions. These range from strategies relying on individual human memory and transmission from human to human, through archival and computer storage of documents and date, to organizational policies and procedures and even physical infrastructure. This list is similar to Walsh and Ungson's proposed "bins" of memory: individuals; culture; transformations, which include training of recruits, standard operating procedures, budgeting, marketing, administrative systems, etc.; structures, which include both individual roles within an organization and "institutionalized myths that are sustained and legitimized by members of an organization" (66); and ecology: physical structure and design. Though informed by this taxonomy, I do not use it directly since "culture" is a concept that is perhaps even more difficult to define than "memory." (See Borofsky et al. 2001.)

Human transmission of the past includes, obviously, people telling stories, and most importantly, as we shall see in chapter 5, their listeners taking up the stories and reusing and retelling them themselves. It is this form of remembering that this book examines in detail. There are other, more formal structures to ensure the transmission of knowledge that exist within institutions as well. The most obvious are personnel policies: mentoring, apprenticeship, succession planning. Such policies set up relations between people that intentionally allow for opportunities for story telling. But they have other, more formal institutional consequences as well: projected career tracks for junior employees; legitimate access by junior employees to sources of information within the organization that would not otherwise be available; opportunities for apprentices to shadow experts as they go about their business, deliberate organizational creation of the infrastructure for communities of practice, etc. (DeLong 2004).

Within institutions, perhaps the most obvious resource for remembering is the production and maintenance of written records. A few examples of the myriad types include: documentary and numerical records, official forms, databases, libraries archives, contracts, authorized biographies and histories, and scriptures. These are resources for remembering. However, remembering does not happen until these written materials are actually used in ongoing interaction. As memory is a currently fashionable topic, there is an unfortunate tendency to discuss any or all of these written resources as memory, which is a category error. Files in a warehouse, in someone's office, or in a database are not memory, but rather resources for potential remembering. Files become part of active remembering when they are used. Thus, the practices for use are as important as the actual form of storage. Recently, databases have become part of an interest in "knowledge management" (Schwartz 2005; Brown and Duguid 2000). This rapidly moving area is not the direct concern of this study. However, it is of interest to examine the relation between narrative and technology. There is currently a technological dream that narrative knowledge can somehow be data-based. Thus far, in my experience, a lot of stories are being videotaped, some are being put into databases, but few are ever consulted again. For a review of the relation of narrative and databases, see Linde (2001).

An important issue about written records within an institution is that they are not produced and preserved only as records of a putatively existent and stable past, but rather are representations of the past which project a probable future use for these records. Even archives that attempt to keep as extensive a record as possible, for example the Library of Congress, must decide what documents and artifacts are likely to be used in the future, in order to decide what to collect in the present. For example, Bowker (1993) offers a detailed examination of the prospective use of record keeping: Schlumberger, a French oil engineering consultancy, altered their record-keeping practices to keep their records in English rather than in French as they began to enter the U.S. market, in order to have records in the court's own language in case they found themselves involved in patent litigation.

Indeed, advances in the kinds of record keeping possible allow for changes in the ways that business can be done. Crosby (1997) argues that invention of double entry bookkeeping, in the early Italian Renaissance, allows for more complex business ventures, because it allowed merchants to keep track of multiple complex transactions over many years and determine which of them had actually made a profit. Yates (1989) has shown the development of modern business records from chronological ledger-based records that allowed users to check old transactions, to topically organized records making use of new technologies such as stencil duplication and vertical filing (and, of course, the much earlier innovation of alphabetical order). These new forms of storage and retrieval led to the development of record keeping as a management tool for forward planning. This move was initiated in the nineteenth century by the needs of railroad companies to manage their business more tightly, because of the demands of knowing where every train was at any given time, and more globally, to predict costs and profits in order to plan the complex business of running many railroad lines, charge appropriate prices for freight, and passenger business, etc.

There is a potential argument here about technological determinism that we will sidestep. I do not want to claim, as some software designers do, that a change in technology will cause a change in work practice. I only note that such development of new forms of representation and storage allow for, and may lead to, new practices. It is all too clear that an institution may mandate a certain type of record keeping, but it is much harder to mandate its actual use. For example, many business and government organizations have attempted to institute the use of "lessons learned" databases, in which problems and their solutions are recorded. They have had some success in getting people to fill out records for the database, for example, by requiring it as part of the process of formally ending a project. But there is evidence that these databases are rarely consulted and do not in fact constitute institutional learning.

Mandated policies and procedures, as well as informal practices, form part of the way that institutions learn and remember. Many formal and informal policies are the result of a decision made during or after a problem. Sometimes these policies remain with no one left to remember the reason that they were instituted; sometimes an older member of the institution can tell the origin story of the procedure. Academic readers may have experienced faculty meetings in which a policy was questioned, and a senior professor served as the oral memory of the department by recounting the situation that gave rise to the policy. Or readers may recall the often-told story of an extended family whose members always cut off the wing tips of the Thanksgiving turkey before roasting it because "that's how grandma always did it." And they would argue for why this made the turkey come out better. And then somehow, some old great-aunt explains that grandma did this because she did not have a big enough roasting pan to hold the full wingspan of the turkey. The discarding of the wing tips is part of the family's memory of grandma, with or without the accompanying story. However, such policies and practices form part of the topic of this book only when they serve as an occasion for a narrative.

Conclusion: The approach of this study

I have just sketched a very rapid survey of the many fields that treat the related issues of institutional memory, cultural memory, national memory, family memory, and, of course, individual memory. This book differs from them in that its central concern is the social and linguistic mechanisms by which forms of representation of the past are produced, the links between these forms of representation of the past, and the ways in which they are used in the present. How does an institution represent its past and work its past, and how does an individual come to take up and use a story of a collectivity as their own? Most of the current flood of studies leaves one suspended in the presentation of the proposed memory of a collectivity, without a link to the adventures of these stories as they go from mouth to mouth. This book attempts to tell an integrated story about stories within institutions: how they are formed, retained, passed on, changed, and used to affect both the narrators and the institution being narrated.

It is important to make clear immediately one of the important claims of this book: institutions and people within institutions do not mechanically record and reproduce the past. Rather, they work the past, re-presenting it each time in new but related ways for a particular purpose, in a particular form that uses the past to create a particular desired present and future. These forms of representation of the past are not identical, but their differences themselves are important to study. There are important patterns in both in the ways stories are reproduced and the ways they are changed, and the patterns observed in an insurance company can inform us about the ways in which very different collectivities work their pasts.

Finally, I would like to acknowledge briefly the contrasts between the subject matter I am writing about and much of the subject matter of the literature on institutional memory or collective memory. I use an insurance company as my main example. Much of the research on collective memory has considered appalling events such as the Holocaust, the suppression of colonized people, ethnic cleansing, etc. In some ways, it is almost impossible to hold these topics together in the same mind, let alone in the same book, and it is possibly offensive even to try.

However, studying the way an insurance company works its past allows us to see structures and patterns in an environment that does not break the heart. My hope is that this can be of value in learning to understand how the past is worked in situations where there is much more at stake, and where the heat of the situation sometimes obscures the light that would make it possible to see more clearly.

Data for the Study

The MidWest Insurance Company

The first chapter discussed how institutions work their pasts and the key role that narratives play in this work of remembering. In order to study this in detail, we need an institution to examine. Thus, we come to the insurance company that furnished the data for this study. This chapter begins by describing the process of how we did an ethnographic study of MidWest Insurance. It then describes the insurance industry as a whole and MidWest as a particular company at a particular time of change. This description provides the background necessary to understand why MidWest used stories as it did and what those stories meant. Finally, I discuss the ethical and practical issues involved in doing ethnographic fieldwork on a corporation with financial sponsorship by that corporation.

MidWest Insurance is a major U.S. insurance company, which initially came to the Institute for Research on Learning with a question about disappointing levels of life insurance sales: Was sales agents' failure to sell as much life insurance as the company desired a problem of learning or a problem in motivation? As our relation with MidWest developed, they asked us to research additional questions as well.

My colleagues and I carried on a three-year ethnographic study, which included extensive observations of the training and work of insurance sales agents and their offices, as well as observations of ongoing training programs, sales conventions, regional meetings, special task forces, and corporate meetings. The fieldwork included ethnographic observation, audio- and videotaping in agents' offices and sales calls on clients as well as participation in a variety of local, regional, and national meetings and conferences. The fieldwork was conducted by a team of ethnographers that ranged in size, at various points in the project, from three people to thirteen. (This is a very large project. Most ethnographies are performed by a single researcher. Team ethnographies are rare and the teams are usually two or three people.) As discussed later in this chapter, we came to MidWest at the beginning of a time of considerable structural change and had the opportunity to see both the previous system and the process of change.

Description of MidWest insurance

In order to understand the stories of the company, and the world they represent, it is necessary to understand something about the insurance business in the United States. When I began the project, I thought insurance was rather boring. However, I did not see this as a disadvantage of the project: there is knowledge about the world that can only be learned by studying the mundane rather than the extraordinary. The mundane is, after all, mundane because it is common, frequent, and therefore close to unseeable. I have come to believe that insurance, far from being boring, is one of the unseen organizers of the social and economic world. Startlingly often, when one asks why some economic or social structure is the way it is, the answer is "because the insurance requires…" An example that most of us are familiar with is medical insurance. It is common, in the United States, to hear stories of people choosing new jobs, or staying in disagreeable jobs, because of the need to obtain or retain medical insurance. Medical insurance decisions organize what conditions are recognized as legitimate diagnoses, what treatments will be paid for, what kinds of training and certification will be accepted. For example, Bowker and Star (2000) offer interesting examples of psychiatrists and patients working together to agree on a diagnosis that would satisfy the psychiatrist's sense of what the problem is, how it can be legitimately described within the categorization of reimbursable conditions by the patient's insurance company, and the patient's reputation if the diagnosis came to be known by the patient's employer.

All this is to argue that insurance, though mundane, has its hidden fascination and hidden power, and the reader would be wise not to skip the following discussion of MidWest's business.

National, regional, and local organization
of MidWest

Let us begin with a brief description of the organization of MidWest Insurance. MidWest is a mutual company rather than a stock company. Mutual companies are owned by the policyholders, a form of private ownership. Stock insurance companies, like all publicly held and traded companies, are owned by stockholders, who need not own policies. (Insurance is the most common type of business organized as a mutual company, though even in the insurance industry, this form of organization is becoming less common.) This form of organization has many consequences, one of which is most important for the study on which I am here reporting.

Because a mutual company is privately held, it is less subject to the urgent pressures which face stock companies. Publicly traded companies are profoundly influenced by the judgments of stock analysts, who weight their analyses heavily in the direction of quarterly returns. Since they have no stockholders who require them to respond to this immediate pressure, MidWest's upper management was more easily able to do long-term planning, and to make decisions that might cause a short-term drop in revenues, in order to avert what they identified as coming problems. In publicly held companies, this is very difficult. While management may see a problem developing in the next years, the pressures from stockholders virtually require them to focus on quarterly results. Several of the programs we observed at MidWest were large scale changes intended to avert problems management saw coming in the next five to ten years.

MidWest was organized into units at the national, regional, and local levels. National headquarters was located in the small town in which the company was founded. (The symbolic importance of this will be discussed in chapter 5.) The national headquarters performed the usual functions of a corporate headquarters: formulating policy, deciding on the range of products to be offered, developing training, overseeing regional units, and making high-level personnel decisions.

MidWest was divided into five regions, each with its own regional vice president. From the point of view of the agent, regional management was much more immediately relevant to their experience than national management at headquarters. Many agents had never visited headquarters, while all agents attended many functions held at their regional headquarters, or organized and run by regional management.

Finally, each region was divided into a number of local management districts. Generally, a local manager managed approximately thirty agents. Managers recruited, trained, and supervised agents. The local manager was the agent's immediate contact to the parent company, and the other agents in the local district were the agent's immediate peers. As described below, this system of local management was in the process of change from a relatively personal relation between an agent and a single manager to a more corporate-style management team.

MidWest as a multiline insurance company

Another important aspect of MidWest's business is that it is a multiline insurance company. This means that it does not specialize in a single type of insurance, such as automobile insurance or life insurance. Rather, it sells almost all types of personal and small business insurance: automobile insurance, home insurance, disability insurance, and life insurance. (It also offers health insurance, but this is not a significant part of its business, and during our three years there, I never heard it discussed.)

Being a multiline company has several consequences. Insurance companies focusing on a single line of business tend to use employee sales agents, rather than independent contractor agents, and tend to have a very high turnover rate (Leidner 1993). (Knocking on doors or cold-calling customers at dinner is a horrible job; few people last at it for more than a year.) Also, both the company and its agents aim to sell more than one type of insurance to clients: the more different types of insurance a customer has with a given company, the more likely they are to remain with that company for years or even generations.

Historically, MidWest's core business was automobile and home insurance. Many established agents had found that they could make excellent returns on these two lines of insurance, without making much effort to sell life insurance, unless it was requested by clients. As I have already mentioned, this was contrary to what upper management hoped to see agents sell.

There are reasons for the difference in orientation between management and (most) agents: the process of selling automobile and home owner's insurance is quite different from the process of selling life insurance. Both automobile and home owner's insurance are mandatory, either legally or in practice. All U.S. states require automobile insurance in order to register a vehicle. Home owner's insurance is required by banks before they will issue a mortgage. In contrast, buying life insurance is an individual choice; it is not required by any law or institution. Thus, for the sales agent, it is not necessary to sell the need for automobile or homeowner's insurance; only the particular policy must be sold. In contrast, agents complain, life insurance takes much more selling. People need to be convinced of the need for it, which can take many long conversations. Additionally, the options in life insurance, agents say, are more complicated to explain than those in home or auto insurance, since there are two basic types of life insurance: term insurance and permanent insurance (also called whole life, straight life, or ordinary life insurance), as well as mixed policies combining features of each.

The sound bite (or "word track" to use the MidWest term) that agents often use to explain the two types of insurance is that term insurance is like renting a policy, and permanent insurance is like buying one. Term insurance provides a death benefit for a specified term, usually one, three, or five years at a time and is typically used to cover a short-term need for insurance. The buyer must qualify medically for such insurance each time it is bought, and the rates go up as the buyer gets older. Term insurance usually provides the largest death benefit for a minimal initial premium paid, since term insurance provides insurance only, without cash value. Therefore, term life insurance costs less in the early years of a policy. But should the buyer stop paying for the policy, there is no return of the premiums paid: thus it is like renting, because rent paid is money gone.

In contrast, permanent insurance is initially more expensive, because it accrues a cash value. The cash value the policy accrues is like equity in a home mortgage: it remains the property of the owner. In addition, the cost of the insurance remains level: it does not increase with the policy holder's age or medical condition. Permanent insurance may pay off in one of three ways: Either the policy holder dies, and the death benefit is paid to the survivors; at some point, the policy is cashed in, and the policy holder receives the cash value of the policy; or, the policyholder may borrow against the cash value, and the borrowed amounts are deducted from the death benefit or cash value.

There is a great deal of debate about the value of life insurance at all, and of the comparative value of term and permanent insurance. Sales agents, MidWest management, clients, and outside financial advisors differ in their opinions, and these differences are framed in terms that are both practical and moral.

From a business standpoint, MidWest management wanted agents to sell more life insurance, for several reasons. First, at the time of our study, the company had temporarily stopped offering homeowners policies to new clients because of the heavy losses they had incurred from major earthquakes, fires, and floods in the previous few years. They could not write new business because they did not have sufficient reserves to cover new risks. Life insurance, they felt, would be the ideal way to replace this lost business. The actuarial figures for death rates used in pricing life insurance were believed to be more accurate than the calculations for natural disasters. Therefore, they felt that increased sales of life insurance policies could smooth out some of the fluctuation in income caused by natural disasters. Many MidWest customers bought their auto and homeowner's insurance from MidWest, but they bought life insurance from another company. This was a source of great frustration to management: their own customers did not know that MidWest offered life insurance or did not request it from their MidWest agent. Finally, MidWest (like all other insurance companies) had found that the greater the number of policies a customer held with a company, the greater the chance that they would stay with that company and not change companies in search of lower prices. Thus, adding life insurance to a customer's holdings increased the chance overall of retaining that customer.

Although some agents agree with management on the business importance of life insurance, particularly for retaining clients, others disagree. For the latter group of agents, management's argument about the importance of life sales is not convincing because they differ from management in their ways of assessing the profitability of life insurance sales for their own businesses. While one of management's arguments focuses on the beneficial effects that life insurance sales have on long-term retention of clients, agents who prefer not to concentrate on life insurance sales focus on the fact that life insurance sales take a great deal of time, much more than other kinds of insurance, since life insurance is not obligatory. Therefore, the agent must raise the question of life insurance, rather than the customer coming in requesting it. The agent must spend time explaining why life insurance is important and how the different kinds of life insurance work. All this can take several conversations with a client, where most automobile or home insurance can be sold in only one meeting. One agent we studied, who sold life insurance very seriously, told us that it could take up to seven introductions of the topic before the client became interested in pursuing the issue. She was willing to take this time, because she felt it was important, both for her own success and for the best interest of her clients.

However, there are also agents who believe that they can make more money selling other forms of insurance, if they do not have to take the time to pursue life insurance sales. Additionally, for agents to concentrate on life insurance sales, it was usually necessary for them to hire more staff. Trained and qualified staff could concentrate on service issues and simple automobile and home insurance sales, leaving agents free to do the more complex selling of life insurance and other financial products. This required more staff members than many agents employed. A number of agents were unwilling to spend the money to hire and train more staff on the possibility that a possible increase in life insurance sales would lead to increased income in the future.

Moral issues in life insurance

Thus far, I have discussed the business issues in life insurance sales. But life insurance is not only a practical issue but a moral matter as well, and this has been the case throughout the history of life insurance. Zelizer (1979) provides a history of attitudes about life insurance in the United States. Until the 1840s, life insurance was considered irreligious, or at least morally dubious both throughout Europe and the United States, although England moved to favor it much earlier. Indeed, in the nineteenth century, France even had laws against life insurance.

The religious ground for the moral argument was that someone who insured his life was insufficiently relying on Providence. According to Zelizer (1979, 73), citing a nineteenth century historian of insurance:

> As Standen recalls: "Thousands of persons of religious influence turned their backs upon life insurance as an impious institution that they dared not countenance for fear of perpetrating some unpardonable sin." Speculating wth the solemn event of death seemed to many a degrading, sacreligious wager, which God would "resent and punish as crime." By insuring his life a man was not only "betting against his God" but, even worse, usurping His divine functions of protection. Life insurance misled men into taking "future consequences or results into their hands, which is God's prerogative." (quoting William T. Standen, *The Ideal Protection* [New York: U.S. Life Insurance Co., 1897, 119])

The practical ground for the moral objection was that life insurance would make men lazy, since they could buy insurance instead of working hard to build up assets to provide for their families. Both objections are based on an unstated fear that there is something sacrilegious or uncanny about putting a money value on human life.

Historically, these attitudes began to change some time in the late nineteenth century, at a point when the majority of families were no longer supported by a family farm but by the wages of a single wage earner. Morally praiseworthy hard work might build a family farm into an inheritance for the family, but no amount of hard work in a factory would allow the average wage earner to accrue assets to support his family after his death. There was a danger that wives and dependent children, bereft of the breadwinner, would have to rely on public or private charity. At that point, the moral meaning of life insurance reversed. Buying life insurance proved that the buyer showed a commendable foresight about the possibility of his own premature death, and that he was doing what he could to provide for his family.

In a conversation about life insurance between a client and an agent, there can be moral issues for both parties. For the client who is the support of their family, the moral issue is providing for the financial welfare of the family after their death. For insurance agents who believe in the value of life insurance, the moral issue is their duty to convince their clients of their own responsibility to ensure that their families would be financially stable "in case something happens to you." Since life insurance is likely to be essential for the financial stability of most families in case of disaster, management believes that it is the obligation of agents to push the matter, even if they do not like selling life insurance or find it difficult to begin the conversation or persist with it if the client does not immediately respond positively.

Indeed, at the time of the study, there was even discussion of the possibility that the courts might find insurance agents legally negligent if they did not at least attempt to discuss life insurance with their clients. This moral and possibly legal obligation was particularly an issue for MidWest agents because of the multiline nature of their business. An agent who sells only life insurance cannot hesitate about discussing it: that is the only product on offer. But for MidWest agents, since they could choose to concentrate on other products they found easier to sell, they had to make a choice about bringing up the issue of life insurance. At the same time, this brought a legal risk. If MidWest marketed the agents' services as providing full service expertise in all forms of risk management, they could not leave the issue of life insurance to someone else. They were obliged to attempt to help the client manage all of the risks that could be managed, which necessarily includes the risk of premature death of a bread winner.

However, the moral and financial arguments about the value of life insurance can be argued in the opposite direction. In particular, there are strong disagreements about the value of permanent life insurance. Management at MidWest particularly wanted an increase in permanent life insurance sales, since this was the most profitable line of insurance for them, and the most likely to be retained through the client's entire life. They argue that for the client, permanent insurance is the most valuable product because of the cash value: the client gets not only insurance protection, which might be paid as a death benefit, but also, depending on circumstances, might instead get back the premiums paid, plus some interest on them. The disagreement turns on the question of the cash value: is it an investment or is it not? A financial instrument which offers the return of the client's payments plus interest sounds very much like an investment.

However, MidWest management and the agents who sold permanent life insurance were careful not to use the word "investment." There are complex legal reasons for this avoidance, which are not immediately relevant here. But the immediate practical reason was that, at the time of the study, the guaranteed rate of return for the cash value was very low, compared to the soaring rates of return on the stock market. Trying to sell the cash value of a whole life policy as an investment would have been foolish.

At that time, the accepted wisdom among most financial advisors was that permanent insurance was a bad idea, benefiting only the insurance company, and that the best choice was term insurance. A typical argument of this sort is given in *Personal Finance for Dummies* (Tyson 1994):

> In the next ten seconds, I'm going to tell you how you can save hours of time and thousands of dollars. Ready? *Buy term life insurance....*
> *Cash value life insurance is the most oversold insurance and financial product in the history of the industry.* As you'll soon discover, there is only a very small percentage of people for whom cash value life insurance makes sense. You would think that the vast majority of life insurance that is bought by people like you—and therefore sold by agents—is term. Wrong! The last numbers I saw showed that about 80 percent of life insurance that is sold is cash value because many people don't know any better. Don't make the same mistake....
> Life insurance tends to be a mediocre investment anyway. The insurance company quotes you an interest rate for the first year only. After that, it's up to the company's discretion what it pays you. If you don't like the future interest rates, you can be penalized for quitting the policy. Would you ever invest your money in a bank account that quoted an interest rate for the first year only and then penalized you for moving your money in the next seven to ten years?

>Many agents argue that a cash value plan is better than nothing—at least it's
forcing you to save. This is silly reasoning because so many people drop out of cash
value life insurance policies after just a few years of paying into them....
>
>**Remember** Purchase low cost term insurance, and do your retirement investing
separately. Life insurance is rarely a permanent need, and over time, you can gradually reduce the amount of term insurance that you carry as you accumulate more
assets and savings. (351–55)

Management and agents at MidWest who believed in the value of permanent life
insurance had many detailed arguments to counter this position. One of their strongest was the issue of rate of return: MidWest does guarantee a minimum rate of
return, and often provided a higher one. And, they argued, these doubters have never
seen a downturn in the stock market. When they cannot get double digit results in the
stock market, they will come to realize the value of a guaranteed rate. At the same
time, for both legal and rhetorical reasons, agents were counseled by management to
describe permanent life insurance to potential clients not as an "investment" but as
"what you do **before** you invest."

The insurance sales agents

The study I am describing focused on the work of the sales agents, and so I now focus
on the agents themselves. I begin with a discussion of their legal status as independent contractors, since this status is the key factor that organizes the relation between
the agents and the parent company. I then discuss what the agents are like, since most
readers are likely to have stereotyped and incorrect views of insurance sales agents
(as I and all the rest of the team did, before we met them.)

Independent contractor agents

Perhaps the most important aspect of MidWest's business, for the purposes of this
study, is the position of sales agents within the company. Unlike many insurance
companies, MidWest's sales agents are not employees but independent contractors. This means that after an initial probationary period, agents do not receive a
salary from the company, but they receive a commission calculated as a percentage of the policies they sell. Additionally, they do not work on premises furnished
by MidWest, but rather lease or buy their own offices, their own equipment and
furniture, etc.

The definition of contractor status versus employee status is mandated by federal income tax law. There is a complex list of over twenty factors which determine
whether someone is genuinely an independent contractor or, in fact, an employee.
These include whether a contractor doing work for a company maintains independent
premises; controls, hires, trains, and pays their own staff or uses staff furnished by the
company; has discretion over how and when the work is performed, etc. The decision
about whether someone is an employee or a contractor has tax consequences both
for the employers and the contractor: an employer must contribute to social security

and Medicare payments, and usually contributes to health and retirement benefits for employees, while independent contractors pay their own taxes and benefits.

In the case of MidWest, the independent contractor status of agents is a central cultural value, which is constantly discussed by both management and agents. This relation is termed the "marketing partnership." Both agents and management of Mid-West are proud of this arrangement and consider it to be a major part of what makes MidWest unique. For management, it is a value because it is a way of demonstrating that the company is founded on salesmanship. The founder was preeminently a superb salesman, and sales ability is still the cornerstone of the company. Almost all of the managers have been sales agents; it is a credential that gives them credibility with agents. For agents, their independent contractor status is a matter of great pride. Most of them are proud to be independent business owners, entrepreneurs rather than wage slaves, and feel that this demonstrates both their courage in not relying on a guaranteed salary, and their ability at sales.

This description of agents as entrepreneurs might seem odd at first. These sales agents have not invented a new product or started a new business from scratch. However, there are a number of ways of defining entrepreneurship (a term of high prestige both at the time of the study and at the time of writing). In a discussion of direct sales organizations (DSOs) like Mary Kay Cosmetics and Amway, Biggart (1989) discusses this question:

> Most [economists] following Schumpeter, see innovation as essential. Entrepreneurs do something different that has economic consequences: they invent a product, refine a production process, develop a new marketing scheme. Some others believe that risk bearing is critical to entrepreneurship. An entrepreneur puts money on the line.
>
> By even a generous interpretation of economists' definitions, distributors are not entrepreneurs. They perform highly routinized selling and recruiting behaviors. Innovation is neither necessary nor welcome. Financial risk is purposely kept low...Distributors risk only the absence of a paycheck, and while that may be personally risky, it is not of the same order as putting one's savings at risk. What distributors do is not entrepreneurial to any economically significant degree.
>
> Entrepreneurship, however, is more than a type of economic action. It is a powerful social ideal that came about with the emergence of capitalism....Direct selling organizations emphasize less what distributors do than who they are as being entre–preneurial....For example, they remind distributors that real entrepreneurs persevere even in the face of difficulty, and that booking more parties during a slump is a sign of the entrepreneurial spirit.
>
> More than anything, though, within the industry entrepreneurialism represents the strength of character to avoid the security of wage or salaried labor. DSOs take their single most significant liability—the absence of a paycheck—and interpret it as an advantage. Direct selling entrepreneurs are willing to risk their financial security on their own ability to sell the DSOs' products." (163–64)

Indeed, during our first meeting with MidWest management, when they were determining whether to commission a study from the Institute for Research on Learning, they were trying to explain their business to us. It was stressed that "The most important thing you have to understand about MidWest is that the agents are independent contractors." At the time, I had no idea why this was important, or even what it meant. But in the course of the study, I came to realize that in fact this was the single most important aspect of the agents' business. (As a methodological note, I have observed that this is a frequent pattern in such projects. On first introduction to a new field setting, one is told what the participants consider to be the central fact about their organization. Coming to understand what this means and what its consequences are forms a major part of the fieldwork and analysis process. It is humbling to spend several years coming to a conclusion that was expressed in the initial meeting. The hope, of course, is that one has come to understand it more deeply or in different terms than it was initially expressed.)

The independent contractor status of agents structures their relations to MidWest in obvious and less obvious ways. The most obvious issue is that sales agents are paid commissions rather than salaries. A less obvious but very serious consequence has to do with agents' staff members. One of the provisions of the income tax law determining whether someone is genuinely an independent contractor is that they recruit, hire, train, and pay their own staff. If a legal issue arises about someone's contractor status, the fact that the person supervises employees of the company employing them would make it more likely that the Internal Revenue Service would determine that the person had employee rather than independent contractor status. This is a serious issue for MidWest agents. They all agree that finding and retaining good staff is a central factor in the success or failure of an agency and that this is a very difficult task. Many agents feel that they are not skilled at finding or training staff and would like MidWest to do this for them. MidWest is aware of the inefficiencies caused by rapid staff turnover and poor training but has been reluctant to aid agents in selecting and training staff, since this could lead to a challenge of the agents' independent contractor status.

The most important consequence of the independent contractor status of agents, and the specific terms of the contract they signed with MidWest, is that agents may make their own choice of which of MidWest's insurance products they sell. Agents may only sell MidWest products, unlike independent brokers, who sell insurance products of the many companies that distribute through brokers. However, of the many forms of insurance offered by MidWest, each agent may sell those products that their clients seem to require, or that the agent understands and believes in. MidWest does not require them to sell a particular mix of products or a specified amount of any one product. This was the initial impetus for the study MidWest asked us to do: MidWest felt that agents were selling much less life insurance than the company wished and wanted to know if this was a problem of learning or of motivation. However, whichever it turned out to be, it was a problem made possible by the fact that agents could choose what products they offered their clients; unlike employees, they did not have specific quotas of specific products to sell.

What sales agents are like

Think of an insurance sales agent. Most readers will probably be imagining these sales agents in images shaped by *Death of a Salesman* or *Glengarry Glen Ross*. Indeed, I began this study with just that prejudice. The general culture has an image of a sales agent as a driven, maniacal, conscienceless bulldog, and, when one studies the culture of sales organizations, this image seems to have some grounding in fact. An example of this type of sales staff is given in Dorsey (1994), a journalistic account of a year in the life of a successful first-line sales manager at Xerox. This is a sales culture in which agents are pushed to do whatever they need to in order to meet their yearly or quarterly sales quotas, including fairly unethical practices such as churning accounts: replacing existing customers' equipment with more expensive equipment that they do not need. Managers stage major sales promotional events, with large rewards to incent the sales force. ("To incent" is an important transitive verb in the business of salesmanship.) Within this culture of sales, it is considered reasonable for sales agents to wreck their health to get that last account in December needed to make the quota for the annual trip. At the same time, there is a tension between the actual culture of sales, which is driven by structural factors in the compensation and reward system for agents, and the attempt by top management to introduce a training program called "Total Quality" selling. This is a sales system which emphasizes the sales agent's responsibility to determine what the customer's actual needs are, rather than selling them whatever they can be persuaded to buy.

This picture of Xerox's sales culture is quite typical within U.S. businesses. However, the sales culture of MidWest is quite different, and as a result, the agents are as likely to see themselves as professionals, like tax accountants or lawyers, as they are to see themselves as crack sales agents. While MidWest's culture of sales certainly includes promotional events and prizes for meeting sales goals, and agents are subjected to a certain amount of pressure from their managers to sell certain products or a certain dollar amount, there is one crucial difference. As independent contractors, MidWest agents are free to choose whether or not to participate in these sales competitions. The rewards are symbolic, conveying prestige; they do not lead to monetary bonuses. Some agents participate enthusiastically, while others do not accept the importance of the symbolic ranks and rewards and do not participate.

The ideology of MidWest Insurance is that clients need insurance and that agents should work to provide them with what they really need. Consonant with this ideology, most Midwest agents do not engage in high-pressure sales tactics; management discourages it and most agents dislike it. There are a number of structural reasons for the absence of high-pressure sales techniques.

Because agents are independent contractors, they can choose what level of profit they themselves find satisfactory. Thus, agents are not required to achieve sales goals specified by management; they are able to set their own desired level of sales and choose whether to attend to management's suggested sales goals. Because of the way agents' offices are placed within a geographical area, the agents do not compete for sales with other MidWest agents but with other insurance companies. In order to reduce internal competition, MidWest attempts to limit the number of agents within a single zip code. Internal MidWest competition is recreational: for prestige and symbolic honors, rather than for money. This is different from the case of the Xerox sales agents described above, where substantial bonuses depend on the outcome of internal sales competition. MidWest management felt a strong sense of competition with other insurance companies and a particularly strong threat from new forms of insurance sales: internet companies, 800 number insurance sales, and insurance sold by banks, brokerage firms, etc. However, at the time of the fieldwork, agents did not perceive these as their personal competition. For them, the perceived competition was other traditional multiline insurance companies. (There was a class of jokes we heard from agents that began "An Allstate agent, a State Farm agent, and a MidWest agent met at a golf course/a church...." Such jokes indicate the inhabitants of the agents' symbolic universe.) If agents mentioned Internet companies or telephone sales companies at all, their comment was that if management would lower the rates on policies, the agents would have no problem with this form of competition.

As many of them indicated to us, agents themselves dislike the stereotype of the driven, amoral salesman. They did a considerable amount of work to reframe this image into something that fit their own sense of self.

For example, one agent had begun as an employee and was encouraged to become an agent. She mentioned that while deciding, she looked at agents and said, "If they can do it, I can too. The question was whether I wanted to." The problem for her was that she could not see herself as a sales person. Her husband, a sales agent for another insurance company, encouraged her by telling her that in her service position, she was already selling people on MidWest. This reframing made a great difference to her, since she had not looked at herself in that way. Rather she had always thought of sales as what used car salesmen did. She came to understand that MidWest was really a service business: "You don't really **sell** a service, you **provide** a service. You help them fulfill a need." She used this reframing to get herself into training as an agent, and it became the central theme in how she organized her office, trained her staff, and related with clients. For example, unlike many agents, she encouraged clients to drop in, rather than insisting on a more professional model of setting appointments.

Another agent discussed his initial perception of sales agents as high pressure salesmen, like used car salesmen, which he expressed using a discussion of the semiotics of clothing. Before entering training, he stated, "I mean, can you trust a guy who sells you a used car? Can you trust a guy who, and so I had this perception of insurance people as they always wore polyester suits and they always had white belts and white shoes." When he had been recruited, and was in the process of training, his manager arranged for him to take the state licensing examination. As he describes it:

> There must have been 500 people milling around this high school auditorium while I was waiting for the appointed time to go in to take the exam along with the rest of the people. And there must have been about 300 pairs of white shoes. (Laughter)...It was like it was all crashing down on me. Here I was with my Levi's and my desert boots on. You know, I'm twenty, pretty young, I suppose, comparatively speaking, but I was 26 and, uh (pause) I was surrounded by white shoes and white belts.
> Interviewer: You thought, boy, am I in the right place?
> Agent: I'm in the wrong, the wrong place. But, you know, I found out very quickly that there's a lot of variety and diversity in the people. There are the people that wear white shoes and white belts and just prototypical insurance person, at least from my perception, but yet there were (pause) some, um, variety as far as their personality traits, approach to people. I was never a very hard sell....I mean, it's not

like there's one way to do it.... And so I never was too high-pressure but, persistent I suppose is probably the only aggressive attribute that I would have with respect to sales.

Perhaps the most dramatic case was an agent who had attended an elite college and said that, initially, she had certainly not considered sales as a possible career. If she had any perception of insurance sales people it was as "boring, boring people. Unnecessary evil, even like a notch just below the lawyer." Her subsequent decision to become an agent was based on her desire to own her own business and the opportunities she perceived at MidWest for entrepreneurship.

However, this speaker was so embarrassed to tell her college friends that she worked for an insurance company that, when asked, she refused to tell where she was working, saying, "You know, I'd prefer not to say." Finally, a friend pressed her: "Oh are you like a secret agent, do you work for the CIA, is that why you have to keep it tight?" The speaker finally told her, "I'll tell you, but keep it between you and I, I work for MidWest." And her friend replied: "Yeah you were smart not to say anything."

Managers are well aware of agents' beliefs about the nature of sales. In one case, two district managers discussed with an interviewer possible agents for field-workers to study. The agent they considered and then rejected was someone who would not sell life insurance because he felt that it required begging and that it was demeaning to beg. One manager notes that "He has told us that he feels that it's almost demeaning to write life insurance, that his image of a life insurance is on the same level as a used car salesman.... What you would find is an office that is, uh, it's a beautiful office and he dresses to the T. You know, you can almost sense the dollar signs walking towards you in his dress and manner. And he prides himself in his office appearance, his personal appearance, his lifestyle with a jazzed-up, shiny Corvette. So he has an image that, uh, well, this is, that is not compatible with being a peddler."

Thus, some agents were able to create for themselves and others an image of a sales professional that allowed them to sell life insurance without feeling demeaned. Others rejected life insurance sales exactly because they could only see it as demeaning. MidWest management was equally sensitive to the stereotyped sales agent. While the culture of MidWest was based on the image of the founder as a super salesman (see chapters 5 and 6), it was equally based on a sense of the ethical nature of insurance sales. Maintaining this balance was sometimes problematic for management, as they created incentives and awards for meeting high sales goals but insisted on the professional nature of the agent and the relation between agent and client.

We came across an example of this tension when we were asked to use our research on mentoring in agents' offices to create training materials on how to be an effective mentor. To do this, we used videotaped examples of real situations handled by agents and trainees. In one example, an agent and trainee were discussing a sales interview they had just had, discussing how they would bring up life insurance at the next meeting. The agent asked how the trainee would bring up the issue of life insurance. The trainee recalled what he had seen the agent do, then complimented him saying, "You're a bulldog. I mean, I saw you. You were out there boom, boom, boom, boom, boom." We used this as part of an example of effective mentoring. However, management asked us to remove the clip because they objected strongly to the term "bulldog," suggesting a high-pressure sales style. Yet they had chosen this agent as an example of an effective life insurance salesman.

MidWest at a time of change

At the time of the fieldwork for this study, MidWest was in the process of instituting a number of structural changes prompted by management's assessment of the changing business environment for insurance sales. Competition from Internet- and telephone- based insurance companies, changes in the law allowing banks and other financial agencies to issue insurance, a series of natural disasters, and, as we have already discussed, disappointing levels of life insurance sales all led to a decision to make major changes in the recruitment and training of new agents, the organization of district management of agents, and the contract between MidWest and existing agents. We had the good fortune to observe briefly the operation of agents' offices and local management centers before the change and then the period during which the changes were instituted. Thus, we were able not only to hear about the "good old days" but also to see them, and to understand better the reactions of agents, management, and staff to the new system. I will describe the changes in detail (to the level that the reader can endure), but I will begin by summing up the overall social effect of them, as planned by management and as experienced by agents. It is important to note that the previous system, these "good old days" do not represent a monolithic past but themselves represented a continuous series of changes from prior states of MidWest organization and of the insurance industry as a whole.

The previous system, as we experienced it, and as old-timers described it, was a system built on personal relations. Most important was the long-term relation between the agent and the client: this was the cornerstone of MidWest's business strategy. Agents justified the somewhat higher cost of their products by citing the benefits to clients of having a local agent—with a face and a name and an existing relationship—to help them to choose the right insurance as their life circumstances changed and to deal with the difficult events that can lead to the need for an insurance payment. Building a relation of trust between agent and client was central to MidWest's business.

Initially, I was rather skeptical: nice theory, but who would trust an insurance salesman? But, in fact, I did observe that the work of sales agents changed when they viewed the relation with the client as lasting for years or generations rather than for a single sale. Thus, I often saw agents reviewing finances and insurance with clients and suggesting that it was now appropriate for them to lower the amount of a particular type of insurance they held or that, given their circumstances, a particular type of purchase was not necessary for them. This led to a short-term drop in revenue for the agent but to the development of trust that ensured a long-term relation with the client. Certainly, I as a client would be much more likely to trust a sales person who told me that I did not need the most expensive product, and I would be much more likely to continue to do business with that person. Indeed, I observed one agent explain to a customer who complained that MidWest's automobile insurance rates were more expensive than other company's: "You're paying the extra $300 a year for *me*."

The desired relation of trust between agent and client was also mirrored in a desired relation of trust between the agent and MidWest as a company. It was expected that agents believed in the honesty and good will of the company and in the importance and value of its products. As I have already discussed, selling and buying life insurance is a moral issue as well as a financial issue. However, although it is less obvious, so is the sale of all insurance. When one buys any type of insurance, one is buying a promise that the issuer of the insurance will do the right thing under the promised circumstances. The client must trust that the company issuing the insurance will do what it promised rather than trying to wriggle out through obscure contractual provisions (the large print giveth and the small print taketh away). Indeed, the client must also trust that the company is stable enough to still be in operation when the time comes to redeem that contractual promise. (U.S. insurance companies, unlike banks, are not insured by the federal government, although most clients do not know this.) Obviously, it is easier for agents to sell insurance as a trustworthy promise if they themselves have experienced the company issuing it to be trustworthy. A feeling of personal connection and trust between agents and MidWest, from the founding to the present, was viewed both by management and agents as central to the way that MidWest chose to conduct its business.

Change in the management system

Under the old system, the relation of trust between agents and the company was mediated by the district manager. The district manager was the one who directly supervised a number of agents in a region, usually about thirty. Frequently, it was the manager who recruited an agent to fill a vacancy in his district, and, after recruitment and training, continued to manage that agent. This could be a very personal relation.

The relation between the agent and the manager who had recruited him or her often had the character of a fictive kin relation, that is, a relation between individuals unrelated by either birth or marriage who have an emotionally significant relationship similar to those of a family relation. A strong bond of loyalty characterized many of these relations. Very often, as part of their introductions at MidWest functions, agents would identify themselves by mentioning who their recruiting manager was. This was clearly the more significant relation if the agent currently had a new manager, either because the agent had moved into the territory of a new manager or the recruiting manager had retired or died. It was considered an obligation to attend the funeral of one's recruiting manager, as much of an obligation as going to a family funeral. Agents also appeared to have a kin-like relation to other agents who had trained with them at the same time, though this was not as strong as the relation to their recruiting manager.

The relation was economic as well as emotional, or to be more precise, loyalty was demonstrated in economically significant terms. Agents felt (or were expected to feel) gratitude to the manager who had chosen them for recruitment into such a desirable professional situation. They could demonstrate this gratitude by their levels of sales in all types of insurance, but particularly in life insurance. Under the old system, district managers were paid a small salary by MidWest, but their income derived mainly from commissions on the commissions earned by the agents in his district. A number of agents told us stories about making an extra effort to sell life insurance so that their manager would qualify for the trip rewarding both agents and managers for life insurance sales. Some agents said that they were not particularly concerned about whether their own reputation would be enhanced by their presence on the trip, but that they did feel a desire to see their manager qualify for the trip. Big-gart (1989) reports a similar reliance on fictive kin ties in direct sales organizations. This fictive kin model is often very explicit, more so than MidWest's. The sponsor, the person who recruited a sales agent is her mother, others she brought in are the sales agent's sisters. People whose sponsor leaves are an orphan line, which can be adopted by another sponsor. This fictive kin arrangement can overlap with biological kinship, since people often recruit relatives. The DSOs described, such as Mary Kay Cosmetics, differ from the fictive kin system of MidWest in that MidWest has only a shallow kinship tree. In the old system, an agent or a manager could recruit a new agent, and an agent can still recruit staff. But agents do not recruit other agents. This contrasts with the DSOs' long kin lines.

It is important to note again that managers had no almost economic leverage to force agents to any level of sales, for any product. They could train; they could encourage; they could hold small local sales competitions of their own, for example sponsoring a day at the races for small, quarterly improvements in sales levels. This could go so far as a manager placing side bets with agents on their levels of life insur-ance sales. But the only direct influence they could have on an agent's career came when another agent in the district retired. It was then at the manager's discretion whether to distribute some or all of that agent's clients to other agents in the district. However, this was a relatively rare event, dependent on an agent's retirement. In gen-eral, agents did not view their district managers as having power over them. Rather, as already mentioned, this was viewed as a relation of personal loyalty. In practice, agents and managers interpreted and played out the relationship of fictive kin in per-haps as many ways as actual kin relations are enacted.

This might all sound quite cozy and charming, quite unlike one's view of heart-less, cutthroat capitalism, and certainly different from the driven sales agents and managers described by Dorsey (1994). Here is a business depending on personal relations rather than on rigid bureaucratic rationality or the brutal logic of the market. Why would the management of MidWest want to change so extraordinary a system? There were a number of reasons, all of which contributed, in management's belief, to the disappointing level of life insurance sales.

The first issue management cited was that this recruitment system inadvertently resulted in a lack of diversity in agents recruited. In general, managers recruited peo-ple whom they knew. It was an informal but generally followed policy not to recruit agents from other insurance companies, since management felt that they would have learned improper or unethical sales practices not compatible with MidWest's prin-ciples. Therefore, managers turned to their personal networks for recruitment: stories about recruiting new agents at church were particularly common. Other agents were recruited into MidWest out of other sales jobs: managers saw how they treated cus-tomers during the sale of a washing machine or a windshield replacement and felt that this particular person would fit at MidWest. In general, recruitment from the manager's network turned out to pick out people like themselves: in particular, white males. MidWest was at this time concerned about a lack of diversity in the agent force (for reasons discussed in chapter 9). Beyond this obvious type of personal similarity, managers picked potential agents who shared the same sales style and approach to the business. This was an effective recruitment strategy when the manager's style and focus was in line with the style desired by MidWest. However, many managers had themselves been recruited at a time when sales skills were highly valued, to the detriment of organizational and business process skills. This led them to recruit and train similar sales aces, who might also lack organizational skills. And as already described, MidWest management believed that it was effective organization of a sales agency that allowed an agent to spend time on life insurance sales.

Management's solution for this problem at the point of the study was to change from external recruiting by district managers to internal recruiting by regional management: they began to recruit agents from within the ranks of MidWest employees. It might appear that internal recruiting would be a counterproductive way to develop a more diverse sales force. However, in terms of ethnicity and gender, the employee force was indeed more diverse than the agent force. It was felt that current claims processors or other employees would already have developed a strong loyalty to the company and would be more likely to follow directives from headquarters. Even at the time, it was understood that this recruitment pool was limited. While there were employees who wanted to become independent contractor agents, not all employees wished to, or would be able to gather the capital investment required to set up an office. Indeed, at the time of the writing of this book, MidWest has returned to recruitment of agents from outside the company as well as internally.

In addition to the change in how agents were recruited, a major change took place in the structure of the task of directly managing the agents of a district. MidWest changed this position from a single manager dependent on agents' commissions to a three-person management team, who were compensated as employees of MidWest. This change was intended to solve two problems of management focus. One was that under the old single-manager system, managers spent most of their time focused on agents who were high producers. Most spent little or no time on middle- or bottom-level agents, whom they called "slugs" or "sleepers." Managers gave most of their attention to high producers who could be induced to do even more and to mid-level producers who might be able to move higher. They had little incentive to spend time with agents who appeared unlikely or unwilling to change their sales practices.

Upper management's hope was that an employee management team would have more reason to work with the bottom half of the sales force. This hope was based on the assumption that the work of the management team was educational: training and assisting agents to develop better business systems and sales strategies. At the same time, there was also an unofficial resigned recognition that some agents would not change their practices, no matter what training, encouragement, or incentives they were offered—management would just have to wait until they retired to replace them with more dynamic sales agents.

Finally, the old management system fostered competition and immediate rewards as a motivation for selling insurance. Managers coached agents in sales techniques and dared them to sell enough to achieve rewards, like sales trips to desirable location. Upper management felt that this type of relation did not work well as a way for managers to train agents in effective business systems, best ways to set up their office practice, or division of labor between agent and staff. (This remained a complex issue; while management wished to see more of a focus on business process, they continued to sponsor sales contests, awards, and trips that encouraged the very habits they were trying to change.)

The new system, introduced as we began the study, replaced the single district manager with a three-person management team. The team's task was to counsel agents in improving their business process, introduce and train new products and policies, provide sales strategies, and assist with new technologies as they were introduced. They were paid almost entirely by MidWest: their bonuses did not depend on individual agents' earnings. Thus, the older agents complained that under the old system, the manager was their employee, whereas under the new system, the managers represented only MidWest. Managers no longer recruited new agents: that was to be done within a program located higher on the management ladder at regional headquarters. This program, called Agent of the Millennium, placed both recruitment and training in the hands of regional rather than local management, and it required that agents be recruited from the pool of people who had worked for MidWest for at least three years as employees. It replaced local coaching by the recruiting manager with classroom-based training at regional headquarters, often conducted by trainers who did not have experience as agents themselves. However, using trainers who taught from standardized materials produced at headquarters was an attempt to inculcate life insurance sales practices early in the agent's training, as well as introducing the office processes and systems that would allow for life insurance sales.

The new contract for agents

In addition to the change in local management structure, MidWest was also introducing a new contract for agents. This contract stated the requirements for what and how agents sold, and what their compensation would be. The proposed new contract was the first major contractual change in over twenty-five years.

Rather than requiring that all agents sign the new contract (as they legally could have), MidWest offered agents a range of choice. New agents were required to sign the new contract in order to become authorized as agents. However, established agents who had signed the earlier contract were given three choices: remaining with the old contract, signing the new one, or a mixed option under which the provisions of the old contract remained in force for existing business, while new business would be compensated under the new contract.

The financial and legal details of the contract, while fascinating in themselves, and riveting for the agents at the time, are not particularly relevant to the question of narrative and institutional memory. Perhaps the most relevant issue of the contract is that new terms of compensation and new requirements for doing business meant that agents choosing the new contract would have to change their way of doing business, including how much life insurance they sold and how carefully they screened their potential clients for possible risk to MidWest. Further, because they would be doing business in a new way, and under new provisions, it was not possible for agents to do a precise comparison between their projected income under the old and new contract provisions. For agents, this caused them to reexamine a question which had already been settled for almost all of them since their hiring: "Can I trust MidWest? Since I cannot calculate precisely how much my compensation would be under the new contract, do I trust management enough to believe that what they are doing is in my best interest, and, therefore, should I take the new contract?"

During the initial period of our fieldwork, it was known that a new contract was coming, but the specifics were not known. Rumors, of course, flew widely, and there was much discussion of all the "what if" scenarios that agents were able to imagine. Upper management was well aware of the seriousness of the issue and devoted a great deal of attention to the way that the new contract was introduced. The new contract rollout was made more difficult by its timing: the old system of managers personally tied to the agents had just been replaced by the more corporate three-person team of managers who had not had time to establish whatever relations of trust and loyalty the new management structure could support. Therefore, rather than relying on the relation between agents and managers, upper management planned a very carefully choreographed rollout, with a great deal of timed staging of the disclosure of information, and careful management of initial impressions.

The contract was initially disclosed to the lead members of the three-person district management team in a series of large meetings held in three locations around the country. This began with a meeting discussing the context and business reasons for the new contract. Most notably, the president of MidWest spoke about the need for change: "You can loose, or if you want to win, you can change." He then showed film clips of a number of CEOs of major companies such as IBM, Hewlett Packard, Ford, Sears, etc., speaking about their experience of change, specifically for this meeting. General explanation of some of the new contract provisions was followed by a presentation by a communications expert to prepare the local managers for the presentation of the new contract that they would make to groups of agents. He provided training in speechmaking, including a somewhat paradoxical training in how to be yourself and act naturally. However, after this training, the regional management decided that they did not want to risk too much change in the message and concluded that the district managers should not inject their personalities into the presentation, but rather should stick to the script, reading it if necessary, be relatively deadpan and business-like, and then "get out of there." Finally, the local managers were given binders with the new contract and explanation of what it provided, what it required, and how it would work, so they could study it in preparation for the local rollout.

The local rollouts were equally elaborately choreographed and had even tighter management of potential emotional responses. In the meeting I attended, the contract was presented to three local groups of agents by regional management and the three lead members of their district management teams. This represented approximately 150 people. The meeting began with a presentation by the regional vice president, the highest ranked manager in the region. He emphasized the reasons for the change, the complex schedule for accepting or rejecting the new contract, and the fact that star agents had been part of the team which developed the new contract. A video was then played of the president's speech which had been given in the managers' meeting described above, and then a video of the senior vice president in charge of agents, the upper manager most known and trusted by agents. He described the outline of the contractual provisions and then added his personal note: "We want agents to take the new contract. It's a good one. It's the right way to go." The general presentation was then followed by meetings between agents and their own district manager: three breakout groups. In these groups, agents asked specific questions about how the contract would affect their particular situations; most of these were deferred by the manager to individual meetings. The last part of the rollout was a series of these individual meetings, also highly choreographed. The initial meeting would be between the agent and manager, no other person permitted to attend. After that, the agent could bring in a second person, a spouse, a lawyer, or an accountant for a follow-up meeting.

This careful staging suggests the gravity of the change in process. Such a major change provided the occasion for a great deal of remembering the past and evaluating the current state of MidWest: Was it the unique company that it had been, or was it changing into something agents did not recognize and might not like? A number of managers invoked the past to prove that contract changes had happened before and had been beneficial. One upper manager recalled that this was his third contract introduction. There had been one about thirty years ago, and a revision of that one six years later. He claimed that the people who did not choose the new contract were sorry: "Those who failed to change failed to advance." Another regional manager invoked a frequently mentioned change: "Look back to when we were asked to move our offices out of our back bedrooms, to bring on trained staff, to incorporate microfiche and then computers." As always, these changes were recalled to make the point that a change that seemed threatening at the time turned out to be entirely advantageous. In these discussions, previous contract changes were mentioned but not detailed—referred to but not narrated. Little or nothing was said about the actual provisions of these earlier contractual changes, since they were not relevant to the issue of what the agents should do in the present.

In the months preceding and following the introduction of the new contract, we heard many agents reflecting on MidWest, and their relation to it, as a way to help make their decision about whether to sign the contract. Some agents felt that they would sign simply because "The company knows what it is doing." One agent who was well known by agents in his district to be highly sophisticated in his ability to calculate the business consequences of the new contract told me before the rollout that if the contract looked at all financially possible for him, he would sign it because he wanted "to be going in the same direction as the company." Another successful agent considered signing because she wanted to be "in sync" with MidWest, even though she felt that she did not understand the direction in which management was taking the company. In spite of her desire to align with the company, she felt she might have to stay with the old contract because the retirement provisions of the new contract would work unfavorably for her. Most agents who had ten years or fewer of tenure felt that there was no real choice for them: not to sign the new contract would demonstrate a lack of loyalty that they believed would probably have unknown but unpleasant consequences for them. Other more disaffected agents cited the new contract as a proof that MidWest had broken with its tradition of valuing the work of agents and that the company was no longer what it had been.

In summary, we were fortunate to carry out our fieldwork at an extremely complex and revealing time. We had a brief period in which we could see the previous system and then immediately after that period, the beginning of the changes which made that system into the "good old days." It was a particularly narrative-rich period, as agents and managers attempted to use the past to understand or explain the present, with varying views about what that past said about the present.

Epistemological and ethical issues in corporate fieldwork

I would now like to turn from a description of the structure of MidWest as we studied it, to a discussion of the issues involved in doing fieldwork financially sponsored by the institution one is studying. Such an arrangement raises practical, epistemological, and ethical issues. The fundamental question is, of course, the quality of the data. However postmodern one may be, it is obvious to question the validity or accuracy of a study paid for by the organization being studied. We may no longer believe in the possibility of strict objectivity, but we are still, rightly, frightened by the specter of the lack of it. However, I argue there are a number of advantages to doing an ethnographic study funded in this way. The first practical advantage is the matter of access. The study reported here involved three years of observations and thirteen different ethnographers at various points in the project. This is a dream project. I know of no independent funding agency that would fund so extensive a study. Only because the ethnographers were performing multiple roles was so long a study possible.

Additionally, because we were sponsored by the highest levels of management, we were given initial access to every level of the corporation. As I shall discuss below, each level of management and the agents themselves had the opportunity to give or withhold permission for our presence. The meetings explaining the project to gain such permission, and even our meetings at headquarters to report our findings, became, themselves, ethnographic opportunities to understand the organization further. It is rare in corporate ethnography to have access to all levels from the bottom to the very top.

Another advantage to so long a study is that it allows time to observe relatively rare events. If one wants to collect a particular type of narrative, as I did, there are several ways to do this. One is to collect the narrative directly by interviewing people. This method is convenient but produces narratives whose context is the interview itself, rather than the narrative in the full context in which it is used. (See Wolfson (1976) for a detailed demonstration of the linguistic differences between narratives collected in interview situations and those collected in naturally occurring discourse.) The other method is to find a situation in which the narrative type of interest occurs and wait for the narratives to appear. This is difficult because the actual stories are rare enough that waiting for them would be frustrating to nearly impossible if that were all one was doing. Thus, collecting narratives in the course of some other study entirely makes a more effective use of the researcher's time. (This of course assumes that the researcher was correct in the belief that situation being studied will contain the narrative of interest. The bird-watcher must know the native habitat of the birds being sought. I guessed right with MidWest Insurance, after a number of wrong guesses: studies in organizations which did not maintain an active stock of institutional narratives.)

I turn now to epistemological issues: how we learned what we did, and the ways in which the conditions of the study affected our learning and understanding. The greatest potential problem in being funded by the institution that is the object of study is that one may produce a biased account to flatter or placate the funder: the problem of the authorized biography. One might think that this type of report to a corporate sponsor must necessarily require flattery, or at least the portrait without warts. But oddly enough, there is a set of cultural expectations within the corporate world that help to prevent this kind of airbrushing of the picture.

When executives hire consultants (and our project was understood to be a somewhat odd form of consulting engagement), they expect to hear bad news. They have brought in a consultant, and prepared to pay for consulting services, because they already know that there is some problem. Thus both the consultants' professional reputation and the needs of the employer work together to permit the presentation of a less than flattering picture. The argument, then, is that within business, there already exists a practice of funding studies in order to receive feedback on potential problems. There is a practical limit on this expectation of bad news: in practice, consultants deliver reports of the kinds of problems they are equipped to help fix. Thus, management's choice of a particular consultant firm already contains assumptions about what kind of problem is probably present and what kind of solution will probably help. Thus, the practice of consulting provides an already understood role for the ethnographer. It also requires the practice of reporting the findings of the study to the people being studied, and they have both the opportunity and the power to agree or disagree with the accuracy of the picture. For example, one agent, interviewed in a later phase of the project, told us:

> By the way, I got a chance to read the IRL report that you guys had. I had never seen it before. And that was a very in depth, that was, you guys did a pretty good job for evaluating MidWest for whatever year, period of time.
>
> Because most of us have been around for twenty five years, you know. Very often you have a hard time putting that whole thing in perspective. But I think you guys pinpointed MidWest pretty well.

Indeed, the accuracy of our initial, small-scale ethnographic description contributed to the extension of the study from a small six-month pilot project to a multiyear effort. At the end of the first pilot project, we had a meeting with upper management in which we described the ways in which agents attempted to fit into the particular communities they served and to display their membership. Thus, we noted that agents drove the most expensive car that someone in their area would drive, but not one which was more expensive, even if they could afford it. We described an event where one agent's station wagon was being fixed, so he drove his wife's Mercedes to work. On visiting a client, he parked it around the corner so that she would not see him in an inappropriately expensive car. Somehow, this example convinced the senior vice president, who was the one to decide whether we should proceed, that ethnographic analysis gave us the capability to understand MidWest agents in a way unlike the methods of other consultants he had worked with, and it paved the way for further work. He felt that we were actually open to learning about the company, rather than providing a standard solution as many of the consulting firms he had worked with had done.

Of course, the opportunity to check one's analysis with one's subjects still does not eliminate another epistemological problem: the need to frame the analysis in terms familiar to the sponsor. Indeed, if anything, that opportunity would tend to exacerbate the use of the sponsor's own category system. There are two ways we attempted to deal with this problem. One was opening up to analysis the taken-for-granted categories of the sponsor. For example, they came to us with the question "Are disappointing levels of life insurance sales a learning problem or a motivation problem?" We concluded that the motivation problem was primary, but that motivation as a concept should be understood in a different way than MidWest understood it: an issue of social membership in particular communities of practice rather than a personal feeling residing invisibly in the individual's heart. This redefinition was one of the deliverables we were able to present to MidWest as part of a series of recommendations on changes in their motivational programs.

The other way we dealt with potential epistemological contamination was the development of parallel analyses: one in-house for ourselves and the other for the sponsor. For example, in the early phases of our exposure to insurance sales people, we were fascinated with the kind of professional friendliness they exhibited and found ourselves wondering about issues of sincerity, authenticity, and the definition of friendship for the agents. Arguing about these questions inside the team became part of our immersion into the culture of sales, but our tentative answers never found their way into our reports to MidWest. It was the part of the culture that was strangest to us, and which we needed to come to understand, but it was the daily bread and butter of a sales organization, whose members required no comment on it.

A final epistemological note: the reader may note my admiration and affection for the people we worked with, and for MidWest itself, and may conclude that I have fallen into the anthropological trap of falling in love with one's subjects. I agree that I am guilty of that. However, I can note that it has been at least eight years since I worked with them: the blindness of first love has had time to wear off. Also, I have studied other corporations where my most positive emotion was an appreciation for the difficulty of the challenges their members faced but not an admiration for the companies themselves. So I suppose I am arguing that MidWest was truly admirable—the reader may believe me or chalk it up to a protracted infatuation. I can only hope that my admiration has improved rather than contaminated the analyses I present.

I have argued for a number of advantages for doing ethnography of this kind. However, there still remain serious ethical issues in doing ethnography on your financial sponsor. These issues must be addressed. The primary ethical issue for any form of ethnographic fieldwork, however funded, is to avoid harming the people one studies. Secondarily, one should help them, if possible. The Code of Ethics of the

American Anthropological Association, approved in 1998 and still current, states this as follows:

> Anthropological researchers have primary ethical obligations to the people, species, and materials they study and to the people with whom they work. These obligations can supersede the goal of seeking new knowledge, and can lead to decisions not to undertake or to discontinue a research project when the primary obligation conflicts with other responsibilities, such as those owed to sponsors or clients.
>
> Anthropological researchers must do everything in their power to ensure that their research does not harm the safety, dignity, or privacy of the people with whom they work, conduct research, or perform other professional activities. (http://www .aaanet.org/committees/ethics/ethcode.htm)

Recently there have been major debates within anthropology about the appropriate guidelines to use: debates which have arisen because national funding bodies are attempting to impose uniform guidelines for all types of research involving human subjects, in fields ranging from cancer research to oral history. (For a review of the underlying philosophical background of these debates, see Hakken (1991).) The problem of devising or adhering to such overarching guidelines does not arise for research funded by the corporation itself, since the procedures required by research grants do not apply. However, this places an additional ethical burden on the research. Since the corporation has few if any requirements on the protection of subjects in the gathering and use of data, it is the responsibility of the researcher to foresee and provide for the possible ethical conflicts and problems

The most important ethical issues for this research center on the issues of informed consent and informant confidentiality. The American Anthropological Association Code of Ethics states this as follows:

> Anthropological researchers should obtain in advance the informed consent of persons being studied, providing information, owning or controlling access to material being studied, or otherwise identified as having interests which might be impacted by the research. It is understood that the degree and breadth of informed consent required will depend on the nature of the project and may be affected by requirements of other codes, laws, and ethics of the country or community in which the research is pursued. Further, it is understood that the informed consent process is dynamic and continuous; the process should be initiated in the project design and continue through implementation by way of dialogue and negotiation with those studied. Researchers are responsible for identifying and complying with the various informed consent codes, laws and regulations affecting their projects. Informed consent, for the purposes of this code, does not necessarily imply or require a particular written or signed form. It is the quality of the consent, not the format, that is relevant. (http://www.aaanet.org/committees/ethics/ethcode.htm)

In the case of a corporate study, just because upper management requests a study of the company and gives permission for it, this does not mean that every member of the corporation has given consent and may therefore ethically be studied. Fortunately, we began our study with an understanding that we would hold informative "buy-in" meetings at the regional and local levels of the organization to explain to everyone who might be involved what we were doing and to give them a choice of participating. Meetings of this sort were part of MidWest's culture: they were the standard method for introducing changes in policy and products. They also reflected one of MidWest's core values that projects were not enforced from above but required buy-in at all levels.

These meetings were, of course, for us, an ethnographic opportunity in themselves, allowing us to see a variety of managers and agents, at a number of organizational levels and locations. At every meeting, we were introduced and the project was explained. We had the chance to explain the work and the value that it might have for MidWest Insurance, to lay out the confidentiality protections we would use, and to request participation. Participation in the study was entirely voluntary for the agents, both in theory and, as it turned out, in practice.

In the first pilot phase of the project, we were asked to study top-selling agents in order to understand how the agents identified by management as the best ran their businesses. Therefore, the agents present at these initial meetings had been preselected by their management as good examples. Thus, participation was seen as an honor, a mark of management's appreciation, and agents gladly agreed to be studied. In later phases, we also studied a wider range of agents, including some identified as average or as poor performers. (The identification of an agent as an average or poor performer was, of course, confidential. Obviously, we did not cheerfully go up to an agent saying, "We've heard you're a bad example. Can we study you?") Agents and district managers were given a choice of whether to participate in the study. Most agreed, but some declined, usually with the explanation that it was a bad time for them to have an observer in their offices. The fact that some did decline was a good sign: it gave me confidence that the choice was a real choice and the consent truly was informed and free and that agents did not feel so pressured by their management that they it was impossible for them to decline. It is important to note here that the independent contractor status of the agents allowed them this ability to refuse a request from management. It would be much more difficult for employees, at MidWest or anywhere else, to decline such a request from their managers.

In addition to consent to participation in a study, the most important ethical issue raised by this kind of research is the issue of preserving informant confidentiality in order to avoid harm to informants. Experience with research in a variety of corporate settings suggests that when management pays for a study of its workers, it will demand access to the raw data about individual workers, which can be used for a variety of ethically dubious purposes, including surveillance or discipline of workers, or even as evidence in wrongful dismissal lawsuits. This type of use was less likely in the case of MidWest Insurance, since agents as independent contractors were not subject to the usual process of detailed performance evaluation. They could be dismissed by management only for acts which grossly breached their contract with MidWest, such as running another business out of their offices while maintaining an insurance business. If there were any agents who were operating in such breach of contract, it is unlikely that they would have allowed any observers into their offices in the first place.

However, because of this general desire for surveillance data on the part of employers, the Institute for Research on Learning made it an unalterable part of the language of all contracts, including our contract with MidWest, that no raw data would be given to the sponsor. This included field notes and audio and video recordings. All reports to the sponsor would keep the names of individuals confidential. Nor would researchers answer any direct questions about individual workers. These contract restrictions served as much for our protection as for the workers—if requested to do so, we would be able to say that the contract prohibited us from furnishing such information.

Confidentiality issues become much more complex when video recordings are involved. It is easy to change names and identifying details in written reports or audiotape transcripts. But participants in videotapes are much more identifiable. Initially, we felt that videotaping in agents' offices would involve both technical and confidentiality issues too difficult to take on. However, it became clear that to understand certain aspects of insurance sales it would be valuable, and in some cases necessary, to have videotapes of sales conversation between agents and clients. For videotaping, we instituted a system of dual written permissions from everyone shown in a video. (Such dual permissions have since become something of a standard in video-based ethnographic research.)

This was a complex, two-stage process. The initial permission form, given to everyone who might be shown in a video, including agents, staff members, and clients, gave permission for the video to be filmed, for use only within the research team, for analysis purposes. At any time during the filming, any participant could request that the tape be temporarily or permanently turned off. Within a week of the filming, any participant could contact us to request that the tape be destroyed. Agents were in general willing to be filmed and were mainly concerned about having the camera sufficiently discreetly placed that it did not interrupt the flow of their conversations with clients. However, some agents did request not to be filmed, as did some clients. Additionally, we had some cases where an agent or a client requested in the middle of a conversation that the tape be turned off and given to them, or called a day later with second thoughts to request that a tape be destroyed. In all such cases, of course, we did stop taping, or destroyed the tapes. These examples were in fact very heartening, since they suggested that we did, in fact, have informed consent: people were paying attention to what they were signing and had no hesitation in revoking the permission they had given.

We used these videotapes for analysis within the research team. In some cases, we found short segments, or whole interactions, that we wished to show to MidWest management as particularly good examples of practices described in our analysis, or to use as part of an academic conference presentation. In such cases, we returned to all participants in the tape with either the film clip we wished to show, or a transcript of it, and requested permission to show this segment to management, or at academic conferences. These permissions were almost always given. This process of second permission for wider showing become quite complex in the last stage of the project when we were producing a training CD on effective mentoring practices. Here, we wished to use a great number of clips. This required a considerable effort of finding, contacting, and explaining the nature of the permission to a wide variety of agents, trainee agents, and clients. Although complex, this process of attaining second permission for wider showing appears to be the minimum required to actually maintain confidentiality with video records.

Even in narrative reporting derived from field notes, ethical issues of confidentiality and privacy arise. We always attempted to disguise identifying details so that it was not possible to tell which agent held a stated opinion or engaged in business practices that management might disapprove of. In some cases this was impossible: if we had only one agent of a particular ethnicity in our study, we would refrain from any analysis or report that mentioned ethnicity. By chance, it happened that one agent chosen for our study was an officer of an organization of disaffected agents, critical of MidWest's current policy. This agent offered us access to this organization, but we were unable to accept this very tempting offer. Because of the oppositional nature of the organization, we would have had to get permission from all the members before we could ethically study it. And we would have been subject to far too much pressure from upper management to report on this organization, whose membership and activities were supposedly confidential (though better known to management than the membership might have wished).

A final reflection on confidentiality: we were concerned about confidentiality and restricting information in order to keep it from being used by management against agents. However, frequently agents saw us as a channel of communication with upper management. Agents often gave us their opinion about some management policy and specifically requested us to tell management what they felt, why they thought management was wrong, and what they thought management should do. This behavior is part of a general phenomenon: if a potential channel of communication exists or develops in an organization, people will use it. But it is also part of the culture of MidWest management, which goes to considerable effort to maintain open communication channels between agents and management. And it is part of the culture of independent contractor agents, many of whom boast of calling upper management directly, when they disapprove of some new policy.

Another important ethical issue that arises in doing ethnography funded by the organization studied is whether the material is confidential or whether the researchers will be permitted to publish in the academic literature as well as provide a final report to the sponsor. This is categorized as an ethical issue because part of the ethical responsibility of the research is to his or her discipline, which includes open publications of findings. In a discussion of contract anthropology, as opposed to university-based projects, Frankel and Trend (1991) describe the problem as follows:

> Worst of all from the standpoint of both external ethical codes and the institutionalized internal norms of any science is the employment that requires one to become a party to secrecy or even to misrepresentation of findings, and to exhibit loyalty not to the truth but to the employer. Everyone is familiar with the notion that science progresses by means of critical challenges to current beliefs. In that case both secrecy and misrepresentation are not just morally shady acts; they are deeply antiscientific and anti-intellectual, for they subvert the progress of knowledge itself. No matter what his or her credentials then, the individual who falsifies or conceals the truth is no longer a scientist—perhaps a spy, a salesman, or conceivably even a loyal citizen and a public benefactor, but not an anthropologist or any other sort of scientist. (180)

While this account of science reads rather naively after recent revelations about medical research sponsored by drug companies, the problems are real ones for the researcher's own professional ethics and standing. In addition, for the Institute for Research on Learning, permission to publish was a business issue for the Institute as well as an issue of scientific ethics for the researchers. Incorporated as a not-for-profit corporation, part of IRL's charter was to contribute to scientific literature; this was part of what distinguished it from a for-profit consulting firm.

For MidWest, this was not a major problem. They were concerned only that we not publish proprietary information about new policies or products, which might lose a competitive advantage for them. (This concern was unfounded, since they had no idea of the slow nature of the academic publication cycle. Long before any proprietary information could be written, peer reviewed, accepted and published, it would long have become public knowledge in the business press.) However, to respect this concern, our contract allowed MidWest right of review of material that we proposed to publish during and six months after the term of the contract. The specific contractual provisions were as follows:

> The second goal [in addition to providing MidWest with research and recommendations on specific issues] is to extend the general state of human knowledge as to the nature of learning, particularly how knowledge is embedded and maintained in organizations and what can be done to enhance that capability. We will focus on the learning of new processes in complex work environments as well as on the effect such learning has on work practices.
>
> IRL will, both during and after conclusion of its participation in the work, participate in scholarly communications, including presentation of findings derived from the work at conferences and seminars, publication of articles in scholarly journals and publication of books. Accordingly, this Agreement grants to IRL a degree of ownership of and publication rights for all data generated by the work for such purposes, including video and audiotapes, slides, photographs, field notes, and documents collected and developed as part of the work, as more particularly set out in detail in this Agreement.
>
> Publication Rights
>
> MidWest grants IRL, and IRL grants MidWest, the right to publish articles in scholarly or professional journals and the right to present technical papers at professional meetings, based on the results to be developed pursuant to this Agreement, provided that: a) any such publications or presentations by either party shall not cause the unauthorized disclosure or reproduction of the "confidential information" as described herein above. To decrease the chances of inadvertent disclosure, proposed publications and presentations will, for a period of six (6) months from the termination of this Agreement, be disclosed to the other for comment twenty (20) days in advance; and b) any publication or presentation by either party will include the acknowledgment of both parties in form appropriate to the circumstances.
>
> Either party shall have the right to withdraw its permission to the other party to publish or present specific portions or all of such articles or papers if the objecting party reasonably believes such publication or presentation will disclose confidential information as defined in section 5 above.

I was the first member of the team to invoke this clause: I wished to present a conference paper based on my initial observations of MidWest's use of narrative. Getting the paper reviewed was a rather strange process for all concerned. I sent it to the vice president who was the monitor for our contract, reminding her of this contractual provision. She clearly had more important demands on her time and delegated it to a subordinate, who was, quite understandably, bewildered about what was being asked of him. I had to walk him through the contract, and through the paper, so that he could formally agree in writing that an academic talk about the seventy-year-old founding narrative of the company did not disclose any proprietary information and could properly be published.

Finally, in work published during the duration of the contracted work, and afterward as well, I and my coworkers have chosen to use the pseudonym MidWest, rather than identifying the actual company. This has become a standard practice in the area of anthropology of work; it was not required or requested by MidWest.

Conclusion

I have discussed in some detail the business issues and the changes in MidWest Insurance, since these form the main data for this investigation of the role of narrative in institutional remembering. As should be clear, we came to MidWest at a time of change. This had a number of advantages. One was that we had a brief opportunity to see the earlier form of organization before the changes—providing a before and after snapshot. More importantly, times of change are rich in occasions when the past is invoked. The past is used to reaffirm a sense of identity, to provide a ground from which to assess the effect and meaning of changes, and to provide a basis for critique of changes. It is at times of change that a particular way of being is constructed as the past. And as people talk about change, they tell stories about this past to understand the present and predict the future. Thus, this time of change was a bonanza for hearing narratives in their natural habitat.

Occasions for Institutional Remembering

In the introduction, we looked at the issue of narratives in institutions and the importance of narratives for institutional remembering. In the previous chapter, we reviewed MidWest Insurance, the institution which provides the core data for this study. This chapter introduces occasions for narration as the most important issue for the life of narratives within institutions. As I have already argued, it is important not to mistake a representation of the past for active memory. Rather, we must discover the activities in which such representations are used to bring the past into the present. We want to know why, how, how often, and by whom they are used. This chapter begins this account by examining occasions for telling stories, the key activity for institutional remembering.

The narratives of a given institution may be collected by a company archivist, or by a historian or folklorist, but if this collection consists only of a rarely consulted archive or unread volume, the narratives have no life of their own, and there is no way to tell whether or not they are actually part of the institution's memory. There have been many such studies, which have a life, perhaps, within their own academic disciplines, but which are not alive within the institution they describe. Therefore, the key question is not what stories can be found, but, rather, what are the occasions which allow for the telling and retelling of the stock of stories which have a life within the institution and which constitute its acts of remembering. That is, when are these stories told, and why.

This discussion focuses mainly on oral narratives and their relation to written narratives, because we are so strongly literate a culture that our unexamined assumption is that institutions maintain their memory in writing, whether preserved on paper, on stone walls, or in databases. After all, there is "history" and "oral history": history derived from written sources is the unmarked assumption in most thinking about institutional memory. Although the main emphasis is on oral narrative, I will also discuss, in this chapter and later ones, written narratives within an institution, the ways in which they are used, and the ways in which stories move from oral to written and back to oral form.

I should also note that my main topic is narratives in linguistic form, whether oral or written. For the sake of completeness, it is important to note that narrative can also be expressed visually, in film or video. While most visual narratives also include dialogue or narration, they need not. I do not discuss visual narratives here, since all of the visual narratives I have encountered in my data set either include a linguistic narration or are voiced by a live narrator. However, it is obvious that a similar investigation could be conducted of the form and use of visual narratives within an institution, particularly as digital video becomes easier for nonprofessionals to produce and manipulate.

Additionally, I do not discuss the existence of written and visual narratives on the Internet. The Internet would appear to form an increasingly popular medium for representing the past. I have not discussed this most revolutionary development in representations of the past, since MidWest, at least at the time we studied it, did not make significant use of the Internet. While they wanted to be, in a cliché of the time, both high tech and high touch, in fact they were much more skilled in the personal touch as part of building relations than they were in the use of existing or developing technologies. Therefore, this important investigation remains to be done in another research site.

The question of how narratives are occasioned is not entirely a new one, although the scope of the current investigation is unique. Previous research on the occasioning of narratives has focused on narrative in ordinary conversation considering how a speaker introduces a narrative into a conversation (Sacks 1992). Sacks shows that in ordinary conversations, narratives are locally occasioned. That is, the storyteller makes use of an immediate event, or a prior story or reference in the conversation, to make a proposed telling of a narrative relevant to the conversation and to the recipient. In fact, one of the important skills of a conversational storyteller is to be able to recognize and make use of local occasions to justify the telling of a story. Similarly, it is a conversational skill to know how to respond to a story with a second story, using the second story to agree with, dispute, or extend the point of the initial story.

Such local occasioning in informal conversations happens within institutions as well, of course; there are myriad conversations that happen within institutions, and stories are told as part of these conversations. But not all of the narratives that are told within institutions happen in a conversational setting. There are many more formal speech events that can serve as an appropriate place for a given story: meetings, speeches, conventions, trainings, etc. The existence of relatively formal or institutionalized occasions for telling particular stories is extremely important for the life of the story in the institution. If there is no time, event, place, object, or practice that provides the occasion for the telling of a particular story within an institution, that story has little chance of entering into the stock of stories known and told by most members of the institution. A few people may find individual reasons and occasions on which to tell it, but it will not become part of the institution's representation of its past.

This chapter's discussion of occasions for narrative remembering uses a tax-onomy of types of occasions for narrative remembering. At this point in intellectual history, it is important to justify the use of such a taxonomy. Both anthropology and linguistics are familiar with the use of taxonomies, since both have a long tradition of structuralism, which posits meaning as arising from the relations of items stand-ing in a formal relation to one another. These are taxonomies that may take the form of a paradigm of grammatical relations, such as familiar verb conjugations or less familiar grammatical items. Or they may be taxonomies of semantic relations, such as a collection of kin terms or color names within a lexical contrast set.

More recently, there has been a turn from using taxonomies as representations of speakers' knowledge of their language and culture to an attempt to describe items in their full cultural embeddedness—an attempt to get the flesh back on the bones. Quinn (2005) offers a discussion of this change in anthropological linguistics as a move from a checklist theory of semantics to a reliance on schemas as a way to remain faithful to the cultural complexity of meaning. Within the field of folklore, there has been a simi-lar move: a change from the initial focus on collecting and categorizing motifs and variants of tales, songs, etc., to an interest in the context of performance: the relation between performer, audience, and the tale or song performed (Bauman 1992).

Historically, we find a similar progression in many sciences and certainly in those social sciences which have used structuralist methods. First is the phase of identifying the phenomena of interest. In later periods, this is sometimes referred to scornfully as butterfly collecting, but, in fact, it is necessary to have some idea of what kinds of butterflies exist before any serious analysis can be done on them. The second phase is structural analysis: classification, creation of taxonomies, understanding the paradigms and contrast sets in which each individual item exists and which give it its meaning. Finally, when the taxonomies or structural descriptions are established, it is possible to ask questions about context, meaning, and use. Linguistics and her older sister, philology, have been working for over two millennia to classify the structural relations of the grammatical and lexical units of language. In contrast, the study of resources for institutional memory is still in the butterfly collecting stage.

In effect, I am recapitulating these intellectual histories. My interest is in describ-ing how institutions use representations of the past, particularly narratives. This is, essentially, a focus on performance—how narratives are used. However, since I am examining a whole range of phenomena that have not previously been considered together as part of a single field, I need to sketch a taxonomy to organize my material. There are an enormous number of ways of representing the past. Rather than dismiss-ing them as an undifferentiated soup that happens to contain a few crunchy bits that I care about, I wish to organize these forms of representation of the past in order to facilitate a discussion of how they are used. This taxonomy is intended as an analytic convenience, both for this work and, I hope, for the work of other scholars as well. However, I wish to make it clear that I consider the status of this taxonomy to be only an analytic convenience rather than a claim about the deep structure of the culture or the mental representations of the members of the culture who use these narratives, memorial statues, and mugs.

Apologia completed, I offer a taxonomy of types of occasions for the telling of narratives. The first axis of this taxonomy is **modality**: time, both regular and

TABLE 3.1. Occasions for Narrative Remembering

	Designed for Remembering	*Used for Remembering*
Time: Regular occurrences	Anniversaries, regular audits, regular temporally occasioned ritual	Annual meetings
Time: Irregular or occasional	Retirement parties, roasts, problem-based audits, inductions, wakes, occasional temporally occasioned ritual	Arrival of a traveling bard, coronations, institutional problems, use of non-transparent nomenclature
Place	Museums, memorial displays, place occasioned ritual	Sites of events
Artifacts	Memorial artifacts, designed displays, photo albums	Artifacts accidentally preserved

irregular or occasional, space, and artifacts. The second axis is **design intention**: whether the occasion was specifically designed for remembering or whether it is has some other primary purpose, but has affordances that also allow for remembering. Table 3.1 shows typical examples, although no cell gives an exhaustive list of possible occasions. Let us examine examples of each of these types.

Temporally marked occasions

Temporally marked occasions are generally what we think of as humanly produced events. They include temporally regular ceremonies, ritual observances, commemorations of past events, annual legal necessities such as the preparation of taxes or the arrival of auditors, etc., but they can also be markings of regular or irregular natural events, such as the cycle of the seasons or astronomical events like the recurrence of a comet or an eclipse.

Temporally marked occasions designed for remembering

We begin with temporally marked occasions. These are occasions that have a regular temporal occurrence: they happen every year, every Sunday, on the anniversary of an event to be commemorated, etc. Some are specifically designed for remembering. For example, the fiftieth anniversary of D-Day was marked by ceremonies created and designed to allow for narrative remembering. Religious liturgies and ceremonies tied to particular dates, such as Easter or Christmas rituals, or the Passover seder, are another example of this type. One type of regularly scheduled ritual observances that permit (and often require) narrative remembering are those marking particular historical events: the birth or death of a founder or a saint, the founding of an institution, a martyrdom, etc. All of these can be the occasion for retelling the story of the event, whether in the form of a set reading of the account of the event memorialized, the delivery of a sermon prepared by its speaker for the occasion, or a relatively spontaneous retelling and updating of the story prompted by a written version, as is common in many celebrations of the Passover seder.

There are also temporally regular textual rituals. That is, on a given day of the year, a given text central to the history or identity of the institution is read: a particular psalm, a text of the founder, etc. This is the familiar yearly liturgical cycle of a number of religions, including Judaism and Christianity. To make the practice strange again, I will discuss it in some less familiar contexts. For example, in a Western Tibetan Buddhist community, Shambhala International, one yearly festival is Milarepa Day, an occasion at which community members gather at local centers to read aloud in one day a 289-page volume of the poetry and stories of founders of this particular lineage (Nalanda 1989). This event was traditional in Tibet and was certainly one way of many that the founders' stories were retold and used to work the past. It takes on a new meaning in Western contexts, since it is virtually the only way in which converts get to hear the stories of the lineage founders.

For another example, Waldorf teachers who are anthroposophists recite and meditate on a verse for that particular week each morning. If the majority of teachers at the school are anthroposophists, they may also recite the week's verse at faculty meetings. These verses are taken from the writings of the founder, Rudolf Steiner. They serve to carry on the memory of this textual community, which is organized around the writings of its founder.

Another point to note here is that while I am making a distinction between historical events, and seasonal, recurring events, this is a determination I wish to leave to the celebrants. That is, if the event is presented as located in historical time, I will not try to differentiate whether it is "really" history or not. Similarly, if something people outside a given community would consider history is treated by that community as an eternally recurring event to be memorialized, again I will prefer the members' interpretation. For an example of this, Yerushalmi (1989) discusses the complex nature of the biblical injunction to the Jews to "remember":

> We have learned, in effect, that meaning in history, memory of the past, and the writing of history are by no means to be equated. In the Bible, to be sure, the three elements are linked, they overlap at critical points, and in general, they are held together in a web of delicate and reciprocal relationships. In post-biblical Judaism, as we shall see, they pull asunder. Even in the Bible, however, historiography is but one expression of the awareness that history is meaningful and of the need to remember, and neither meaning nor memory ultimately depends upon it. The meaning of history is explored more directly and more deeply in the prophets than in the actual historical narratives; the collective memory is transmitted more actively through ritual than through chronicle....
>
> With the sealing of the biblical canon by the rabbis at Yabneh, the biblical historical books and narratives were endowed with an immortality to which no subsequent historian could ever aspire and that was denied to certain historical works that already existed....That which was included in the biblical canon had, so to speak, a constantly renewable lease on life, and we must try to savor some of what this has meant. For the first time a history of a people became part of its sacred scripture. The Pentateuchal narratives, which brought the historical record up to the eve of the conquest of Canaan, together with the weekly lesson from the prophets, were read

aloud in the synagogue from beginning to end. The public reading was completed triennially in Palestine, annually in Babylonia (as is the custom today). and immediately the reading would begin again. (14–16)

In particular, in many periods of Jewish history, current events are remembered by placing them within a recurring pattern:

> On the whole, medieval Jewish chronicles tend to assimilate events to old and established conceptual frameworks. Persecution and suffering are, after all, the result of the condition of being in exile, and exile itself is the bitter fruit of ancient sins. It is important to realize that there is also no real desire to find novelty in passing events. Quite to the contrary, there is a pronounced tendency to subsume even major new events to familiar archetypes, for even the most terrible events are somehow less terrifying when viewed within old patterns rather than in their bewildering specificity. Thus the latest oppressor is Haman, and the court-Jew who tries to avoid disaster is Mordecai. Christendom is "Edom" or "Esau," and Islam is "Ishmael." Geographical names are blithely lifted from the Bible and affixed to places the Bible never knew, and so Spain is "Sefarad," France is "Zarefat," Germany is "Ashkenaz." The essential contours of the relations between Jews and gentiles have been delineated long ago in rabbinic aggadah, and there is little or no interest in the history of contemporary gentile nations. (36)

In contrast to the detemporalization of a historical event, we can also find the regular commemoration of events not located in historical time. From what we know of the classical Greek mysteries, they appear to have had this character: an annual retelling and reenactment of mythical events, tied perhaps to the seasons, such as the return of Persephone from the underworld.

Moving from religion to accounting for a different kind of example, U.S. corporations are required to do regular audits that are legally mandated occasions for a specific form of remembering. They have a conventional pattern, requiring personnel within an institution to present specific records in a specific form to outside auditors. But they are also an occasion for new members of the institution, particularly those involved with record keeping, to ask questions and share stories about why the records are as they are: How are the records set up? Why did we set up a separate project number for that part of a project? Why was there an under-run or over-run? Why are the old procedures different from the current ones? We did not have the opportunity to observe this kind of remembering at MidWest Insurance, since we did not do fieldwork at the headquarters offices at which these reviews take place. While agents also must file taxes, and interrogate their records in preparation for preparing their taxes, we did not have the opportunity to see any agent doing so. However, I suggest that an ethnographic study of the accounting practices of a U.S. corporation would furnish a treasure of narrative remembering.

Temporally regular events used for remembering

Other temporally regular events can be used for remembering, although that is not their primary purpose. For example, MidWest holds annual sales conventions in each region as well as nationally, which form regular occasions for narration, although this is not their primary purpose. These conventions have formal talks by executives of the company, which regularly invoke the past to explain the present and future. One of the main functions of these conventions is to announce new products and new programs to the agents. If these changes are likely to be unpopular with agents, it is common for management to try to show that they are actually completely in harmony with MidWest's past, which requires telling stories of this past. Another function of the convention is to honor the achievements of individual agents. This too leads to storytelling about their history and contributes to the company's ongoing narrative of what a successful career is. (See chapter 7 for a discussion of the generic, or paradigmatic, narrative of a successful career.)

In addition, we have observed, the convention is also an occasion for the display of many other forms of representation used for remembering. For example, we saw a psychedelic-style light show featuring photos of the history of the company, mounted blowups of historical photos, a videotape loop of the company's history, a contest in quiz show format featuring questions about company history, etc.

Events like this kind of large convention also form an occasion for smaller communities to come together. These conventions are often held in desirable vacation destinations and thus form the occasion for the creation of additional institutional memory for these smaller communities: for example, "the time we went to Rome and the regional vice president gave his speech in a toga." These new events are then retold at subsequent meetings of the communities. For example, a MidWest agent told us about the adventures of the "Road Rats," an informal group of agents and their wives (at the time he is remembering there were no women agents) who met regularly at trips for high performing agents, renting motor scooters to explore the exotic locale of the trip. He told a story of bad weather, bad hotels, bad cab drivers, and nearly missing the boat back. As the following excerpt shows, much of the fun comes in remembering past excursions, even difficult and uncomfortable ones:

> And now, of course, that's the greatest trip we've had. Every time we get together we talk about this wonderful time we had in Capri. And it was just a disaster but of course now it's hilarious. We had a great time. So all the people who were on this trip were at dinner last night. All the Capri Road Rats. John Smith, you know, the white haired guy, the big dog [the regional vice president], he's a member of the Road Rats. There's eight couples, agents and their spouses, that are official Road Rats. We even have t-shirts with two big rats sitting on a motorcycle.

Temporally irregular events

Like temporally regular events, events which happen irregularly, prompted by occasions or circumstances, can also be divided into those specifically designed for remembering, and those not designed for remembering as their main purpose, but incidentally used for memory work.

Temporally irregular or occasional events designed
for remembering

Temporally irregular or occasional occasions are events whose exact timing cannot
be predicted but recur within an institution and require certain types of narration.
One common example of this type designed for remembering is the class of rituals
of liminality, like inductions or retirements. Inductions are a particular class of occasions on which a new person, or new group of persons, is admitted into an organization or a new status within it. These occasions can include orientation meetings and
presentations in a business context, administration of oaths of office in a political or
military situation, etc. For example, at MidWest, part of the training of new agents
and employees includes an account of the founding and subsequent history of the
company. This is not a pro forma event. It takes a considerable amount of time and is
delivered with great liveliness.

For example, I observed a training session for new employees in which the first
morning and part of the afternoon of a three-month-long training covered the history and values of MidWest. The video history was shown, and the manager doing
the training then asked the students what in the video stood out for them, throwing a
small roll of hard candy bearing the MidWest logo to each person who mentioned a
striking fact. She then passed out sheets of company milestones by decade and went
through them, discussing high points in the company's history, interspersed with
stories of her own involvement with MidWest.

One former trainer, now an agent, described the importance of this kind of training for new agents:

> Agent: I don't know about The Agent of the Millennium Program, but I hope that
> someone is telling them it's not a job. My real concern is taking our agents from
> employee ranks only. I think it's good in most respects, but the danger is that you get
> people who see the agency opportunity as another job, as no different than moving
> from clerk to underwriter. Maybe that's what MidWest will want. But I don't think
> if you do it right that it is at all. They may not be prepared for us if they think of it
> as a job.
>   Interviewer: You came through it that way, but didn't see it that way.
>   Agent: All of us see what we do as more than a job. The responsibilities that come
> with it. Because we are a service business you take work home with you. Everybody
> know that Sally works at MidWest, it follows her wherever she goes. Everywhere you
> go there's someone who needs something from you. We've had people who have left
> us, moved, but keep in touch, think of us as friends. It's refreshing to develop these
> side relationships. That doesn't come with the job. It's a way of life.

Training is a fairly routine form of institutional induction. For a contrast, let us
examine a rather more operatic induction ritual involving the recounting of history is
given in Bonanno (1998). This is an account by the son of the head of a U.S. Mafia
family of his formal joining of his father's Family:

> I took my "oath of office" in a large warehouse in Brooklyn.... After the initiation,
> we all gathered at an Italian restaurant, the Enchanted Hour, which was across the

street from the warehouse.... There were speech and toasts and endless plates of food as the waiters came and went through the entire day and into the night. The speeches were about the old country and about our traditions, who we were once and always would be. It is a sacred component of our tradition that, from time to time, on certain occasions, we all hear, once again, like parishioners in a church, the old stories, the biblical sagas about what made us who we are. This was one such occasion.

"Sicily, our country, was the invasion route of conquerors," said one speaker. "In the eight century B.C., the Greeks landed in our country and pushed the native Siculi and Sicani inland, and then the Romans came and then the Byzantines. We were sacked by the Vandals and the Goths; then the Saracens invaded the island. Our people detested the Saracens, but we took their culture to heart, its beauty, its passion for secrecy and revenge..."

And so it went through the Sicilian Vespers up to the period when our people moved out and away, went to Europe and Australia and the United States. One of our group captains stood up and got the attention of everyone in the room. He turned and looked at me. Then he spoke, in Sicilian.

"Salvatore, I will remind you of your great-grandfather Giuseppe Bonanno, a friend and helper of Garibaldi himself...."

I knew the story, set in 1870, when Garibaldi's ragtag army was on the verge of being wiped out by the occupying and far more powerful Bourbon armies. Our Family, which by then had become prominent in the area around Castellammare del Golfo on the western tip of the island, came to Garibaldi's rescue. The story was a reminder of who the Bonannos were, of the blood that connected me in 1954 to my forebears, going back for centuries.

"Remember the Battle of Segesta, [actually fought in Calatifima]? Who was there to help Garibaldi? Who did he turn to for help when the Bourbon armies were ready to annihilate him?..." The words came tumbling out, but it was more in the manner of a church service than a narrative. "They turned to the *piciotti*, 'the boys.' And so, Salvatore, your great-grandfather rounded up a herd of sheep and cattle and drove them toward the Bourbon army so that they raised a cloud of dust as they went...."

There was excitement in the speaker's face, his skin was flushed, and his hands moved before him almost as if he was leading an overture to an opera. "A great cloud of dust was raised, the Bourbon soldiers could not see, and so Garibaldi's men, few though they were, moved in and around them, destroyed them, once and for all.... The great and historic Segesta...it is with us today. But it was not liberation, only the illusion of liberation, for Sicily has never been free."

Another person got to his feet, rapped a glass with a spoon, calling for attention. I was reminded about my father's success in this life and how it should always be my guide, my model. Someone else told a story about the Beati Paoli, the Blessed Pauls, and Corleone della Forresta, who worked for the government during the day but who wore a hood over his face like a modern Robin Hood; there were stories about his contemporaries Count Blasco and old Don Raimondo...on and on into the night.

The speeches finally ended. The ceremony itself, simple, stark, and chilling began. I was asked to write a number down on a little piece of paper, a number larger than the number of people in the room. I wrote down 115 (my birthday is November 5: 11/5). Then everyone in the room held up one, two, or three fingers of one hand. When the number I selected was reached, the designated person drew blood from my finger with a pin-prick. The drops of blood were spattered onto a picture of Saint Sebastian; the picture was then burned while I held it so that I could feel its heat, feel what would happen to me if ever I broke the vow I now was taking. (13–17)

This is presented as a true memoir, but it sounds, as I have said, quite operatic. Certainly the speeches could not be verbatim, since they are recalled forty-five years after the event by a historically minded author whose main theme is the honorable past and subsequent moral decline of the Mafia. Even if the induction happened as described, there is considerable argument about the degree to which popular beliefs about the Mafia in the last two centuries have been shaped by fictions about its nature, ceremonies, and rules. However, the veracity or not of the story does not vitiate my point. What Bonanno has written here at least sounds exactly like what we think an initiation should be, and it contains an enormous amount of remembering of the past. *Si non è vero, è ben trovato.*

Creating the institution by remembering it

In the previous examples of induction as an occasion for remembering, what is retold is the story of the whole institution. A minor theme is the trainer telling her own story and how it relates to the story of MidWest Insurance, but the main point is the story of the institution as a whole. Similarly, in the Mafia induction, the speaker and his family are located within the entire political history of Sicily. Both are definite and highly reified institutions. While we quite properly speak of the continuous reproduction of an institution by the minute-to-minute and day-to-day processes and activities that constitute it, an institution like MidWest Insurance is also reproduced by its continuous seventy-five years of ongoing activities, as well as its buildings, its file cabinets, its location in a larger net of laws and regulations. In contrast, let us now look at an institutional occasion for remembering in which the theoretical issue of interest is exactly the creation of the institution by the act of remembering.

The example we will consider here is the high school (or college) reunion. I treat these as temporally irregular because although their structure could be regular—the tenth, twentieth, or twenty-fifth reunions after graduation, in fact class, reunions are not always held at these landmark dates, and more importantly, many people attend only one class reunion (Vinitzky-Seroussi 1998; Ikeda 1998). Following Zussman (1996), Vinitzky-Seroussi calls these reunions "autobiographical occasions": situations in which people who share a past have the opportunity to co-construct this past in the present by re-narrating it. An important point about class reunions is that the institution remembered was not the salient unit at the time being remembered. That is, a high school (or college) class is not experienced by its members as their collectivity of primary allegiance.

The class, the cohort as a collective, is a formal delineation of age and academic placement rather than a substantive social unit. It is not the major framework in school, where both social subunits (cliques) and units that transcend the cohort (e.g., the football team) constitute more palpable social entities. A glance at various high school yearbooks confirms this. The pictures of the graduates are arranged alphabetically, while most of the group photos are shots of different school clubs and teams (e.g., photo club, band, football team). Other collective student activities pictured in the yearbook—such as plays and other performances—bring students together only briefly.

Moreover, the class is not a unit that existed in the minds of its members to begin with. It should be noted that the returnees indeed have no doubt that they graduated from a specific class and that they will remain members of that class for the rest of their lives. But how do they recall this unit?

From the interviews I conducted it seems that in most cases the memory of the class is remarkably vague—"we used to have fun."...In most cases, detailed memories of high school have very little to do with the class as a unit; rather they are memories either of oneself or of specific encounters with others.

The collective celebrated by the high school reunion has its foundation on shaky ground: the class as a social unit is invented and reified at the reunion, the event itself may not provide evidence that there was a collective in the past, past leaders may not take the roles other returnees expect of them, the notion of community is based on a partial foundation at best, and the entire collective may never meet again. (Vinitzky-Seroussi (1998) 41)

Thus what is remembered is not the institution of the high school class, since that collectivity has little stable long-term existence. While the members were attending high school, it had an administrative existence for the school, as "The Class of N Year." But it was not a salient social institution for the participants. Rather, an ephemeral institution has been called into being for the occasion, and it serves as an opportunity for personal, individual remembering. One might think that although the high school class is not the salient unit, the high school itself would be. However, high school reunions are most commonly held in restaurants or banquet halls, not at the school itself. The reasons are legal: most high schools are forbidden to serve alcohol on the premises and do not carry the liability insurance to permit gatherings like a reunion. This means that the building itself is not available to participants as a spur for remembering. The impersonal and unrelated setting of a banquet hall tends to restrict participants to the memories they came in with, rather than triggering forgotten stories about this gym or these halls. (Although I have not yet attended any of my own class reunions, I am always struck, on entering a school, by how frighteningly evocative the smell is.)

In spite of its somewhat accidental nature, the high school reunion has power for the participants because it may contain at least some of the right people to remember with. That is, it can be an occasion for remembering one's past with some of the people who shared that past and either receiving their confirmation that the past was as one remembers it, or learning a different version of one's personal past. (See chapter 8 for a discussion of second-person stories: stories told about oneself by others.) For many of the participants interviewed, a successful reunion was one in which the proper co-rememberers were present and confirmed or improved one's account of oneself back then.

As Vinitzky-Seroussi describes it, remembering the high school past is only part of the work of remembering. The other part, and perhaps the most salient aspect of the reunion, is the contrast between the past and the present: bringing people up to date on what has happened between then and now. All returnees wished to show a successful trajectory. This show is not only and perhaps not even primarily narrative: a slim attractive appearance, appropriately expensive clothes, and a desirable spouse are as much a part of demonstration of one's success as a narrative of what one has been doing. Indeed, the stories tend to be short, and conventional. Short, because people tend to circulate and talk to as many others as possible, so that long, detailed, and nuanced stories are rarely possible. And conventional, since the demonstration of success is not to a community of people with whom one has had the opportunity to work out shared values. Therefore, the definition of success must be the default values of the larger society: marriage, children, a conventionally successful job. The implicit hope, for many returnees, is that one will finally be able to "show them," or admit one's disappointments to "them" because the appropriate "they" will be in the room. But for at least some returnees, the event brings them to suspect that there is no "they" that can serve that function, and that perhaps there never was one. In contrast, updates of one's activities written for an alumni newsletter permit more creative framing of one's activities as successes. However, they lack the opportunity to receive direct confirmation from their recipients.

Ikeda (1998) extends the analysis of proper recipients, arguing that for Americans, one's high school classmates are the most relevant people with whom to explore the meaning of progression through the life course.

> At the core of my analysis of high school reunions are the phenomenological interplay between high school past and adult present in the drama of human development and the forming and re-forming of the high school class as a community of memory in order to collectively create meaning. In the high school reunion, Americans are, to paraphrase Fernandez (1986), thrown into a room full of mirrors in which they can see themselves. Through the arrangement of the light and shadow of the high school self seen in classmates' memories, as well as the silhouettes of adult classmates that have been drawn by inescapable life processes—biological, social, and historical—Americans seize images of their present selves in relation to others and place their biographies in the context of the larger processes that embrace them. In the struggle over meaning that emerges in each high school reunion, Americans construct new symbols and stories uniquely fitted to their high school class as they participate in meaning-making activities as memory-bearing persons situated in specific historical and lifecourse positions. In the process, the high school reunion mediates individual meaning with collective meaning and enriches the individual biography with a sense of connection to culture and history. (151–52)

Temporally irregular or occasional events used for remembering

Certain occasions may arise at irregular intervals that are used for remembering. For example, in committee meetings, someone may propose changing a policy. This is often, though not necessarily, the occasion for someone else to object by recounting the story of previous problems that the policy was designed to prevent. Similarly,

irregularly scheduled audits, like an IRS audit of an individual's taxes are an opportunity within a household for narrative remembering of financial actions and their
reasons. In oral cultures, or cultures maintaining a strong oral element, the arrival of
a traveling bard may be an occasion for the singing of epics or tales foundational for
a given group but not known in full or not sung except by designated specialists. In
some documented cases, but not all, bards travel from place to place. For example,
in Tibet, prior to the Chinese invasion, there were traveling singers reciting the Gesar
epic, as well as local amateur singers, who, however, knew only fragments of the
enormous epic. Thus, the arrival of traveling singer, dressed in a distinctive Gesar
bard hat, was the main way most people had the chance to hear parts of the epic,
which singers in their own village did not know, and for local singers to learn more
of it (Kornman 1997; Enhong 1999).

In the case of the extensively studied oral bardic tradition of the former
Yugoslavia, singers were local and not professional; most were farmers, herders,
coffee house owners or workers, who performed for local audiences. However, Lord
(1965) argues that in the medieval period, there were traveling minstrels:

> In an account of the occasions for singing and of the audience which fosters it,
> mention at least should be made of the courtly entertainment of the earlier days
> in Yugoslavia. What we have been describing up to this point was in existence in
> Yugoslavia in the 1930's and to an extent still continues. In medieval times, before
> the Turkish conquests, the Christian courts had undoubtedly fostered the minstrel's
> art as had the courts of other countries in Europe at that time. When these courts re-
> emerged, however, after the expulsion of the Turks, they were no longer interested
> in the bards but sought their entertainment from abroad or from other sources. Hence
> in the Christian courts oral narrative poetry played no role for many generations.
> The local Moslem nobility on the other hand with its rich estates had fostered the
> art, and since this local nobility was still alive in some districts such as Novi Pazar,
> Bijelo Polje, and Bihac¢ in the 1930s, it was still possible to obtain firsthand infor-
> mation about the practice.... The records of the Parry Collection abound in stories,
> some fairly full, of how the Moslem bards used to sing at the "courts" of the Turk-
> ish nobility. Here the professional or semiprofessional singer was afforded the best
> opportunity for practicing his art. There seems to be little evidence, however, that the
> beys and aghas actually maintained a court minstrel. They not infrequently called in
> singers for special occasions when they entertained guests, but they did not keep a
> singer in their courts. In the old days the ruling class of Moslems celebrated the feast
> of Ramazan [sic] in its courts rather than in the kafana [coffee house]. (16)

A much more local and small-scale example of a temporally irregular occasion used for remembering is the use in conversation of a specific and odd piece of
nomenclature. Unusual terms may provide the opportunity for the narration of parts
of the institutional memory. For example, I have heard several accounts of the term
GO's [Gentil Organisateurs] for the staff of Club Med, told by former staff members
who were told them during their training period. In one version, the term is said to go
back to the earliest founding when conditions were Spartan, and the staff had to be
exceedingly gentil to deal with the complaints of customers. In another version, the

term is said to derive from founding idea, revolutionary for a French company, that its staff should be *gentil*.

An example at MidWest Insurance is the pair of terms MOC and SOC, pronounced "mock" and "sock," which stand for "moveable object collision" and "stationary object collision." Although all auto insurance now protects against both, initially MidWest only provided protection against moveable object collision, since the founder felt that someone who hit a stationary object was an incompetent driver and should not be driving. Stationary object coverage was therefore added only several years after the founding of the company. These terms are revived in stories about the founder to provide occasions for stories about how many changes the company has undergone and about the moral and somewhat idiosyncratic character of the founder.

Another example of the use of terminology as an occasion for narrative at Mid-West is the following, an explanation of the numbering system of the corridors in the headquarters building. The event at which this was told was a speech to new managers by a veteran manager described as the unofficial company historian. (See chapter 5 for a fuller description of this event.) He told this story as part of a series of stories about the enormous growth of MidWest, requiring the building of offices that seemed absurdly large at the time of their construction but which rapidly required additions, including the inclusion of separate buildings:

> The original building was built in 1929, and then it was added to in 1935, and just before the war, we purchased the property on the North side and built the eight stories. Just after the war. So as I say, it looks like a single building. And I don't know if you have ever had this experience, but the dotted line down the middle, there used to be an alley way there from E Street over to Downs County courthouse, which you can see in the background. And honestly today, I wrote a letter the other day to Sam Jenks, 12 South Fire building. And I wrote one also to Samantha Smithers, Southern North Fire Building. And I saw, what's this North South jazz. And North South means whether you were north or south of the alley, and that alley has been gone for darn near sixty years and it still hangs on as a tradition around here.

What is interesting about the use of this story is that the narrator uses a small and probably unnoticed detail of the nomenclature of the layout of the headquarters building to illustrate his grand theme—the unstoppable growth of MidWest.

An example of the complexity of this kind of memory comes from my own experience at the Institute for Research on Learning. For a long time, the governing committee was called G-Wiz. This odd term was questioned by most new employees. The question formed the opportunity for the retelling of a complex story about changes in the governance of the institute. Initially, the governance committee was small, consisting of four, and then five, founding members of the Institute. In somewhat ironic recognition of the exclusivity of the size of the group, the committee was nicknamed the Gang of Four, shortened to G4 and then G5. As more members were admitted, it grew to G8. Meanwhile, there was also a committee of the whole, called G-All, or GALL. When it was decided that all researchers should be part of the governing committee, the question was raised as to whether it should be named G14, after the current number of researchers, or Gang of All, which would then preempt the name of the committee of the whole. At this point of confusion, someone suggested naming it G-Wiz, and the name stuck. The name and the story were perpetuated partly because of the oddity of such a name for a governing committee. But it also continued to be told because it furnished a moral demonstration of improvement from an exclusive to a more representative method of governance and was thus one means for inducting new members into both values and the history of those values.

Finally, an additional type of temporally irregular occasion that allows for remembering the history of MidWest comes when agents are attempting to sell insurance to clients, and they tell or reference the history of MidWest as a guarantee of the company's stability and quality. In the following example, the agent is talking with a client, new to her, who is transferring her insurance from another MW agent in another state:

> Agent: So we're going to do auto insurance today? First let me give you an introduction to the company and myself so you know something about us. Have you ever done business with MidWest before?
>
> Client: Yeah. I recently moved to the area from the East Coast.
>
> Agent: Oh great.
>
> Client: So I still have my insurance from there.
>
> Agent: Terrific. And you were with MidWest there. You may know we were founded in Smallton [STATE] in 1923 so we've been around for more than 70 years now which is a sign that we're doing something right for our policy holders. We are a multi-line company so we do auto, life, health, disability, annuities, IRAs, just about everything really. Sometimes people think of us exclusively as an auto insurer, and there's a good reason for that since we're the largest in the country. We insure one out of every six cars, one out of every five homes, and we're one of the fastest growing health insurers...And I'm really proud we've been ranked number one out of all the life insurance companies in the countries. not only by the [?] group and just about anyone you talk to.
>
> One advantage to our being so big is that we have claims offices all over the United States and Canada so if something does happen while you're away from home there's always a MidWest claims office. Most times they can write you a check on the spot. Also if you were to move from one place to another like you're experiencing it's very easy to transfer your policy to a new and different agent. The flip side of our being so big and having those benefits is that MidWest really tries to personalize service. That's very important to our policy holders. So as your agent I'm available to answer any questions that you have. If you were to have a loss we'd take the initial report right here in this office. And we're available to make sure the process goes smoothly. Our claims people are wonderful and they do a terrific job. So usually we aren't too involved in that process.

In this example, the history of MidWest is referenced, not told in full. This is characteristic of the way in which agents use the history. It is primarily used as a warrant for the stability and trustworthiness of the company. As the agent here spells out, the size and the stability of the company is an advantage for the client—the most important lesson of history for a client.

Places as occasions for remembering

We turn now to places as occasions for remembering. As with events, I divide these into places intended and designed for remembering, and places used for remembering, but not designed to be so.

Nora (1989) has produced a widely influential exploration of places as memory sites. However, his use of the term "sites," or "*lieux*," is much broader than my intended use. I really do mean places as physical locations: buildings, locations within buildings, statues, former battlefields, islands, etc. In contrast, Nora describes his project on the relation of history and memory as an attempt to study national feeling not in the traditional thematic or chronological manner, but instead by analyzing the places in which the collective heritage of France was crystallized, the principal *lieux*, in all senses of the word, in which collective memory was rooted, in order to create a vast topology of French symbolism:

> Though not really a neologism, the term did not exist in French when I first used it.... I took it from ancient and medieval rhetoric, as described by Frances Yates in her admirable book, *The Art of Memory* (1966), which recounts an important tradition of mnemonic techniques. The classical art of memory was based on a systematic inventory of loci memoriae, or "memory places." In French, the association of the words lieu and mémoire proved to have profound connotations—historical, intellectual, emotional, and largely unconscious (the effect was something like that of the English word "roots") (xv–xvi).
>
> If the expression lieu de mémoire must have an official definition, it should be this: a lieu de mémoire is any significant entity, whether material or non-material in nature, which by dint of human will or the work of time has become symbolic element of the memorial heritage of any community (in this case, the French community.) The [original] narrow concept had emphasized the site: the goal was to exhume significant sites, to identify the most obvious and crucial centers of national memory, and then to reveal the existence of invisible bonds tying them all together. As revealing and sweeping as this approach was, however, it tended to create the impression that lieux de mémoire constituted a simple objective category. The broader conception...placed the accent instead on memory, on the discovery and exploration of hidden or latent aspects of national memory and its whole spectrum of sources, regardless of their nature. This simple change of method, this natural extension of the original notion of a lieu de mémoire, in fact gave rise to a far more ambitious project: a history of France through memory. (xvii–xviii)

Thus, for Nora, *lieux de mémoire* can have three senses—places, sites, causes. They can include what I am considering as places: geographical sites marking remembered events, pilgrimage sites, and memorials for the dead. But he also includes textbooks, the new calendar adopted during the French Revolution, standard histories in wide use, geographical divisions such as the division of France into Paris/provinces, or North/South, landscape paintings, generations (such as the generation of '68), etc. I will not discuss in Nora's goals as a historian considering the writing of history and the relation of history and memory. He is concerned with the acceleration of history: "The metaphor needs to be unpacked. Things tumble with increasing rapidity into an irretrievable past. They vanish from sight, or so it is generally believed. The equilibrium between the present and the past is disrupted. What was left of experience, still lived in the warmth of tradition, in the silence of custom, in the repetition of the ancestral, has been swept away by a surge of deeply historical sensibility. Our consciousness is shaped by a sense that everything is over and done with, that something long since begun is now complete. Memory is constantly on our lips because it no longer exists" (1).

I consider this a mistaken and romantic construction: we used to have organic memory; now we only have history. It is romantic in its view of a traditional and cozy past. It is mistaken in believing that processes of memory have changed fundamentally, or no longer function at all. I will discuss this issue elsewhere, in discussing the persistence of folk tradition and oral memory processes in the heart of the corporation. Here however, I will simply note that in contrast to Nora's extremely broad notion of *lieux de mémoire*, my use of the term "place" is intended in a much more limited sense as specifically spatial.

Places designed as occasions for remembering

Sites like historical museums or memorial statues and displays are the most obvious form of places for narrative remembering. These may be extremely public forms of narration, as in the memorized stories told by museum guides or available in invariant form in taped tours. Even here, though, some freer and more personal stories may be occasioned. For example, White (1997) describes tour guides at the Pearl Harbor museum, as part of the official tour, describing their own war experiences in relation to the bombing of Pearl Harbor.

Designated memorial places may accomplish several types of remembering. One is personal remembering. The most vivid example I can offer is the Vietnam Veterans Memorial Wall, a wall of the names of the dead at which individuals, families, and survivors gather to leave offerings such as flowers, photographs, beer, cigars, medals, discharge papers, at the part of the wall where the name of the person remembered is written (Lopes 1987). One also sees letters addressed to the dead and small groups of people sharing their memories of the dead. The relation between the personal and the institutional is complex here. The memorial's design allows for and encourages personal remembering: the names of the dead are the central design element, and they are situated so that the carved name can be touched, Post-it notes can be attached, offerings can be left at the base of the wall. Though the letters and offerings are personal and intimate, they are left at an official place. Interestingly, this practice of leaving letters and memorial objects, using the Wall as a place to visit and communicate with the dead, was apparently not planned or expected by the designer, or by the group of Vietnam veterans who sponsored the building of the memorial. The designer, Maya Lin, described her intention for its use as an opportunity for people to take a journey, a pilgrimage: "When you leave the memorial, you have to walk back up into the light. You must choose to do it, to go beyond. To me, it is very much a journey. You have to walk out and leave it in the end" (Maya Lin, quoted in Palmer (1987), xviii). This description does not include the practice of leaving letters and artifacts, a practice derived from vernacular American practices of grave visiting (Noyes and Abrahams 1999).

Initially, the practice of leaving messages appears to have been spontaneous: letters were left on hotel stationery, or on paper brought to make a rubbing of a name. However, once the practice was publicized and became known, people were able to prepare in advance: they bring letters printed on computer paper, objects belonging to the dead, or intended for them, like champagne for a twenty-fifth wedding anniversary, and letters addressed to the curator of the collection kept by the National Park Service (Sturken 1997, ch 2).

When the design chosen was initially unveiled, it drew a great deal of criticism for its unheroic or indeed antiheroic nature. It was described as a "black gash of shame and sorrow," a "degrading ditch," a "tombstone," a "slap in the face," a "wailing wall for draft dodgers and New Lefters of the future," a "sad, dreary mass tomb," and "Orwellian glop." However, once the memorial itself was unveiled, criticism ended as the possibilities the design allowed for remembering and healing became clear. At the same time, the very absence of a symbolic institutional statement about the meaning of the war is itself a statement of the national dilemma of drawing a single agreed moral to the story of the Vietnam War. (There is a statue of three infantrymen, a more conventional war memorial, but it is sited to the side of the Wall, and appears to attract nothing like the attention the Wall gets.)

Even apparently conventional memorial sites can support a wide variety of institutional ceremonial occasions, given the existence of groups committed to a particular version of memory. Prost (1997) discusses the phenomenon of antiwar ceremonies by World War I veterans at war memorials: "The idea of treating monuments to the dead as important sites of republican commemoration may seem paradoxical. At ceremonies at war memorials, men festooned with decorations parade, and the tricolor flaps in the breeze above the strains of 'La Marseillaise': symbols such as these might seem more appropriate to a meeting of right-wing nationalists than to a republican memorial" (307).

Prost first discusses the design of local monuments for the dead of World War I:

While some used conventional designs, such as Victory crowning a soldier with a laurel wreath, or a soldier brandishing a flag aloft, others show the horrors of war by symbols of grieving wives, children and parents, or a soldier holding a dead comrade. Similarly, the ceremonies had a dual character, which caused continuing contestation between government or Army officials and veterans' groups. While the officials wished to have the ceremonies commemorate the military victory, the veterans groups were unanimous and successful in carrying out funerary ceremonies, remembering the dead, and marking the horrors of war, and the desire for peace. Both the design of the ceremonies, and the speeches themselves had this dual character.

Two groups of people had a claim on the right to speak in these ceremonies: elected officials, because they embodied the entire community, and veterans, because only those who had fought in the war were entitled to draw its lessons. In fact, those two groups often overlapped, and compromises were always possible: perhaps the mayor had fought in the war, or perhaps there could be two speeches instead of one. For the veterans, however, the very idea of delivering a personal speech was shocking. Whoever spoke on Armistice Day must not speak in his own name but in the name of all veterans, living and dead.... The very form of the Armistice Day speech was the first significant thing about it. The medium reinforced the message. Neither the victorious army nor its leaders were mentioned. Not a word was said about Foch or Joffre or Pétain. The spirit of the occasion was hostile to militarism or any cult of personality. Revanchist demands and Alsace-Lorraine were rarely mentioned. Defeated German never figured as a nation or a people: it was always imperial or militarist Germany, and France, fighting for right and freedom, stood ever ready to respond to militaristic and imperialist aggression.

Most Armistice Day speeches were constructed in two parts. Part one: the past, the war, the dead. Part two: today, peace, the living. The first part invariably consisted of a panorama, which could be more or less lengthy and detailed, of the horrors of war: victory was never mentioned without a reminder of what it had cost. For the veterans present, this would have been a grave omission, for it would have meant overlooking both the death of their comrades, and their own suffering. It was repeatedly stated, therefore, that war kills, that war is carnage, slaughter, massacre, and butchery.

The second part was introduced by a transitional passage, which could take two forms: the speaker might ask his listeners to behave today in such a way that yesterday's sacrifices would not have been in vain, or, in a related strain, he might exhort the living to show themselves worthy of the dead. The first transition placed the accent on the meaning that the combatants themselves gave to their sacrifice: they were fighting the war to end all wars, and this justified a pacifist conclusion.... The second transition placed greater emphasis on the virtues of the dead, whose example justified every moralistic appeal. The lesson to be drawn from their sacrifice varied from orator to orator and moment to moment, but it was also civic in nature. The need for absolute devotion to public affairs, for giving precedence to the general interest over any special interest, for loving an obeying the law and the duties to the community that were created by the rights the law guaranteed for every citizen. For others it was the concrete equality before blind death that revealed the true meaning of the formal equality of citizens before the law.... Last but not least, there was the fraternity of the trenches, no doubt somewhat polished up for the occasion but at times felt with sufficient conviction to kindle memory. Keeping faith with that memory implied tolerance and respect for one's fellow citizens, which meant an end to sterile conflicts like the religious disputes of the turn of the century and to politics insofar as it created artificial divisions. Shaken by the death of so many citizens once mutually hostile to one another, the Republic now signified reconciliation. (326–27)

However, this somewhat subversive memorial celebration of the horrors of war changed as the survivors of the war being memorialized died and as the lesson of the need for devotion to the ideals of the Republic became dryly conventional, or disbelieved. Without the actual ceremonies that included critique or opposition to the war, conducted by people who had a moral right to object, the monuments could only be occasions for the most conventional remembering of victory in a war whose cost was no longer vivid for its survivors.

The construction of such sites are often the center of a great deal of contestation of historical meaning. Current arguments about Holocaust memorials or the prior disagreement about the building of the Vietnam Wall show the deep passion involved. The rebuilding of the World Trade Center site, and the appropriate memorial statement, has given rise to extremely passionate arguments, complicated by the price of Manhattan real estate. Whether an event should be memorialized at all can give rise to complex arguments. One side may argue that the event is not worthy of memorialization, while the diametrically opposed interests may argue that the event is so appalling that its memory must be preserved outside the normalizing process of erecting statues that will be covered with pigeon droppings and ignored by passersby. Even if there is agreement on building a memorial, enormous difficulty is increasingly common in deciding on a design, since the design decision provides an official meaning for the event, and such a meaning can always be contested.

Thus far we have discussed memorials: symbolic places designed for remembering. But there are also places designed to function as occasions for remembering by some form of re-creation of past places. Familiar American examples of the fullest attempt at re-creation are the reproductions of towns such as Colonial Williamsburg, Sturbridge Village, Plimoth Plantation, etc. These can be full working reproductions, with staff in period costume, engaged in period crafts such as blacksmithing, weaving, etc. A slightly less extensive form of reproduction is restoration of past buildings or streets, with narration by a guide, or by a *son et lumière* display. A minimal form is the preservation of a historic building, with a plaque attached, explaining its history.

These types of attempted reproduction or re-creation have been discussed by Lowenthal (1998) and Samuel (1994) as part of the desire to preserve and propagate a national or ethnic heritage. The term "heritage" as currently used covers a wide and ever-growing set of inheritances from the past to be preserved and celebrated as showing a particular "us" where we came from and who we are: stately homes, national monuments, landscapes and wonders of nature, antique furniture and household articles, local dialects, national or local literature, distinctive cuisine, genealogical records, abandoned coal mines, etc. The discovery, revaluing and display of such materials constitutes the heritage industry, which is sold through souvenirs, historical movies, auctions of Napoleon's letters, and Elvis's lounge suits, as well as the constructed or reconstructed destinations of tourism.

For historians, the distinction between proper history and the illegitimate heritage industry is that the practice of history is believed to be a dedication to the discovery of the truth, whereas the practitioners of the unearthing and preservation of heritage are attempting to produce a useable and usually sanitized past for a nation or a people, a past which is inspiring for that collectivity, which makes its members understand their current membership in terms of past glory. As Lowenthal (1998) argues:

> The crux of most aspersions against heritage is that it undermines "real" history, defiling the pristine record that is our rightful legacy. Critics who idealize this unsullied past view history as true because innate, heritage as false because contrived. History is the past that actually happened, heritage a partisan perversion, the past manipulated for some present aim. Substituting an image of the past for its reality, in the typical plaint, heritage effaces history's intricate coherence with piecemeal and mendacious celebration, tendering comatose tourists a castrated past. (103)

What counts as a real place is thus quite complex. In fact, places need not stay in their place to be used. MidWest uses design elements from a small town of the 1930s as an icon of its history and its character. To some extent, these elements are taken from familiar photographs of the actual town of its founding. These elements are used in many ways. First, in the 1970s, MidWest commissioned a painting called "Main Street Memories, 1939," which includes in the foreground a street of gabled brick buildings, including a MidWest agent's office, a barber shop, a fire station, and, in the background, a church and a number of private houses. Many agents hang prints of this painting in their offices. Further, a line drawing taken from this print adorns the MidWest mugs agents give to clients and use themselves. MidWest has also produced a stage set incorporating elements of this small town, which is used on stage during national conferences. Agents and managers to be honored come onto the stage through the door of the agent's office, labeled MidWest Insurance, Robert E. Boyd, Agent. They walk across the stage, shake hands with the president of the company, who hands them their award and thanks them. They leave the stage through the door of the barber shop. I have also seen these design elements used in a regional training department, which included a corridor of classrooms designed to suggest this same main street. Design elements include false building fronts along the basement corridor that memorialize the name of the town and the founder of the company: The McBee Bookstore, The Smallton Town Hall, etc. In addition, the arches of the windows of the original building are repeated as painted design elements over the classroom doors and false windows. The brick of the original building is echoed in facing for the corridor, although the mauve and gray color scheme is much more typical of the late 1980s than of the late 1920s.

Places used as occasions for remembering

We turn now to places not designed for remembering, but which come to be used for remembering. For example, sites of notable events may allow for the retelling of those events, while not being specifically designed for memory: "That's the cave where Luigi and his men hid out from the government when..." Fentress (1992) quotes Levi (1963) as follows:

> The peasants of Gagliana were indifferent to the conquests of Abyssinia, and they neither remembered the World War nor spoke of its dead, but one war was close to their hearts and constantly on their tongues; it was already a fable, a legend, a myth, an epic story. This was the war of the brigands. Brigandage had come to an end in 1865, seventy years before, and only a very few of them were old enough to remember it, either as participants or as eye witnesses. But all of them, old and young, men and women, spoke of it with as much passion as if it were only yesterday. When I talked to the peasants, I could be sure that, whatever the subject of our conversation, we should in some way or another slip into mention of the brigands. Their traces are everywhere; there is not a mountain, gully, wood, fountain, cave or stone that is not linked with one of their adventures or that did not serve them as refuge or hideout. (Levi 1948, 138)

They argue:

> The peasants of "Gagliano" (Carlo Levi's pseudonym for Aliano in Basilicata, the instep of Italy) in 1936 remembered the days of the brigands in the 1860s because

they had some meaning for them, whereas World War I had none; the latter was just another mortal affliction imposed by the government, but the brigands fought for them, against the newly formed Italian state, in the peasants' last resistance to the modern world. That is to say, even the Risorgimento of 1859–70, in Levi's time the mythic historic moment for Italians as a whole, particularly the middle classes, was simply remembered by those peasants as something that had to be opposed. We have seen that social memory exists because it has meaning for the group that remembers it. But the way this meaning is articulated is not a simple one. We have been concentrating on narrative context as a guide to how the forms of memory can be structured, and therefore unpicked. What sorts of things are remembered in the first place, and why, is an equally important issue, however. Events can be remembered more easily if they fit into the forms of narrative that the social group already has at its disposal; many peasantries, for example, have well-established ways of recounting local revolts against the state, just like Aliano's brigands, as we shall see. But they tend to be remembered in the first place because of their power to legitimize the present, and tend to be interpreted in ways that very closely parallel (often competing) present conceptions of the world. (87–88)

Reading Levi more closely, we see that he mentions numerous occasions on which the brigand wars are recounted: books about the brigands sold from pushcarts (167), comedies staged by the peasants—"Sometimes they told the deeds of knights or brigands" (231). Thus the places as occasions for remembering form part of a much richer web of activities of remembering salient revolts and resistances.

Basso (1996) has described the extensive use the Western Apache make of places and place names as occasions for stories that function as moral instruction in how to behave. He cites examples such as the following to indicate the connection between places, place names, stories, and the learning and remembering of moral behavior:

The land is always stalking people. The land makes people live right. The land looks after us. The land looks after people (Annie Peaches, age 77, 1978).

Our children are losing the land. It doesn't go to work on them anymore. They don't know the stories about what happened at these places. That's why some get into trouble (Ronnie Lupe, age 42; Chairman, White Mountain Apache Tribe, 1978).

We used to survive only off the land. No it's no longer that way. Now we live only with money, so we need jobs. But the land still looks after us. We know the names of the places where everything happened. So we stay away from badness (Nick Thompson, age 64, 1980).

I think of that mountain called Tséé Łigai Dah Sidilé (White Rocks Lie Above in a Compact Cluster) as if it were my maternal grandmother. I recall stories of how it once was at that mountain. The stories told to me were like arrows. Elsewhere, hearing that mountain's name, I see it. Stories go work on you like arrows. Stories make you live right. Stories make you replace yourself (Benson Lewis, age 64, 1979).

One time I went to L.A., training for mechanic. It was no good, sure no good. I start drinking, hang around bars all the time. I start getting into trouble with my wife, fight sometimes with here. It was bad. I forget about this country here around Cibecue. I forget all the names and stories. I don't hear them in my mind anymore. I forget how to live right, forget how to be strong. (Wilson Lavender, age 52, 1975, 38–39)

In Basso's analysis, Apache place names either describe the environment, often as it was when the ancestors arrived rather than now, or "allude to historical events that illuminate the causes and consequences of wrongful social conduct" (24). Particularly names of the latter sort can function as the occasion for stories that can either teach traditional modes of conduct or can be told as a rebuke to someone who has transgressed these norms. The following is an example of how such stories can be used:

> In early June 2977, a seventeen-year-old Apache woman attended a girls' puberty ceremonial at Cibeque with her hair rolled up in a set of pink plastic curlers. She had returned home two days before from a boarding school in Utah where this sort of ornamentation was considered fashionable by her peers. Something so mundane would have gone unnoticed by others were it not for the fact that Western Apache women of all ages are expected to appear at puberty ceremonials with their hair worn loose. This is one of several ways that women had of showing respect for the ceremonial and also by implication, for the people who have staged it. The practice of presenting oneself with free-flowing hair is understood to contribute to the ceremonial's effectiveness, for Apaches hold that the ritual's most basic objectives, which are to invest the pubescent girl with qualities necessary for life as an adult, cannot be achieved unless standard forms of respect are faithfully observed. On this occasion at Cibecue, everyone was following custom except the young woman who arrived wearing curlers. She soon became an object of attention and quiet expressions of disapproval, but no one spoke to her about the cylindrical objects in her hair.
>
> Two weeks later, the same young woman made a large stack of tortillas and brought them to the camp of her maternal grandmother, a widow in her mid-sixties who had organized a small party to celebrate the birthday of her eldest grandson. Eighteen people were on hand, myself included, and all of us were treated to hot coffee and a dinner of boiled beef and potatoes. When the meal was over, casual conversation began to flow, and the young woman seated herself on the ground next to her younger sister. And then—quietly, deftly, and quite without warning—her grandmother narrated a version of the historical tale about the forgetful Apache policeman who behaved too much like a whiteman [a tale linked to a local place.] Shortly after the story was finished, the young woman stood up, turned away wordlessly, and walked of in the direction of her home. Uncertain of what had happened, I asked her grandmother why she had departed. Had the young woman suddenly become ill? "No," her grandmother replied. "I shot her with an arrow."
>
> Approximately two years after this incident occurred, I found myself in the company of the young woman with the taste for distinctive hairstyles. She had purchased a large carton of groceries at the trading post at Cibeque, and when I offered to drive her home with them, she accepted. I inquired on the way if she remembered the time that her grandmother had told us the story about the forgetful policeman. She said she did and then went on, speaking in English, to describe her reactions to it. "I think maybe my grandmother was getting after me, but then I think maybe not, maybe she's working on somebody else. Then I think back on that dance and I know it's me for sure. I sure don't like how she's talking about me, so I quit looking like that. I threw those curlers away." In order to reach the young woman's camp, we had to pass within a few hundred yards of Men Stand Above Here and There, the place where the man had lived who was arrested for rustling in the story. I pointed it out to

my companion. She said nothing for several moments. Then she smiled and spoke softly in her own language. "I know that place. It stalks me every day." (56–57)

Basso's examples are very rich cases, in which there is a regular and complex link between narration and places, mediated by a particular genre of place names, which summarize events which happened at those places. The corporate examples I have observed are not as dense. But they share the link between places and remembering, both of the institution's past and of the individual's past within that institution.

In order to occasion remembering, a place need not be the site of a dramatic event; it need only be a site relevant to the rememberers. In a business context, one frequent type of remembering comes in passing a salient place. A member will indicate it as "the first building, where we started," or "the old fire company building." This is frequently an occasion for a story about the founding or the early days. Such spatial marking is also used for personally significant spaces: "That's the office I used to have." "Oh you have Cindy's space." These encounters can form the occasion for a story about one's own career: pointing out a cubicle on the way to a corner office can be a way of indicating a successful trajectory. Or pointing out the many locations one used to occupy can form the occasion for describing how much the company has changed, or for dropping ironic remarks about the company's "annual re-org."

Artifacts as occasions for remembering

Artifacts frequently serve as occasions for remembering. As with times and places as occasions for remembering, I also differentiate between artifacts specifically designed to occasion remembering and artifacts not designed for remembering which come to be used in that way.

Let me here distinguish between what I have called spatial occasions and what I am calling artifacts. I am making a simple and perhaps artificial distinction: memorial places are large and stationary objects. One does not regularly move a statue or a house marked with a plaque commemorating the birthplace of someone judged worthy of being remembered. In contrast, artifacts are smaller and more portable objects. The distinction is not an absolute one, of course; statues and even buildings can be and are moved, and the more highly valued they are, the more likely they are to be moved if necessary. But such movements are rare events. In contrast, objects like photo albums, mugs, family bibles, etc. are easily moved, and many of their affordances for remembering arise from the fact of their portability. (See Linde (2001) for a fuller discussion of memorial places and artifacts.)

Artifacts designed for remembering

Some artifacts are specifically designed for remembering. The most central example of memorial artifacts is photo albums and, more recently, family videos. (I discuss photo albums because I have my own experiences with their use in families. Since home movies or videos were not part of my family experience, I have nothing to say about them until someone else takes up the marvelous opportunity to study how they are used.) Photo albums are frequently, perhaps usually, looked at by more than one person at a time. They are an occasion for parents to tell children about their relatives, about their parents' pasts, and about the children's own pasts. They can also be a way of inducting a new family member into the family's past. Part of the process of being engaged or newly married can include the new member of the family being shown photos of family members and being told who they were and what they did. It is also an opportunity for family members to tell stories about the prospective or new spouse as a child, including the ritual embarrassment of showing baby pictures, or the more real embarrassment of dealing with pictures of former spouses. Such pictures can also require editing, either verbal, or physical, to remove traces of a past that participants do not want to be required to narrate. (This used to be done with scissors; digital technology has made it a much smoother operation.)

Note that while photo albums provide affordances for family remembering, they also shape it. The conventions of the family photograph and the family photo album project a particular image of an ideal family. Photographs both capture images of family rituals and form the occasion for reflexive metarituals of remembering and conveying those stories to others who were not present for them (Hirsch 1997).

There are also less formal memorial artifacts: T-shirts, mugs, posters of past events, baseball caps that mark local milestones or events, briefcases or plastic portfolios distributed as souvenirs of conferences. Certainly within a corporate context, these things are everywhere. I am considering here artifacts designed to be distributed to members of a given institution, as a mark of events they have attended or milestone events they have helped to enable. I am not discussing souvenir items distributed across institutional boundaries, for example, pens marked with a business's name and phone number, given to customers or potential customers. This is a whole industry in itself. However, the remembering it is attempting to provoke is simply the memory of AAA Acme Company when you need a second mortgage, a bail bond, or a windshield repair. A typical example we observed was sales agents of companies wanting referrals from MidWest agents regularly providing their offices with pens, mugs, etc. with their logos, as well as gifts of candy, cookies, etc. Many agents, as a matter of policy, give these gifts to shelters, retirement centers, or throw them away. (Check your doctor's office for drug company pens.)

MidWest Insurance offers a wide array of such artifacts to sales agents for purchase, to be given to customers: gum and candy with the MidWest logo, key chains, pens, note pads, road atlases, teddy bears, etc. The memory which the gift is intended to trigger can be as simple as using a pen and remembering that your insurance agent represents MidWest. Or it can be a more complex memory about relationship: seeing a teddy bear wearing a little T-shirt with the MidWest logo can remind you that your agent is a caring person who remembered your child's birthday with the gift. In addition, MidWest offers for sale to agents a wide variety of clothing marked with the MidWest logo: hats, shirts, jackets, etc. I was always puzzled about the use of such objects until I heard a former agent turned manager lecturing about how valuable it is to wear a MidWest sweater or jacket as a means of starting conversations with strangers in public places or at public events, which could lead to new business. In contrast, the institutionally internal artifacts I am considering occasion a remembering of past events within the institution.

There is a great deal of study yet to be done on how such artifacts are used. One use is the opportunity to display one's history within the company. As one employee of a high-tech company explained (in an e-mail response to my query):

As we say here, "It's not a job, it's a wardrobe." The only thing I have to buy is pants, pretty much. Clothing is to celebrate various product releases. Sometimes it's easy to get and sometimes not. Recently I had to do some quiet negotiations to get a full-leather jacket for a product I used to work on; my former [Company] jackets were one that is part-cloth and part-leather and a silk one, and the full leather was highly coveted—not just for the leather, but the recognition that you were part of that team. We had some [Company] friends over last weekend, and one of them was wearing a nice jacket. We complimented him on it and he said, "Look, no logo!" It was probably his first non-[Company] jacket in some time.

Another type of use for commemorative artifact is the effort to establish commonality between members of an organization. For example, a person seeing a commemorative mug on someone's desk has the opportunity to say, "Oh, I was at that meeting too." This can be the beginning of narration of each person's trajectory through the community and of the search for other times and places that their paths have crossed before. I once observed a designer in an engineering firm telling a story about how the team passed a production milestone of 84,000 units shipped in one month. As he told the story, he waved at a baseball cap on a high bookcase shelf that memorialized a prior milestone of 50,000 units shipped in a month. Although the cap was not mentioned in the conversation, it is referred to in order to demonstrate both of the prowess of the designer and his team and of the impressive nature of achieving a goal of 84,000 units, when even 50,000 units was worthy of memorializing.

A particularly important type of commemorative artifact is the plaque, certificate, pin, or statue that serves as the emblem of an institutional award. At MidWest, these are widely used as the center of the motivational system. In fact, the MidWest term for the whole sales incentive and awards program is: "pins, points and plaques." Such awards represent a match between an occasion and an artifact. An award for high levels of sales achievement is given at some public meeting, whether it is a district, regional, or national meeting. The successful agents are displayed, praised, and thanked in front of their peers and given an award whose memorial symbol can then be displayed.

In addition to serving as the focal point of a ceremony, a collection of such artifacts can serve to establish a person's history within the organization. At Mid-West, over the course of a career, an agent may collect an array of memorial artifacts including pins, plaques, certificates, model automobiles, shadowboxes with a display of many artifacts, and other memorabilia, all of which mark various levels of sales achievements. Almost all the agents we have observed display these prominently and may use them to narrate the stages of their careers. One agent I spoke with had placed his award plaques immediately facing the front door so that they are the first thing that a person sees upon entering the office. The agent says that clients' response is: "I'll go with him, he has all those stars." Similarly, another agent explained that she displays her plaques because "people notice them. They are more confident if they feel I'm accomplished at a certain level."

The display of awards may be more subtle. In one example we observed, after paying his bill, a client noticed a coffee table-sized book "Hawaii: The Big Island" on a table near a couple of chairs. He looked through the book and asked, "Who's been to the big island?" The staff person responded that the agent went there on a Top Sellers Club trip recently. However, there was no further question from the client on what a Top Sellers Club trip was.

MidWest designs and displays many memorial artifacts, particularly photographs and plaques, that represent the past of the institution as a whole. At corporate, regional, and, frequently, district headquarters of MidWest, corridor walls are lined with photographs: pictures of previous buildings, pictures of the original main headquarters building at regional headquarters, pictures of present and past executives, pictures of outstanding agents and service people, pictures of various graduating classes of agents and managers. These photographs serve as an occasion for stories. Prominently displayed in the main headquarters building of MidWest are low-relief bronze busts of the first five presidents in the main atrium, which are used by tour guides and in training sessions as occasions for narratives about these men. This is not unusual. Many institutions have busts or paintings of founders and leaders in lobbies. In some cases, these are dead objects, unnoticed and unknown by the people passing them, while in other institutions, they serve as live links to narratives. Samuel (1994) offers examples of English brokers and banks that maintain "mini-museums" in their lobbies. These go beyond the internal history of the company to photographs or wax models and memorial objects of famous clients, such as memorabilia of Florence Nightingale or Lord Nelson, or a letter from Lord Byron asking for an extension of credit.

Another important occasion for memory is the use of photographs and plaques. At both corporate and regional headquarters of MidWest, corridor walls are lined with photographs: pictures of present and past executives, pictures of outstanding agents and service people, pictures of various graduating classes of agents and managers, pictures of awards ceremonies. Like the busts, these photographs serve as an occasion for stories. For example, as we walked through the building on our way to our next meeting, we passed a photo of a now-retired vice president and were told that he was the father of someone we had met. This occasioned stories about the careers of both men.

Artifacts used for remembering

The next class of occasions for narrative remembering is artifacts not designed for remembering but that come to be used in that way. Virtually any artifact can be used to remember with, if it lasts long enough. The original design intention is not at issue here. One may carefully press a floral corsage to remember the giver and the event on which it was given. Or one may casually stick a ticket stub in a coat pocket and years later find it and remember the performance.

As institutional artifacts age, they can become worthy of display. Some institutions, including MidWest, use public spaces to display memorial artifacts. For example, the main lobby of the main corporate headquarters contains a small museum. This includes the first rate chart drawn up by first president on a piece of brown paper, a gleaming fire engine, from 1935, the year the fire company was founded: the "Mack Pumper," posters of radio and television programs sponsored by the company, examples of gifts given as performance incentives and recognitions to sales agents over the company's long history, including top hat and white gloves, leather purses containing gold pieces, and old and new plaques, pins, and statuettes used as rewards for agents, and posters advertising the radio and television shows which MidWest sponsored. Initially, this exhibit was designed as a special traveling exhibit for national conventions.[1] It was so popular with agents that it was permanently installed at headquarters. Regional conventions continue to feature traveling exhibits of the history of the company, including video loops of old film footage of the company as well as many of these incentive artifacts, for show, not for sale, which attract lively interest from visitors to the exhibition. This practice is not exclusive to MidWest. Many companies which work their pasts intensively have such public displays.

At a more individual level, it is quite common for engineers and designers to store and display in their offices prototypes of designs they have worked on (if the objects are not too small or too large to display). Framed and mounted patent grants can be similarly displayed. Both of these types of artifacts are used as the support for stories about the person's career or about the particular issues that arose in the process of the design. Prototypes are often taken down, handled, dismantled, as part of such stories. In one example I have observed in a design firm, an engineer working on a particular widget had a box of widgets of the same type manufactured by many competitors. As part of explaining the history of his design, he picked up particular designs to show their defects and excellences, in contrast to what he eventually came up with.

Conclusion

This discussion of occasions for remembering contains the key point for understanding how institutions work their past: what we need to analyze is not memory, but remembering. Remembering is an event. It may be a solitary and internal event for an individual. But for an institution, it necessarily is a social event, involving at least two, and perhaps millions, of people. Retelling and remembering of this sort require proper occasions. Without the occasion, the story rarely or never gets told. In this chapter we have surveyed the range of occasions for narrative. In the next chapter, we turn to an examination of the narratives that are repeatedly told on these occasions.

Retold Tales

*Repeated Narratives as a Resource
for Institutional Remembering*

T he previous chapter discussed the importance of occasions for institutional remembering. A story has no real life in an institution if there is no occasion on which it can be or must be told. The current chapter begins to look at the narratives themselves. Of the many types of narrative found within institutions, this chapter focuses on the class of narratives that institutions use to work their pasts: that is, to retell the past in the present in order to influence the future.

Within the boundaries of any institution, many, many stories are told daily. Social life is an ocean of stories, and life within institutions is no exception. Of these uncountable stories, the ones which are the most useful in understanding the work of stories in institutions are repeated narratives, rather than narratives which are told only once, however dramatic they may be. In previous work (Linde 1993), I examined the life story of the individual, showing that the life story is a discontinuous discourse unit, composed of just those narratives that have long-term repeatability. These are the narratives which a speaker tells and retells over the course of his or her life, the narratives of the most important events, the events that have made the speaker who he or she is. These narratives are reworked as circumstances or understandings change; they are told differently to different hearers at different times. They thus form an important part of the socially transacted memory of the speaker.

In studying narrative in institutions, a similarly valuable starting point is to ask which narratives have an extended life. For institutional narratives, an extended life means not only that they are retold over a long period of time by a single speaker, but also that they are retold by narrators other than the original protagonist. Within institutions, there are many ephemeral narratives: the stories in the lunchroom about this morning's computer crash, the terrible traffic, or a manager's momentary fit of generosity or bad temper. These are stories that can be told during the course of the day or perhaps the week but will not survive the weekend. Such narratives can certainly tell us a great deal about the ways in which membership and identity within institutions is created through ordinary and ephemeral discourse. However, the discussion of this book will concentrate on a particular class of institutional narratives that are repeatable and repeated both through time and across tellers.

I call this class of narratives retold tales: narratives told by a speaker who was not a participant or witness to the events narrated but heard them from someone else. It is, of course, possible for a narrative to be repeated by a nonparticipant only once. A piece of ephemeral, or not very important, gossip may function in this way. However, in this study, I examine those tales that are told repeatedly within institutions and the institutional support for their telling. Such retold narratives have a special status within institutions because, as I shall show, they form an important part of the way that institutions remember their past and use that remembering to create current identities for both the institution and its members.

Why is retelling so important? There are two reasons, one methodological and one more fundamental, having to do with the appropriation of the story by a new speaker who was not present at the events.

Methodologically, when a researcher hears a story told in an institutional context, it is important to be able to establish whether that story is ephemeral or whether it forms part of the repertoire of stories active within that institution. There may be stories some members of an institution know but rarely or never tell: these are not part of the institution's working memory, although they might be elicited by a researcher attempting to gather as many stories as possible. Similarly, stories told just once are not part of the institution's active memory. It might be possible to tell whether stories are retold by doing a decades-long study of an institution, waiting for retellings of even very rare stories. This would be methodologically admirable but is, in practice, impossible. Therefore, the research must attempt to find ways to discern whether a story has been retold.

The most obvious evidence that a story has been retold is that the teller cites the original teller, or the teller he or she heard it from. An example would be "My first manager told me...." There can also be a citation that indicates that a story is a story: "There's an old story about Mr. McBee." There is also the indirect evidence furnished by cues within the story that the speaker could not have been present at the event: therefore, he or she must have heard the story from someone else. A very striking example, heard frequently at MidWest, is "We were founded in 1925." This clearly is a retold tale; none of the speakers were old enough to be present at the founding. All of these are examples of the kind of internal evidence that can show us that a particular narrative is a retold tale.

In addition to the issue of how to recognize a retold story, there is the more important issue of how a new narrator takes on the telling of a story of someone else's past. Whether the story is the founding story of a religion, or an account of how an insurance company moved from selling only automobile insurance to a full line of property and life insurance, the most important moment in the career of that story is the point at which it moves to a new generation of tellers: when someone who was not present at the original events told the story. If a story does not acquire new tellers, it can have no life beyond the life of the original person who experienced the events and first formulated them as a story.

When a story moves to a new teller, we may say that appropriation has taken place. This appropriation can be viewed from either side. One could say that the teller has appropriated the story—taking on someone else's experience as relevant to the teller's own experience. Or one could say that the story has appropriated the teller— acquiring another link in the chain of transmission. Both perspectives are, I believe, both useful and true. Chapter 8 discusses the issue of the appropriation of a new teller in greater detail. (Linde (2000) provides an earlier discussion of the acquisition of a speaker by a story, including the history of this understanding of acquisition.)

Why "retold tales?"

Let us now consider "retold tales" as an analytic concept. What is a retold tale and why is yet another distinction needed? Within discourse analysis, we already have the time-honored category of grammatical person. Wouldn't it serve to talk about third-person narratives: stories whose main protagonist is he or she or they rather than I? But grammatical person is not an adequate way to describe the category I wish to pick out, because the distinction I wish to make using the notion of "retold tales" does not correspond exactly to grammatical person. I wish to examine the set of repeated narratives told within an institution by people who were not present at the events narrated. The grammatical person of these narrative can be third-person singular or plural: stories of he, she or they. Or the person can be first-person plural: stories of we. The key definitional point is that the speaker is describing events that have in some way been learned through the narration of others. (Of course a first-person narrative also may be retold many times by the person who originally experienced its events.)

Typically, any narrative is described as having a person that corresponds to a grammatical person: first person, third person, etc. However, the establishment of the person of a narrative is more complex than a simple person marking. Almost any first-person narrative has more characters than the narrator alone, and hence will contain third-person characters and verbs. Some third-person narratives will include the narrator as a minor character or observer and will thus contain first-person verbs. What determines the person of a narrative is not the simple presence or even numerical preponderance of a given grammatical person. Nor is it necessarily the person of the main character or protagonist. Rather, the deciding factor is the point of view from which the narrative is told. The identity of the point-of-view character determines the person of the narrative.

Within literary theory, identifying the many types of narrator is an issue of great complexity. Careful attention is paid to the distinction between the protagonist and the narrator of a first-person story, to the extent of knowledge that narrator purports to have and actually has, to the reliability of the narrator, and to subtle shifts in tone that may suggest without explicitly announcing a new point of view and thus implicitly a new narrator. The issues are simpler in oral narrative but still require attention. Discourse analysis has traditionally focused on the first-person narrative of personal experience, that is, the narrative in which the point-of-view character and the protagonist are identical to the speaker. In fact, that is how oral narrative has been defined, beginning with Labov's classic work on narrative, which locates the definition of oral narrative in the narrative of personal experience, which must necessarily be a first-person narrative, since it requires personal experience (Labov 1972, 359; Linde 1998). Obviously, there are other persons possible for oral narratives of personal experience, although they have not been studied in the detail that the first-person narrative has received. Studying narratives told in second or third person involves not only the form of the narrative but also social factors of constraints on reportability and on storytelling rights, as well as some rather complex issues of elicitation and context of telling. Because narratives told within institutions are not restricted to first-person singular narratives, I here sketch some of the social constraints on second- and third-person narratives.

Second-Person narratives

Second-person narratives are stories in which the protagonist is "you," the addressee. They are quite rare in written text. They are found in text-based interactive games ("You enter a dark tunnel...") and in some textbooks. There are a few short stories and novels written in the second person: many people find them quite irritating to read. Most written narratives are in either the first-person singular or the third-person singular. Within spoken discourse, we can find some second-person oral narratives, but these are also fairly uncommon. Conventions of storytelling rights require the person who best knows the story to tell it (in the absence of other factors such as institutional rank, which we will discuss below). This means that in most cases people have the greatest authority about their own lives, and therefore other speakers would not be in a proper position to tell narratives about those lives (Shuman 1986). However, there are circumstances where a person is not in command of all the facts, or all the meanings, and therefore can be told a second-person narrative.

The most common of these circumstances is the situation in which children are told stories about themselves. This can happen either because the events of the story happened when the child was too young to remember them, or because the storyteller is using the events of the story to instruct the child in what is tellable, or in how the moral meaning of the events should be understood. Thus, Ochs and Capps (2001) show many examples of family conversations in which parents conarrate the events of the day with a child or provide evaluations of the events children report, thus framing for the child what events are tellable and what responses are appropriate.

It is common, at least in American culture, that there are stories told to children, as well as to other family members, about the children's own actions. The narratives of this type that persist within the family form a particularly important kind of personal myth. Such narratives point to central events or to examples of typical character traits. These childhood narratives thus form one important way that parents convey to their children their characters, their position in their families, and their similarity to, or difference from, other family members. Miller (1994) describes the functions of such stories:

A related narrative practice in South Baltimore that is relevant to self-construction was the telling of stories about the child. This participant structure may be thought of as a variant of telling stories around the child in that a caregiver told the story to another person in the child's presence. That is, again the social configuration required at least two persons, narrator and listener, in addition to the child. The difference is that the child herself was cast as the protagonist....

At the level of content, for example, narrators conveyed particular images of the child protagonist in action, images that recurred across stories and across children. The children were portrayed as active, spirited, mischievous; as speaking up or talking back; as "mouthy," feisty, and sharp. The mothers thus created child protagonists who resembled the self-protagonists in their stories of their own experiences.

In addition, stories about the child conveyed messages about the significance and organization of the child's experiences. By consistently telling stories about some experiences rather than others, caregivers conveyed which ones were reportable. By creating a particular rendition of the experience, they showed what the component events were, how the events were related, and what was important about them. (168)

While I have not done a formal study of the persistence of this type of second-person narrative into adulthood, informal questioning suggests that at least half of the people I asked remember at least one story told to them as children about their actions as babies or younger children. See Stone (1988) for a discussion of such stories as family folklore.

Though children may not have full storytelling rights as the final authority on their own lives, adults normally have such authority. It requires unusual circumstances for someone else to be allowed to tell an adult listener a story about the listener's life. These are usually situations in which the protagonist is not the best authority on what happened, or what it meant.

First, the protagonist was drunk, unconscious, or otherwise insensible. This can lead to the classic request: "Tell me, what happened last night? What did I do?" This question is reasonable because the addressee may have a better memory of the events than the protagonist does. Or for some other reason, the protagonist may not remember the details of some event she was involved in and may ask another participant to tell her the story again.

Next, a second-person narrative may be appropriate in situations where the protagonist did not understand the consequences of what happened, or has a very different view of them than the narrator does. For example, I was once told a story about myself by a friend about a situation in which I, as editor of the college newspaper, bravely confronted a complaint from the wrestling team about lack of press coverage of their events by inviting them to join the paper and write sports stories. I was astonished at hearing this narrated as an act of courage on my part. My friend, who was present but silent during the exchange, was a judo champion: he perceived a physical threat in the complaint from which he might have to defend me. I perceived only a correct complaint about a shortage of sports coverage, which I tried to remedy. When my friend told me this story years later, I was astonished at his agonistic and highly dramatic version of an event I barely remembered. He had formed the events into a story; I had not.

A more complex case is the one in which the protagonist does not know what is happening to, or being said about, her behind her back. These have been extensively described in Goodwin's work on he-said-she-said sequences. These are complex sequences in which A tells B what C is saying that B did (Goodwin 1990). These accounts can have serious social consequences for the future relations of all the parties involved.

Next, there is the case in which the protagonist's actions had later consequences unknown to her. For example, I have had narratives told to me about how some purported action of mine as a graduate student was told as an exemplary narrative, an instruction in how to behave, by later generations of graduate students. This is a narrative about and within a narrative: someone telling me a story about how a story about me was used.

Third-Person narratives

Third-person narratives, stories of he, she, and they, are important in the study of institutional memory because they extend the range of narration, allowing for stories about people and events not experienced by the speaker or addressees. Although third-person narratives are more frequent in conversation than second-person narratives, they still do raise a question about the circumstances under which they can be told. First, there are specific constraints on the reportability of third-person narratives, depending on the relation of the third-person protagonist to the speaker and addressees. Such narratives are more reportable if all interlocutors know the protagonist. A third-person narrative with a protagonist unknown to the addressees must have events which are extremely reportable, because of their drama or because they are extremely relevant to some topic already discussed in the conversation. In institutional contexts, a protagonist need not be a personal acquaintance to be known. The founder of MidWest, Mr. McBee, is a character who is assumed to be known to all members of the company. And within the storytelling practices of MidWest, Mr. McBee is always salient; that is, if there is a story about him that could be told on a given occasion, it is taken as automatically relevant. As we shall see, learning his stories is part of the process of becoming a member. (There is valuable future research to be done on the category of hyperrelevant individuals within a given community. For example, I have observed, any scholar of Elizabethan England who has a train of argument that could be relevant even tangentially to Shakespeare will bring Shakespeare into the argument. Possible narratives about current celebrities are similar: the issue is which individuals are relevant within a given community.)

Finally, there is a serious issue of the nature of knowledge implicit in any third-person narrative. There is an important difference, as I shall show, between a third-person narrative in which the speaker was a minor participant or silent witness of the events and one in which the speaker did not witness the events, but rather came to know them in some other way. I reserve the term "retold tales" for narratives of events not experienced by the narrator, whether they are told in the third-person or the first-person plural. The same story may be told in the third person—"MidWest was founded in 1925," or in the first-person plural—"we were founded in 1925."

(In previous work, I have called these "non-participant narratives" (1998), but the neologism is too graceless to reuse.)

It might appear that the factor defining retold tales is not grammatical person, but rather evidentiality: linguistic markers that indicate the source of a speaker's knowledge of the event narrated. There are languages in which marking the source of knowledge is an obligatory grammatical category, just as in English, marking the time of an event is an obligatory category, encoded in the tense of every verb form. English has optional evidential markers: "as I've heard," "apparently," "it seems that," "as the old story goes," etc., all of which mark the fact that the speaker did not directly experience the events being narrated. The issue of marking evidentiality is discussed in more detail in chapter 8.

However, the narrator's source of knowledge is not the main issue for these retold tales. In fact, what speakers mark is not the way they came to know the events of the narrative, but rather their stance towards, or relation to the events narrated. There are certain stories that I may tell as events distant in social time or space, which are unrelated to me. There are other stories from an equally distant past that I tell as part of my story, because they are a necessary part of understanding who I am and in what groups I claim membership.

Appropriations of the past

Having discussed the notion of retold tales, and how they relate to other aspects of narrative such as relevance and person, I now turn to the question of how these retold tales are actually told. How do people tell a story of events they did not witness? How do they make it both relevant to themselves and to the situation at hand? This is quite an important issue in how a story is framed. A new teller coming to tell a story could tell it as something that happened back in the past, interesting as a museum piece or a nostalgia item, but no longer really part of the present. Or it can be told as relevant to the present and to the person telling it. It is the latter case that is of interest here: the framing of past events not experienced by the teller as relevant to both teller and audience.

One very common way for a narrator to do this is to project himself or herself backwards into the events of the narrative. That is, the narrator recounts past events as if he or she had been present, even though this was not the case. In some cases, the speaker could have been present, in others, as already mentioned, the events of the story may have happened before the speaker's birth or entry into the group.

I offer a story about a story as an example that I have witnessed. When the last director of the Institute for Research on Learning first assumed that post, he had to preside almost immediately at meetings with potential clients, where the form of the meeting required that he tell the story of the origin of IRL in order to explain what kind of organization it was. Often, this happened in the presence of IRL researchers who had been there at the founding or who had had a much longer tenure there than he had. Yet because of his position as director, he was the correct person to tell story, having greater storytelling rights to this story than lower-ranked, though more institutionally experienced, participants. At first he handled this difficult discourse demand by telling the story with strong evidential markers of nonparticipation: "I've only been on board for three weeks, but I've been told that..." These markers indicated his somewhat delicate position. He was the director, and hence the person who should properly tell the story, but he was also a newcomer to the institution who had not been present at the events. In addition, he was telling the story in the presence of some of his staff members, who had either been present since the founding or who had heard many more tellings of the story. This was an effective but temporary strategy. Over the course of time, as he became more and more centrally a member of the Institute and an owner of its history, he dropped the markers of nonparticipation, telling the story with no marking of how he came to know it. Although he still told the story in the third person, he told it vividly, with a camera's eye view, including details of motivation, direct quotations, etc. It is details of this sort that indicate he had come to appropriate the story as part of his own past.

Furthermore, over the years, IRL researchers' versions of the story were changed by the director's version, even those employees who were present at the original events. Originally, the researchers who told the story focused on the intellectual reasons why learning rather than education or training should be the focus of study: the deficiencies of schools of education, the need for a social counterpart to cognitive science's focus on individual learning. The director added in business reasons that explained why the CEO of Xerox chose to give a large grant for the study of such issues: his fear that schools were not educating the kinds of workers that businesses would need. As researchers heard this addition to the story, in the course of many retellings, some of us added it to our own versions, particularly when speaking in business contexts, although not in academic contexts. (With the demise of IRL, I note that my own accounts of its founding have returned to the research-based story I and other researchers used. This is not surprising, since I am now telling the story to other researchers, not to potential business clients.)

What differentiates these retold tales from simple accounts of the past is exactly the linguistic details that indicate the speaker's inclusion in the account. These include use of the first-person plural "we," quoted speech (which could not have been heard by the speaker), description of actions, feelings, and motives of characters, exploration of the point of view of one or more of the characters in the narrative, and explicit indications of the relevance of the story of the past to some current situation. In the following chapter, we will explore these characteristics in great detail.

What tales are retold in institutions?

Within a given institution, what tales are retold? Are there differences between institutions in how many tales are retold and in what those tales are about? Are there any commonalities—tales we can expect in almost any institution?

Certainly there will be differences between institutions. For example, a classic work on oral history, Vansina (1985) shows that different tribal and national groups in Africa maintain different scales of memory, where scale is measured by how many generations of memory a given group maintains. Describing a culture maintaining only one generation of adults:

"Historical consciousness works only two registers: time of origin and recent times. Because the limit one reaches in time reckoning moves with the passage of generations, I have called the gap a floating gap (24)."

Interestingly, this is not a restriction on how far back into the past a group can remember. Both the number of generations and the starting point remain constant for each particular social group. Rather, groups have an origin story, a floating gap of indefinite length, and then stories of as many generations of memory of the recent past as each particular group maintains.

Similarly, I believe that institutions in a literate society differ in how much of their pasts they maintain and use. In particular, the issue here is how much of its past an institution works, that is, invokes and retells for present purposes. This is a new set of questions about institutional memory, and so we do not have available comparative ethnographies of retold tales in different institutions. I would hypothesize that different types of institutions work their pasts quite differently. For example, I would expect that technology companies, by the nature of their business, are less likely than insurance companies to refer to the past rather than to the changing future. Although even here, I would expect differences between startup technology companies and long-established technology firms like IBM, which was founded in 1911. A comparative study of this type would be extremely illuminating, but it probably must wait until many individual institutions have been studied with an emphasis on their use of narrative.

In the comparison of technology and insurance, two contrasting forms of business that I am familiar with, I hypothesize that insurance companies will tend to work their past more intensively than technology companies do. Insurance is an inherently conservative business, since its function is to conserve its clients' assets, and to do so, it must be conservative with its own assets and careful about the risks it takes. In contrast, technology is inherently future-oriented, focused on the next development and the next product.

However, even given the conservative nature of the insurance business, insurance companies differ in the degree to which they make use of their past in public or internal representations. While I do not have detailed ethnographies to compare, a simple comparison can be made by checking the Web sites of insurance companies. This allows us to examine what each company chooses to present about itself to the public. I have examined MidWest and eleven of its competitors, choosing the companies most often cited by MidWest as chief competitors, as well as all those insurance companies listed on the insurance comparison site Insweb (www.insweb.com), which sell the same lines of insurance as MidWest. Four of the twelve companies make more than a one sentence mention of their histories: four of them, including MidWest locate their history three screens in from the home page. The one company that has its history on its home page has only that single home page. The only company with a more extensive company history than MidWest has been in business for fifty years longer, and many companies as old have no mention of history at all. Such a comparison is only a quick summary of the use the companies make in presenting themselves to the public, based on a single form of data. It cannot, of course, tell us what use of the past exists within the companies for their employees or to their customers. However, this quick comparison does suggest that companies of similar age do indeed differ in the use that they make of their past.

In support of the comparison made above about the difference between technology versus insurance companies in their relation to the past, I note that doing a similar search on IBM, a relatively old technology company, often thought of as conservative, finds no link to a history of the company. Only the IBM research department offers a paragraph about its history, four pages in from its home page. Let us grant, then, that both types of institutions and individual institutions differ in the number of stories they maintain. Given this, I propose a further hypothesis that the choice of which stories they maintain is not arbitrary but can to some extent be predicted. Many scholars of business narrative have noted the frequent presence of stories about the founding and the founders. This analysis goes beyond that simple discovery to suggest that this is the most likely story to be found within an institution. That is, if an institution maintains only one story that everyone must know, it will be a founding narrative. If it maintains two, the first will be a founding narrative and the second will be a story about turning points in the history of the institution. Turning points include averted disasters, changes in direction, and exemplary past triumphs. This prediction about the presence of story types in an institution has, in fact, the form of implicational hierarchy.[1]

The first story that any institution will maintain is an origin story, since this is "The Story of Us." Origin stories may specify the origin of the group or may focus on the character and actions of the founder. Origin stories are a commonplace in anthropology: we expect that every tribe or human group has an account of the origin of the world and of the origin of that particular group.

The presence of a founder's story also differs from one group to another. Some institutions have founders whose presence is still strongly felt; others have founders who may be present as an oil painting in the main lobby, but whose story is not known to many members. Let us take universities as an example.

When I first began teaching at Stanford University, founded in 1891, I was struck by the strong presence of the founder, Mrs. Jane Lathrop Stanford, still very much alive in campus discourse 100 years after her death. Students knew stories about her; editorials in the student paper criticized actions of the administration as not being consonant with Mrs. Stanford's vision; the campus bus service, I was told by a student, is called the Marguerite, named after Mrs. Stanford's favorite mare. She is invoked in jokes: for example, students in a dorm took as a mascot a plaster dog that they claimed was a statue of Mrs. Stanford's beloved dog; at one point, this dog was kidnapped by students from another dorm as a prank. The Stanford Founders' Day celebration has Mr. and Mrs. Stanford look-alikes leading the parade in a horse-drawn carriage. Students hold a Halloween rally at her tomb. Even in communications outside the institution, her vision is referenced. For example, a job description for a position as assistant dean of the chapel discussed her vision of ecumenism. Stories abound: the choice of Palo Alto as the location of the university over the now-defunct town of Mayfield, because Palo Alto was willing to become a dry town in response to Mrs. Stanford's demand, while Mayfield would not give up its saloons; the Stanfords' choice not to donate money to Harvard, but to found their own university in their own home state. Undergraduates learn some of these stories as part of their formal orientation process as freshmen; graduate students do not have the same depth of knowledge since they do not go through a similar orientation process.

Certainly not all universities have founders who are so present. I attended Hunter College High School and Hunter College in New York City; I knew the name of the founder of Hunter College only because I knew someone who held a Thomas Hunter Scholarship, named in his honor. It may be that the difference can be attributed to the relative reportability of the founding stories. Stanford University was founded in honor of the Stanford's son Leland, who died of typhoid at the age of seventeen, a dramatic story indeed. (Many people telling this story narrate this as a death by drowning in a sailing accident, or even more dramatically, in the sinking of the Titanic.) It was only after I became interested in the issue of the presence of stories of university founders that I researched the founder of Hunter College and discovered that the Reverend Thomas Hunter had been a supporter of the women's suffrage movement and a pioneer in advocating higher education for women, starting the college as a normal school in 1870 to train women as teachers. An interesting story, surely, and one I was never told when I attended his schools. The lack of presence of the Reverend Hunter may be part of the general erasure of women's history. Or it may be the case that Stanford University is an exception and that universities typically do not vividly remember their founders. (Columbia University, where I did my graduate work, memorializes its pre-Revolutionary War founding in 1754 as King's College, but not its founder.) If that is so, it would be the memory of Mrs. Stanford that needs to be explained, rather than the absence of Thomas Hunter. This is an empirical question; it could be answered by comparative ethnography/historiography of various universities. I would add that I take as my examples universities I have attended or taught at, since I am interested in the stories that members remember and retell, not in stories written in an official history but not part of the regular discourse of and about the university.

As we shall see in the next chapters, MidWest Insurance strongly remembers its founder, George McBee. Mr. McBee, as he is generally referred to at MidWest, is present in stories, in pictures, and in exemplary tales about how to behave. The official corporate history is structured as a biography of the founder. Again, as with universities, many businesses maintain and use stories of their founders, but this is certainly not universal. It is a common way to establish a corporate identity, but not the only way.

Returning to the proposed range of stories that institutions maintain, if an institution has a second story in addition to a story of the founder, it is likely to be a story about a major turning point for the institution. Turning point stories can be stories of averted disasters, or more generally, major changes in direction for the institution. MidWest has an averted-disaster story about how they almost went bankrupt after World War II because of a rapid growth in auto insurance sold to bad drivers or drivers of bad cars, as drivers returned to the (dangerously unrepaired) roads after the war years of rationed gasoline and no production of new cars. This story is told by and to agents as a tale of how the agents saved the company by checking their books of business and pruning out drivers with bad records or bad cars. (See chapter 5 for a fuller discussion of this story.)

A more recent story of this sort comes from the Xerox Corporation: In the 1980s, Xerox's core copier business was seriously threatened by Japanese rivals such as Canon, Minolta, and Ricoh. The company focused on improving the quality of its products and after-sales service. The resulting turnaround is part of the lore recounted inside Xerox itself, as well as being a classic case taught in business schools. Note that this story with a happy ending is quite different from the stories told about Xerox's inability to market technologies developed by its research center: the personal computer with graphical interface, later developed by Apple Computers, and initially, the laser printer. These stories are told about Xerox from the outside, and unofficially inside, but do not form part of the official story of the company. [A well-known book about the Xerox Corporation, *Fumbling the Future*, has made this story a business commonplace (Smith 1988).]

In a history of a government-funded British nuclear physics laboratory, Law (1994) establishes a distinction between evolutionary and heroic institutional narratives. Bureaucratic narratives tend to be evolutionary and present an account of the rational and orderly development of the institution. Heroic accounts obviously require a hero and obstacles for the hero to overcome. For the laboratory Law describes, a heroic narrative requires an account of revolutionary change and the role in such revolutionary change of crucial individuals. These are genius stories, whether the genius is scientific or managerial, and the obstacles to be overcome are caused both by outside forces—and by the absence of such genius.

MidWest's stories of averted disasters are heroic narratives, though the heroes are not only the founder and president but also the sales agents as a group. The tone of these stories, however, speaks of an everyday heroism rather than a heroism at the limits of human capability: though the company faced bad times, the sterling character of its members made it almost a foregone conclusion that these obstacles would be overcome. (Of course, if an institution does not overcome its obstacles, it will not survive to retain the relevant stories.)

After averted disasters come stories of changes in direction: not necessarily prompted by difficulties, but nonetheless causing the institution to change and presumably grow. MidWest maintains two major stories of change. The first came early in the company's history: the company's change from selling only automobile insurance to selling a full range of insurance products, including homeowner's insurance, life insurance, business property insurance, and health insurance. While this change is sometimes referenced by upper management in speeches, it is not a particularly salient story for most members of MidWest, since it happened so long ago, with the new lines of insurance added within a decade or two of the company's founding. There are no agents or managers now working who can remember selling only automobile insurance. A more recent change of direction came in a move to professionalize agents, beginning around 1950, which was referred to as the "Full-Time Agent" concept. Agents were asked to work full-time, where before, many agents were farmers or shopkeepers who sold insurance on the side. The new agents were given formal training when first taken on, a contrast to the old policy of "hire and hope" that the new agent would be able to sell effectively. Agents were asked to rent or buy office premises for their businesses, and newly recruited agents were required to have, at first, a high school diploma, and later a college degree. The changes were implemented gradually: existing part-time agents were encouraged but not required to become Full-Time Agents.

This change in the status of agents is frequently retold or referenced both by managers and by agents. Indeed, there is a formulaic way of referencing it: "when we were asked to move out of our dining rooms into real offices." The story is used as an example of a change in direction that was initially felt as burdensome and unnecessary, but which ultimately profited the agents who did make the required changes, as well as profiting the company. At the time of the fieldwork, we met some agents and managers who were old enough to have begun their careers working from their dining room tables, but most of the people who cited the story were too young to have experienced this change.

Finally, in the hierarchy of types of story retained by an institution's memory are possible stories of exemplary past triumphs. MidWest's exemplary triumph is the story of a sales campaign begun during the period of the Depression and successfully concluded during the middle of World War II. In 1939, Mr. McBee, the founder and president of MidWest, decided that the company should more than double the number of policies it held within a period of five years. This campaign was given a slogan: "A million or more by '44," and rolled out to the agents. As the story goes in retrospect, it was an apparently impossible goal. The first obstacle was the economic climate of the Depression, in which many insurance companies went bankrupt. And then there were the war years, during which gasoline was rationed, and automobile production was stopped as automobile factories turned to the production of war supplies. During this period, the slogan was sometimes restated as "A million or more in spite of the war." But given such conditions in the world, how could the company possibly hope to sell enough policies to double its holdings? And yet the company and the agents, working together, added new agents, developed advertising campaigns, and made great efforts to sell new policies and get lapsed policies reinstated. And the goal was reached by March of 1944. The story is remembered and retold. In fact, a new sales campaign was begun during our fieldwork: "A billion or more by 2004." This is not, in itself, a stirring slogan. But it carries with it the resonance of its prior text: MidWest has accomplished such a feat before and we can do it again.

In this section, I have proposed a potential ordering for the stories held in an institution's memory. This argues that institutional memory is not an unstructured bin that can contain anything. Rather, it has more and less likely stories, and if it does not contain the most likely story, an origin story or a story of the founder, it will not maintain a story about a later exemplary triumph. Whether this proposed predictability of narrative types is a valid generalization is an empirical question is testable with more research on narratives within institutions.

I would add that the examples I have proposed come from corporations and universities and therefore tell the civil triumphs and disasters of these types of institutions. Origin stories, averted disaster stories, triumphal achievement stories of nations, peoples, or religions have a much more monumental character. The disasters are more disastrous, and even the triumphs likely to be more bloody. One of the virtues of studying institutional memory in an insurance company is that the relative mildness of the material makes it easier to see the patterns of narrative. It hurts the heart to take a sufficiently distanced view that would allow one to classify the Holocaust or the Trail of Tears as one example of a class of disaster stories within a predictable range of institutional narrative types. And yet, there are common patterns in what kinds of stories people and groups remember, and it is important to understand these patterns.

Relation of an institution's story to larger narrative patterns

MidWest's origin story is not *sui generis*. Rather than being a unique story, it forms part of a larger body of similar American business stories. These business stories are always success stories. Usually, success is linked to virtue: the Protestant ethic enacted in narrative. At the same time, each institution has its own flavor of this larger American story, and its particularities. A business school library will contain many business histories: browse HG8963 for insurance company histories, HD9651 for automobile company histories, etc. These histories include both authorized company histories and outside histories. A related genre can be found in business magazines such as *Fortune*, *Forbes*, *Money*, *Inc.*, and *Fast Company*: hagiographic accounts of successful business executives and currently successful companies.

Within this genre of business narratives, the authorized history of MidWest Insurance has several interesting particularities. One is its handling of the paradox of the founder's story. Usually, corporate narratives face a problem in presenting the founder as a model to be emulated, since the daring entrepreneurship valuable for a founder may not be the more routinized behavior of a desirable employee (Martin et al. 1983). (Current business rhetoric would deny that this is a problem, calling for innovation on the part of "intrapreneurs." That is, employees, working within the company, are advised to innovate, to start new projects, to act like entrepreneurs within their own companies. But even the business press advocating this idea admits that it is, in practice, a difficult position to accomplish, given the inherent conservatism of large companies, even those that profess to reward innovation.) However, in the case of MidWest, its sales agents are contractors, not employees, and thus the stories and rhetoric of the entrepreneurship of the founder can apply to them directly, rather than risking being heard as an unintended exhortation for the agents to leave the company and start their own businesses.

A second particularity has to do with the way that the MidWest stories handle the question of risk. In many business narratives, risk is presented as a necessary part of the road to success. The risks the founder took are highlighted as part of his heroic journey. However, for an insurance company risk is not valued. Rather, risk is what insurance is designed to manage: would you want your insurance company to present itself as taking heroic risks? Therefore, neither the founder's story nor the agents' stories of their starting their own offices focus on the risks this required. Rather they highlight early hard work, paying off in steadily growing business.

A final particularity of the MidWest story is its claim that MidWest is a family, and that family values are embodied in how the company does business. As a value, this seems rather bland: surely the discourse of family is part of all American business narratives? However, this is not the case. While the discourse of the corporate family as well as the importance of the personal family may have been a commonplace at one time, now it is just as common to hear stories of success coming as a result of working twenty-hour days, maxing out credit cards, wrecking health and families in the process. In Silicon Valley startup-company stories, for example, such events are proudly recounted. However, at MidWest, a story about starting one's own agency and destroying one's family in the process could not be told proudly, and certainly not about oneself. While such cases exist, we were told about them privately, as gossip about people who were considered dubious characters or failures within MidWest's culture. These stories were certainly not told to demonstrate that their protagonists had shown impressive proof of their single-minded determination to succeed, but rather to indicate their failure to craft a well-rounded life in which they were able to take their families seriously.

Why this is not a master narrative

Theoretically, one might be inclined to call the story of MidWest a master narrative (or *grand recit*, grand narrative, or metanarrative). I choose not to use this terminology for two reasons.

One is a technical reason: as discussed by Lyotard (1985) and those following him, master narratives seem to be everything but narratives. Frequently cited examples of master narratives include: the belief in progress, the idea of the Enlightenment, the survival of the fittest. But these are not, in the technical sense of discourse analysis, narratives. They may offer a plot trajectory or an ideology or a schema or a script for actual narratives, but they are not themselves narratives. This contrasts with the official and unofficial stories of MidWest Insurance, which are actual narratives in words or visual images, actually told or presented on specific occasions.

The second reason for not calling them master narratives is that I would prefer to avoid the intellectual baggage that goes along with that argument. Currently, it is a term of abuse within postmodernist thought. (For a useful definition of the difficult term "post-modernist," see Newton 1989). Master narratives are said to be totalizing, hegemonic, controlling. This is the widely accepted view, although there is a growing critique of this position that argues that the absence of some form of master narrative leads to increasingly fragmented identity politics, which makes large-scale political action impossible.

Rather than use the term "master narrative," I prefer an analysis of nested narrative types: MidWest's narrative is a particular instantiation of American business success narratives, which are themselves particular instantiations of American success narratives, etc.

Conclusion

In this chapter, I have attempted to define a class of narratives that exist within given institutions: the retold tale. These are the stories that are repeated within an institution, taking on tellers who were not present at the events. The stories of this class are important because they represent a mechanism for continuing the past into the present; by developing new tellers who were not present, the stories are not temporally restricted to the lifetime of witnesses.

Fundamentally, this chapter has been a discussion of the mechanisms that allow for the formation of an oral canon. Usually, the term "canon" is used to describe an authorized collection of texts, which a given community of practice uses as the carrier of its knowledge, its values, etc. The two most prominent kinds of textual canons are religious canons and literary canons. An example of a religious canon is the Bible, the Old and New Testaments that form the scriptural canon of Christianity. An example of a textual canon is the somewhat less clearly delineated entity "English Literature," that is, those texts that are included in classes given by English departments.

The choice of items in a canon is the result of a historical process of selection. Typically, the process of selection is not publicly available as part of the knowledge of the canon. Rather, the choice of works in a canon has the appearance of a natural process. That is, the books of the Bible are believed to be included because they are the word of God. Most members of the community of practice who are taught this canon are not taught the historical selection process by which certain works were included and others excluded, and the resulting inclusion or exclusion of communities of practice that become labeled as orthodox or heretic on the basis of their definition of the canon. Similarly, a literary or artistic canon is presented as if it were a self-evident fact: these works are included in the canon because they are great works. Most readers are not aware of the social and political processes by which the canon arose, although academic "canon wars" have brought this process into greater prominence. In a discussion of the relation of the professionalization of literary studies to a preference for ambiguous literary works (since ambiguity gives the professional something to work on, and a social justification), McCrea (1990) notes the mystification of the social construction of the literary canon: "[The canon of literary works] exists, but its formation is not a subject for discussion or debate. For all the recent willingness of the dominant figures in English studies to engage in metacommentary—to discuss how they do what they do—there has been no corresponding surge of interest in judging the texts to which they do it" (140). Apparently, part of the authority of a canon comes from the belief (or the presentation) that it is a self-evident fact. Specific attention to the process of its social constitution would undermine that authority.

The canon of stories at MidWest, or at any institution, has a similarly opaque origin. The stories exist; they are told, officially and unofficially; someone writes them into the president's annual speech or articles in the official newsletter; but the process of how these stories are chosen is not available to members. At the same time, there is a grassroots component to the process of continuing the canon: if district managers and agents do not themselves retell the stories in the institution's repertoire of stories, those stories cannot function as live carriers of the institution's memory.

We may also distinguish between open and closed canons. An open canon is a canon that may be added to. A closed canon is fixed; it will have no further additions. English literature is an open canon: we expect that further great books will be written, and will become part of the canon. While additions to the canon require adjustment of representations such as the curriculum of literature courses, or anthologies like the *Norton Anthologies*, such adjustments are possible and expected. We do not believe that literature is over.

In contrast, the Bible is a closed canon. The nature of the text, and of the communities that sustain it, means that no further books will be added. In fact, the treatment of the discovery of the Dead Sea Scrolls is an interesting commentary on the closed nature of this canon. The Dead Sea Scrolls are being used as material for further study of the Bible, providing additional archeological, sociological, and even theological knowledge to be used for an improved interpretation of the canonical books of the Bible, and the process of canonization. But it is unlikely that they will be included in new editions of the Bible itself. Another example of a canon closed by historical factors, rather than by the social process of religious canon formation, is the canon of Latin literature. Since Latin is no longer a living language, we do not expect any new masterpieces of Latin literature to be composed.

The collection of stories at MidWest is an open canon. While the institution continues, we can expect that new stories of averted disaster, triumphs, and changes of direction will be added. Perhaps there will even be a new hero added to the canon. At the same time, if Vansina's theory of the floating gap is correct, there is a limit to the number of stories the institution can sustain: if new ones are added, some old ones will be dropped.

Finally, I would like to clarify the status of my argument about the existence of an implicational hierarchy of retold tales. It is clear that it is useful to postulate the existence of a class of retold tales within an institution, and that this class of stories functions like other, better known types of canons. An internal organization of these stories, both within a single organization, and across institutions, may be discovered once the material is available to do comparisons. I suggest that this internal organization takes the form of an implicational hierarchy. This is subject to further empirical confirmation or disconfirmation. However, the existence of the class of retold tales does not require the existence of the implicational hierarchy of narratives; its existence is already well documented.

Multiple Versions
of MidWest's History

The previous chapter introduced the notion of retold tales: the stories within an institution that are known to most members, and that persist because they can be told by people who were not present at the original events. I also argued that it is useful to think of an institution as having a core stock of stories, which is the collection of the retold tales that are most frequently told. This chapter goes further to examine the stories that make up the core story stock of MidWest Insurance and to explore the relation of the position of the story's teller to the choice of stories, and to the way these stories are framed for an audience and an occasion.

In understanding how an institution remembers, one must attend not only to the stories that are retold, but to who retells them, and the stance or positioning towards the institution that the teller expresses. There is obviously a continuum of possible positions a speaker may take towards a representation of the past. For the present, let us distinguish four useful levels of stance. The first stance is an official representation of the past produced by an authorized spokesman for the institution. The second level is a semiofficial representation of the past. This is a story produced by a speaker located within the institution whose position does not permit him or her to represent the institution officially. Or the story may be produced on an occasion in which a speaker of whatever position within the institution presents only a personal stance, although the representation of the past is consonant with or not contradictory to official statements. The third level is an unofficial and oppositional representation by a speaker located within the institution. Here, the speaker or producer marks the representation of the past as being in intentional opposition to the official version. The final level is a representation of the past of an institution presented by an individual outside the institution or by another institution. These external representations may be intended as commemorative in an approving sense or in opposition to the institution's version. The official or unofficial status of a representation is thus a complex combination of a speaker's position within or outside an institution, the medium and genre of the representation, and the occasion on which the representation is offered.

There is a great deal to be said about speaking unofficially or oppositionally. Representations of an institution's past can exist outside the institution as well as within it. And these representations can be relatively well aligned with the institution's own representations, different, or consciously oppositional. Chapter 9, discussing silences, will consider consciously oppositional accounts. However, in this chapter I will focus on positions taken by speakers within MidWest Insurance as a way to examine both the function of speaker's stance and the very important question of whether one can speak of a single institutional memory, or whether there are multiple ones, perhaps as many as there are members of the institution. As I have found for MidWest, a core institutional memory does exist: an account of the most salient events and evaluations of the institution's past. What constitutes it as core is that all versions of the institution's past, told from whatever stance, include these events and evaluations. This is the part of the past that anyone in the institution can be expected to know as part of their membership. By a stroke of methodological good fortune, my observations contain five temporally complete tellings of the history of MidWest, produced on different occasions, for different audiences, and in different genres. When we examine ways in which the past is represented at MidWest, we find two basic forms. One, the more frequent form, is the retelling of some single past event to illustrate some point that bears on the present situation at the time of the telling. Another form of representation of the past is an attempt to tell the complete story of the institution. Complete here does not mean that it includes every story ever told about the institution, but rather temporally complete, providing an account of the entire span of time, from the founding, or before, to the present time of telling. Given this complete time span, the choice of events to include is particularly revealing of what the teller believes to be salient about the institution's past. This is similar to the ways in which the stories of individual are told. One way individuals represent their lives is to tell accounts of the past singly, on different occasions. Of these, the frequently retold stories form a life story as a temporally discontinuous unit (Linde 1993). But there are also occasions on which accounts of the past are told as a single, continuous unit, on a single occasion, composed of the most important and most frequently retold events of the discontinuous unit, as well as other stories that may be rarely or never told on any other occasion. The analogy between individual speakers and institutions is this: most of the stories individual speakers tell about their lives are stories about single events. Some of them are ephemeral and are repeated only a few times. Others are about central events that the speaker repeats on many occasions to many addressees. And occasionally, a speaker may be asked to tell "the story of your life," a request that produces a single account containing those events and evaluation from the life story that are relevant to the occasion of the request. The temporally complete tellings of the history of MidWest are the analog of an individual telling "the story of her life" on a single occasion.

It is an unusual opportunity to have as many as five different versions of the history of MidWest. The comparison of so many different complete tellings allows us to make two important analyses: first, it permits us to determine what the core memory is—the part of the past assumed by all versions. Second, the comparison of complete tellings also permits an analysis of the different ways in which a particular telling is shaped to represent the position, point of view, and current circumstances of its teller and its audience. To describe this in terms of positioning, the core memory is known and usable by anyone in any position within the institution. The other parts of the past included in a particular version are relevant to the specifics of a particular position within the institution at a particular time and circumstance.

Versions of the five complete tellings of the past of MidWest

The five different versions of the past of MidWest from the founding to the time of their telling include two printed books, one series of articles in the MidWest magazine distributed to agents, one lecture to trainee managers, and one unsolicited narrative by a district manager told to a field-worker as part of an interview. A description of each version follows.

First is an authorized history of MidWest and biography of the founder, published in 1955. This history was commissioned by MidWest, and issued by a major commercial publishing house. As the author describes the process:

> This book ... was undertaken at the request of the [Automobile Department] of [MidWest Insurance]. It is, therefore, an authorized biography and history. I should like to point out to the general reader, however, that in the preparation of this typically Midwestern story and in its writing I have been given the fullest latitude and utmost freedom in the choice of material and the use to which I have put it. The executives of the company opened its files to me and let me examine them without direction.

This book is in wide use at MidWest. Although it is not easily available to the public, it is still reprinted and available for purchase within MidWest, where it has a very active life. It is displayed by many managers on their bookshelves, turned outwards so that the front cover rather than the spine is visible. When we first met with upper management at MidWest, they showed us the book and told us that in order to understand the company, we must read it. I began to wonder whether the book was displayed as a talisman of loyalty or whether it really was read. When I mused on this question to a district manager I had come to know, she assured me that she used it all the time. I asked what she used it for. Her answer was that she "mined it for stories" for speeches, since she had come to the company relatively recently, and that she didn't know the history "by blood," that is, she did not come from a MidWest family, and had joined MidWest in the middle of her career.

This book is a typical example of the American genre of authorized business histories in its optimistic tone and tale of ever-increasing success. It is unusual, although certainly not unique, in recounting the biography of the founder and the history of the company in parallel. I refrain from citing publication data in order to protect the confidentiality of the actual insurance company I have called MidWest.

The second temporally complete version of the history of MidWest is a privately published memoir of the founder of MidWest, produced as a small hardbound book, to commemorate his seventieth birthday. This memoir appears to have served as one source for the authorized history, although it is referenced in the authorized history only in passing and without publication information. This volume appears to function more as source material for the complete tellings circulating within MidWest, rather than as a complete telling in itself. In contrast to the ubiquitous status of the authorized history, I have never seen the memoir displayed at MidWest or heard it mentioned by anyone at MidWest. Thus, although it has a physical existence in a few libraries or private collections, it is not part of the practice of how MidWest works its past, although it may serve as source material for some tellings, particularly those produced by speakers who have a research department backing them (for example, senior vice presidents) or whose job or inclinations lead them to detailed historical research. (I obtained a copy myself through a Web search that led me to a used book store in the city where MidWest is headquartered.) I include it in the comparison since it may have served as a source for the authorized history, and it appears to be the source for at least one story of the founder present in version three, but not in the authorized history.

The third complete telling is an eight-part series of articles in the company's newsletter for agents. This series was produced in honor of MidWest's seventieth anniversary. It contains eight articles, printed in consecutive monthly issues, which give highlights of the company's history, with each article covering one decade. The articles appear under the name of a senior vice president, but they were almost certainly prepared for him by the headquarters' research staff. This material is mainly taken verbatim, or with light editing, from the official history, with additional heavy use of reminiscences by older agents and photographs from the archives. It does contain one story present in the memoir, but not the official history.

Most of the articles give a paragraph of framing historical events for each decade. Although some of these are business developments directly relevant to the economics of insurance sales, some are recognizable cultural events of the time: landing a man on the moon, the Beatles, etc. These attempt to give a flavor of the times. For example:

> Hundreds of auto insurance companies [in the 1920s] were doing business in North America. Still, throughout the Midwest, farmers were complaining about the difficulties they encountered in acquiring adequate affordable auto insurance.
> The stock market had crashed in 1929. By the end of 1932, a quarter of the workforce was unemployed. Thousands of banks had failed. Blue chip stocks were selling for pennies a share. Soup kitchens and bread lines were part of city life. In the country, drought ruined farmers. Auto sales dropped from 4.5 million in 1929 to 1.1 million three years later. The number of cars registered in the United States declined 10 percent during those years.
> The 1940s were turbulent. On Dec. 7, 1941, Japan 'awakened a sleeping giant' at Pearl Harbor. Canada had declared war on Germany two years earlier. Although there was no fighting on U.S. or Canadian soil, the countries felt the effects of the war. The auto insurance market was severely impacted. By the end of 1942, no new cars were being produced, gasoline was rationed, no new tires were available and most people cut their travel to a minimum.

> During the 1960s, violence rocked the country as civil rights advocates and pro-
> testers against the Vietnam War took their messages to the streets. The popularity of
> television and frozen TV dinners zoomed. Youth culture simmered, fueled by the music
> of the Beatles. Above it all, Apollo II astronauts took man's first walk on the moon.

Although these framing events give a historical flavor of each of decades, the majority of the articles are devoted to business developments at MidWest.

The fourth version of MidWest's history we collected is a videotape of a speech
given at the main headquarters of MidWest to a group of newly promoted regional
managers. The speaker, who was in charge of sales promotions programs, was
described by a senior vice president introducing him as "Someone who knows an
awful lot, maybe more than anyone else around here about MidWest's history. He
really makes [the official history] come to life." Indeed, that has been part of his job.
He is the person who designed the lobby display and traveling exhibits of MidWest
memorabilia described in chapter 3. The speaker begins: "I'd like to talk about Mid-
West through the years. I've made a kind of hobby of it." He described himself to me
in an interview as "the unofficial MidWest historian."

This speech came as part of a training program for the new regional managers.
Many of the stories in it are ones that they must have heard before, since they are
ubiquitous in MidWest, and certainly formed part of the managers' initial orientation
when they were hired. The purpose of this occasion of telling is therefore not to tell
them something entirely new, although the account does contain some details not
present in the written versions, which the managers may never have heard. Rather,
I argue, the telling has two purposes. The first is inspirational: to get the managers
even more enthusiastic about the great past and even greater future of MidWest. The
speaker at times gently parodies the inspirational genre of his speech. For example,
in telling the story of the famous slogan "A million or more [auto policies] by '44"
he ends by saying: "Now brothers and sisters, that's *sales leadership*. If you want to
say 'Amen' go ahead." The second purpose of the telling, I believe, is to induct new
managers into the practice of using stories of the history of MidWest as a source of
inspiration for the agents and employees whom they will manage. The event could be
seen as a ritual of permission, so that the addressees are now themselves authorized
to tell these stories at formal events. (See the discussion in chapter 8 on storytelling
rights within an institution.)

The speech was extremely lively and well received by the audience. They looked
alert and interested, laughed heartily at the many jokes in the speech, and at the end
rose to a standing ovation. (As an outsider, viewing the video alone in my office, not
constrained by politeness or politics, I will note that I too found it an effective and
entertaining talk, somewhat to my surprise. The humor is midwestern and MidWestern, with jokes about Sunday school and small town life. Not precisely my form of
humor, but effective nonetheless.)

As a speech, this version lies somewhere between an oral and a written production. The speaker works from notes, which include items from the authorized history.
At some points he reads his notes verbatim. At other points, he speaks freely, without
consulting his notes. Additionally, he uses slides of photos of the founder, the first
and subsequent headquarters buildings, charts of the standings of various insurance
companies, including MidWest, and graphs of MidWest's growth, and the effect of

various natural disasters such as Hurricane Andrew and the Northridge earthquake. All of these features are characteristic of business speeches as a genre.

The fifth version is a purely oral version, which comes from a field-worker's interview. The person interviewed is a district manager who had worked for MidWest for forty years. As a district manager, his job is to manage agents, and like almost all managers, he was promoted to this job after some years as an agent himself. The field-worker did not request an account of the history of MidWest. Rather, she asked him about if he had been an agent and why he became a manager. Part of his explanation of why being a manager is fun is that "Our business never stays the same, it always changes." The field-worker's follow-up question about what the changes have been prompted a long account of MidWest's history. This telling is detailed and knowledgeable. It is clear from the complexity of the account of the details of the insurance business, and the polished quality of some of the component stories that this is not the first time this manager has told these stories. Rather, I speculate, this is a version, produced for the interviewer, of a story he has told to agents many times before.

Comparison of versions as a method

Before turning to the comparison itself, let us consider the method of comparison of versions: what it is and what it can show. This data set consists of five complete tellings of the history of MidWest, collected by chance in the course of our fieldwork. Additional fieldwork would almost certainly have collected additional versions. However, this is a good sample: three official written versions in two different genres, a staged oral version, and an impromptu oral version. These provide valuable materials for a comparison.

There are two main purposes for doing such a comparison of versions. One is to determine the contents of the core institutional memory: those parts of the past are worked in all of the versions. The other purpose is to discover how a retelling of the past is shaped by the present position of the teller and addressees and by the present situation on which the past is brought to bear.

Comparison of variant versions of a text is a standard and time-honored method in both philology and history. While the present comparison uses some of the same methods and questions, there are also differences. First, unlike the process of producing a critical edition of a particular text, I am not attempting to discover the earliest or purest version of a single work. I do not posit a single original text: there was no such urtext. The authorized history was produced by standard methods of historical composition: examining earlier histories, consulting original documents, and interviewing participants. At least some of these documents, and many of the stories of the people interviewed, remained as direct sources for later versions independent of their use in the authorized history. Oral stories were written down and distributed in the official history but also remained as part of the oral story stock, and may have contributed directly to later tellings. An additional reason for not trying to reconstruct an original text is that the producers of later complete versions were not trying to reproduce an original text. Rather they were each attempting an account of the history of MidWest appropriate for their time, their position, their audience, and their genre. Thus the comparison of these kinds of texts is more like the work of a folklorist or redactor of oral epic attempting to map the range of versions, rather than that of a philologist attempting to work back past scribal corruptions to an original pure written text.

Further, unlike the work of the historian, this comparison does not attempt to discover which parts of which versions are factually verifiable. When the authorized history recounts that MidWest was first chartered in 1925, this is independently verifiable in state records. When a manager recounts that the founder sold the first policy, this is verifiable in MidWest's records. Such work of verification is the standard spadework of historical research and is essential for creating the historical record. However, I am not concerned with the verifiability of the stories recounted. My study of memory is concerned with how an account of the past is worked in the present, what is remembered, what stories are told, by whom they are told, how they are told, and how they are used for present purposes. This is not to argue against the importance of the process of historical verification. The existence of Holocaust deniers, for example, has taught us that. However, it is the use of stories within an institution that I am concerned with; their verifiability against a larger historical record is another investigation.

There is another possible set of questions about historical verifiability: how do the stories told within the memory of an institution compare with stories told about the institution by tellers outside the institution. Such a comparison would tell us a great deal about the boundaries of institutions, the effects of outside information, and how parochial or permeable an institution's account of itself is. These would be valuable questions to pursue in order to understand how an institution's memory functions within a social setting larger than the institution itself. I have not pursued these questions in the case of MidWest, since before it is possible to make a useful comparison, it is first necessary to understand the workings of the internal memory. I will, however, return to this issue in the discussion of silences in chapter 9, since a silence in an institution's account of itself may often be detected by reference to accounts maintained by other institutions or individuals.

In doing any comparison, one looks, of course, for similarities and differences. To determine the core institutional memory, I look for versions of the retold tales, direct reproductions of parts of particular versions, and different stories making the same point. In particular, I look for those retold tales contained in both oral and written versions. These are the central element of the institution's memory: the parts of the past that are so important that they are always included. This consensus tells what is most important in the story of the institution: what anyone must know about us to know who We are. Oral tellings of these stories are extremely important for arguing for the existence of a core institutional memory. We might find a story that appears in all official written versions but in no oral version. Such a story might be part of the official version, but it would be hard to argue that it is included in the working memory of everyone in the institution. For example, the three written versions agree in including the holding of the first sales convention as an important milestone for the company. However, neither oral version includes this. I would argue that this event is probably not as important to members of the company as those events represented in both the written and oral versions.

The next level of comparison has to do with similarities of evaluation. A number of the versions compared contain different stories about the founder, which, however, have the same evaluative points: they demonstrate his probity, his concern for the welfare of others, his sales ability, his ability to choose and manage able and committed associates. Such statements about the particular character of the founder are frequently part of an institution's memory, worked again in the present to inspire such virtues in hearers. It might be argued that this is a hagiography that contains no actual content, since such virtues are posited of all American business leaders. However, when one examines accounts of many business leaders, their posited virtues differ, and they differ according to the type of business they founded. Thus, within Microsoft, as well as in the business press, stories about Bill Gates are framed to demonstrate that he is awesomely smarter than anyone else in the company and possibly in the world. For example, *Wired Magazine* Readers' Choice poll named Bill Gates as "Wired Visionary Architect of the Future." "So why is Bill king of the mountain? Brains, agility, tenacity and singular leadership. Bill's prescience—it's the software, stupid!—has resulted in Microsoft's dominance across the globe" (*Wired Magazine*, December 1999, vol. 7, issue 12, 366). This form of hagiography was common before the antitrust lawsuit brought against Microsoft in 1999. Since that point, articles in the business press have been more critical of Gates's business practices but still do not question his intelligence. In contrast, overwhelming intelligence is not the defining virtue ever posited of MidWest's founder. However, it is the appropriate central virtue to recommend to employees of a software company, just as probity and salesmanship are the appropriate central virtues for an insurance company. (It might be argued that this is represents a general shift in American values, rather than differences particular to specific industries. But I believe that however much we may want our software, and hence our software designers, to be intelligent, the value we still desire most for insurance, insurance companies, and insurance sales agents is reliability or trustworthiness.)

Finally we come to the examination of differences: the stories contained in some but not all accounts or present in only one version. This is the part of the comparison most resistant to analysis. There are many reasons why a particular story may not be included in a given version: Lack of time or space for inclusion, lack of relevance to the occasion of telling, lack of knowledge by the teller, deliberate obfuscation of the historical record. Thus, although it is possible to speculate about the reason for an omission of a story, it is not possible to be certain. But inclusions can be analyzed. The inclusion of a story in one version at least suggests that it was important to that particular teller, and one may attempt to analyze the reasons for this importance. This is possible even for the authorized history. Although this genre might appear to be an attempt at the full story, any history, however long, is shaped by the author's decisions on what is relevant and what can be formed into a story. Without such shaping selections, one would have an archive, and an interminable one at that, but one would not have not a history.

In addition to investigating the collection of stories that forms the institution's memory, comparison also allows us to investigate issues of point of view and institutional position. Each version is told by someone in a particular position in (or outside) the institution to an actual or projected audience. The point of view of teller and audience shape the choice of stories, the way they are framed, and the choice of evaluations. I will show some examples of these kinds of point-of-view issues in the comparison of complete tellings. I will examine it in more detail in the next chapter, which does a detailed microcomparison of three versions of a single story.

The core memory: The stories everyone knows

We turn now to the parts of history of MidWest present in most or all versions, and particularly, as discussed above, present in at least one oral version.

1. The founder was a retired midwestern farmer

This is the core fact in the institution's memory. It is one fact that everyone in the institution knows. In this comparison, it is present in all five versions. It is used in the institution's memory work in a number of ways. One is that, initially, the company was founded to offer insurance to farmers in states in the Midwest at affordable rates: the founder's background as a farmer is a warrant for his understanding of the problems of farmers. A second reason links to the meaning of the farm in the wider American story, which contrasts the virtue of the farm to the wickedness and corruption of the city. Farm origins are taken as an indication of honesty, probity, and down-to-earthness, all characteristics that MidWest predicates of the founder and of the company he founded. For example, in an interview one agent told us: "MidWest was started by a farmer. And I think of farmers and country folk as very friendly, very down to earth."

What is interesting about this characterization is that the speaker was born in a large city and has spent all his working life in either cities or suburban areas. However, here he echoes an American belief in the moral nature of farms and farmers that can be traced back to Thomas Jefferson (and indeed back to Roman nostalgia for a virtuous pastoral past).

2. The character of the founder

The founder's farm origins are tied to his character, which is described and/or illustrated in all five versions. He is described as being honest, hardworking, and possessing integrity and determination, as having great ability to persuade others, impressive salesmanship, ability to choose the right people and motivate them, ability to deal with opposition and obstacles, a paternal care for his employees, and a broad vision of the possible growth of his insurance company. All of the complete tellings contain some stories about the founder. Although the choice of particular stories differs, they all illustrate this cluster of virtues.

Note also that the versions are in agreement on what is *not* said about his character. He is not described as an expert in the details of the insurance business, nor as having the mathematical ability to calculate complex actuarial systems. Rather, he is described as having the crucial founding ideas about what kind of insurance should be offered to farmers and the ability to attract the law-yers, accountants and other experts who could handle the technical end of the business. As the veteran district manager (version 5) describes it: "McBee was a, uh, innovator and motivator. Uh, smart enough to hire people that could get things done that, you know, he didn't have the skills to do." The meaning of the account of the founder's vision, salesmanship, and ability to choose and motivate others, rather than technical expertise has changed over time within MidWest and had become a somewhat problematic issue at the time of our study. For-merly, technical business skills were not highly prized. Most of the older agents we studied had been recruited on the basis of character and sales ability rather than technical or managerial skills. In fact, we were told humorous stories about the last few dinosaur agents who had not yet adopted computers in their busi-ness, although MidWest had introduced them twenty years ago. At the time our study began, MidWest had become concerned that current economic conditions of intense competition required agents to have a level of business expertise they had not been recruited or trained for. Rather than the old model of a supersales-man, with one or more "girls" supporting him in the office, the new agent was to be the "CEO of their business," putting in place business systems and procedures that would allow for sales, particularly life insurance sales, based on system rather than personality or raw sales skill. This is a model not supported by the story of the founder, or by the skills of the veteran agents, and the company found it a very hard sell indeed. An emphasis on the ability to recruit and motivate personnel and to use the skills of others to set up a business-like business was at this time not a bland point of hagiography. Rather, it was a hotly contested issue about the identity of the ideal agent.

Finally, the founder was not notably a churchgoer. None of the versions have any account of his religious life or preferences. However, the virtuous character of the founder has developed into a preference for church membership for MidWest agents and managers. A number of agents and managers described being recruited by a fellow church member, and this appears to be a highly valued way of coming into MidWest. However, this seems to be a case of church attendance as a demonstration of virtue, rather than a demand for church affiliation or a preference for any particular church.

3. Background on insurance business showing
   the founder's revolutionary ideas

All but the headquarters trainer's speech (version 4) contain some background on the state of the insurance business at the time of founding as a way of indicating just how revolutionary the founding ideas were. The authorized history, as one would imagine, gives considerable background on the commercial insurance business, as well as the relation between farm mutual associations and insurance sales. More surprisingly, the district manager (version 5) describes in detail how insurance bro-kerages then worked, and the relation between their expenses and commissions, and the consequent high cost of their insurance.

In contrast to the prevailing practices of the 1920s, the founder envisioned a company that allowed for a semiannual premium, rather than an annual premium, which would be easier for farmers to pay. He wished to market to farmers and to charge them a lower premium than current commercial companies, because, as the district manager describes the founder's thought: "It doesn't seem fair to, to charge a farmer the same rate for his auto insurance policy as the guy driving to Chicago every day. So he, and so he came up with what they called a farmer's discount, and they gave ten percent off if you were a farmer."

Another innovation was an initial fee and direct billing: automatic renewal of policies, rather than rewriting each policy each time it came due, with a concomitant charge each time. I doubt that all members of MidWest know the founding business concepts in this level of detail; in fact, I am amazed that anyone does. This account contains a startling specificity of changes from practices long obsolete (since the insurance industry eventually adopted most or all of MidWest's innovations). Indeed, many of these practices were no longer in force when the speaker himself began working at MidWest.

4. Founder told to start his own insurance company

Three of the versions contain a story about the founder initially being asked to join a local insurance company. When he made suggestions for how it should be run (in line with the ideas sketched above), he was told to start his own company. They all contain not only the same story but the same punch line, although they differ on the exact date. As the various versions put it:

Version 1: The Memoir

> He didn't have any trouble selling policies; in fact, he made as much as $1,500 a week, but he was bothered because the company didn't, in his estimation, settle claims fairly. The company officials only laughed at him when he complained and said: "Well, Tom, if you don't like the way we run things, go start your own company. You'll find your ideas aren't practical." So he quit.

Version 2, the official history, draws on Version 1:

> Thomas McBee experienced no difficulty in selling automobile insurance policies for this struggling young company. Inexperienced in salesmanship though he was, he is said to have made "as much as $1,500 a week." Although this undoubtedly was an exaggeration, there is no question that he showed unusual aptitude for the business.... One thing about his new field of endeavor bothered him. Inexperienced as he was in insurance technicalities, he could not see eye to eye with his new employers on details of their operations. Always outspoken, Thomas McBee one afternoon expatiated on how *he* thought things should be done. [The owner] laughed at him and said "Well, Tom, if you don't like the way we run things, go start your own company. You'll find your ideas aren't practical."

Version 3, the newsletter articles, does not contain this story. It moves directly from the founder's retirement from farming to his plans for a new insurance company.

Similarly, Version 4, the headquarters manger's speech to new managers does not include this story.

Version 5, the veteran district manager:

> And somebody (?) said "Hey look, you think you know so much about the business, go start your own company. Leave us alone, we're doing fine."

5. Founder sells first policy and boasts, "if I can sell one,
   I can sell a million"

Symbolic of his sales prowess, the founder is noted as having sold the first policy. This is present in all the versions. The written versions include the name of the buyer and the car he was insuring.

In the words of the headquarters trainer:

> This tradition of sales leadership had its beginning from the very first day. It was June Fifteenth, Founder's Day. Our founder's birthday, 1925. T.D. McBee was then forty five years old. Prowling up and down the streets of Jefferson, Broadway, and Euclid and Main there, talking to everybody he could find about this honest insurance company he was going to start. And somebody said to him, a lot of people didn't think we would live six months, certainly not a year. And that day, somebody said to him "you know Tom, I think you better give up the idea of starting an insurance company." "Why?" "Cause you can't write any insurance, you are a tractor salesman." "But I've already got some" McBee said with a grin. "How many applications do you have?" the friend persisted. "One" and he had it in his pocket. "What does a single application amount to?" And Tom McBee said the famous words we have all heard a hundred times "Well if I can sell one policy, I can sell a million." And so it began.

In the words of the district manager:

> Manager: And, uh, McBee wrote the first policy and, of course, that's pretty famous within MidWest. He said, if I can write one we can write a million. And, uh, little did he know that, uh—
>
> Interviewer: He was right.
>
> Manager: He was not only right but I don't think he had any idea how big this company would get. Maybe he, maybe he did.
>
> Interviewer: What, when did he say that?
>
> Manager: Oh, when the, when he wrote the first policy back in 1925....So it went from there.

While the authorized history barely notes the quote, the memoir gives it more fully:

> There were cynics, of course, who predicted that the company wouldn't last more than six months; others who foretold its end within a year. But Thomas McBee wasn't worried. Some one asked him that first day how many automobile insurance policies he thought he could sell.

"Well," he replied with a twinkle in his eyes, "I guess if I can sell one policy I can sell a million."

The memoir also uses this quote to motivate another incident that forms an important part of the institution's memory: the drive to sell a million automobile policies (discussed in point 9 below).

He thought back to a conversation he had on the day he wrote the first policy in MidWest—*his forty-fifth birthday on June 15, 1925*. A few minutes after he had obtained that first application he met a friend on the street.

"You know," the friend advised, "I think you had better give up this idea of starting an automobile insurance company."

"Why?"

"Because you cant write any business."

"But I already have some," McBee said with a grin.

"How many applications do you have?" the friend persisted?

"One."

"Huh! What does a single application amount to?"

"Well," came the reply, "if I can write one policy I can write a million."

By the end of sixteen years the company had less than half a million automobile policies in force. Thomas McBee decided it was about time to do something about it.

This attitude is one that many agents share. For example, one agent told me that one of the things he really liked about being an agent was that if he found he or his family needed more money in a given year, he could always sell more policies. And if they had enough money, he could go duck hunting.

6. Entry of ruling dynasties into MidWest

One piece of the past which all the five versions include is the entry into MidWest of the men who formed the first generation of leadership, along with Mr. McBee, and whose sons and grandsons continued to lead the company. In particular, all versions mark the entry of the current president's grandfather as a lawyer for MidWest. Interestingly, both oral versions agree with the official history in including the entry of the father of a recently retired and very well-regarded vice president in charge of sales agents. He is salient in an account for agents exactly because of the position his son achieved.

One thing which none of the versions mention, though, is the idea that there are or should be ruling dynasties. It is assumed that MidWest hires members of the same family, at every level of the organization. (See the discussion below, as well as chapter 9.) The idea that upper management positions tend to run in the same few families is not officially discussed, although it is a striking feature of the history of the company, and one that is at odds with American democratic ideology. It is, however, discussable unofficially. See chapter 9 for an examination of what one employee called MidWest's practice of "monarchism."

7. Expansion to other states

All the versions include some account of the geographic expansion from the initial state in which MidWest was chartered to additional states and ultimately nationwide. This account of the expansion is a way of specifying the enormous growth of Mid-West from small local business to an international company. This story of growth is a central theme for MidWest and indeed for any business history. Success in business necessarily means growth, and growth is easily and dramatically described by geographic expansion. This part of the history includes both the expansion of insurance sales into new states, and later, a change in the management structure to an organization into regions, with regional headquarters reporting to central headquarters. As one would predict, the details of the expansion are given by the four versions that are official, or which issue from headquarters. The district manager notes the expansion in general terms, but he does give an account of the first regional headquarters. This detail is salient for him because the first region was the region in which he is located: its history is his history.

8. Building the main headquarters building

An account of moving from rented quarters is included in all three written versions and in the version by the headquarters-based manager. In telling this part of the story, he is able to give local details: that the naming of corridors as east and west corridors reproduces the naming of the alleys that the new building replaced. This telling is salient for the occasion: it describes the building in which the speech takes place.

The district manager does not mention the building of the headquarters building. This building is not particularly important for agents. No events take place there that they must attend. Some agents may have visited the headquarters building as part of their participation in various teams and task forces, but this is not particularly common. For the agents, it is the regional headquarters building that is important. They visit this building for training, educational and motivational events, and it is the managers at the regional headquarters whose decisions have the most immediate effect on agents.

9. "A million or more by '44"

All versions include the universally known sales slogan, invented by the founder: "A million or more by '44." As I have already discussed, this slogan refers to the goal of writing a million auto policies. At the time this was announced as a goal, in 1938, the company had less than half a million automobile insurance policies in force; the announced goal required more than doubling the number of policies. In 1938, the Depression was limiting the number of new automobiles being bought and operated. By 1941, World War II brought about even stricter limits on automobile use, due to gasoline rationing, unavailability of new tires, and conversion of factories from the production of automobiles to the production of military supplies. Still, the goal of a million auto policies was reached half way into 1944. The problems of the

Depression and the war years form part of the story; it is thus not limited to the bare fact of a goal and its accomplishment but includes the apparently overwhelming obstacles to achieving the goal.

This story is very widely told within MidWest. I have heard it, not only in these versions, but in speeches, video histories, and virtually every account of the past of MidWest. It is usually used to illustrate the company's determination and ability to overcome difficulties and even impossible odds to accomplish visionary goals. It is frequently used as an encouragement to further efforts. The implicit argument is: "If we could accomplish such an apparently impossible goal, we can certainly accomplish the current goal."[1]

10. Difficulties after World War II: How the agents (or somebody) saved the company

Another working of the past that occurs in all five versions, and that I have also frequently heard in other contexts, has to do with MidWest's difficulties immediately after the World War II. With the ending of gasoline rationing, and the return of large numbers of former soldiers, many more cars returned to the road. Many of these were old cars, in bad condition, and accident rates soared. After paying out many claims, MidWest found itself with dangerously low financial reserves. MidWest's management changed its rules for the eligibility of older cars for insurance, and the agents were asked to reinspect every car they insured to eliminate unsafe older vehicles. All the versions tell this story but differ in the degree to which they credit the agents with the turnaround.

The official history concentrates on the difficulties involved in increasing staff at headquarters and in developing systematic new procedures for dealing with a flood of policies and new claims. It also discusses changes in the underwriting rules, which specify the required age and condition of insurable automobiles and explains the reasons for these changes. While the agents' role in reunderwriting existing business is mentioned, the focus is on reorganization, changes in the operations divisions to accommodate the numbers of new underwriters and claims processors needed, and the development of new procedures. Indeed, the agents are dismissed in the surprising phrase "down to the lowliest agent." The underwriting crisis is described as everyone's crisis:

> In the crisis years of 1945 and 1946 the increased frequency of claims and the increased cost of almost every type of claim produced a staggering underwriting loss for the every casualty company in the industry....For a few months in 1946 MidWest was losing money at the rate of $1,000,000 a month. The company's surplus by that time had dipped to about $10,000,000. The simple arithmetic of this was frightening. But through the concerted effort of almost everybody connected with MidWest, from Thomas McBee down to the lowliest agent, the turning-point came in 1947, when the company's underwriting experience was once again raised to a satisfactory level.

The headquarters trainer, speaking to managers, gives an account of this crisis with the founder as hero, stressing his leadership, and in particular, his ability to gather the right team of executives to solve the problem. The role of agents is not mentioned at all:

> This move to total decentralization began in the late '40s. The war is over now, and our fantastic growth during the war brought on fantastic problems following the war. You had severe severe severe claim problems. And then after the war, it took a year and a half for all of the GIs and people from the central industries to get back from their (?). And they needed a breathing spell and instead what we got at that time was a flood, an absolute flood of automobile insurance applications. The war is over, GI's are home, tire and gas rationing is off. Cars are being manufactured for the first time in half a dozen years. People can drive for the first time in a dozen years, if you count the depression years and the war years together. And we were just flooded with applications. We couldn't do it all from Smallton, there weren't enough people, there weren't enough buildings, there wasn't enough space. So Thomas McBee once again to the rescue. He appointed a twenty one person planning committee, headed by the then young A.J. Brown Senior. It was sort of a [Facing the Millenium] Group of 1947. [The Facing the Millenium Group was a future planning group that had recently been chartered at the time of this speech.] And he said this to them "We have got a problem and I want you to do what ever is necessary to solve the problem. But don't depart from the principles on which we built MidWest." And they are, he's talking automobile insurance of course, they are the membership plan of continuous policies, the six months premium, and the happiness of our agency force. "Beyond that there are no restrictions."

As he describes it, the innovations developed by this team included processing innovations and structural changes. The processing changes he mentions are the picturesque ones, which are frequently featured in visual representations of MidWest's past: pages on roller skates rapidly moving applications around the headquarters building, and "sew to file girls," who used sewing machines to sew files together rather than pasting them, since sewing was considerably faster. The structural innovations he mentions are the move from a single central headquarters to regional offices and the change from part time agents to the "Full Time Agent concept." Thus the credit for saving the company goes to the founder and to the team of innovators he convened. This version does not include the work of agents in saving the company from its underwriting crisis.

As would be expected from his position, the district manager's account of this crisis is a great deal more agent-centered, and he also explicitly makes the evaluative point that this story is just one instance of how the agents share with the founder the values of determination and loyalty:

> Manager: And then when the war was over well then the, uh—you know, everybody hits the road, they all have held back for years, vacationing and...and so, uh, in 1947 all of a sudden the statistics stuff start coming in. Come to find out, based on the number of losses we were paying and everything else, we were about, uh—we had twelve million dollars in assets. And we were losing money at the rate of a million dollars a month. So, in twelve months we (would be) broke. And they slammed on the brakes and, you know, did some drastic things.... So, um, they literally canceled

out, uh—well, first they canceled out the entire state of Minnesota because they were losing money like crazy.

Interviewer: Why was that?

Manager: Well, inadequate roads, people were sliding and slipping and—and driving too fast and, you know, number of accidents.... Then he went out in the field to the agents and said, "We need your help, we've got to do this thing, we've got to re-underwrite, people have more than their share of accidents we need to cancel them, we need to get them off the books, we can't continue with (?)." So we've had some rough spots. They overcame that, uh... the agents dug in and worked like heck. Some of these guys would pick up the entire account (from) regional office and sit down with their underwriter. There were no (?). Looked through every single file: well, what do you think about this one? What do you think about that?... And all those agents, uh, uh, they had that one common denominator. They had the same enthusiasm and the same determination.

These are the two extreme versions of this story: heroic efforts by the central office and heroic efforts by the agents. The other versions lie somewhere in between these in their focus. Clearly, the identification of who the heroes were is affected by the occasions of the tellings, and the audience for them.

11. Birth of the "Full-Time Agent" concept

One of the highlights of the history of MidWest, from both the agents' point of view and from that of management is the move from part-time agents, often farmers, who sold insurance as a sideline, to full-time agents whose only business was the sale of insurance. This milestone is present in all relevant versions compared. (The memoir ends before this policy was instituted.)

The official history focuses on the requirements on the new professional agents: the level of sales they were committed to produce and the increased levels of training that MidWest undertook to provide for them. This milestone is also described as part of the professionalization of the sales agent. The Full–Time Agent program required a high school diploma for new agents and preferred a college degree: a change culminating in the early 1990s in a requirement for a college degree for new agents.

The newsletter articles describe this change as a way to generate policyholder loyalty, improve service, and grow with the postwar "boom." It includes the relation between the concept and the new contract, which affirmed the agents' status as full-time, exclusive independent contractor agents for MidWest. This status is still extremely significant to agents and MidWest, both for symbolic reasons revolving around the powerful role of the agents and their freedom from managerial constraint, and for the important legal and tax consequences both for the agents and for MidWest. This version does not frame this change in the way we have usually heard older agents describe it: "We moved from doing business from our dining room tables to having our own professional offices." Instead, the story features the names of the members of the committee who came up with the concept—all people who were involved with the Life Insurance company, whose names at least older agents would know. The headquarters trainer also cites the "birth of the marketing partnership":

And this was a time also when we departed from our part time insurance agents. Our part time farmer agents. And we got agents out of their homes and into professional offices for the first time. People said: we are going to go do away with the part time farmer agents that gave us a million automobile policies and a billion dollars worth of life insurance? And we said YES, the time is right. Just like today our saying, we are going to go to the [Agency of the Millennium] program. And the answer is yes, where the time was right when we did this, the time is right now to do what we are doing, I firmly believe. And it was at this time, of course, that the marketing partnership was born, when we had professional full time agents instead of part time farmers. And as Paul Harvey says, you know the rest of the story.

Finally, the district manager describes this professionalization as linked both to growth, and to the need for agent training:

So, you know, and then ultimately what happened then is that, uh, after World War II and after we got our feet back on the ground, uh, we decided to start recruiting. If we wanted to continue to grow, uh, we had to do a couple of things. One is that we had to train our agents a lot better than (?) because the other guys had not really trained very well. They were just given a rate book and some applications and a little instruction and that was about the extent of it. Um, so in 1951 they came out with what they called then [the Full Time Agent concept]....[This concept] was a way of bringing somebody in full-time. And they had a what they called a subsidy program. In other words, they would subsidize them income-wise until they could build their business up to a certain level....And then there was a training program and they started getting into the, uh, training and how to sell and how to service the business.

12. MidWest is family

Perhaps the most prevalent theme in all these accounts, and in every story we have heard about MidWest, is the idea that MidWest is family. This is not an event or a story in itself. Rather it is an evaluation of the character of the company, which many stories are told to demonstrate.

As I have already discussed, there a number of ways in which this is literally true. Although official figures are not available, my informal questioning suggests that at least half of the agents and employees of MidWest have kin who currently work or previously worked for the company. The leadership of the company has concentrated within a small number of families. This is true at the highest levels, which I have already discussed. It is also the case that the sons and daughters of district managers are likely to become agents and then rapidly move into district or regional management positions. Within MidWest, having a parent in the company does not raise a problem of nepotism for a young recruit; rather it is taken to suggest that the recruit is likely to have the appropriate attitudes, loyalty, and knowledge necessary to succeed.

"MidWest is family" is also taken to mean that the company takes a benevolent interest in its members that goes beyond the purely financial logic of most corporations. MidWest is proud of its extremely low turnover rate; it boasts that during financially difficult times, it did not downsize or lay off workers (although it did move some operations centers to new geographical locations, which caused the resignation a number of employees who did not wish or were not able to move to those locations.) Both the memoir and the official history recount many stories about the founder's paternal care for his employees. The official history describes his initial relations with his first employees as more like a family than an office staff, with a paternal understanding of their needs and an ability to elicit strong loyalty and commitment. It describes the first few years of life in the main office as similar to life on the farm, where the founder and his hired men had worked in close harmony, with the founder never asking anyone to do anything he could not or would not do himself. As the company grew in size, this informal paternalism evolved into a "scientifically controlled welfare program," which worked to promote employees' physical and financial welfare, morale, and training. This included the establishment of a company medical office, a sick leave program and vacation schedule, a schedule of recreational activities, the construction of sports facilities and a park in the headquarters town, chartering buses or trains for transportation to nearby sports events, establishing a credit union for employees, etc.

What is of interest here is not just the employment policies of the company, but the reasons given for them. These policies could be described, for example, as examples of progressive labor policies as compared to the general trends in U.S. businesses of the time. Instead, though, they are described personalistically as the result of the founder's paternal interest in his employees, mainly instituted and overseen by one of his sons who had an aptitude for this kind of personnel work. There is some discussion of the economic issues of attracting and retaining employees as the business grew and the problems of doing this in a small Midwestern town, rather than in a large city. However, even this discussion is framed as a concern for the welfare of young female clerical staff members. Since there were not enough potential staff members in the main headquarters' town, clerical staff were recruited from surrounding farms and towns. These are described as young women, away from home for the first time, who appreciated a rose and a card remembering their birthdays, and who needed help with finding medical care and establishing proper credit and savings accounts.

13. Stories about Mr. McBee

As I have already mentioned, all of the five versions contain stories about Mr. McBee. Obviously the memoir celebrating his seventieth birthday and the official biography would necessarily revolve around stories of the founder. But the newsletter series, the speech, and the oral interview all contain such stories as well. The newsletter series focuses mainly on accounts by veteran agents about Mr. McBee, showing his character and also the high regard which his agents felt for him. For example, one such story describes an agent who sold the first policy in a new state into which MidWest was expanding. He sold a policy immediately but then waited several days to write and file it so that it would be dated on Mr. McBee's birthday.

The district manager told a long story about Mr. McBee that gives indications of his character, determination, and skill in handling people. It is analyzed in detail in the next chapter as part of a comparison with two written versions of the same story.

14. Recent stories

Thus far, the stories I have discussed center on the early period of MidWest's history. The written sources do not cover the recent decades: the authorized history was published in the late 1950s, and the newsletter series covers only the decades up to the 1980s. It is too early to tell, then, what parts of the more recent past will form part of the institutional memory shared by everyone at MidWest. We have already discussed Vansina's (1985) argument that institutions and group will tend to have a "floating gap" in the accounts of the past they maintain. That is, they will have detailed accounts of their founding, and of some number of generations past that, plus an account of the recent past. But each group has a particular set of memorial practices that allows them to remember in detail only a given number of generations. Over the life of a group, a certain amount of history in the middle will disappear, causing an expansion in the floating gap in the timeline of the remembered past.

One such example of a floating gap I have observed comes in the memory of previous contracts and contract negotiations between MidWest and its agents. When we began our fieldwork, the company was engaged in the process of changing its contractual arrangements with agents: offering those agents already under contract a choice between their current contract and a new contract whose complexity made it difficult for agents to project its effects on their business. During this period, there was a great deal of discussion of the advantages and disadvantages of the new contract, both by management and by agents among themselves. This included discussion of previous contractual changes. Managers and some veteran agents who had been through the previous negotiation made reference to the immediately prior contract change, arguing, for example, that agents who took that contract were benefited, not harmed. But we saw no evidence that any of the newer agents knew anything about the existence or details of the prior contract change. It appeared not to have passed into the institution's ongoing memory.

However, we did see some events I believe will become part of the institution's core memory. First among these is the series of natural disasters in the early 1990s that cost MidWest and every other insurance company severely: the earthquake in Northridge and the Oakland Hills fires, both in California, and Hurricane Andrew in Florida. The costs of payments for the losses due to these disasters caused MidWest to place severe restrictions on the sale of new homeowners policies for a number of years and to raise the cost of its homeowners and earthquake insurance policies. For the management of MidWest, the effects of these disasters showed that their actuarial calculations about the likely impact of natural disasters had been too optimistic. The memory of this actuarial error is encoded in the new price structure as well as in the stories about the change. For the agents, especially in California where particularly strict restrictions were placed on the sale of new homeowners policies, "since Northridge" became an ethnomeasure marking a boundary between a particular version of the good old days when it was easy to sell insurance and a more difficult present sales climate.[2]

To give an example of how this piece of the past is used, in the headquarters trainer's speech, the disasters are described in relation to the sinking of the Titanic:

Now everything I've said this afternoon was true of MidWest until a day in August in 1992. It was true before hurricane Andrew. And now of course, it's after hurricane Andrew, and our company history will be written in a manner different after hurricane Andrew than it was before hurricane Andrew. Hurricane Andrew was, as you know, a real wake up call for us. A slap on the side of the head so to speak. We tried in the '80s to slow things down, but MidWest has never been very good at slowing things down. It took that slap on the side of the head by Andrew to get our attention. If, and you have all heard this before I'm sure, if Andrew had hit a few miles further North in the Miami or Fort Lauderdale area, it would have roared across the state and exited Tampa, picked up steam across the Gulf and slammed into New Orleans. And if two weeks later there had been an 8.5 Richter scale earthquake in the West Coast, MidWest would be very badly bent.

One time I was a teacher of history. And maybe my mind runs in channels like that, but I made a connection between the managers and directors with the White Star steamship line in the early part of our century, and today for us, eighty years later. At that time, the White Star Line was in fierce competition for the transatlantic trade with Cunard and other European steamship companies. And their boldest venture in that direction was the design and the construction of the RMS Titanic. She was the largest, grandest ship afloat when she was launched in 1912. And she sailed proudly from South Hampton to the heart of France and then to go across the ocean for her maiden voyage to New York City.

Never mind that she had too few lifeboats and that she overlooked other safety matters. Why should she bother? Why should they bother? She was three football fields in length, she had a double steel concrete reinforced haul with sixteen watertight compartments. The captain of the ship wrote "This boat is unsinkable, I cannot imagine any condition which would cause the ship to flounder. I cannot conceive of any vital disaster happening to this vessel. Modern ship building has simply gone beyond that." And of course it was on that same, April night in 1912, Good Friday night that she slipped to the bottom, hit an iceberg: 1,513 men with her, mostly men with her. Women and children first in those days of course. And then captain, A. J. Smith was a veteran sailor. Forty years on the high seas. But then on that Friday night, he was down in the lounge playing bridge with some of the other passengers, and no one had heeded radio reports of an ice field not far ahead. It bothered nobody that another ship just fifty miles west of the Titanic had anchored for the night. Reluctant to sail in a sea of ice. Titanic didn't slow, but stayed at twenty six knots, anxious not to lose any time on her maiden voyage to New York City. Now this disaster wasn't the fault of the ship. It was the fault of those in charge. It was the fault, it was complacency and over confidence were greater dangers that night than was ice. I think that sometimes you and I are the Captain Smiths of the RMS MidWest, and you and I and the people we influence can help save our ship.

Invoking the sinking of the Titanic is a strong argument indeed for taking recent disasters seriously.

A number of other internal changes of the 1990s may also enter into the institution's core memory. One was the change in the district management system. As described in detail in chapter 2, under the old system, a single manager recruited and trained agents for his district, receiving his compensation from commissions on his agents' commissions. The new system moved to a team of three managers, who received salaries rather than commissions. I believe that this change is likely to remain salient to the agents who were initially recruited under the previous system, since they felt that their manager was, in effect, their employee and would represent them to the management of MidWest. The new system, they felt, moved the management team to the other side of the line, so that they represented the company rather than the agents. From the managers' point of view, it marked a change from a period in which the relation between agents and their managers was a relation between individuals. For example, agents told us that under the old system, they would make efforts to sell more life insurance than they might want to so that their manager would be able to attend the vacation trip. Something we heard frequently was "I didn't want to be the one who kept my manager from traveling." Under the new system, the manager's role became much more bureaucratic, without the structural incentives for the managers to consider the relation as a personal one. However, it is less likely that agents recruited under the new system will know in any detail what the previous system was like, since they did not experience it.

Finally, a major change occurred in the system of recruiting new agents. Under the old system, recruitment was one of the primary responsibilities of the manager, who looked to the outside to find, enlist, and develop promising sales recruits. Under the new system, only employees of MidWest are eligible for training as agents. This has removed the recruitment function from district management and has put an end to a powerful system of fictive kinship, or lineages of recruitment. Under the old system, agents were very aware of who had recruited them, were indebted to them, and had a particular connection to other agents recruited by the same manager. For example, it was an understood obligation for agents to attend the funeral of the manager who recruited them. The change in recruiting policy has made a powerful change in the relations between agents and their managers, which I believe will remain in the institution's memory, just as the change from the part-time agent to the full-time professional agent has remained in the institution's memory long after the retirement of the last of the part-time agents.

Topics of the stories of core memory

Thus far, the stories I have identified as constituting MidWest's core institutional memory have focused mainly on issues of identity: who founded us, who are "We," and how did we get that way, how have we preserved our essential identity through periods of change. This seems to be the case for most institutions. The absolutely central part of an institution's core story stock will be about its identity. But identity is not just a matter of the virtues of the founder and values of the organization. There is also the matter of what the institution actually does, and how it does it. Therefore, we now turn to another set of stories that focus on the "what" of the business: in this case, the details of how insurance is actually designed, marketed, and sold.

While there have been a number of studies of the function of narratives in creating and maintaining the identity of an institution, there has been almost no attention given to the ways in which narratives are used to do the actual work of the institution. Indeed, there is a prior question requiring investigation: What are stories good for?

What kinds of knowledge of the past do they convey easily? What kinds of knowledge is it difficult or impossible to convey with narratives? Because of their basic structure, narratives easily convey past events and their meanings. Information that is not heavily weighted with moral meaning is less easily made narratable. Therefore, topics of identity such as stories about a charismatic founder or an institutional turning point travel easily through an institution and can become part of the memory of the entire institution. In contrast, stories about the details of the work often remain within the limits of the particular group that did that work, and they do not become part of the memory of the institution as a whole. While the details of a particular form of work can be narrated in such a way as to have moral meaning for its practitioners, it is difficult to form them into stories comprehensible to a broader audience.

The one case I know of which examines stories about the details of actual work is by Orr (1996; 1990). These studies provide important insight into the work of copier repair technicians, showing that this type of narrative forms a major part of their work practice. These technicians could not properly do their jobs without participating in a community that tells endless stories about copiers, clients, and repair technicians as part of the work of maintaining an ongoing community memory of difficult problems, unexpected and undocumented solutions, and heroic diagnoses. What is particularly interesting about this study is that, unlike many studies of white-collar work, the work described is **not** primarily linguistic. After all the talk, these technicians have to fix cranky, dirty, aging machines. But they also have to represent the situation to the client, keep the client happy, and possibly even teach the client(s) to use the machines properly. And they also use narrative to pass along knowledge about particular models, particular machines at a given site, tricks for repair, and all the information that is supposedly, but not actually, covered by the procedural documentation:

> [These stories of copier repair] are also told in the pursuit of more purely social functions than diagnosis. They preserve and circulate hard-won information and are used to make claims of membership or seniority within the community. They also amuse, instruct, and celebrate the tellers' identity as technicians.... In more normal social discourse, the problematic quality that occasions the telling of the stories seems to stem primarily from a wide range of occasions on which technicians are called upon to account for their activities, and secondarily from a need to represent themselves in a heroic or at least competent perspective. In these tellings, past problematic circumstances are made publicly and collaboratively inspectable by one's peers, and one's experience is made reproducible and reusable on subsequent occasions by others. Such tellings are also demonstrations of one's competence as a technician and therefore one's membership in the community. (126)

Orr (1996) offers one transcript and analysis of an extended narrative about problems in diagnosing an unusual problem in a difficult machine. What is particularly interesting about this example is not so much the events, which are arcanely technical, but the evaluations, the meanings the speakers draw from them. All the overt evaluations center on the surprising and tricky nature of the problem, because of the unreliability of the diagnostic codes built into the machines. There are none of the evaluations of the speaker as skilled or heroic, which we normally expect from tales of performance above and beyond the call of duty. However, this kind of evaluation of the self is present, though implicit. Since all the participants in the telling are skilled technicians, they can be assumed to know, without being told, the meanings of specific breakdowns and repairs. These stories, in the form in which they are told, are not likely to travel beyond the community of practice of repair technicians exactly because understanding them requires so much technical knowledge.

Turning to MidWest, the nature of the actual work has to do with selling strategies, business strategies and practices for both the company as a whole and for each agent's office, and strategic and financial planning. These issues are differently narratable and narrated. For example, there are a number of stories about Mr. McBee's sales prowess, which are intended as instructional for all sales agents. I have heard agents exchange stories about difficult sales they have accomplished, unusual sales, sales techniques. Such stories are part of the regular discourse within this community. Few if any of these stories become part of the institution's official memory, but they do have some circulation within smaller communities of agents. In contrast, there are also parts of the agents' business that are rarely represented in narrative: how the agent arranges office procedures, sets up and maintains filing systems, recruits, trains, and motivates staff, etc. (Although stories complaining about difficulties after the loss of a trusted staff member are quite common and elicit recognition and sympathy from other agents and managers.)

It might be argued these are topics that cannot be made into the subject of stories, simply because narratives require dramatic events and morally distinguishable characters. That is, the details of bookkeeping, for example, can be conveyed didactically, by description or explanation, but not by narrative. This is partially true—it is difficult to tell stories about the details of bookkeeping. However, whether a topic can be narrated appears to depend at least as much on the skill of the narrator in shaping it into a story as it does on the nature of the topic itself. For example, we observed a series of training programs by one former top-selling agent turned trainer, who attributed her sales success to her ability to design and implement business systems and procedures. She created and taught training programs for agents that used stories and examples of how she worked with staff, maintained discipline over her time allocation, etc. Indeed, she produced riveting narratives illustrating how to deal with drop-in customers, how to train staff, how to allocate time: all issues of developing appropriate business processes. She was able to do so because she was passionate about issues of business process and believed that agents should institute and follow proper business processes as part of their moral duty to serve the customers and the company. This example shows that such issues are narratable—it is possible to form them into stories. However, within the culture of MidWest, it is the case that they are very rarely narrated, and even these rare narratives about business process and practice remain at the level of individual or small group memory rather than becoming part of the memory of the institution as a whole.

By its nature, insurance is a particularly memory-rich form of business. A company must retain records of policies and policyholders over the course of lifetimes. This is not, and could not be, done only in narrative. Much of what MidWest (and any insurance company) must remember is embedded in its actuarial formulae, investment and reserve fund decisions, underwriting policies, and, of course, in records in file cabinets and databases, in ways mandated by law or carried on by custom. Only a very small part of this kind of memory is represented the story repertoire of the core institutional memory. However, given the general observation that the "what" of a business is rarely narrated, perhaps we should be surprised at how many of the insurance details do make it into the story.

As we have discussed, the details of a number of the founder's business innovations are present in the central story of the company: lower rates for farmers because they were better risks, semiannual rather than annual premiums, an initial membership fee but no annual fee for purchasing insurance. At the same time, the founder is described as having a talent for seeing the big picture, for salesmanship, and for finding the right personnel, who would understand the minutiae of the insurance business at a technical level, which he did not. As the district manager described him, Mr. McBee was an "innovator and motivator. Uh, smart enough to hire people that get things done that, you know, he didn't have the skills to do."

As a side note, it is interesting that instances when the founder's lack of grasp of the minutiae of the insurance business caused difficulties have not entered into the institution's core story repertoire. For example, there is a story in the authorized history about a problem caused by the way that the company's first secretary chose to calculate reserve funds. In the somewhat vague description of the error, she used the average number of policies in force over a six-month period rather than the mean of the number of policies in force at the beginning and the end of the six-month period. This problem is mentioned but not described in detail. The secretary is described as having left the company after a struggle for control with the founder. The reason for the error is unknown: it may have been her mistake, or she may have chosen a method of calculation that would keep apparent costs low in order to encourage sales. But in this telling, the blame for the mistaken form of calculation is limited to the secretary, who is described as having prior experience in the insurance business. The biographer does not blame the founder, who chose her as the secretary of the company, and who did not catch the error. However, although this is an account of the details of the business, the main point I wish to make is that this whole story appears only in the authorized history. I have never heard it referred to anywhere else. It thus does *not* form part of the core institutional memory.

We might also ask why one might even be concerned about memory of the details of the business: why not just assume that these are known by the appropriate members of the hierarchy and need not be known by everyone? In particular, why should a sales agent understand the actuarial calculations of risk that underlie the company's decisions about where to set rates and what kinds of risks the company will and will not insure? In fact, this is a point of tension between the agent and the company. It is in the agent's interest that rates be set as low as possible, since this make it possible for the agent to sell more insurance. Similarly, when an agent has a potential client, it is in the agent's interest that the company be willing to issue insurance on an old car in poor repair, or life insurance on a client in bad health, so that the agent need not turn away a potential sale. Getting the agent to understand something about the actuarial calculations is a way for the company to get the agent to understand the distinction the company makes between short-term and long-term benefit. In the short term, the agent and the company may benefit from selling as much insurance as possible, no matter what the risks may be. In the long term though, writing insurance on bad risks can harm the company financially and thus ultimately harm the agent.

Our observations showed that these tensions are actively discussed. Agents complain about rates that are too high and about restrictions on the insurance they may sell. The company complains about agents' not doing the proper field underwriting, that is, not doing thorough inspections to determine that cars, houses, and clients are in appropriate condition to be insured. However, when agents and managers complain about this issue, they are never explicit about the fact that there is a short term conflict between the interests of the agent and the interests of the company. Management stresses that the agents cannot prosper if the company does not prosper, which requires appropriate choice of clients. However, there is a difference between the agents en masse and any individual agent. An individual agent can attempt to get the best possible price for a valued client by bending the rules without projecting the effect on the company if all agents did this. This is, of course, a version of the tragedy of the commons. Neither agents nor management wish to discuss the possibility of such a conflict of interest might exist.

I have already described the story of the agents saving the company after World War II by hastily reunderwriting all of the cars they insured. Although this is framed as a tale about heroic efforts, either by the company as a whole or by the agents in particular, it is also a story about the nature of actuarial calculations of risk: under new conditions that included a sudden increase of cars, many of them in poor repair, on ill-maintained roads, it was necessary to change previous company decisions about what cars could be insured, and the change had to be implemented quickly. It is thus one story that teaches agents about the long-term consequences of actuarial decisions.

A similar teaching tale, this one within the memory of most agents working for MidWest, is the consequences of the series of natural disasters in the early 1990s: the Northridge earthquake, Hurricane Andrew, and the Oakland Hills fires. As I have described, these disasters required a reworking of the actuarial calculations about the likely impact of natural disasters. It caused a moratorium on the sales of new homeowners insurance for several years, and then a rise in prices, particularly for earthquake insurance. Both the management of MidWest and the agents discuss these changes, although they seem to have different meanings for each group. For the management, the effects of the disasters demonstrate the crucial need for correct calculations of risk—without them, the company's reserve funds can be drained to a point that could cause the company to fail. For the agents, the changes mark a boundary between the good old days and the present. The good old days were a time, they say, when it was easy to sell insurance, because the rates were low and because one could propose the purchase of life insurance to a client who had come in seeking to buy homeowners insurance when purchasing a new house. Currently, the job of selling is more difficult because home insurance rates are high, and MidWest is asking agents to sell more life insurance policies than home insurance policies, requiring them to place much more energy in marketing and selling of life insurance than they had previously had to do.

At the time of the research, agents still understood the reasons for the changes, even though they bemoaned their consequences. In fact, they had to understand these reasons, since they were the ones who had to explain to their clients why rates for homeowners and earthquake insurance had risen. Thus, the actual rates and the story of the reasoning behind them were linked in stories for clients. However, as time passes and the rates are no longer a change and a shock to clients, it is quite possible that agents will not continue the memory of the relation between these disasters and insurance rates. It would be interesting to know whether actuaries have longer memories for such changes: finding this out would require an ethnographic study of the work of actuaries and underwriters.

Position and rendition

Thus far, the analysis has concentrated on stories and themes that occur in the core of the institution's memory: the stories that appear in both official and unofficial, written and oral versions. I now turn to the stories and themes that appear in only a subset of the renditions of the institution's memory. As I have already argued, the fact that a story is absent from a particular complete telling is quite resistant to analysis since there are many reasons why a particular story may not be included in a given version. Yet it is possible to suggest reasons why a particular story is or is not found in a particular telling by examining who was doing the telling, to whom, the situation of the telling, and the possible effects which the teller intended for the telling. In particular, we may look at the formal position of the teller within the institution, as well as the way that the teller positions him or herself in and towards the telling, as a way of analyzing the differences between versions.

Positionality is a concept that has recently become quite important, both in studies of narrative and in studies of individual identity as a discursive creation. Within social psychology, the concept of positioning as the dynamic and linguistic construction of identity has been suggested as a way to avoid the problems of a static, entirely determined, identity caused by the notion of "role" (Davies and Harré 1990):

> In moving from the use of role to position as the central organising concept for ana-lysing how it is that people do being a person, we have moved to another conception of the relation between people and their conversations. In role-theory the person is always separable from the various roles that they take up; any particular conversa-tion is understood in terms of someone taking on a certain role. The words that are spoken are to some extent dictated by the role and are to be interpreted in these terms. With positioning, the focus is on the way in which the discursive practices constitute the speakers and hearers in certain ways and yet at the same time is a resource through which the speakers and hearers can negotiate new positions. (62)

The concept of positioning has its origins in the field of marketing, where prod-uct positioning refers to the ways in which a seller attempts to place and differenti-ate a particular product within field of similar products (Harré and van Langenhove 1991).

While the analysis of positionality focuses on the creativity of the individual, speakers do not have an entirely open field in which to position themselves. They work within a field of existing power relations, other speakers, also trying to position themselves and others, existing forms of dominant and resistant discourses, and their own varying abilities to work within these constrains. More recent studies on positioning attempt to show the ways that speakers attempt to maneuver their positionings within such fields. In these studies, identity is thus not entirely static, as is suggested by the notion of role. But it is also not entirely fluid and manipulatable, as a naïve reading of the notion of positioning might suggest. For example, Holland (1998) shows detailed examples of how people work to negotiate identities within a variety of cultural worlds: the caste system of Nepal, Alcoholics Anonymous, the culture of romance and dating in U.S. colleges, and the diagnostic categories of the U.S. mental health system. In each of these worlds, the authors show how members are both constrained into particular subject positions by the existing category system, and at the same time move creatively both within and outside the cultural system to establish a position that is not entirely determined by others. Similarly, Berman (1998), in a study of Javanese women's narratives, offers a detailed study of the complex work of positioning in a protest by women factory workers, as protesters, their families, and their managers each attempt to frame the events, and shape the positions of the participants.

In my comparison of complete tellings of the history of MidWest, I wish to use the notion of positioning as a tool that allows me to analyze reasons for the inclusion or omission of a given piece of the institution's past. I use the notion of position in two ways. Each of these tellings is produced by one or more authors, who have a particular formal position within MidWest. And in each telling the author takes a particular stance with relation to the material and to the addressees. The telling is thus shaped by the speaker's institutional and personal allegiances, as well as the proposed position of speaker that the speaker attempts to represent and the effect the speaker proposes for the telling. (Note that all of these versions, both written and oral, are essentially monologues. Even in the two oral versions the addressees have very little opportunity to dispute, shape, or change the version of the past presented as relevant to them. Thus the work of positioning in these cases is not a dialogic activity, as it usually is in more interactive settings.)

Positionings of each telling

I now sketch the positioning of each of the five complete tellings. I then describe a number of stories or themes present in only a subset and the reasons I ascribe to the presence or absence of these themes.

The official history

The official history and biography of the founder was commissioned to represent the authorized version and still is used as such within MidWest. As such, it purports to speak for the entire company rather than for one sector of it such as the agents, the employees at headquarters or regional headquarters, or the management. Of all the complete tellings examined, it is the most complete. This is trivially true in the sense that it is the longest: book length, rather than a short monograph or a forty-five-minute speech, etc. It is also the most complete in the number of different types of topics it covers, topics that may be relevant to only one segment of the members of the company. Thus, it gives considerable coverage of the business details of how MidWest was founded: where the money came from, how the company was incorporated, how the legal firm representing it was chosen, the false starts, etc. It contains the widest cast of characters: all the initial members of the board of directors, all of the sons of the founder, the first agents. As I described above, it even contains a problematic character about whom all other versions are silent: the original secretary, who left after a "power struggle" with the founder. It is also the most complete in that it attempts to tell the history from a point of view relevant to anyone in the company. It is not written for agents alone: it represents a view from the standpoint of upper management that is presented as relevant to anyone within MidWest. Since I did not have the opportunity to study operations staff, I cannot say whether they take the authorized history as their history, or whether it is irrelevant to them. I can, however, report that agents, and particularly all levels of management, use the authorized history as a representation of their past.

The memoir

The privately printed memoir of the founder of MidWest, produced to commemorate his seventieth birthday, is a short work of about 100 pages. Its position is similar to that of the authorized history (which it precedes by about ten years), presenting an account from the point of view of management. It differs in focusing mainly on stories about the founder and the human side of the business. It does not include much of material on the history and development of the insurance industry that is present in the authorized history.

The newsletter articles

The newsletter articles are mainly reworkings of material from the official history, with additional frequent materials from reminiscences of older agents. The positioning of this series is management's effort to give a history of the company that would be relevant and instructive to agents. Thus its focus is on the history of agents within MidWest. For example, this is the only version that includes the names of the first three agents: the founder and two others.

This series includes a considerable amount of material on the history of agent training, and on the development of record-keeping forms, and later the computer system. This is the part of management's decisions whose impact on agents is most obvious: they take the training, they are required to use the computer systems. I would mention that both of these are topics of interest to agents. Older agents spontaneously told us about their training and particularly about the introduction of new record-keeping systems and the great change imposed on their work by computerization. (In many of the organizations studied by IRL, we have found this kind of use of technology to mark one's history. Thus, people note the technology in place when they joined the company or the first technologies they helped to develop: "When I came in, we were still using the D40s." "I go back to the days of the X75." The

Xerox Corporation displays its history in the lobby of its headquarters building by an exhibit of successive generations of copiers and printers.)

In particular, the newsletter series is unique in pointing out the role of agents in milestones of company history. For example, the series includes forms of agent participation not included in any other version: The company's logo was chosen from entries in a design contest among agents. The newsletter was similarly named by a contest for best name, which was won by an agent's wife. The slogan "A million or more by '44" was developed by an agent. None of the other versions include this detail; this agent's contribution is usually subsumed to an account of the founder's genius and vision in devising the goal. Similarly, we are told that the new contract was developed in consultation with an elite group of top-selling agents. This is a reference to the frequently used task force method, in which upper management consults with highly ranked and respected agents to get their opinions and suggestions about potential decisions. Such a mention of the task force serves to remind agents that the contract, about which many of them had complaints, was at least partially devised by the most respected agents. It is a tacit argument by management that agents cannot complain about the contract as something imposed on them by management, since there were agents involved in the process of shaping it.

Additionally, this version, the most recent of the written versions, contains a number of slightly distanced references to the farm origins of the company. Thus, it contains cute stories about how MidWest used to insure 4-H club members' calves and colts, once offered poultry insurance, etc.

The headquarters trainer's speech

The next version is the speech given at the main headquarters of MidWest to a group of newly promoted regional and district managers by a headquarters-based manager in charge of sales promotions programs. Devising and administering sales promotion programs is part of the work of managing agents, because these programs provide incentives for high level of sales, such as prizes, attractive travel packages, sales conventions, etc. Producing these requires this manager to stay in touch with the agents' point of view about what is an attractive reward and what is an appropriate incentive for a given level of sales (although the actual sales level is set by upper management). In giving this particular speech to new managers, the speaker's point of view is that of someone located within central headquarters, whose current task is to appeal to the managers of agents. He represents management as it works with the agents (as opposed to the management work of forming policy, managing the employees who process claims, etc.) This is a mid-level management position—he implements policy but does not make it. His positioning of his talk draws not only on his function within MidWest but also on his age. He is near retirement age, has worked at MidWest for his entire career, and is one of several people we met who describes himself as MidWest's unofficial historian.

His version uniquely includes information about the national headquarters, various headquarters buildings, and the survival of the names of alleys in the designations of corridors in the new headquarters.

The district manager's interview

Of all the five tellings of MidWest's complete history, the field-worker's interview with the district manager provides the version that is the most agent-centered. The manager takes the agents' point of view to the degree that he does not give a history of the management system, even though he himself is a manager. (Note that the newsletter articles, also focused on appealing to agents, do give this development.) This manager had been with MidWest for over forty years. He began his career as an agent but rapidly became a district manager, supervising agents. As already discussed, the position of the district manager (under the old system of management) was a complex one. He was the link between the agents, who were independent contractors, and the insurance company. The district manager (unlike sales managers in most corporate settings) had virtually no control over the activities of the agents he supervised. Thus his role with existing agents was to train, to motivate, to "incent," to be a cheerleader or coach, rather than a boss. Most of the manager's compensation came from commissions on his agents' commissions, rather than from a company salary. As already described, agents have told us that under this system, they considered the manager their "employee," responsible for representing their interests to the company and dependent on their success for his success. These details about the position of the manager are important because they give the economic and structural basis for my claim that the manager is representing the agent's point of view when he tells the story of MidWest to the field-worker. My argument is that representing the agents' point of view is exactly what a manager's position has required him to do. This particular manager had been extremely successful at this for over thirty-five years, and he was highly regarded by agents. Further, the skilled nature of the telling, and the formulaic nature of the appropriate parts of the narrative, suggests that he is reproducing for the field-worker a story he has often told in the past to his agents.

One interesting point about the manager's telling of MidWest's history is that it is not strictly chronological. It begins with his own entry into MidWest, which he tells in full. He then tells stories about the executives in power when he entered MidWest. He then moves to a story of about how the current president, the son of the previous president, came into office. After discussion about those events with the ethnographer, he moves backward by noting: "It's been a family-run company since the beginning." From there, he moves back to the founding of the company, citing the initial members as Mr. McBee and two others. The two others were the fathers of two important dynasties in the company. One became the third president, and his son and grandson the fourth and fifth president. The other was a senior vice president in charge of agents, and two of his sons later became important local and headquarters managers. In fact, the two others joined a few years after founding. But their importance for the subsequent history of the company leads the speaker to project them backwards to the moment of founding. (This is a classic example of the tidying of facts to make a shapely story.)

Positionings and choice of events for narration

Once the positionings of the various versions have been established, it is possible to show the relation between position and the choice of events to include within a version of a complete story. I now discuss events presented in only one or a few of the versions, with an attempt to show how this is consonant with their positionings. I end with an extended example of how a minor detail in an early version became important and was foregrounded in a later retelling because of changed business practices.

As I have already discussed, only the official history attempts to give the full story of the business decisions involved in starting the company: how the company was chartered, how reserve funds were calculated, how a law firm was chosen, etc. Obviously, these are required for a comprehensive business history but are of little or no relevance for subsequent generations.

An important landmark in the history of the company was the expansion from sales in the first, founding state to nearby states and then to the entire United States. This eventually required the development of regional offices to supplement the founding office, which became the main headquarters. All of the written versions detail this expansion. However, the district manager's oral version covers only the founding of the first regional office. This is a detail that has local interest, since it was located the district manager's region.

As I have already discussed, an important value at the company is "MidWest is family." However, only the authorized history and the memoir include details of the paternalistic management system at the headquarters office. Neither the oral versions nor the newsletter articles, all of which take the agent's point of view, include these details. I argue that this is the case because the treatment of employees is not relevant to agents. As contractors to MidWest, their relation to MidWest is very different from that of employees. As I have already shown, the agents' status as contractors has great practical and symbolic importance, both for the company and for the agents themselves. Agents are always concerned to emphasize differences between their status and that of employees. This distinction means that agents do not take the history of employees of the company as relevant to their own history.

At the same time, though, certain details of employees' work in the past have become visual icons, recognizable by agents, and useable to symbolize the nostalgic charms of the past. For example, after the war, when business at headquarters increased dramatically, in an attempt to speed up interoffice delivery, deliveries were made by young women on roller skates. Similarly, to speed production, thick files of paper were sewn together rather than stapled. Images of the skaters and the "sewing machine girls" are frequently displayed at MidWest as icons of the past. The authorized history includes stories and pictures of both of these. (The memoir ends before these innovations were introduced.) The newsletter articles include pictures of them, without explanation, and the district manager does not mention them. They are not directly relevant to the work of agents, and there is no reason that agents in that period would ever have seen the originals. The headquarters trainer does mention them as part of what went on here, at headquarters. He also has a personal interest in these icons, since he is the person responsible for designing displays of the past:

> We started sewing our policies together, we had a test and found that we could paste
> 150 policies together an hour, and we could sew 1,000 policies together an hour. So
> some smart guy said "lets buy all the Singer sewing machines we could" and these

started appearing back then in the early 50's. And none of you all are old enough to remember, but they were out on the floors until the mid 70's. So they were with us a long time. I was giving a speech one time, and a lady was sitting where you are Diane, and she said, "I used to be a soda file girl." And I said "What," "A soda file girl." And I said, "I don't dig." She said, "The superintendent would give me a bunch of papers and it said 'sew to file' and it gotten shortened down to soda file girl." And she said "It was the neatest part of my job." She also told me that she would probably pre-decease me because she is older, but I could have her body stuffed and put out there behind the sewing machine, we'd have a whale of an exhibit.

Although these images are not directly relevant to agents, they do recognize them, since they have become visual icons frequently used in company displays. For example, I have heard the roller skate girls referred to by agents. The story was not told in full but indexed very sketchily. Thus, I heard one agent say to another, looking at a very long buffet table, "You need roller skates to go down this thing."

Life insurance requested by agents

The way the various versions handle the introduction of life insurance into the line of products offered by MidWest provides a particularly clear example of how the speaker's positioning works in the selection of individual stories to be told. At the time of our study, and for most of its history, MidWest was a multiline company. That is, it sold every form of personal insurance: automobile, homeowners insurance, life insurance, and health insurance. However, when it began, it sold only automobile insurance, and for most of its history automobile insurance was the backbone of the business. As already described, at the time of our study, the company was attempting to get agents to sell more life insurance, a demand many agents resisted or ignored. Many agents viewed the demand to sell more life insurance as an unreasonable request, which would require the investment of a great deal of time and effort for an insufficient financial return.

Against this background, let us examine the different ways the different complete tellings handle the introduction of life insurance into the product line of MidWest. Life insurance was the second type of insurance introduced, after automobile insurance. Life insurance products were added to MidWest eight years after its founding as an automobile insurance company. Both the newsletter articles and the authorized history make the following point: the life insurance product line was added by MidWest because of requests by agents who felt there was a market demand for life insurance, and that during the Depression, life insurance was a more easily saleable product than automobile insurance. However, the authorized history recounts the agents' request and the addition of life insurance in a flashback, located in the narrative's timeline twenty-five years after the institution of life insurance as a product. In contrast, the newsletter articles place it in its chronological order in the history of the company's products.

The difference in temporal placement is important. At the time the book was written, life insurance sales were not a major issue for the company, and the role of agents in requesting life insurance was a minor detail, of no particular importance to the history of the company. However, as I have already described, the articles were written at a time when the selling of life insurance was a contested issue between agents and the company. When the articles foreground the introduction of life insurance as an agent-instituted product, this implicitly presents a subtle warrant for the reasonableness of management's demand that agents sell it. In effect, it says: "Look you guys, quit complaining about being asked to sell life insurance. This was *your* idea, not ours." I also note that this covert argument appeared to have failed. In three years of research within MidWest we *never* heard this point made, either by agents or by management. The role of the agents in requesting the introduction of life insurance does not appear to be in the working memory of the company, although it does appear in print. Rather, it is part of the particular positioning of the newsletter articles, written by a senior manager, for agents, at a particular time when life insurance sales had become a contested issue.

Conclusion

Having five temporally complete tellings of the history of MidWest has allowed us to begin to understand the contents of the core story stock of the institution and to investigate the effect of the position of the teller, the addressees, and the situation on the choice of stories told and the way that they are framed.

Positing the notion of the core story repertoire allows us to think about the set of retold tales that recur frequently within an institution. Having examples allows us to consider their content and the kinds of topics that are likely or unlikely to be expressed in the most frequently told stories in an institution. MidWest has, as one would expect of any institution, stories about the founder, the growth and expansion of the company, and the difficulties overcome by perseverance and effort. It is the details of the stories that characterize the institution: the particular virtues of the founder, the particular types of effort required. More generally, we see that there is an issue about exactly what kinds of events and knowledge can easily be formed into narratives and which are difficult or impossible to convey by narration. MidWest is not unusual in having its narratives focus on identity: who the company is, what qualities the company and its members are expected to exhibit, how the changes in the present are necessary to preserve the fundamental nature of the company. More technical issues of exactly how the business of the company is done are difficult to convey using narrative. It is possible but takes an unusual narrator, and business details are more usually conveyed by other means.

Having five different version of a temporally complete account of MidWest's history also allows us to explore the ways in which the narrators use their position in the company as well as their relation to their addressees to shape the details of their tellings of particular stories in a way that is appropriate to the occasion, or to make points particularly salient to the time of the telling. Thus, the core story repertoire is not an inert archive. It is a set of stories that are retold again and again in ways that make them continuously relevant.

Three Versions of One Story

A Comparison

In the previous chapter, we saw a comparison of multiple versions of temporally complete tellings of the company's history, looking at large-scale similarities and differences between them. A comparison of the similarities between versions allowed us to determine the collection of stories that constitute the core memory of the entire institution. An examination of the differences between versions also allowed us to begin to investigate the effects of positioning on choice of stories.

Moving from the previous analysis of the similarities of the structure of temporally complete tellings, we turn now to a detailed analysis of different forms of a single story of the early days of MidWest Insurance. By yet another stroke of methodological good fortune, the fieldwork data includes three different versions of a single story about the founder: a written version, which appears both in the privately printed memoir published in the late 1940s as well as in one of the series of articles on history in the company newsletter published in the early 1990s, and an oral version of the same story told by the veteran district manager in his interview with a field-worker in the mid 1990s.

I will use a comparison of these versions to demonstrate two separate dynamics in the life of a narrative within an institution. The first is to extend the analysis of the relation of positioning to the shaping of narrative, begun in the previous chapter. In this chapter, I show in detail how the positioning a speaker takes shapes the microstructure of the narrative—that is, how a given story about an adventure of Mr. McBee is told either as an account by management of Mr. McBee's management skills, or as an account for agents of Mr. McBee's care for his agents, and the admirable skills and character traits his agents still share with him. The second important issue is the complex relation between written and oral narrative within an institution—the continuous movement of a narrative from oral form to written form back to oral form, which continues without a necessary ending point at which the process is complete.

The three versions and their textual history

The story being examined here is a tale about problems that MidWest experienced in its early years when criticisms and rumors were spread by competitors, and the way in which Mr. McBee, the founder, dealt with such unscrupulous rumors. It is a story from the very late 1920s or early 1930s, which has survived over sixty years within MidWest. As I have said, the data from our fieldwork contain two written versions and one oral version. Interestingly, the official history does not contain a full telling of this story. It does, however, reference the version given in the earlier memoir: "In [the memoir], [the author] tells how Mr. McBee forced a rough Western newspaper editor to quit 'rawhiding my agents out here every week' in his newspaper. Such attacks were not infrequent; sometimes they were of the nature of blackmail, inspired with the hope of forcing MidWest to buy the editor off through advertising. Thomas McBee always refused to do this."

I have no external evidence for whether the oral version is derived from the written version, whether this written version copies or adapts an earlier written version, or if this is an oral story extant in the company that the written version has preserved and extended. It might be argued that the fuller form of the confrontational conversation in the oral version of the narrative suggests that oral tradition in the company has preserved details of the story not used in the written versions. However, the existence of this detail does not prove that the oral version reproduces an early oral tradition from which the written versions derive, since these are the kinds of details skilled narrators frequently add to elaborate on the bare events of a known story.

Mr. McBee and the editor: Three versions

The stories follow, arranged in temporal order. I have titled and numbered the episodes in order to allow for easier comparison between the versions. Only the third version contains all of the episodes. The numbering of the first two versions is matched to the numbering of the episodes of the third version, and therefore the numbering of the first two versions is not completely consecutive.

Memoir version

1. Mr. McBee's Determination

> Thomas McBee was on the road almost as much of the time as he was in his office in Smallton. The entry into the various states were preceded by trips that brought him before meetings of Farm Bureaus and other organizations. Many times it was necessary to go in and set up an insurance organization for the state, training agents for the job. It was the kind of work that meant living out of a suitcase, catching sleep

on pullman jumps, being away from his home and family most of the time. It was hard, nerve wracking, grinding work that took a quick mind and a strong body—but Thomas McBee, fortunately, had both.

3. Mr. McBee Steps In

On one of these trips occurred an incident that revealed another facet in his characteristic ability to handle men and situations. He dropped off of the train in a small western town and found his way to the newspaper office. Walking in he asked for the editor.

4. Mr. McBee Meets the Editor

"My name's McBee," he said by way of introduction. I'm the president of the Mid-West Automobile Insurance Company.

"Oh, you are, eh?" came the crusty reply.

"Yes, sir," McBee came back genially, "and I'm looking for the fellow who has been rawhiding my agents out here every week in this paper."

5. Editor Says "So What?"

"Well, I'm him. What are you going to do about it?" the editor snapped.

6. Mr McBee Thanks the Editor

"Nothing," McBee said with a grin. "I just want to shake your hand. Here, have a cigar. You're a fellow after my own heart. You know, you've got those fellows so mad that they're writing more insurance than I ever dreamed they could. Don't say that I talked with you, but just keep on riding them." With that he left the office.

7. Final Evaluation

But the newspaper failed to grant his request. It had no more to say about the matter.

Newsletter version: "Silencing the Guns"

2. Slanders of MidWest

In addition to the Depression, other challenges had to be met during the '30s. Mid West had become big enough for people to begin taking "pot shots" at the organization.

Anonymous letters and pamphlets were sent to policy holders by competitors. Rumors and stories were circulated to discourage interest in Mid West.

3. Mr. McBee Steps In

One of the blasts was handled by T. D. McBee personally.

4. Mr. McBee Meets the Editor

Stopping in a small western city, he went to the editor of the paper and said, "My name's McBee. I'm president of MidWest Insurance. "

"Oh, you are, eh?" answered the editor.

"Yes sir," said Mr. McBee, "and I'm looking for the fellow who has been rawhiding my agents out here every week in this paper."

5. Editor Says "So what?"

"Well, I'm him. "What are you going to do about it?" snapped the editor.

6. Mr McBee Thanks the Editor

"Nothing," Mr. McBee said with a grin. "I just want to shake your hand. Here, have a cigar. You're a fellow after my own heart. You know, you've got these agents so mad they're writing more insurance than I ever dreamed they could. Keep up the good work. Don't say I talked with you, but just keep on riding them."

7. Final Evaluation

The newspaper's guns fell silenced.

Oral version

1. Mr. McBee's Determination
[Final evaluation of a previous story about how the agents saved the company in the late '40s.]

And all those agents, uh, uh, they had that one common denominator. They had the same enthusiasm and the same determination (???). And, um, without that, uh (???) motivating (???) and, uh, boy, if you said anything about MidWest, you know (???) to a MidWest agent them was fighting words. And I was the same way, still am.

2. Slanders of MidWest

And then, um, oh, one story about McBee was
some editor
because the newspaper was getting a lot of advertising from one of (the brokerage firms)
and, uh, so the editor, the broker guy
(???) Mid West and so forth
and started really giving him a bad time (to pay for it).
So the broker got the editor to write this about
Don't put your money into Mid West,
Don't buy insurance from them,
They'll cancel you.

3. Mr. McBee Steps In

So the agent was really getting
uh, taking the heat.
He called, uh, finally called McBee and said,

Well, it's
this guy on this newspaper is killing me and I don't know how to—I don't know how
to get around him.

4. Mr. McBee Meets the Editor

McBee got on the train in (?)
and the story goes that, uh,
he walked into the editor's office and said, uh
I understand that you've been giving the Mid West agent out here a bad time.

5. Editor says "So what?"

And the guy said Yeah, so what?
He said, My name's McBee, I'm the uh president of this company.
And he said, Well, yeah, what do you expect **me** to do about it?

6. Mr McBee Thanks the Editor

He said, not a **thing**.
He reached over, he had a cigar in his pocket and put it in **his** pocket and he
said,
Keep it **up**.
He said, uh, uh, "He's written more business just from that than you can imagine"
And walked out the door.

7. Final Evaluation

So the editor's guns fell silenced. [LAUGHTER]
So, He was that kinda guy
He would do that kinda stuff.

Comparison of the versions

Let us begin with a close examination of the three versions themselves. This
analysis will allow us a more detailed look at the issues of positioning raised in
the previous chapter: how the speaker or writer of the story uses a range of linguistic strategies to position both the story and himself with respect to a particular
audience.

Common features of the three versions

Since the versions are not identical, either in their wording or in the events and evaluations they include, let us begin with an examination of the features the three versions
have in common, those features that lead me to call this the "same" story.

All three versions begin with a problem. The newsletter and interview version
specify that the problem was that as MidWest expanded, threatened competitors

began to spread slander and libel about MidWest Insurance in the form of rumors, pamphlets, and newspaper stories. The memoir version of the problem is more general: the expansion of MidWest into additional states forced the founder to spend much of his time on the road handling the administrative work and problems that this expansion required. This particular problem of libel was one instance of these many problems.

All the versions have the problem of libel personally handled by Mr. McBee. Only the oral version specifies that the problem began with a rival insurance broker who was threatened by MidWest's success and induced a local editor to criticize his rival. But all three versions show the founder's way of dealing with the libels by personally confronting the editor and revealing himself as the president of MidWest Insurance.

All the versions have the editor belligerently refusing to change. All the versions contain a reversal in the punch line: the surprising element of Mr. McBee thanking the editor for his good work, since the libels served to spur the agents on to sell more insurance, and giving him a cigar as a gesture of gratitude. All the versions agree that the editor thereafter stopped printing such libels. Two of the three versions include the evaluative closing: "the editor's/newspaper's guns fell silenced."

Thus the event structure of the three versions is entirely similar, as is the overall evaluative structure. However, there are a number of salient differences between the oral and the written versions of this narrative, and these differences can be related to the positioning work being done by the producer of each story. The previous chapter has given an overall account of the differences in positioning of the versions. Let us now turn to an examination of how this positioning plays out with regard to these versions of a single story.

Differences in positioning

The earliest of the three versions, the memoir, is specifically an account of the life of the founder, written so as to indicate the relevance of his life for everyone in the company. Its audience is thus not specific—it is an account of the character and actions of the head of the company, framed so as to be taken as relevant by everyone within MidWest. The story is occasioned by an account of the personal problem faced by him in the early years—the crushing burden of work required to spread his insurance company:

> Thomas McBee was on the road almost as much of the time as he was in his office in Smallton. The entry into the various states were preceded by trips that brought him before meetings of Farm Bureaus and other organizations. Many times it was necessary to go in and set up an insurance organization for the state, training agents for the job. It was the kind of work that meant living out of a suitcase, catching sleep on pullman jumps, being away from his home and family most of the time. It was hard, nerve wracking, grinding work that took a quick mind and a strong body—but Thomas McBee, fortunately, had both.

In contrast, the newsletter story is a history of the company produced for agents. Thus it occasions the story by an account of challenges facing not the founder but the company as a whole;

> In addition to the Depression, other challenges had to be met during the '30s. Mid West had become big enough for people to begin taking "pot shots" at the organization.
> Anonymous letters and pamphlets were sent to policy holders by competitors. Rumors and stories were circulated to discourage interest in Mid West.

The founder comes in to the story as the person who had to deal with these challenges, but the initial framing of the story is of problems arising from the successful growth of the company, not as an example of the virtues of the founder.

A third positioning is evidenced in the oral version told by the veteran district manager. His version is framed as a story particularly relevant to agents, which tells their history, since it demonstrates the valued qualities that agents share with the founder. His telling of this story follows an immediately preceding story discussed in the previous chapter: how MidWest Insurance faced serious business difficulties just after the end of World War II and was saved by the actions of the agents, who showed the same enthusiasm, determination, and dedication to the company as the founder. The narrator concluded this story about the attitude of agents at this time: "And if someone ran down MidWest Insurance, them's fighting words. I'm the same way. I still am."

He then moved immediately to the story of Mr. McBee and the editor, which shows how the founder dealt with someone criticizing the company. He does not explicitly mark the connection of this story of the founder with the previous story of the action of the agents. However, his placement and framing of this story shows these virtues in the actions of the founder, and thus demonstrates how agents and managers continue to share with the founder the same qualities of determination and loyalty to the company.

One key detail, which shows that this version is specifically both for and about agents, is that in this version the action is initiated by an agent, who calls on the founder to defend the company against criticism and libel. In contrast, both written versions, which are framed more generally as being about the founder or the company, contain no specification of how the founder became aware of the offending editor or chose to deal with him in person. There are no agents as actors on stage; only the offstage agents who have been incited to greater sales efforts by the libels about MidWest.

Linguistic differences between the versions

I now turn to the linguistic differences between these versions.

Markings of evidentiality

First, let us consider the presence or absence of evidential markers in the three versions. As already mentioned in chapter 5, evidential markers are linguistic indications of how a speaker has come to know the events being discussed (Chafe 1986; Aikehnvald 2004). There are languages that have obligatory marking of evidential status. That is, every verb or every sentence must contain a linguistic element indicating that the speaker knows the event narrated by direct experience, by having heard about it, or because it can be inferred, etc.

English does not have obligatory markers of evidentiality. However, like all languages, English has resources available in the language for speakers to mark how they acquired their knowledge of events, if they choose to do so. For example, the following is taken from a mother's story about how her child got separated from his babysitter when they went to an outdoor art show: "And he looked and he looked and he looked for her, and finally he came home and in the process *evidently* got lost twice, but he did make it home." *Evidently* here is an evidential marker. It marks the fact that the speaker was not there: she derives her knowledge of her son's getting lost from his later account of what happened, not from firsthand knowledge. It is the speaker's choice to mark the indirect nature of her knowledge. She marks the most dramatic part: the boy getting lost. Her knowledge of the fact that he repeatedly looked for his babysitter is similarly indirect, but she does not mark it.

Even in languages that have obligatory markers of evidentiality, these markers do not entirely represent accurate reports but rather represent one more rhetorical resource for speakers to manipulate. Mushin (1998) offers a valuable comparative study of the use of evidentials in three languages: Macedonian, English, and Japanese, which differ in the number and type of evidentials. In a study of staged retellings of narratives by native speakers of these languages, she found that evidentials were not used simply to mark that the speaker was retelling a story heard from another speaker. Rather, they were used to indicate epistemological stance: "the conceptualizer's assessment of information according to the nature and status of its source" (39). As Mushin uses the concept, the cognitive notion of epistemology, how the speaker knows, blurs towards social issues of stance or self-presentation. By retelling a story, the speaker is not only doing a task of reproduction of a story previously heard but is also showing herself to be a competent understander and teller. However, the laboratory nature of the data makes it difficult for this study to actually study how speakers actually manipulate stance. For example, in a discussion of English speakers' use of nonreportive stances, Mushin reports:

> One explanation for the lack of reportive coding is that it interferes with the reteller's autonomy as a story teller. To adopt a consistent reportive epistemological stance in English implies that the reteller must commit to being faithful to their source. They can achieve this either by reporting what someone else has said with evidential reported speech, or at least by reporting that the information they had was acquired via what someone else said with adverbials that imply reportedness (e.g. *apparently, supposedly.*) The representation of narrative information thus threatens the autonomy of the storyteller since it implies that they are bound by whatever they were told. It downplays the storyteller's creative role in the reconstruction of a narrative. (223)

However, because this study is based in a paradigm of narration as a cognitive task, and because it uses staged laboratory data, it is not able to analyze in any detail the storytellers' work of taking a stance toward the material being retold (since they have been requested to retell it as a laboratory task), or toward the addressee (who is the experimenter).

Within anthropological linguistics, there has been more attention to the social aspects of retelling and to the marking of the nature of knowing. For example, Hill (1992) argues the primarily social rather than epistemological function that the use of evidentials plays in discourse:

> Evidential elements obviously function in the manipulation of responsibility for knowledge. But Du Bois (1986) has suggested that it is misleading to think of evidentiality in the strictly cognitive or epistemological terms preferred by "personalist" accounts. "Knowledge" is instead a social phenomenon, an aspect of the social relations between people. This state of affairs is evidenced linguistically in the famous ambiguity of the English modal "must" between so-called epistemic modality, where "must" indicates certainty of knowledge, and deontic modality, in which "must" constitutes a directive. Furthermore, the decision about which is meant requires interpretation by the hearer, drawing on evidence from context. (17)

The papers collected in Hill and Irvine (1992) examine a wide range of cases involving issues of speakers' knowledge and responsibility, showing that these are always negotiated issues, with serious social consequences. Aikehnvald (2004) demonstrates the ways in which the use of evidentials mirrors cultural assumptions. For example, a number of Amazonian languages typically describe the dreams of ordinary people in sentences using the evidential marking events that were not visually experienced. On the other hand, the dreams of shamans are described using the evidential that marks direct experience, since shamans are assumed to be omniscient and, therefore, the language suggests that descriptions of their dreams are to be understood as factual statements about what they see.

This chapter's comparison of three versions of a single story considers optional marking of evidentiality as only one resource of many that speakers use to construct a telling that is coherent with their position within MidWest, their stance toward the material, and the kind of response they wish their addressees to have. This is a demonstration of the major claim of this book at the most detailed linguistic level: institutions and people within institutions do not mechanically record and reproduce the past. Rather, they work the past, re-presenting it each time for a particular purpose, in a particular way, that uses the past to create a particular desired present and future. Of the three versions, only the oral version uses markers of evidentiality: "One story about McBee," as well as "and the story goes." These are an indication of a narrative that has become institutionalized. Not only was the speaker not a participant (since he was not born at the time of these events), but he is telling a story familiar within his work world in both oral and written forms and has a canonical shape, including key incidents and key phrases. It is interesting to compare this usage to quotatives like: *As the old saying goes*, used to introduce proverbs and proverb-like material. (I include "proverb-like material" because I have heard the phrase used to quote lines from song lyrics, short passages from Shakespeare and the Bible, and advertising slogans.) It appears that there are genres of speech that must be marked as such. In particular, this speaker uses evidentials of this sort when he tells personal third-person narratives about key characters in the history of the company. He does not use them when he produces more chronicle-like accounts of the march of large-scale events in the history of the company.

DIFFERENCES IN WORD CHOICE AND SYNTAX   I now turn to some key differences in the actual word choice in the three stories. The oral version expresses the problem as "giving the MidWest agent out here a bad time" while the two written versions describe this as "rawhiding my agents out here." While the *American Heritage Dictionary* defines "rawhiding" as "to beat with a rawhide whip," with no indication that it is either regional or obsolete, I have never heard the word used in California, where the oral version was produced. It is probably an older form, which has dropped out of the oral version.

As would be expected, the written memoir version contains a number of syntactic forms characteristic of written text. These include the following subject-verb inversion: "On one of these trips occurred an incident that revealed another facet in his characteristic ability to handle men and situations."

An additional written feature is the following sentence, which contains an inversion of narrative order: that is, the order in the text does not match the temporal order: "The entry into the various states were preceded by trips that brought him before meetings of Farm Bureaus and other organizations." Such an inversion of narrative order is a marked form, but not unknown; it is more frequent in written than in oral narrative. The syntax of the newsletter version is less complex, but it does contain a series of passives: "In addition to the Depression, other challenges had to be met during the '30s. Anonymous letters and pamphlets were sent to policy holders by competitors. Rumors and stories were circulated to discourage interest in MidWest." The most interesting linguistic feature is the sentence that concludes the newsletter and the oral version: "So the newspaper's/editor's guns fell silenced." This is an extremely literary phrase, which sounds old-fashioned, if not archaic. The phrase is most frequently used in descriptions of World War I: either the Christmas truce of 1914, or Armistice Day, November 11, 1918. It is also used commonly in discussions of battles of the American Civil War. I have found instances of it describing the end of World War II (a campaign speech by World War II veteran, Senator Bob Dole) and the end of the Gulf War (a congressional speech by President George H. W. Bush), both of which are highly rhetorical in tone. It is certainly unusual in conversational narrative. As I shall discuss in the next section, the district manager's use of it suggests a complex interplay between written and oral versions of the story.

Finally, of the three versions, the oral version is the only one containing an explicit statement of exactly what libels were being spread about MidWest. These are organized in the familiar folktale pattern of three escalating statements:

Don't put your money into MidWest,
Don't buy insurance from them,
They'll cancel you.

This is an example of an artful and well-practiced narrative structure.

DIFFERENCES IN ARGUMENT STRUCTURE   I turn now to differences in the argument structure of the three versions: that is, the different points that are either explained in full or left for the addressees to construct their connection to the rest of the narrative.

Two of the versions give reasons for the spread of the libels. The newsletter versions explains briefly *why* libels were being spread: MidWest had become big enough for people to begin taking "pot shots" at the organization. This explanation is linked to the newsletter version's general theme. The entire series is framed as an account of the rapid growth of MidWest; the problem of libel is thus presented as one consequence of this growth.

In contrast, the oral version gives a much more detailed account of the reasons for circulation of the rumors: a brokerage firm whose business was being hurt by MidWest's success incited a newspaper in which it advertised to print detrimental stories. This fuller account ties back to an earlier topic in the interview. Here, the manager explains the structure of the independent insurance brokerage system prevalent at the time when MidWest was founded and the reasons why it was an inefficient distribution system that was unfair to the consumer compared to MidWest's model. Thus, the prior discourse had already set up brokerage firms as potential villains.

Finally, the two written versions give a nearly identical explanation of the founder's dealings with the editor: the founder wanted (or claimed to want) the editor to keep writing such stories because it got the agents mad enough to write more insurance: "You've got those fellows/these agents so mad (that) they're writing more insurance than I ever dreamed they could." In contrast, the oral version simply describes the effect without explaining the motivation: "He's written more business just from that than you can imagine."

CHANGES IN EVALUATIVE STRUCTURE   Thus far, I have discussed issues of overt positioning of the three versions. I now turn to an issue of the evaluation of the story, which indicates a change in the value of particular kinds of actions over the history of MidWest. In particular, the issue is the acceptability of deception to achieve a worthy end.

All the versions frame this as a story about the determination of founder and agents, their fearlessness, their willingness to stand up to criticism, the trust agents had in Mr. McBee to help them when they got into difficulties. But the story can also be read as an instance of a double deception of both the editor and the MidWest agents: the founder's willingness (or apparent willingness) to collude with an outside critic to keep up the pressure that motivated agents to sell more insurance, and his apparent praise of the editor's behavior as a way of getting him to change it. This issue of deception is problematic within MidWest, although many readers may assume that this kind of deception is exactly what one would expect of a salesman, and that therefore it is to be expected within the sales culture of MidWest.

However, this sort of deceptive cleverness is not a value MidWest would currently approve and would not wish to show in its past—particularly in the actions of its revered founder. Our fieldwork suggested that there has been a partial change in

MidWest's view of the acceptability of certain sorts of sales techniques that include an element of deception. Although MidWest managers say that MidWest always was the most honest and ethical insurance company, at an early period it was considered legitimate to use sales tactics that pressure clients into buying the insurance, particularly the life insurance that the agent knew clients actually needed. Even this statement is somewhat ambiguous. In many cases, managers pressured agents into selling life insurance they believed or claimed to believe clients needed; some agents then sold such insurance to please their managers or to win rewards such as vacation trips and other prizes. (Some other agents did believe in the need for life insurance and sold it because of their own convictions; others ignored the entire issue and did not push life insurance on clients who did not request it.)

Because there were a number of serious legal judgments brought against other insurance companies for deceptive sales practices, MidWest at this point in our research wished its agents to sell insurance to clients only when the clients genuinely needed it and understood what and why they were buying. MidWest management was concerned that agents not trick or pressure clients into insurance sales. Current training programs stressed the importance of discovering clients' actual financial situation and trying to sell them only what they actually needed. Indeed, we observed one case in which a trainee agent, spending time in a veteran agent's office, said that he would like to emulate that agent's "bulldog tenacity" in selling. When we told this story to the directors of training as an example of successful mentoring on the part of the veteran agent, the training directors were extremely upset by the phrase. "Bulldog tenacity" sounded too much like high-pressure sales tactics, which they emphatically did not want new agents learning.

In general, in our observations, MidWest agents do not pressure, trick, or flim-flam clients. We have observed almost no examples of high-pressure sales tactics. In fact, we have seen a number of cases in which agents did a financial review with clients and recommended that they lower the amount of insurance they were carrying, since their financial situations had changed. But we have also observed some few older agents who use a range of routines with clients that comprise a sales style we have called the trickster. Such an agent, for example, purposefully places his chair higher than the client's in order to maintain a stronger control over the interaction, something that a more equal seating arrangement does not automatically support. He maintains control of the conversation using questions whose answers can lead directly into a sales pitch. For example, such an agent will ask, "How much life insurance do you have?" in order to get a precise answer which he can then analyze for financial adequacy. MidWest's current practice prefers that the agent begin with a complete financial review of the client's situation, in the course of which the actual need for life insurance can be determined and then examined against the amount of the life insurance the client may currently carry. (I have used "he" to describe this style of sales, since the few examples we observed were all older men, holdovers from an earlier period.)

However, not all agents proceed in this way. In one example of the trickster that we observed, the agent had printed copies of two stew recipes on his desk: one chicken and one beef. When a client refuses to buy life insurance, he shows the two recipes to the client and asks, "Since I won't be bringing a check to your funeral, what kind of stew would you like me to bring for your family, chicken or beef?" Senior managers wince when they hear this story (or try to guess which old guy it was, since our confidentiality agreement prohibited us describing any agent behavior in a way that would allow management to identify them). But they admit that this kind of sales style is present at MidWest, although they argue (and hope) that it is an older style that current training will eradicate.

To return to the story of the founder, there is a certain element of this kind of trickster behavior present in the events, although it is not currently highlighted as a virtue within the company. Thus, the two earlier versions specifically include the founder's double trick on the editor: "Don't say that I talked with you, but just keep on riding them." This could be viewed as a benign deception. The founder requests the editor to conceal their conversation and continue his inflammatory editorials, knowing that he will do just the opposite, and so actually benefit the MidWest agents whom he is trying to protect. The most recent version, however, does not specify this part of the deception, but only notes that the editor was silenced, and thus the agents and the company were benefited. This omission is consistent with the company's recent more stringent policy attempting to eliminate any form of deceptiveness or trickery in sales practice.

Oral and written life of a retold tale within an institution

The comparison of these three versions allows us a unique look into the life of a retold tale within an institution as it cycles between oral and written forms and back again. Such a comparison allows us to consider issues of orality and literacy in a somewhat different way than the discussions current in the fields of anthropology, folklore, and cognitive psychology.

The history of this narrative is partially attested by the forms we have preserved here and is partially conjectural. The version originally printed in the memoir was presumably initially told as an oral story about events in the early 1930s. If we take it as a true story, it was probably told by Mr. McBee, the only person from MidWest present at the events, to at least one other member of MidWest: a colleague in the home office, the agent who complained about the behavior of the editor, perhaps one of his sons, in short, someone inside the institution who was not present for the drama. (It is possible but much less likely that it was originally told by the editor, either to someone at MidWest or to some member of the general public as a story about a good trick that was played on him.) If we take it as fictional, it was invented by someone at MidWest, either Mr. McBee himself or someone using him as a character to illustrate a point about the history of MidWest and about desired personal characteristics for its members. Almost certainly it was not invented in the late 1940s by the memoir writer; he probably obtained it from the oral tradition of stories circulating in the company as he compiled his work; the memoir contains many similar anecdotes, although the writer does not indicate their sources.

The story does not appear in the official history, written in the mid-1950s. However, this says nothing about this particular story as such; there are a number of additional anecdotes of the founder given in the memoir but not present in the official history. However, it is entirely possible (although not documented) that it also continued within MidWest as an oral story. In either case, it reappears in the newsletter history series in the early 1990s as a written story, obviously taken in form from the memoir version, repeating many sentences word for word. It is then told to the field-worker as an oral anecdote by the veteran line manager in 1997.

What is particularly important about this oral telling is that it was not prepared. The interview was an unscheduled, on-the-fly event.[1] The field-worker was shadowing the manager, and in the course of a break in his schedule, he began telling her about his history in the company, which he then linked to an account of the company's history and the life of the founder. It is extremely unlikely that he had consulted the memoir or the historical series to prepare for this conversation, since there had been no arrangement that he would be interviewed about the history of the company. Such consultation of the written record would be quite likely in the case of a prepared speech. We have heard managers telling us that they "mine" the official history to find just such useful stories. But in this case, it appears that this story is part of the manager's repertoire, available for telling on appropriate occasions without a return to the printed sources to brush up on his knowledge. Yet, as already mentioned, he does reproduce word for word one extremely literary feature of the more recent written version, the overall evaluation of the story: "So the editor's guns fell silenced."

This documented availability of the story for the manager raises the fascinating question of the relation and interplay between oral and written versions of the stories in the story stock of an institution. In discussions of the relation between oral and written cultures, oral and written transmissions, there has been a common assumption that the directionality goes only one way. The standard view is that an oral culture becomes, by whatever processes, a written culture, and orality is crushed by the juggernaut of literate modernity. This argument focuses on claims about the results on cognition of acquiring literacy: there is said to be a "Great Divide" between the oral and the literate mind, because the affordances of literacy allow for processes of decontextualization, reflection and critical thinking not possible in an oral culture. (The key arguments of this extensive literature are to be found in Ong (1982) and Goody (1969).) Recent critiques of this theory argue that it is based on an insufficient analysis of language practices in both oral and literate societies: all the forms of critical thought claimed as literate can be found in oral societies, and the forms of uses of literacy are not determined by the technology of writing itself, but vary widely from society to society. See for example Street (1995). Thus, if one asks questions about the social structures supporting literacy and orality, rather than cognitive questions about mental processes of oral and literate persons, a very different picture emerges. In the case of narrative, the questions to ask are exactly those questions suggested by the early discussion in chapter 3 about occasions for remembering: when and how does a society, or a particular institution within a society provide occasions on which a story can be retold orally, a text read silently or chanted aloud, a particularly valued picture displayed and described?

Thus, if we turn from the issue of orality and literacy, and rather look at the adventures of stories as they move from one modality to another, we must again beware of assuming that the directionality is always from oral to written reproduction of texts. Here, perhaps, the fullest literature on this movement is found in studies of oral epics. The classic study of the nature of oral epic tradition is Lord (1965), Milman Parry and Albert Lord's study of the survival of a oral epic tradition in the former Yugoslavia into the 1930s. The authors studied the Yugoslavian bardic songs in order to understand the oral origins and oral survivals in the Homeric epic, which had previously been studied as a written poetic composition. Therefore, their emphasis was on the oral aspects of the Yugoslavian tradition, since they considered it a fascinating and invaluable opportunity to see an oral tradition still alive and in action. On first reading, it is easy to take their description as a case of a pure oral survival, a living fossil, which one can indeed use to try to understand how Homer composed. However, on a closer reading, it becomes clear that even for the village bards of Yugoslavia, there was a parallel written tradition that influenced the oral tradition, just as the oral tradition influenced the written. Thus, for example, the authors note that side by side with the oral bards, there were also songbooks circulating, which the oral bards used to learn new songs. While traditional folklore methodology would regard this as an unfortunate corruption of the pure oral tradition, on another view, it provides us with a complex example of the mutual influence of oral and written sources, with neither one superseding the other.

For example, Lord (1986) discusses the use of songbooks in the former Yugoslavia, attempting to distinguish an oral world from a literate world (a version of the Great Divide theory). He argues that although some of the singers he studied in the 1930s and 1940s used songbooks, they treated them as part of the world of orality. That is, they used them to learn songs, just as they would from another singer, but did not assume that they had to reproduce them verbatim:

> Some of the songbooks contain bona fide oral traditional epic written down from singers, usually somewhat edited, but not necessarily. Through these little books, which often tell nothing about who dictated the songs, who wrote them down, or where, songs, or versions of songs, may become distributed in places where they were not previously known. The effect is that of the wandering singer, if you will—with the one difference, which may or may not be important, that a fixed text is thereby being propagated. To the traditional singer in the world of orality this may make no difference at all, because the reading of the text to him would be like the hearing of it from a singer, and he would treat it accordingly...that it was fixed would be of no interest to him, unless the person reading it to him indicated that this was the way it must be told or sung. Otherwise he would not hear it as fixed, even if he could read it himself, provided he was still a citizen of the world of orality. But for those in the world of literacy, this printed version would likely become "the version" of the song, rather than simply one performance. To them the fixity would be important. (41)

Similarly, in reanalyzing some of Parry and Lord's data to foreground issues of performance, Foley (1995) also found more complex relations between orality and literacy:

> Our joint research uncovered several traditional oral genres, some of them unreported or not very well known, but very little in the way of extended narrative poetry, which in this region would be the shorter, Christian variety of epic. The Halperns

had recorded a version of the *Udovica Jana (Widow Jana)* narrative some years earlier, but by 1975 there were few older men who claimed or were reputed to be able
to sing to the *gusle*, and fewer still who were actually willing to do so. One man who
did perform for us, for instance, proudly announced that he had learned a particular
song from a *pjesmarica* ("songbook"). When we asked to see the published source,
he produced a well-worn pamphlet entitled *Borba Jogoslavenskih Partizana (The
Battle of the Yugoslav Partisans)* that he had laboriously pored over and crudely
marked, indicating deletions and the like. Nonetheless, comparison of his acousti-
cally recorded performance to the text revealed that the integrity of the register had
superseded his avowed fidelity to the printed source: the actual version he sang followed the songbook only occasionally and loosely. (104)

Furthermore, there were written versions of the oral epics written down, mainly
by learned nationalistic clerics in the nineteenth and early twentieth centuries, and
these written versions again spawned new oral versions. For example, Judah (1997)
describes the nineteenth-century nationalistic process of making collections of
Serbian songs and epics, and then examines their use in the formation of Serbian
justifications for the wars of 1991–1995:

> In the first published collection of Serbian epic songs, we find "The Downfall of
> the Serbian Empire" in which Lazar makes his fateful choice between the eternal
> "empire of heaven" and the temporal "empire of earth." He chooses the empire of
> heaven, "that is to say truth and justice, so that the state would one day be resur-
> rected. An earthly kingdom was rejected in favour of nobler ideals—victimhood and
> sacrifice—and this choice is to be compared with the temptations of Christ." (37)

The epic argues that the Serbs were betrayed by traitors in their ranks, although
the historical record differs: "The Brankovi'c myth of treachery was needed as a way
to explain the fall of the medieval state, and it has powerful seeds of self-replication
contained within it. Throughout the war of 1991-5 no Serb ever ascribed a defeat to
loosing a battle fair and square. With monotonous regularity losses were always put
down to secret deals—and treachery" (36).

I would note that this history of the Yugoslavian oral epic is not just a fascinating glimpse into a past world. As Judah (1997), among others, indicates, these epic
songs played a role in justifying Serbian nationalism after the breakup of the former
Yugoslavia. These issues of the destiny of a nation or a people remain serious matters, and the stories about them can be part of bloody events.

On another continent, and another life world, Kornman (1997) describes the
Tibetan national epic, the story of Gesar of Ling. This is an epic that continues a
vigorous oral existence in parallel with many different written versions. For example,
one Western-educated Tibetan in exile has describe his childhood experience of the
epic as follows:

> When I was young my father use to sing the Gesar Epic quite often. In 1985 my
> mother went to Tibet and when she returned, she brought back about 4 different
> Gesar Epics, the one I personally remember the most is the battle of Ling and Hor's.
> My parents use to tell me that by reading or singing the Gesar Epic, would invoke
> the auspicious omens, such as the dakas and the dakinis [supernatural protectors].

Some of the other reasons were, to keep us in touch with part of our culture and heritage, second it really brings back lots happy memories of their past lives, third the whole epic has a very intense inspirational and motivational character to it and fourth it is just too interesting to ignore, isn't it?

I remember specially during the Dokham parties, group of elders use to come together and sing the Gesar Epic. They use to make recordings to listen later. My father usually use to sing after the lunch or dinner because my sister and myself we use to ask him to tell us stories. I remember my sister use to join in with my dad in singing the epic.

When I went home (India) to visit my parents in 1997. I found that my father still treasures those books very much. My father is around 82 years old he can't sing so well, so he was reading it almost everyday whenever he had time and he was feeling good. (Personal communication, via e-mail.)

In this complex example, we see the traditional epic as a sung text, a tape recorded text, and a written text, all functioning within one household.

At the same time the Gesar epic has been written down by Tibetans at least twenty times, for at least five centuries (Karmay 1998). But the process of writing has not provided a final version of the form or the canon of epic. To this day, new episodes continue to be written in response to current political or religious needs. For example, when told by an English visitor stranded in Tibet about the ongoing World War II, a revered Tibetan lama, Khamtrul Rinpoche, responded in sympathy by composing an episode about King Gesar conquering the Germans.

On yet another continent, and another life world, Finnegan (1988) describes the complex interplay between oral and written forms in contemporary uses of traditional Maori literary forms. While these forms are thought of as primarily oral, in fact, in modern times, they show the same two-way movement between oral, written, and electronic representations. Pieces may be composed in writing but performed and transmitted orally, or performed orally from notes. Families may preserve song books and genealogy lists. Poetry is performed on radio programs, and preserved in phonograph records, and recirculated through Maori language newspapers and magazine. Similar forms of mixed transmission have been found in the Pacific for other groups, including Ifaluk, Tongan, Fijian, and Samoan forms (111–12).

This has been a long excursus into some life worlds far removed in place, feeling-tone, and central problems from the world of MidWest Insurance. But I am not just taking the opportunity to tell interesting stories about interesting stories. The main point I want to make is that the oral tradition is not exotic and it is not dying, at least not in large U.S. corporations. Oral culture lives and flourishes side by side with written culture, and each feeds the other. This is particularly important in understanding the functions of narratives within institutions, since narratives pass through these apparent barriers of modality perhaps more easily than any other discourse form.

Further, I suggest that the most valuable question to ask is not "What is the oral culture at MidWest?" Or, "What is the written culture?" Rather, the questions that yield the more interesting answers, for MidWest or any other institution, are, What is the life of a particular narrative or group of narratives within an institution, as it moves between modalities? What is the stock of narratives? Who are the tellers? What are the uses? To summarize the life of narratives at MidWest using the particular case we have just examined as an example and the complete tellings we examined in the previous chapter. Narratives abound at MidWest, and narratives of the founder and the early days are particularly popular. These stories exist in both oral and written form. People learn these stories from previous oral tellings, from the written sources or from both. However they learned these stories, they have the written versions available to them to refresh their memory or to find a story appropriate to a given occasion. (This is a situation that comes up for anyone faced with the task of making a speech; this is usually a manager's job, but it can be a job for an agent as well, if the agent has been invited to address a district meeting, a task force, a training class, etc.)

There is one process that is conspicuously absent in this discussion: verbatim memorization and recitation. While that is not a process in use at MidWest, it has certainly not disappeared in the modern world. This kind of activity is likely to be found in any institution constituted around a central body of highly valued texts. These are most often religious institutions but need not be. Waldorf education, which I have already discussed, makes heavy use of the memorization of texts, particularly texts composed by its founder.

Conclusion

Narratives have multimodal lives within institutions. They move from water cooler sessions to print to formal speeches to videotapes and back to the water cooler. There is no final form, no ultimately authorized version. The analysis of three forms of a single story has tried to suggest some of the ways stories are occasioned, move from one modality to another, and from one point of view to another. Thus, it is not simply the existence of a narrative within an institution that is important, but rather the occasions and the forms of transmission that allow for its movement and continual reproduction within that institution, in whatever form of representation the members actually use.

Paradigmatic Narratives

Exemplary Narratives of Everyman

T he previous chapters examined the retold tales of an institution, analyzing both their events and evaluations and the ways in which these are shaped by the position of the teller and addressees. These are stories of the founder and of major events in the life of the company. They are framed as exemplary narratives, teaching tales about how a member of the institution should act under a variety of circumstances. In contrast to these heroic tales of the founder discussed above, we now turn to a different kind of exemplary narrative: stories about ordinary members of the institution told both by the protagonists themselves and by others in a way that presents the story to the addressee as an example to be followed, and as one piece of a life course to be emulated. I call these stories that offer patterns for a model life course "paradigmatic narratives," exemplary narratives of Everyman. The gender is intentional, since, as I shall explain later, at MidWest these were indeed men's stories.

Within MidWest, the paradigmatic narrative consists of stories that show instances of what a successful career at MidWest consists of, and how it was achieved by specific, real-life agents. These stories are intended to be taken by members as a detailed model of success and as a promise that such success can be accomplished by any member of the institution. They present the institution's model of ordinary success. These are stories not of heroic and unusual accomplishment but of the success that can be accomplished with ordinary aptitudes and perseverance, and the absence of unusual bad luck.

This chapter begins with a definition of the paradigmatic narrative. It then considers in detail the status of the paradigmatic narrative as a discourse unit and the methodological question of how one discovers a paradigmatic narrative within

141

an institution. From there, it discusses the paradigmatic narrative at MidWest and changes in the career structure that may change not only the details of the paradigmatic narrative, but even the existence of a predictable life course that can be narrated as a reliable prediction of what is possible for new members.

The notion of the paradigmatic narrative arose directly from our observations at MidWest. In the course of our fieldwork, we found that we were constantly told stories about agents' careers. Agents told us stories about their own careers; managers told us stories about their prior career as agents; managers and agents told us stories about other agents' careers. Further, we heard each of these types of story told to other agents, particularly newer agents, during both private conversations and large official meetings. While some of these were presented as unusual stories about an idiosyncratic character, others were clearly framed as typical illustrations of a possible agent's career, or an ideal agent's career. In particular, as a regular part of the process of recruiting a possible new agent, managers would try to demonstrate to the potential new agent what a good career choice it would be by pointing to other agents in the area, describing their enviable businesses, and then telling the stories of how they had arrived at these positions. The patterns formed by these exemplary stories constitute the paradigmatic narrative. Thus, the paradigmatic narrative is defined as a discontinuous unit, consisting of the narratives told on a variety of occasions within a particular institution, which collectively constitute the model for a career within that institution.

We on the research team found that we needed this concept both to understand the kinds of stories we were hearing at MidWest and to communicate to upper management agents' beliefs and expectations about career tracks and opportunities, stages of life and concomitant responsibilities, and rights at each stage. As we shall see, however, although the term and the definition were invented to describe and make vivid a particular situation at MidWest, in fact, such paradigmatic narratives exist in many institutions. The notion of the paradigmatic narrative will be more precisely defined below. At this point, we will focus on its most important defining characteristic of the paradigmatic narrative: the presentation of a narrative as exemplary. The paradigmatic narrative is a representation of the ideal life course of a given type of person within a given institution, including its stages, preferred time for attaining each stage, preferred age at beginning and end, possible options, etc. It is this exemplary character that differentiates tellings of component stories of the paradigmatic narrative from tellings of other first- or third-person narratives. When Tom tells Dick a story about Harry, depending on the framing, it can be understood to be just a story about Harry, presumably relevant in some locally occasioned way to the situation of the telling, but having no wider relevance. But Tom can also tell Dick a story about Bob, who is admired in their community, and frame the story as exemplary. Such a story presents its events both as an example of good practice and as a promise of a possible career to its hearer.

Readers may be most familiar with the model of an academic career: the move from graduate student to tenure-track position to promotion and tenure, and status within a department. Not every graduate student achieves this career, and many may add steps such as postdoctoral fellowships, lateral moves into administration, etc., or may take unusually long or short periods for each stage. However, the steps of the standard pattern are clear, even if individual ways of working it out differ.

For example, Traweek (1992), in her ethnography of particle physics, describes the paradigmatic course of the physicist's career, including the different types of behaviors, attitudes, and skills valued at each stage. Like the paradigmatic account of the MidWest agent's career, these narratives are gendered—Traweek calls her account "Male Tales Told During a Life in Physics":

> Undergraduate physics students, to be successful, must display a high degree of intellectual skill, particularly in analogical thinking. The students learn from textbooks whose interpretation of physics is not to be challenged; in fact it is not seen as interpretation.... It is not until graduate school that avuncular advisors introduce the older students to the particle physics community and cautiously allow them to see themselves as members of it; through stories of success and failure, stories about the work of the generation now in power, they teach the novices a style of "doing" physics and a "nose" for good issues. Graduate students are also learning to be meticulous and very hard working.
>
> Self-assertion and bravado must be added in the third stage, when the "students"—having earned their Ph.D.'s—become research associates.... The "postdocs" begin to learn and communicate about physics orally, rather than through books and articles. They cultivate competitive and acerbic conversation to display independence and a contempt for mediocrity. They learn stories about those in recent generations who have "made it"; from these stories they realize how important it is to anticipate the future.
>
> At the end of their fifteen-year training period, young particle physicists hope to become full members of the research community. However, only about a fourth of the American students will be sponsored for positions at major universities or laboratories where they will be able to continue research. Those remaining have three options, which like the less successful Ph.D.'s they take in approximately equal numbers: they can leave the field, or work at peripheral schools and cease research, or take a staff position at a major lab in which they will manage the production and maintaince of detectors (what one group leader calls "engineering management). (75–94)
>
> [The next stage of success is to become a group leader.]
>
> During his career, a group leader accumulates considerable wealth in the form of detectors, targets, and computer software, as well as his less tangible—but perhaps even more significant—reputation in the community. This reputation is the power that the leader wields in the community as a whole; it is symbolized by his membership on laboratory program advisory committees, which determine which experiments will be accepted, and by his control of a network cutting across laboratories and physics departments around the world. This wealth must be maintained assiduously; it is not clear that it can be inherited. Every powerful senior physicist can invoke a lineage of which he is a part, naming his teacher and his teacher's teacher. It is direct descent from one leader to another in this lineage and the attendant privileges, rights, and duties that a leader will try to bequeath to one of the postdocs who have worked with him.... During the old days of funding expansion they could start new groups for their heirs. Now the only group their heirs might lead is their own. (94)
>
> [The final career stage is becoming a statesman in physics.]
>
> The first stage in becoming a science statesman is administering a laboratory. Each laboratory is thought by physicists to reflect the necessarily powerful personality of its director.... Statesman no longer actually do physics; they recruit students. They get money for the lab; they get money for science; they attend to the public

understanding of science. It is utterly inappropriate for junior persons to be doing any of these things. Only a senior person can do this. Furthermore, only a senior person who has made a significant discovery can do it, one who has manifestly been able to avoid for an entire career the corrupting enticements of extrascientific power. On the other hand, interacting with people on the outside is itself a kind of corruption. Teaching, administration, and consulting for the government are potentially contaminating because they require the cultivation of skills not thought to be based on reason—in particular the power of persuasion. The scientists themselves usually claim that they no longer do research because they have no time; other scientists believe that these science-statesmen chose their new role because they no longer had "any science left in them." (101–102)

In the case of an academic career, the stages are institutionally reified, with most stages named, and achieved through institutional decisions and announcements. While new or prospective academics may be told stories about exemplary, unusual, or failed careers, the telling of such stories is not necessary in order to lay out the career track and the expectations at each stage. Instead, universities have formally defined and made explicit (to some extent) the stages, the times appropriate and allocated to achieving them, the formal requirements for achievement, etc. That is, a new faculty member can be told explicitly: you will come up for tenure in seven years because this is mandated in the university regulations. There is less need to tell stories about how Professor Smith and Professor Lee navigated the tenure process to establish what that process is. Such stories are more likely to be used to communicate exceptions or unusual cases, or to give oblique advice about those parts of the process that are not formally named, described, or discussed.

In contrast, the career of a sales agent at Midwest has only two named and institutionally defined stages, both of which occur at the beginning of the career: the decision to become a trainee agent (who has the status of an employee of MidWest), and the successful completion of training and move from trainee agent to independent contractor. However, there are additional stages, which are socially recognized although not legally defined. These form an important part of the expectations and the social practice of the agents and the company, although they are not named, and do not form part of the contractual arrangement between the agent and the company. Part of understanding these stages includes what kind of work an agent is likely to have to do, what kind of revenue can be expected at each stage, when the agent's business has become stable, etc. These stages are identified and conveyed by narratives told both by the agent in question and by others.

The paradigmatic narrative of an agent's career is presented from the point of view of the agents. As described above, a move from being an agent to becoming a manager is **not** part of the ideal career course of an agent. Because this is a move from being an independent contractor back to being an employee, agents who have not moved into management consider it a lateral move or even a move down. This evaluation is both economic and symbolic. Economically, a highly successful agent may have a higher income than the first few levels of management. Symbolically, since agents value their independent status as entrepreneurs so highly, a move into management is seen as an abandonment of the courage it takes to rely on one's own efforts to bring in revenue and a reversion to dependency on a salary granted by a corporation. The symbolic meaning for agents is very similar to the implicit criticism, in an academic context, of professors who leave research to enter university administration: they have abandoned the main value of undertaking such a career in the first place. However, for agents who have become managers, the paradigmatic narrative of the agent's career is somewhat different. They present themselves as having been successful in the first stages of the agent's career. Most then describe the move into management as an intriguing new challenge. Parenthetically, the stages of a manager's career are considerably more formally defined than those of an agent, but I am not able to describe it in detail here. Our ethnography focused on agents and so did not reveal a paradigmatic narrative for managers' careers. It would take more extensive ethnography among managers to discover whether such a paradigmatic narrative does exist, or whether the institutionally typical career structure for managers of climbing a defined career ladder makes a paradigmatic narrative unnecessary.

Why we invented the term "paradigmatic narrative"

As described in chapter 2, we were initially asked to study MidWest agents to answer the question of whether the disappointing level of sales of life insurance was a motivation problem or a learning problem. We began our ethnographic study of agents with the assumption that it was probably a learning problem, since we were the Institute for Research on **Learning**, not the Institute for Research on **Motivation**. However, as we came to understand the situation better, we concluded that although there were learning issues, the root problem was in fact motivation. However, it was not motivation in the various senses described by psychologists. Nor was it motivation as understood by the management of MidWest, whose approach to motivation was the typical strategy of attempting "motivate" or "incent" sales agents with promised rewards of "pins, points and plaques," or vacation trips to desirable destinations. We argued that these ideas of motivation were too exclusively focused on motivation as personal, ignoring the entire social dimension of the nature of motivation.

Our key finding on motivation was that agents' motivation was to a large part created by imagined and actual career trajectories. Agents are motivated not only by the inner prompting of their hearts, but also by possibilities of what kind of business they want to have, what kind of business they believe they can and should have based on the example of others, and what others believe they should have. They are also motivated by how they want to be seen by others and what subcommunities of agents they wish to be members of. That is, agents' imagined career trajectories are primarily social creations: What one sees as possible, and what one is told is possible, powerfully shape what one believes it is possible to achieve, and thus one's motivation to achieve it. The importance of role models is exactly this: They show existing career trajectories one can imagine as possibilities for oneself. This analysis allowed us to expand the discussion of motivation from an understanding of motivation as something in the heart of the individual to something that the organization presents as an example of the kind of success possible, and the time course for that success. Such a model of a career details the measuring stick against which current agents measure their own progress, feel satisfied or dissatisfied, and are persuaded by or distrustful of management's attempts to change their practices.

This issue of imaginable trajectories for agents at MidWest is particularly important because MidWest as a company tends to be extremely insular in its definition of success. That is, most agents and managers compare themselves to other agents and managers at MidWest. Very few agents look outside the company to other independent insurance agents or to other small business owners for a sense of what counts as success, what is possible in the prevailing economic climate, etc. Similarly, most managers have spent most or all of their careers at MidWest and do not consider managers at other companies as a reference for what counts as success. They do not regularly come into contact with such people, and if they do meet them by chance, do not consider their careers relevant in measuring their own success.

Some of this insular inward-looking quality of MidWest arose in the 1980s and early 1990s when MidWest was in a period of growth, in contrast to recession and downsizing in the economy as a whole. One of the great problems facing upper management, the problem we were brought in to address, was how to communicate to agents the urgency of the pressure from competitors. Management saw competitive threats not only from established competitive insurance companies, but particularly from new ways of selling insurance: Internet sales, sales by companies who functioned without agents or offices, selling only through 800 numbers, sales of insurance by banks, professional associations, etc.[1] For most agents, though, these worries of management were not credible as immediate threats or as reasons for changing one's way of doing business. Their current experience did not immediately reflect the economic trends about which management was warning them. (In a study of interviews with middle managers at eight companies undergoing reorganization and downsizing, Heckscher (1995) has discussed similar discontinuities of communication between upper and middle management. He shows that although upper-level managers attempted to communicate what they saw as "the big picture" to employees at all levels of the organization, these communications were usually failures. Middle managers and line workers either did not understand them, did not see them as relevant to the work that they had to do immediately, or did not see what they could do to make a change in the predicted dire future.)

At MidWest, the experience of established agents was that MidWest Insurance had long held out a promise of a stable, attainable model for success, which had indeed been true in the 1970s, 1980s, and through the early 1990s. Agents had prospered. As one of them told us: "I've made more money than I could have imagined." Agents benefited from MidWest's policy of expansion in the past decades and from the fact that since their commissions were a percent of the price of the insurance they sold, their incomes were in fact inflation-proof. Thus, MidWest agents had been insulated from the inflation of the 1980s and the wave of corporate downsizing in the early 1990s.

However, by the late 1990s, as we concluded our fieldwork, management was beginning to challenge the entire idea that agents could continue to count on a stable career model. Concerned about competition from many sources, upper management began to fear that MidWest had permitted a habit of entitlement for agents, that agents believed that once they had built their business, they had a right to maintain insurance sales at whatever level they chose, rather than attempting to expand continuously, or to sell whatever product MidWest currently was trying to expand. They also found that their accustomed motivational practices did not work to change agents' behavior. Many agents believed that they had been recruited with a covert promise that they could work hard to build up a good business and then reap the harvest of it—"invest and then rest." From the point of view of management, too many agents had "plateaued," reached a personally acceptable level of sales and then stopped striving for further growth. This led to a situation in which management saw agents holding on to a sense of unjustified and economically dangerous entitlement in the face of strong competitive forces in the market, while agents felt that they had a justified entitlement to what they had been promised and had worked for. Hence, they resented and resisted management's new emphasis on the need for expanded life insurance sales.

After our fieldwork and analysis of this complex social construction of motivation, we needed a way to communicate to upper management the disconnection between their understanding of motivation and how to motivate agents, and what the agents were actually experiencing. We developed and made explicit the paradigmatic narrative as a way of demonstrating to management that agents were relying on a career model management had promoted for decades, a model that precluded the kind of energetic sales efforts now requested from agents at all stages in their careers. Although economic conditions had changed, and management felt that the model was no longer reliable, it had become a deep part of the beliefs and the business practices of MidWest agents. This meant that it could not be changed simply by exhortations or by fine-tuning the system of symbolic rewards.

As a tool for explaining the mismatch between managers' and agents' expectations, we drew together and presented to managers and agents our observation of the paradigmatic narrative of the typical MidWest agent. We called this "The Story of Bob." This turned out to be a surprisingly effective strategy for making explicit to managers and agents what we meant by assumptions and expectations that had become integral to the culture. For example, we used it to explain the reason for certain problems managers experienced in attempting to counsel and motivate older agents who were not selling life insurance at the level management desired. It made explicit the recognized stages of development in an agent's career and showed how this determines what any agent will see as a legitimate or illegitimate demand by management. For example, agents find it entirely appropriate for a manager to ask a first- or second-year agent to spend evenings and weekends making cold calls in order to develop new business. However, the same demand made to a fifteen-year agent, even one who is quite unsuccessful, violates the stages of the ideal career, and thus will be seen as an insult by most older agents and will be resisted strongly. We were able to use the paradigmatic narrative as a way to show management that such expectations and resistances on the part of agents were not the unjustified complaints of overpaid whiners with too strong a sense of entitlement, as many exasperated managers believed, but rather were an exact reflection of the structure of the model career for sales agents that management (and several decades of economic expansion) had built.

What kind of discourse unit is the paradigmatic narrative?

We now turn to the structural question of what kind of discourse unit the paradigmatic narrative represents. I distinguish the paradigmatic narrative from a myth or folktale, because the entire paradigmatic narrative is never told on any given occasion.[2] Rather, pieces of it are told on occasions relevant to the current situation and interests of the recipient of the narrative. Thus, a manager recruiting a possible new agent might cite the beginning part of the trajectory expressed by the paradigmatic narrative: "You'll work hard for the first seven years or so, and then you can start to reap the rewards. You can invest and then rest. Look at the kind of business Bob built. He started from scratch, worked nights and weekends, did thousands of cold calls to build up his book of business. And you've seen him now. His efforts were so successful that now he's driving a BMW, and takes every Wednesday off to play golf." Additional stages are described, in the form of narratives of the careers of others, as they become relevant for a particular individual whom the manager was attempting to mentor.

The paradigmatic narrative is also distinguished from a developmental or institutional list of stages, whether such a list forms part of a psychological theory of human development or an institutionally reified list of career stages and their requirements. The difference is that the paradigmatic narrative is expressed by the telling of stories of particular agents' careers, rather than by a theory of human development, a list of the stages of a life course, or a set of rules for retention, promotion, and tenure. Within an institution, not all careers reflect the paradigm, and so not all stories form part of the paradigmatic narrative. As Goffman (1981) has pointed out, it is the task of a narrator to justify the apparent egotism of telling a personal story by making it the story of Everyman, the story of what any reasonable person would do in similar circumstances. The paradigmatic narrative represents the work of an entire institution to create such universal relevance for particular narratives, that is, to create the story of the Career of Everyman.

As mentioned above, the paradigmatic narrative is a temporally discontinuous unit, which is never told in its entirety in a single telling. In Linde (1993) I introduced the notion of a temporally discontinuous discourse unit, specifically the life story of an individual, which is composed of a lifetime's telling of personal narratives. The paradigmatic narrative adds another dimension of discontinuity. In addition to being temporally discontinuous, composed of stories told on many occasions, it is also a narrative with discontinuous characters. Stories about different agents may be told to illustrate the various stages. Thus, an agent may learn the full paradigmatic narrative by hearing how Bob started, how Ralph decided to move to a larger office, how Tom handled problems with his staff, etc. While virtually all districts have an exemplary agent who is most frequently used as examples by managers and other agents, most districts have more than one such exemplary agent who are currently usable as the protagonist of such stories. Indeed, they must have more than one in order to be able to tell stories of agents at various career stages. Thus, the paradigmatic narrative is not only temporally discontinuous but also has a protagonist with a discontinuous identity: the ideal agent, as exemplified in different narratives about Bob, Ralph, and Tom, etc.

Now a methodological note on the nature of the unit I am describing. The usually scholarly process of discovery is to observe a phenomenon in a community being studied and then to describe it to a community of scholars, which is usually distinct from the community being studied. More recently, ethnographic studies have included checks with members of the community studied as to the accuracy of the representation. (This issue of representation, who has the right to produce representations of a given group, is a hotly contested issue in anthropology and cultural studies.) In the case of the phenomenon described here, we observed the materials that form the paradigmatic narrative and produced a representation of it first for the members of the community we were in the process of studying. We presented it to managers and agents at MidWest as a way of describing aspects of their culture that we argued formed a significant barrier to the kind of changes they were attempting to bring about. It was thus our attempt to represent in a single story a collection of stories usually told discontinuously, with different parts told on different occasions.

To draw the paradigmatic narrative together for a single telling, we personified the paradigmatic agent as "Bob," a name that matched the generic agent name usually used by MidWest: "Robert Boyd," and that also was an acronym for the frequently used term "Book Of Business," the agent's collection of clients and their insurance policies. Using materials from many stories we had heard, we constructed the paradigmatic narrative as a rhetorical device in our discussion of management's newly constructed model for how agents were to sell. We argued that this model, embodied both in management exhortations and in compensation provisions of the new contract, contradicted the expectations that agents had of how a paradigmatic career should proceed. In this unusual telling of the entire story in single meetings, we had the great advantage of presenting the story to a great many agents, managers, and executives, who were able to give us a check on the accuracy of our construction. Indeed, it was almost terrifying how quickly agents and managers recognized themselves and their associates in the paradigmatic narrative: "Oh, I was a Bob," "I wish I had a hundred guys like Bob," etc. The only objection we received was from a few upper-level managers who made the objection that "we never promised them that." This objection was always countered by their peers, who reminded them that while the company had made no legally binding contractual guarantees of such a career, in fact, the informal promise of the paradigmatic career as we described it was exactly what managers had used to recruit new agents. This recognition, and subsequent appropriation of the terms and phrases we had used, suggested to us that our construction indeed reflected the assumptions and discourse practices of MidWest Insurance.

Determining the elements of the paradigmatic narrative

I turn now to the question of how one recognizes and explicitly formulates a paradigmatic narrative. As we worked through the narratives we heard in the course of our fieldwork at MidWest, we used the questions below to determine which of these narratives formed part of the paradigmatic narrative:

Who tells it?

Is the story told only by the protagonist or by others as well? That is, is it a retold tale? If it is a retold tale, what is the status of the narrator? Narratives that are told by someone in authority, such as a manager recruiting a new agent are likely to be instances of the paradigmatic narrative. Authority may be positional, as in the case of a manager telling a story. Or it may be moral authority, as in the case of agents who are generally respected in their community of agents. A story told by someone other than its protagonist is more likely than a first-person story to have entered into the story stock of the paradigmatic narrative, especially if it is a story of success. However, not all stories in the paradigmatic narrative need be retold tales. Some are cases in which older agents or managers tell stories of their own work lives to younger agents as examples of what kind of a career is possible.

What is the narrative's intended scope of relevance?

The narrative may be told in such a way as to indicate that it recounts idiosyncratic events or that it demonstrates a general pattern. It is instances of general patterns (or what are believed within an institution to be general patterns) that form the paradigmatic narrative. Sometimes this recurrent quality is made explicit within the paradigmatic narrative: indications that "this usually happens" or "most agents have this experience at first." At other times, it is necessary to know the culture and the stories told within it to recognize the recurrence. For example, in MidWest's individual agency structure, the loss of a long-time staff member is known to be extremely disruptive for the agent. An outsider hearing a story about "then his receptionist left to get married" may not recognize a potential exemplary story about how to handle a serious problem that happens to most agents in the course of their careers.

What are the events?

The paradigmatic narrative is composed of many stories, all of which have very similar event structures. For the paradigmatic narrative of MidWest, all instances contain an effortful beginning and very hard work leading to a successful business, which allows the protagonist to relax and reap the rewards of his labor. Agents boast of having been "scratch" agents, that is, having started from scratch and built up a clientele, rather than starting by taking over a retiring agent's office or being given policies from a retiring agent's book of business. (In fact, when we probed agents' stories of starting as scratch agents, the stories would often become more complicated. Agents who said they started from scratch would often reveal that they had in fact been given some number of existing policies to start with. But they would still claim to have been "scratch" agents if that beginning book of business was not large enough for them to live on.) Part of recognizing a narrative as forming part of a paradigmatic narrative is recognizing repetitions: kinds of events that are often narrated.

What are the evaluations?

The narratives that form the paradigmatic narrative have evaluations that exemplify the core values of the institution. In the case of MidWest these are the same values exhibited in the story of the founder: hard work, honest dealing, sales skills, family relation between the agent and the company, and strong, long-term relations between agents and clients. There are events, actions, and decisions, which would be highly valued at other companies that are not valued at MidWest, such as radical innovation, extreme risk-taking, and sacrificing of one's personal life and family relations for the sake of the job. For example, stories of Silicon Valley success can include a divorce as a routine consequence of the long hours required to build a new technology business. If any such narrative were told at MidWest, it would be censured as extremely aberrant and would not form part of the paradigmatic narrative. In fact, we did hear such stories: their protagonists were described as bad examples—"not really MidWest."

What is the relation of the paradigmatic narrative to the promotion and reward structure of the organization?

The career described by the paradigmatic narrative is not created by narratives alone. Rather it is also closely tied to the honor and reward structure of MidWest. MidWest honors agents by publicly presenting them with awards at regional and national meetings, by profiling them in a monthly magazine, and by asking them to teach other agents, serve on task forces, etc. These honored agents generally have careers matching the paradigmatic narratives, and their careers are narrated at such events. Further, regional and national awards match to various stages of the paradigmatic career: early hard work and small initial achievements are recognized and rewarded at the district level by local managers; long-term career achievement is recognized and rewarded at the national level by upper managers. This reward structure of "pins, point and plaques" (described above in chapter 2) is extremely meaningful to those agents who have chosen to take the paradigmatic narrative as a yardstick for their own progress.

What are the occasions for the telling of the paradigmatic narrative?

Certain types of occasions conduce to the telling of narratives that form part of the paradigmatic narrative. Instances of the paradigmatic narrative are very likely to be heard on formal, ceremonial occasions. An important part of the reward ceremonies at conventions and meetings is a senior manager narrating the story of the agent being honored as the agent stands on stage with his wife, who is given a bouquet of flowers. Another important occasion on which they were told is during conversations about recruitment: a manager tells stories to a potential candidate to suggest what an agent's career could look like.

Paradigmatic narrative: The story of Bob

Having defined the paradigmatic narrative, I here present MidWest's paradigmatic narrative, as we presented it in a written report to agents and managers. We called this "The Story of Bob." The choice of name is deliberate: this story is definitely gendered. This narrative is a composite of narratives told directly to us, or to agents, by agents and managers. Specific details are particular to the particular stories. For example, not all agents were recruited by a manager who was a fellow church member (although many were). These details are included for aesthetic reasons: to give the flavor of what these stories sound like. It is the overall structure and stages of the story which is common to the paradigmatic narrative.

Recruitment

Bob became a MidWest agent in 1957 when he was twenty-seven. He and his wife Helen became friendly with Doug, a fellow church member, who had just moved to the community as a MidWest manager. Doug talked to Bob about the insurance business and eventually recruited him to become an agent. When Bob left his former employer, Montgomery Ward, his boss told him, "You'll starve."

One motivation for Bob's interest in becoming an insurance agent was an event that had happened many years before. When Bob was in high school, his father died of pneumonia, leaving Bob's mother and the family "behind the 8-ball." What was especially catastrophic about the event was the fact that Bob's father had canceled his two life policies just two months before he died, for economic reasons. Many years later, Bob reflected on his decision to leave retail sales: "The last one to help a bereaved person is the MidWest insurance agent."

In the fall of 1957, Bob and Helen were interviewed by MidWest. About the interview, Helen said, "MidWest interviewed both of us. They hired the both of us." In the late 1950s, MidWest was looking for a "team," and a supportive spouse (almost always a wife) proved invaluable to the success of the new agent.

Hungry agent

As Bob's manager warned him, the first years were tough. Bob worked out of a small office, with his wife as his only staff member. In the beginning, Bob "banged on doors" during the days, a strategy he says would not work now because so few women are home during the day. He also left brochures in the handles of parked cars but never on windshields because he, personally, "hates that." Bob spent five years slowly and methodically building his book of business.

After four years of this, his book of business grew to the point where he could afford to hire a full-time staff member, and his wife was able to stay home with their children. Bob began to look for a larger office in a better location, which would allow him to house a larger staff and attract more business.

At his point, MidWest attempted to recruit him into management. Bob was asked to become a manager at a time when he had proved himself to be a solid, capable agent but before he became so successful that his income would drop if he left agency for management. In Bob's case, he was approached on two occasions to leave the agency. And in both instances, Bob declined, unwilling to give up his independent status to become an employee of the company, but proud to have been asked. (For agents who do move into management, the correct way to do so is to be asked. It is considered somewhat improper for an agent to request to be considered for management. As one manager told us: "MidWest seeks all management people out. In fact if you ask to be considered for management you're kind of put on the back burner.")

Mature agent

No longer did Bob make cold calls or knock on doors. Rather, the business was feeding itself through numerous referrals and long-term clients. Also, Bob only occasionally worked on weekends. Instead, business, and people, came to Bob, and to Bob's office. He developed different, increasingly sophisticated business strategies more consistent with his notion of what it meant to be a "mature" agent. Less concerned with simply "making it financially," Bob was now motivated by other rewards: peer recognition, Top Sellers' Club, trips with friends who were also top sellers, etc. He enjoyed the prestige of being known as a top-selling agent, enjoyed showing his plaques to his clients, enjoyed the company of other top sellers, enjoyed being able to take time off to golf with fellow agents.

Senior agent

After more than twenty years as an agent, Bob slowly moved to being a senior agent. He took on additional responsibilities in the company, including mentoring young agents and teaching classes when invited by his manager. Finally, after thirty-eight years of running an agency, he retired from MidWest. Attending Bob's retirement party, hosted by MidWest, were dozens of clients that he had serviced during his years in agency. He was especially pleased that his first manager, who recruited him all those years ago, was at the event.

How is the paradigmatic narrative created and learned?

As described above, it was the research team that created this explicit formulation of the paradigmatic "Story of Bob." We took the response of agents and managers as a validation that we had correctly understood the narrative practices of MidWest. But if the paradigmatic narrative was there for us to read, who wrote it? No one person, of course. It was a joint creation, and its shape was only fully understood in retrospect. It was partly created by upper management in its contract and reward structure. The contract defined what kinds of business could be written, and what the agent would be paid for them. In particular, the "Story of Bob" began with the development of the "Full- Time Agent" concept (as described in chapter 5.) At this time, MidWest began to insist that agents work full time at insurance sales, a change from the original model of a farmer working part time as a salesman. MidWest also instituted educational requirements for agents, first high school, and later college graduation. It also instituted a more formal program of training and apprenticeship.

This professionalization of the sales agent intersected with larger economic trends: MidWest was expanding its business at a time of general growth. Furthermore, since agents' commissions were figured as a percentage of premium, they found themselves relatively immune to the effects of inflation. Thus, for twenty or thirty years, MidWest agents' careers were relatively stable, affected only minimally by the fluctuations of the larger economy. This economic trend made it possible for many agents to achieve the promised levels of success. In contrast, turnover of sales agents in other insurance companies was very high. For example, the insurance industry overall during this period showed three-year retention rates of only 25 percent (Berube 1966). (Compare the discussion in Leidner (1993) of door-to-door sales agents of a very different insurance company. This company had a five-year retention rate for sales agents of approximately 5 percent. Although the company offered trainee agents glowing promises of economic success, these promises were almost impossible for agents to achieve.)

The paradigmatic narrative presented the stages of an agent's trajectory, which were defined by the growth of his book of business. At the beginning, an agent had to pursue every possible sale, and he had to work nights and weekends to do it. At a later stage, the agent could be more selective about business opportunities and could "stop begging" for business, an achievement many agents described with pleasure. At a still later stage, the agent's business became relatively self-renewing, with customer referrals replacing business lost by clients moving, changing insurers, etc.

Because the contract did not require agents to sell specified amounts of life insurance, it was supplemented by the reward structure, which was designed to encourage life insurance sales. It offered "pins, points and plaques" for various levels of life insurance. Agents who achieved those levels would receive recognition at local, regional, and national meetings, would receive free travel to appealing destinations, and would be profiled in the company newsletter. This display of symbolic rewards made clear to all agents what kinds of activities the company valued beyond the ones it rewarded contractually.

While MidWest created contractual and reward structures to develop the ideal agent, it did not have complete control over how these structures would actually create agents' careers. Thus, to some extent, the story of Bob was also created by agents as they worked out how to develop their businesses in a changing market. When Bob started his business, there was no "Story of Bob" for him to use as a model. The agents whose careers he could look back on were mainly part-time agents, working out of their homes. (As I have already mentioned, older agents refer to this change as the time "when we moved our offices out of our dining rooms.") Since the "Full-Time Agent" concept had been put in place only a few years before Bob began to work for MidWest, Bob had few models for what his career as a full-time professional could be.

As an example of how the model changed, we can look at the changing meaning of "the supportive spouse." MidWest did not require or even expect that part of the Full- Time Agent concept would be that the agent's wife would work in the office in the early stages, and then be replaced by paid staff when the business began to prosper. The wife's support mentioned in the "Story of Bob" above was the expectation that the wife would accept her husband's long hours and low income in the early stages of building a business. Having one's wife work as staff in the office was a pattern that agents and their wives worked out in practice as they established their own businesses. However, later agents did have this example, and many other details, as part of the model, since that is what a paradigmatic narrative offers within a given institution. I would mention that spousal support was still sought in the latest round of recruiting we observed as part of the new internal recruiting program. However, by the late 1990s, the meaning of spousal support had changed yet again. Both men and women were being recruited as agents; therefore, support was required both from wives and husbands. It was assumed that both wives and husbands of prospective agents were employed, and so could not necessarily be expected to function as office staff. They were still interviewed to determine whether they understood the financial and time demands that would be made on a new agent, whether they were willing to see their spouse go for periods of training at regional centers that would take them away from home, and whether they were in favor of the venture. The details of what kinds of support were needed from a spouse were changing, but the need for a supportive spouse remained part of the new model that was under construction.

When the story does not fit

The "Story of Bob" was a powerful one, but it did not fit everyone. What happens when the model does not fit a given agent? This section describes both agents who either explicitly or in their practice rejected the model, and those agents, mainly women and minorities, for whom the model did not work. The following section discusses the possibility that institutions may be coming to the end of predictable models such as the paradigmatic narrative, as economic conditions change too quickly to allow the prediction of stable trajectories.

Agents who reject the model of the paradigmatic narrative

It was certainly not obligatory for agents to take on the "Story of Bob" as a model for their professional aspirations. Some agents chose to develop their own definitions of success. Some defined their own form of success by choosing to specialize in areas of insurance sales other than life insurance, for example, commercial insurance, which MidWest offered but did not concentrate on. These agents considered themselves small business owners and measured their success against that of other such self-employed professionals in their area, rather than participating in a model of success entirely defined by the company.

Other agents, remaining within MidWest's definitions of success, contented themselves with the substantial financial rewards and smaller symbolic rewards of selling automobile and home insurance. For example, we heard one agent compliment another who had achieved a somewhat less emphasized honor: membership in the group of agents specializing in high levels of auto insurance sales. He welcomed him to this group of agents and told him that this was a much nicer group than "those life insurance jerks." This is a clear example of an agent defining an alternate model of success.

Finally, some agents accepted in principle the company's definition of success but did not attempt to achieve it, contenting themselves with more modest efforts and modest returns than the company wished. Such agents might give lip service to their managers' exhortations that they should work harder in order to bring in a great deal more revenue than they currently achieved. However, a number of such agents told us in private that in fact their current level of revenue was sufficient for their needs, or that they could bring in as much net income for themselves by employing only one support staff person, rather than hiring the second person they would need in order to engage in a more active marketing campaign. This was a phenomenon MidWest's management considered a problem, which they described as "plateauing." Agents described as having plateaued were those who reached a level of revenue sufficient for their needs but lower than MidWest's management considered possible or desirable, and who did not choose to work harder to earn more. We note that "plateauing" is a description from the company's point of view, particularly as they contemplated a changing and more competitive market. From the agent's point of view, it could as well be called "contentment," a virtue that is virtually un-American, if not contrary to the spirit of capitalism.[3] In general, agents who had plateaued did not defend their position to management. Rather, they would listen politely to management's exhortations and then continue to do their business at their chosen level. This silence is a typical politeness strategy much in use at MidWest: silence or avoidance rather than overt criticism. But it is also part of a general difficulty, in the U.S. economy, of criticizing the discourse of the desirability of continuing growth and ever-expanding success, by saying that one has enough for one's needs. This claim is too likely to be heard as the sour grapes of a loser, rather than as the enviable position of a person satisfied with their situation.

Agents for whom the paradigmatic narrative did not work:
The case of women agents

We turn now from agents who did not choose to take on the paradigmatic narrative as their own, to those who could not take it on. In particular, the "Story of Bob" did not work for women, who began entering the agency force in significant numbers late in the 1980s. (The entry of a large number of women came as the result of the settlement of a discrimination lawsuit, which is discussed in detail in chapter 9.) The reasons the paradigmatic narrative did not work were both gendered, specific to women agents, and generic, applying to all agents at this time. I will discuss the gendered reasons here and the generic reasons in the discussion of changes in agent identity.

As already noted, much of the "Story of Bob" was actually the story of Bob and his wife. In contrast, women agents in general could not expect their spouses to serve as unpaid or minimally paid staff in the early years of establishing their business, as male agents routinely did. Women agents were less likely to find trips to golf resorts a reward. The older generation of male agents with wives who either worked in the agency office or who did not work outside the home, were more likely to make their social life within MidWest. Both such agents and their wives tended to have as their friends other agents and their wives. These social connections made company-sponsored sales conventions and trips appealing to both husband and wife, since they were an opportunity to travel with one's friends. Women agents with working spouses were much less likely to construct their social lives within MidWest. In addition, changes in the economic climate affected both male and female new agents. Most agents now have working spouses, which means that arranging vacations around the schedule of sales trips is more difficult and perhaps less appealing than it once was. All of these factors lead to the erosion of the appeal of the sales convention as a reward for top-selling agents. And yet this reward system was a primary way in which the paradigmatic narrative was embodied and administered.

In general, the "Story of Bob" does not work for women agents, and yet there is no official story of Roberta. But although an official woman's version of the paradigmatic narrative did not exist at the time we did our fieldwork, as we talked to women agents, we found three recognizable career trajectories and identities, based on how the women agents had entered the company. One was the woman agent who "came to it by blood," that is, whose father had been an agent. These women had worked in their father's offices, were familiar with MidWest, and moved to become agents as soon as MidWest began actively recruiting women. Such women were most likely to reproduce male models of the relation between agent and staff members and were also most likely to be deeply embedded in the culture of MidWest. The second trajectory was that of women who had worked as a staff member in an agent's office and who was encouraged by the agent or by a manager to apply for a position as an agent when these positions opened up to women. These women were more likely to develop a relatively egalitarian relation with their staff members, rather than reproducing the model of the offices that they had worked in. The third was a woman "from the outside," that is, someone who had had a previous career and came to MidWest for the entrepreneurial opportunity to own her own business. These women were the most likely to look outside MidWest for models of success, since they already had seen other models, had friends and business contacts in other industries, etc. Each type of entry point led to a different way of conducting business, a different identity, and a different type of relation to MidWest. Yet these three trajectories are *not* paradigmatic narratives because they are not recognized or used as such within the company.

We discovered that these trajectories are not paradigmatic narratives by the ways in which they were received by agents and managers at MidWest. When we presented the "Story of Bob" at meetings, the women present immediately asked: "What about Roberta?" We then offered them accounts of these three trajectories, calling them the stories of Roberta, Bobbi, and Francine. When we presented them, women agents greeted them with surprised recognition: "I'm a Roberta!" "I'm definitely a Bobbi." Again, this provided a check for us that we had identified actual patterns of experience for women agents. However, these patterns were **not** part of paradigmatic narratives, since they were not known, narrated, or incorporated into the reward structure of MidWest. The women who recognized their own stories in our accounts had not known that their experience formed part of a larger pattern, that there were other patterns based on other entry points, or that different entry points led to different trajectories and professional identities. The men present did not recognize any of the three patterns. Thus, the women's individual narratives remained solely personal: they were not publicly available or understood as models for other women to use. This is a clear example of the difference between a narrative that functions as a part of the paradigmatic narrative and one that is understood as purely individual, even if statistically it represents an instance of a larger class of narratives.

Agents for whom the paradigmatic narrative did not work: The case of minority agents

The "Story of Bob" also did not work for many minority agents, most of whom were recruited at the same time as the women agents. Most obviously, the visual representations of the ideal agent in brochures, television advertising, etc., and the living examples pointed to down the street or on the stage at conventions were older white males, since they were the ones who had the time in the company to achieve the kind of stable success that the paradigmatic narrative was intended to exemplify. This was a problem that minority agents had pointed out to management, and that management was attempting to remedy.

However, the defining factor for whether the paradigmatic narrative could work for minority agents was the kind of neighborhood in which their agency was located. Minority agents in prosperous areas had to deal with the problems of visual representation in MidWest materials, that is, a predominance of white male agents in graphic materials from MidWest. And of course, they had to deal with whatever racism they might meet from prospective clients. But because of their location, the economics of their business was not markedly different from that of white agents.

However, frequently minority agents were placed in inner-city areas. (New agents opening their first office were given a particular geographical area for their new office or were assigned to the existing office of a retiring agent. There was some effort to match the agent's ethnicity and language skills to that of the area, although this was not an official policy.) Agents in inner-city offices found that the economic conditions in their area, and the kinds of demands placed on them by their communities, precluded writing the kinds of business that would allow them to achieve Bob-hood. The obvious problem was that potential clients in their neighborhoods had less money to spend on insurance. But there was also the more subtle problem that agents in inner-city areas had more difficult and complex problems of time management than agents in prosperous areas. For example, agents in inner-city areas found that they had to spend a great deal of time doing much more extensive house inspections before agreeing to write home insurance, since the housing stock in the inner city was older and less well-maintained than that in suburban areas. This meant that they were able to insure a smaller percentage of the houses they inspected than was the case for suburban agents. It also meant that they had less time to spend on the more time-consuming life insurance sales. (This issue of differing time demands on agents in inner-city areas was one MidWest found extremely problematic and had not found an answer for.) Similarly, when inner-city agents did write life insurance, it was usually for much smaller amounts than those written by agents in more prosperous areas: insurance that clients intended for use in covering funeral expenses, rather than large policies to pay off mortgages and cover children's college expenses. Even writing a large number of such policies might not bring the agent to the dollar amount required to be eligible for life insurance sales awards. Finally, a number of the minority agents we studied took on a great deal of community work, both formally in outreach and education programs, and informally in providing extensive financial advice for financially unsophisticated clients. This kind of work also took time away from the sales efforts necessary to achieve the paradigmatic career. MidWest supported community outreach work for all agents, and most agents did participate in quite a lot of this kind of activity. The difference for minority agents was that often community groups, as well as their own clients, explicitly requested their participation in this kind of activity. In contrast, for the older group of white male agents, it was their own choice as to how much time to spend coaching Little League, attending Rotary Club meetings, etc.

What happens when the career model no longer applies?

In the previous section, I described a situation in which the paradigmatic narrative is not appropriate for certain groups within MidWest. Initially, it might appear that the correct response to this problem would be for MidWest to develop multiple narratives with different heroes: that is, add to the "Story of Bob" the "Story of Roberta," the "Story of Roberto," etc. This model had an initial appeal to MidWest's management because it would represent no fundamental change, but rather an incremental growth in existing practices. However, as they considered this proposal, they found that it had two related problems: problems with the model itself, and more broadly, problems with the very possibility of proposing a stable model for success.

The first problem was that the "Story of Bob" was no longer appropriate or probable even for the white males for whom it had been developed. For many reasons, it is a story of the past, which management believed would not work unchanged in the future. First, MidWest believed that the kind of agent it produced would not be able to succeed in the current and coming markets, which are becoming increasingly competitive and unstable. To counter increasing competition in the insurance market, MidWest was considering offering expanded financial services, such as investment products like variable life insurance (in which customers determine how their premiums are to be invested), Individual Retirement Accounts and annuities, and banking products, such as mortgages and credit cards. In order to sell such products, agents would have to engage in much more professional training, including classes to obtain new licenses, and would have to expect that they would be involved in continuous learning of new types of products and new types of business practice to support them. The "Story of Bob" was not a model of continuous learning. Bob learned to be a salesman and to run his business. He might at times take refresher courses in sales skills or learn about a new product MidWest had added, but the ability to continue to learn was not part of the presentation of Bob's virtues. The model of Bob is also not a model of a financially sophisticated risk manager and advisor: Bob knew the basics of the business, and was a trustworthy, stable and friendly advisor on matters of insurance, but not an overall financial expert. The move from insurance advisor to risk advisor or investment advisor would require a major change both in knowledge and skills, and in beliefs about risk, prudence, etc. In addition to these specific problems with the "Story of Bob," MidWest faced the issue of whether a paradigmatic narrative, or a family of them, would be possible at all in the future they predicted. The use of paradigmatic narratives to define a career course presupposes a relatively stable situation, one in which stories about past careers can be used to model future ones. However, at present, the entire notion of a predictable model for a successful career is being called into question. This doubt about the possibility of stable careers is an issue not only at MidWest but in the entire U.S. economic market.

Both during the time of the fieldwork, and even more at the time of writing, there has been considerable discussion in the general business discourse about the erosion of the possibilities of careers that are stable and predictable enough to use as models for the future. This discourse predicts a vision of a stable past, in which one could know what the career ladder was within a given corporation, where one stood on it, and what one's chances were of rising. The assumption is that at one time (a posited Golden Age), most people (that is, middle-class white men) worked for a single corporation for their entire careers, and that a successful career consisted of rising within that corporation. While this is widely believed, in fact, it may be true only for a single generation: the post–World War II generation. For example, Cappelli (1999) argues that the labor relations of nineteenth- and early twentieth-century businesses were closer to the current model of outsourced and contractor labor than to the stable corporate model of the 1950s through the early 1980s.

Whatever the historical truth about the stable past may be, the more recent business discourse claims that the predictable career ladder or the paradigmatic career is over. Because of changes in the workplace, including downsizing, continuous mergers and reorganizations, and the rise of whole new industries, to stay afloat in this ocean of change, one must constantly reinvent oneself. Slogans that encapsulate this view, current at the time of the research, include: "You Are Your Projects" and "Free Agent Nation." Some examples of this discourse follow, both taken from the magazine *Fast Company*, which provides an optimistic, Silicon Valley-centered view of the current landscape of work.

Pink (1997) provides a description of the new rules underlying the world of the work with the worker as free agent, rather than employee:

> The old social contract didn't have a clause for introspection. It was much simpler than that. You gave loyalty. You got security. But now that the old contract has been repealed, people are examining both its basic terms and its implicit conditions.
>
> Free agents quickly realized that in the traditional world, they were silently accepting an architecture of work customs and social mores that should have crumbled long ago under the weight of its own absurdity. From infighting and office politics to bosses pitting employees against one another to colleagues who don't pull their weight, most workplaces are a study in dysfunction. Most people do want to work; they don't want to put up with brain-dead distractions. Much of what happens inside companies turns out to be about...nothing. The American workplace has become a coast-to-coast "Seinfeld" episode. It's about nothing. But work, free agents say, has to be about something. And so, instead of accepting the old terms, they're demanding new ones. Thus the second rule of the road for navigating Free Agent, USA: work is personal. You can achieve a beautiful synchronicity between who you are and what you do.

Peters (1997) makes a similar argument about the need for workers to reinvent themselves as brandable commodities, immediately responsive to market forces, rather than as members of a relatively stable and predictable organization that could serve as the structure within which a career could be planned:

> It's over. No more vertical. No more ladder. That's not the way careers work anymore. Linearity is out A career is now a checkerboard. Or even a maze. It's full of moves that go sideways, forward, slide on the diagonal, even go backward when that makes sense. (It often does.) A career is a portfolio of projects that teach you new skills, gain you new expertise, develop new capabilities, grow your colleague set, and constantly reinvent you as a brand.... Instead of making yourself a slave

to the concept of career ladder, reinvent yourself on a semiregular basis. . . . It's this simple: You are a brand. You are in charge of your brand. There is no single path to success. And there is no one right way to create the brand called You. Except this: Start today. Or else. (94)

This discourse had not gone without criticism. For example, in a special edition of the *New York Times Magazine* (2000) section on "The Way We Work Now," a variety of articles presented the disadvantages to workers of actual free agent work, or of continuously moving from job to job (Munk 2000). It argues that the real winners in this revolution in how workers relate to their employers, besides the advice-givers, are the employers themselves:

> The other big winners are companies in the market for what economists call a flexible work force, which is to say, workers who can be hired and fired over-night, in the blink of an eye. Workers who answer 4-plus incoming lines and to whom you have no obligation whatsoever. Workers who are here today, gone tomorrow.
>
> FreeAgent.com [a Web-based registry for contract workers] knows the score. Its web site includes a page that encourages employers to hire its eager temps. "Top 10 Reasons Why Managers Love Free Agents" is how it begins. And then FreeAgent. com shows its hand:

> 10. They don't need pep talks.
> 9. They don't gripe about their salary.
> 8. They won't stab you in the back.
> 7. They tell you when your ideas [expletive].
> 6. When they're sick, they work from home.
> 5. They don't ask for health insurance, paid vacations, personal days...
> 4. ...401(k) plans, stock options, quarterly bonuses
> 3. NO PERFORMANCE REVIEWS.
> 2. If they're stupid, lazy or incompetent, you can fire them pretty easily.
> 1. They do all the work, you take all the credit. (50–54.)

More recent discussions of the growth of the contingent labor force also include the issue of offshoring. Offshoring is the movement of a business process formerly done at a local company to a foreign country. It was not being discussed at MidWest during the period of our fieldwork. The nature of the insurance business might make it possible for MidWest to offshore the processing of applications and claims but not the sale of insurance, since MidWest considered its competitive advantage to be the face-to-face interaction between customer and agent.

Similarly, within the academic labor market, there are discussions about the erosion of the traditional professor's career track. This includes attempts to limit or eliminate tenure, the increasing reliance on a contingent labor force of adjunct teachers, the growing threat to the traditional university from Internet-based virtual university systems, etc. Both sides of this debate are represented: those who say that new academic arrangements represent an opportunity for university administrations to reduce both the salaries and the influence of professors and those who argue that moving a more contingent academic labor force is a benefit to the cause of education because it allows for the elimination of tenured deadwood. See, for example, Feenberg (1999).

The discourse cited above attempts to give the viewpoint of the worker: whether or not such arrangements are advantageous or not, how to surf the waves of change, how to succeed as an independent agent. There is also the question of how the employer represents this new relation to potential employees. In general, employers increasingly cannot, or will not, promise lifelong employment or job security, since they cannot make long-term predictions about how many employees they will need or what skills those employees must have. However, employers do not wish to describe their employment relation as purely market-driven, since this description provides no incentive for employees to remain when needed, rather than taking advantage of a tight labor market to find the best employment opportunities. As Cappelli (1999) notes, once the bond of loyalty is broken, problems arise on both sides. Employees suffer from downsizing in a slack labor market; employers suffer from excessive turnover in a tight labor market. Many employers have tried to develop a new implicit contract for employees that does not promise lifelong employment, but which tries to offer something more than a purely market-driven relation. According to Cappelli (1999) these deals include the following points:

> At least an implicit acknowledgement that the employer can not longer offer job security. Not even career security; a long-term relation in which jobs might change, can be guaranteed. The most honest of the contracts go further and offer the obvious caveat emptor: Because we cannot guarantee your future, you have to start taking charge of it yourself.
>
> The most important thing the company needs from you is your skills. But the company can no longer be responsible for identifying and developing those skills. You, the employee have to take on that responsibility. Some of the deals go on to argue that the company also expects employees to follow the values of the organization, to embrace them as long as they are in the company's employ.
>
> In return, the company offers several things. Implicit is that it will try to keep employees with the company as long as the economic environment makes that possible. Virtually all of the deals go on to say that the company will also provide employers with the means and opportunity to develop their skills in ways that will help ensure that they can have career advancement, even if it takes them away from their current employer. Many of the deals add that the company will offer the employees more challenging and exciting work than they have had in the past and reward them for good performance. (27–28)

The Apple Computer "Apple Deal" is one of the earliest versions of this attempt to make this new employment relation both explicit and appealing. It gives a good flavor of what this discourse sounds like in Silicon Valley, as well as a relatively unusual effort to make it explicit:

> Here's the deal Apple will give you; here's what we want from you. We're going to give you a really neat trip while you're here. We're going to teach you stuff you couldn't learn anywhere else. In return...we expect you to work like hell, buy the vision as long as you're here.... We're not interested in employing you for a lifetime,

but that's not the way we are thinking about this. It's a good opportunity for both of us that is probably finite. (Etorre 1994)

During our study, Midwest was not contemplating an end to their belief in a long-term relation between the company and both employees and independent contractor sales agents. However, in response to competitive pressures, management was beginning to introduce into their training programs elements of this discourse of continuous change and continuous effort already prevalent in the wider economy. There was, in fact, an attempt by management to convince agents that the future was more uncertain than the agents believed (although it probably held continuing opportunities). Because of this uncertainty, agents should not be working in expectation of a point at which they could relax their efforts and reap their rewards, since individual agency offices might never again develop into this mature stage.

This line of argument was strongly resisted by established agents, since from their point of view, there was no inspiration in the message, but only an exhortation that they would have to work harder in order to stay where they already were. I would note that resistance in this case took the form of ignoring unwanted messages, rather than an explicit critique of management's account of the future. Since the contract with agents did not provide for penalties for lack of new sales, managers could only exhort, and agents could ignore these exhortations. When we asked agents directly what they thought of some of these speeches explaining competitive market pressures and requesting greater sales efforts, their responses usually boiled down to "It was sort of boring. I've heard that stuff before." As I have already mentioned, this is a typically polite form of criticism within MidWest we heard many times in many contexts: unwanted messages are not criticized in detail but rejected overall as boring or repetitive.

However, the trainee agents and newly appointed agents did not have stable books of business that would allow them to ignore management's concerns about the pace of future change. Many of them were beginning to adopt management's message of constant change. They did this, often quite explicitly, as a way of showing their alignment with management and with the company's current direction.

There is a serious question though, about whether such rapid and continuous changes mean that it will no longer be possible to construct a new, more appropriate narrative identity. That is, will twenty-first-century Bob and Roberta need a postmodern rather than a modern self, fragmented and shifting, rather than a self organized around a predictable narrative trajectory. What could that look like? This is a real issue for MidWest. Let the reader try to imagine a shifting, indeterminate, postmodern insurance company. Buying insurance is still primarily buying a promise from an insurer: the client pays money for automobile, homeowners, or life insurance on the assumption that in the case of accident, disaster, or death, the insurance company will pay what it contracted to pay. Can the postmodern self or the postmodern insurance company be trusted to pay off on such a promise? Will it still be there to do so?[4]

It might be argued that the company could offer a model of a postmodern, fluid self to its agents, while continuing to present a public face to its customers of old-fashioned, dependable solidity, a double loop of the postmodern self. This would appear to be quite difficult for the agents to maintain. Strauss (1997), however, argues from interviews that people are in fact able to maintain a presentation of self that is partially integrated, a modern self, and partially fragmented, a postmodern self. The problem with deploying such a strategy at MidWest would be that the company's public face must be presented primarily by agents (although MidWest has some control of the presentation of its image to the public through its advertising.) Because of the major role MidWest gives to its sales agents in representing the company, MidWest management has implicitly taken the position that the agents' experience must match the desired experience of their customers. That is, if the agents cannot trust MidWest's promises to themselves, they cannot sell MidWest's promises to customers. This parallelism between the experience of the agents and the customers has led MidWest to some decisions, which from the standpoint of revenue alone, might appear to be misguided or incorrect.

The clearest example we observed of the company's effort to maintain its promises to the agents came in the offering of a new contract to sales agents. The old contract did not specifically reward agents who achieved high levels of life sales, and it did not require sales of specified products or penalize agents for writing insurance policies that proved unprofitable for MidWest (for example, writing insurance on badly maintained houses or cars). The new contract was much more stringent in specifying rewards for sales of desired types of insurance and penalties for writing unprofitable business. However, while beginning agents were offered only the new contract, current agents were offered a choice between signing the new contract and remaining with the old contract they had signed earlier. MidWest encouraged them to work out for themselves, in consultation with their managers, which option would be most advantageous for them. (The complexity of the contract made this a different situation for each existing agent, depending on amount of time till retirement, exact composition of the agent's book of business, company restrictions on writing home insurance in that agent's area, etc.) MidWest was not legally obliged to offer agents this choice; they could have made the new contract a requirement: take it, or leave the company. While agents were offered incentives for signing the new contract, they were free to remain with the old one. Agents would have interpreted a requirement to take the new contract as a violation of the promises MidWest had made to them. In our analysis, MidWest decided that agents who felt betrayed in this way would not be able or willing to present MidWest as a trustworthy insurer. There is thus a parallel between the relation to the company that MidWest builds for the agent and the relation to the company that an agent builds for the client.[5] If this is the case, it provides strong implicit restrictions on just how fluid an identity the company can support for its agents, if it wishes to retain its traditional corporate identity of solidity and trustworthiness for the public.

By the end of our fieldwork in 1998, we saw a major change happening in the development of agent identity, driven by new forms of recruitment and training. As discussed above, the previous system for recruitment and training was personalistic, done mainly by a manager who identified promising candidates, recruited them into MidWest, and mentored them as new agents. For the last three years of our fieldwork, new agents were recruited from existing employees of MidWest and trained through a specified curriculum of classroom and field experiences. The new system is considerably more bureaucratic than the old one, relying much more on standard curricula and criteria and much less on personal relationships, although there is some attempt to bring exemplary agents in to the classroom to discuss their experience.

What we observed of this system in its early stages is that the new agents it produces are developing an identity but not yet a narrative trajectory. There is, at least as yet, no new story, since agents of the new model have not been in business long enough to develop one. And yet, there is a growing identity based on comparison: the new agents are **not** Bob. Some of our observations suggest that one axis for this distinction is a contrast of "the old and the new" agent. This is an attempt by MidWest managers and trainers to keep new agents from developing attitudes and practices of entitlement MidWest management feels are no longer effective either for agents or the company as a whole, and that are not possible for new agents given the current economic climate for MidWest. At the same time, management must not lose the loyalty of the many agents of the older model, who still are likely to remain for many years and who must not be insulted by criticisms of the older model. Thus, in a discussion of old and new agents, we heard a trainer admonish trainee agents that they should still respect the older agents because they "saved the company" several decades ago by responding to a request to write an extraordinary amount of new business, when incorrect underwriting had led to a financial crisis. (This is a story that forms an important part of the company's history. It was told by someone not born when these events had taken place. See chapter 5 for a fuller discussion.) Similarly, we saw a stress on distinguishing between good and bad agents of whatever tenure with the company. We never heard managers or trainers explicitly distinguishing between an older generation of lazy agents and a new generation of virtuous go-getters. But to some extent this comparison was implicit in their critique, since some of the practices being censured were only possible for agents who had been in business long enough to build a self-sustaining book of business that would allow an agent to put little or no effort in attempting to bring in new business. The implicit contrast was made by trainers' discussion of agents with a "good attitude" or a "bad attitude," those who do or do not "do the work." We also heard the terms "slug," "pond scum," "men of extinction," and "flat-liners," referring to agents who sell no life insurance, and the pair "squeakers and sleepers" referring to complainers and to older agents who have "checked out" of the effort of making new sales. All of these describe ways of being that are presented to trainees as models to be avoided.

While vividly named, these are traits, not stories. They appear to support the possibility that MidWest, like much of the U.S. economy, is moving into a period when a paradigmatic narrative about a lifelong career within a single company is not possible, because conditions are expected to change too fast to predict a career trajectory. This is a conceptual problem for U.S. business in general. It is part of the current general belief about occupational futures that the lifelong career with a single company is no longer possible and that the average worker will have seven different careers in a lifetime—a suspiciously magic number, but one which reflects a belief about the rate of change in the economy. (See, for example, Pink (1997); Wallulis (1998).) As described above, current business rhetoric is just beginning to sketch a paradigmatic narrative for the discontinuous and unpredictable career of the worker as free agent. And while there is an attempt to make this prospect appear exciting and full of potential, there are many criticisms of it as a way for corporations to expand the contingent labor force, shifting economic risk from businesses to individuals. (Bishop and Suchman (2000) discuss more fully the economic issues involved.)

MidWest too at the time of our fieldwork was just beginning to develop a rhetoric about identity in the face of change. Although Bob's career is no longer possible, there is still a promise that the opportunities for agents are still great. A version of this, developed by local recruiters but not yet adopted by MidWest as a whole, is that a career as an employee or an agent at MidWest is promising because MidWest is so large, with so many functions and departments, that you can make your own trajectory, although you now have to take that responsibility yourself, rather than relying on traditional structures, management, or mentors to create your career for you. The great appeal of a job at MidWest in the new economy is not the independence promised by owning an agency, or the traditional stability promised to an employee of such a stable company, but rather the possibility of doing so many different jobs, learning so many different skills, which makes one more employable whether within MidWest or outside it. This is very much the anthem of the Free Agent Nation, transposed into the key of MidWest.

Conclusion

This discussion of the paradigmatic narrative at MidWest has been an attempt to show a particular kind of exemplary narrative. Rather than presenting the narrative of a founder or an extraordinary hero as a model for emulation, the paradigmatic narrative provides a way for a person of admirable but not extraordinary achievement to have their story be told as part of a model of how to act within an institution. When someone's story is told in a way that is presented as recognizably exemplary, it offers an account of success that is not unusual or heroic, but rather a model for emulation because it is demonstrably possible to the ordinarily competent member. It is also a way of linking smaller communities within a larger organization together with that organization. That is, MidWest as a whole supports the paradigmatic narrative, and profiles examples of agents from everywhere in the company in its newsletter and at awards ceremonies. But within the smallest unit of organization, the district, managers and agents profile and narrate the story of exemplary agents who are known to their peers, and who are visibly present for emulation. Thus, the model career is seen exemplified locally, making it appear more seductively possible, though also more of a personal failure for the agent who buys into the story but fails to achieve it.

As I have already discussed, I am certain that the paradigmatic narrative is not a social phenomenon restricted to MidWest. Traweek's description of narratives of physicists shows a similar use of narrative for the socialization of young members. Further research should show additional examples of this phenomenon in other institutional contexts, professional and otherwise. In particular, it would be extremely valuable to have enough studies available that it would be possible to draw comparisons between the paradigmatic narratives of differing types of institutions.

Narrative and Intertextuality

Telling One's Own Story within a Textual Community

$\mathbf{P}$revious chapters have illustrated various forms of narrative used within MidWest to work its past. This chapter moves from the retold stories about MidWest's founder and history, and the paradigmatic story of the ideal life course of a MidWest agent, to an investigation of the relations between these canonical stories and the ways in which agents shape their own stories. To show these relations, I will first describe the theoretical notions of intertextuality, textual communities, and induction into textual communities. Then, I will describe the various intertextual relations that hold between agents' and managers' stories and the stories of the company maintained by the textual community.

Intertextuality and textual communities

Let us begin by introducing some of the theoretical apparatus needed to understand the phenomenon of how someone tells their own story within a field of prior texts produced and maintained as important by their community. To do this, I will rely on two key ideas from the field of literary studies: intertextuality and textual communities. I will then discuss the limits on the notion of textual community and the processes by which someone becomes a member of a textual community.

There have been few, if any, studies of the relations between oral stories within linguistics. Within the field of sociology, Conversation Analysis has investigated the relation between immediately adjacent stories in a single conversation: the ways in which speakers use a second or subsequent story to construct their comments, agreement, or disagreement with what a speaker attempted to do with an immediately prior story. However, these studies do not extend to the relation between stories located in different interactions. In contrast, the data of this study provides a complex example and permits the study of intertextual relations between oral, written, and filmed narratives, over a period of more than seventy years.

Intertextuality

Intertextuality is a concept that allows us to investigate the relation of a story to a prior story, particularly a culturally privileged story. Intertextuality has mainly been discussed in terms of the types of relations that can exist between written literary texts. A more recent term, "interdiscursivity," discusses the relations between oral texts separated in time, or the ways in which a given oral discourse may use stylistic features of some other genre or form of discourse, for example, a speaker in a story using a sentence or even a single word that recalls political speeches, sermons, etc. (Fairclough 1992). In this discussion, I choose to use "intertextuality" rather than "interdiscursivity" as an analytic tool, since the term is more suited for the analysis of relations between specific texts in various media, across time.

The term "intertextuality," first introduced by Kristeva (1984), is used in a variety of fields, but its home discipline is literary studies. Within literary studies there are two views of the important relations between texts. The first, older tradition focuses on a particular text and searches for the prior sources and influences which work to shape that text. Thus, for example, someone studying Spenser's *Faerie Queene* might trace its sources back to Ariosto's *Orlando Furioso* and Boiardo's *Orlando Innamorato*, from there back through medieval romances to the *Chanson de Roland*, and then back to Vergil's *Aeneid* and ultimately to Homer's *Iliad*. In this genealogical view, a text is seen as having various forms of conversational relations with earlier texts of its genre: response, continuation, homage, critique, parody, pastiche, etc. What unites the texts of a genre is a community of readers and writers having a shared concept of what the elements of the genre are and a shared agreement on the constitution of the canon of valued prior texts.

In more recent arguments about intertextuality, the focus has shifted from tracing chains of influence between specific texts to a concern about the necessarily intertextual nature of any text, whether or not it explicitly responds to any prior text. This line of thought, tracing from Saussure, Bakhtin, and a group of French theorists, including Kristeva, Derrida, and Foucault, focuses on the ways in which no text can ever be individual or univocal: that is, the impossibility of complete originality or absence of influence by prior texts. Any use of language necessarily invokes and depends upon prior uses of language. While this is true both of spoken and written language, the issue becomes particularly acute for literary texts, because the ideology of Western literature since the Romantic period assumes a strong and primary value for originality. Yet, this view of intertextuality argues that no author can ever be wholly original.

> Texts, whether they be literary or non–literary, are viewed by modern theorists as lacking in any kind of independent meaning. They are what theorists now call intertextual. The act of reading, theorists claim, plunges us into a network of textual

relations. To interpret a text, to discover its meaning, or meanings, is to trace these relations. Reading thus becomes a process of moving between texts. Meaning becomes something which exists between a text and all the other texts to which it refers and relates, moving out from the independent text into a network of textual relations. The text becomes the intertext.

Intertextuality is one of the most commonly used and misused terms in contemporary critical vocabulary. 'An Intertextual Study of...' or 'Intertextuality and...' are such commonplace constructions in the titles of critical works that one might be forgiven for assuming that intertextuality is a term that is generally understood and provides a stable set of critical procedures for interpretation. Nothing, in fact, could be further from the truth. The term is defined so variously that it is, currently, akin to such terms as 'the Imagination,' 'history,' or 'Postmodernism': terms which are, to employ a phrase from the work of the U.S. critic Harold Bloom, underdetermined in meaning and overdetermined in figuration. Intertextuality, one of the central ideas in contemporary literary theory, is not a transparent term and so, despite its confident utilization of by many theorists and critics, cannot be evoked in an uncomplicated manner. (Allen 2000, 1–2)

The current chapter uses the notion of intertextuality primarily in the sense of the first and older approach, focusing on the study of the prior sources and influences that work to shape a current text and the shared assumptions over time of what constitutes a text of that genre. Thus, in the case discussed in this chapter, agents' and managers' tellings of their own stories represent the current texts; the various versions of the telling of the story of the founder and the history of MidWest, and the paradigmatic narrative of the ideal agent's career (discussed in chapters 5, 6, and 7) form the valued prior texts. As I have mentioned, these prior texts themselves, of course, have yet earlier prior texts of their own, as well as related texts, and competing texts in the wider world of U.S. business discourse. However, this investigation will be concerned less with extending the search for possible other prior and related texts further back into the past than with the question of social processes by which these relations between texts are established. That is, the focus will be on the ways in which speakers take on these prior texts as relevant to their own story and the possible ways in which they can position their own story in relation to it.

There is an important distinction necessary to make here about the relation of the prior text to a current teller's story. I am not claiming that each agent or manager telling their story has the founder's biography directly in mind at the moment of telling, although they all will have heard his story as part of their training. Rather, they are telling their stories in an environment strongly shaped by the founder's story and by other stories that refer back to the founder's story. Such a discourse environment shapes what can be easily formulated as a recognizable story and what can be understood as an appropriate story for a member to tell.

Textual communities

The notion of intertextuality, as described above, discusses relations between texts, but it does not touch on the social relations between people and institutions that create and support these textual relations. From the point of view of an analyst, any two texts can be picked out and compared, even if the analyst is the first person in history who has ever read or heard both texts. But from the point of view of someone producing a story, only certain texts are known and available as plausible as prior texts. The decision about which texts are available to be treated as prior texts is not made by the narrator alone. Rather, it is the work of a community that determines what prior texts are maintained so as to be available and relevant for a current narrator.

The relation between a community and a field of related texts has been discussed as part of the definition of the notion of "textual community." The term is taken from Stock (1983), who uses it in his study of medieval literacy to describe groups of people (often religious groups considered to be heretical by the wider society) whose religious activities are centered around particular religious texts, and often around a particular literate interpreter of those texts.

The term "textual community" has also been used in a broader sense to describe the entire readership, over time, of a particular text or group of texts. See, for example, Riddy (1991), who uses it to describe "the community of people who read the same text [in this case, Arthurian histories and romances composed in England, whether in Latin, English, or French] who are brought together simply by the act of reading (or hearing); a community which the text itself creates insofar as it seeks an audience" (315).

I would argue that this sense of the term is too broad to be useful for the purpose of the current analysis. I would use the term "community" only to describe a group of people who know themselves to be a community by virtue of activities they know that they share. Thus, I would not call the all the viewers or readers of *Star Trek* television shows, movies, and novels a textual community, since any given person may not know any other reader of these novels or viewer of these shows, nor may they know that another person of their acquaintance is involved with these texts. However, the term "textual community" is entirely appropriate to describe those people who are members of *Star Trek* fan clubs, attend *Star Trek* conventions, participate in face-to-face or online discussion groups, write for fan magazines or Web sites, or engage in other social activities and relations constituted by mutual appreciation of *Star Trek* texts. It is also necessary to establish a distinction between a strong and weak sense of textual community. A strong textual community is one primarily constituted around a particular text or set of texts. For example, the heterodox religious communities described by Stock are textual communities in the strong sense: they define themselves as communities by their allegiance to new religious texts or to new interpretations of familiar biblical texts.

Even in this strong sense, no community in the present is purely textual. If people relate with one another at all, there will always be rituals, food, holidays, etc., which the members share, in addition to their allegiance to a particular text and their particular way of interpreting that text. Diachronically, across time, it may appear that there are communities that are purely textual: for example, the community of readers constituted by their appreciation of texts in a literary canon. But even here, there are the social processes that determine how such a canon is constituted, how a person comes to know of the existence of a literary canon, and comes to believe that reading these texts is relevant or valuable. That is, one might read and appreciate *Hamlet* in solitude and know no other person who also appreciates the play. But to make this solitary appreciation possible, there were people who identified *Hamlet* as a valued text, edited its editions, published affordable editions, staged the play, and made movie versions of it available. Further, there is the social question of what sort of person one shows oneself to be by knowing or not knowing *Hamlet*, or any other highly valued text in a literary canon. Thus, even a strongly textual community involves social processes beyond a solitary person's involvement with a text alone.

In the weaker sense, a textual community is a group formed around interests, principles, and practices other than a valued text, but such a community does maintain a set of valued texts and practices for inducting new members into a knowledge of those texts. In this sense, MidWest Insurance is a textual community. As an institution, it has a legal existence, contractual obligations, financial reserves, buildings, reified institutional roles, as well as less formal practices, rituals, relationships etc. However, it does also function as a textual community, organized around the story of the founder and the paradigmatic stories of the ideal agent (as discussed in previous chapters.) Part of becoming a member of such a community means learning to tell one's story as part of an ongoing textual community.

Induction into a textual community

How does someone become a member of a textual community? For many such communities, particularly textual communities in the weak sense, membership comes by birth and by the usual processes of socialization into a culture. Thus, the strongest textual community for many people is a religious community, and their membership develops through their training in their family and their family's religious activities, as well as the educational programs that the particular religious group maintains for children. However, the textual community of MidWest mainly takes in its new members as adults. (This does not include the processes of induction for new members whose families were members of MidWest; for them the process of induction is much more like that of being born into a particular religion.) It should also be noted that from the new agents' point of view, they are not trying to become a member of a textual community, they are trying to attain the legal and commercial status of agent. Agha (2005) makes this point quite effectively in a discussion of the relation between learning of particular forms of language use and developing one's professional role:

> Like the notion of footing, the notion of role alignment does not seek to explain self-descriptions. Take the case of legal register. I argued earlier that the law school classroom is an institutionalized site of socialization to legal register. This suggests that students who acquire the register are performing a kind of role alignment with the characterological figures of legal register.
>
> Such an account is, of course, wildly at odds with any self-description that a law student might volunteer as an account of conscious, strategic choices. Thus a person may consciously intend to go to law school to acquire wealth and power, to serve civil rights causes, or for some other reason; he or she may never attend focally to questions of register acquisition. Yet the capacity of a lawyer to acquire wealth and power (or to serve civil rights causes, or to pursue whatever ends he or she has in learning the law) nonetheless depends on the acquisition of the register. (55)

Depending on one's discipline, and one's political views, the process of induction may be labeled as ideology, hegemonic domination, or socialization. An extreme view of the work of narrative in institutions is to see it as a means for enforcing obedience to the corporate culture on subordinates (Witten 1993; Mumby 1988). However, even if one were to take this view as a complete description of the use of narrative in institutions, it would still remain necessary to examine the process by which someone else's narrative is taken on as one's own. The process may be benign or oppressive; voluntary or coerced. But how does it happen? How does the story of another become relevant to the self? For children, learning to become a member of a textual community is best described as a process of socialization or acculturation. These processes are the material for the massive amount of work in anthropology that describes the reproduction of culture. But for adults, the process of becoming a member of a textual community is somewhat different than that of a child. I therefore use the term "induction" rather than socialization to mark this difference.

In particular, the case I am describing is one in which adults voluntarily choose to become members of a community and determine for themselves the intensity of their membership involvement. While the selection and probation periods for new agents require a strong display of involvement, members' subsequent degree of involvement is their own choice. As discussed above, it is quite possible for an agent to be successful without strong involvement in the textual community of MidWest. These are the agents who are described by their managers and fellow agents as "not really MidWest." They are still legally and functionally agents of MidWest and may run a successful business. It is their style or their degree of allegiance that is in question, not their actual membership. I know of no studies of textual communities for a community like that of MidWest based in a commercial institution. The most similar area of study is the issue of religious conversion and conversion stories. Conversion stories represent an excellent locus for investigation of the induction of an adult member into a textual community. The notion of a conversion story requires a situation in which there is a person who is converting, a religion (or ideology) the person has joined as an adult, and a text or field of texts that religion offers as models. Conversion stories thus represent the best-known case available of how someone takes on a new ideology, a new identity, and a new understanding of their history and their place in the world. All of this change requires a revised personal story, and most religions offer or even require from a convert a preferred form of narrative based on a highly valued narrative of the religion's founder or one of its saints.

Part of taking on such a preferred narrative is learning **how** to tell one's own story in relation to it. Thus, in religious contexts, one must know not only which stories to take as models but **how** the model is to be used. This requires induction into the community's narrative and symbolic practices in order to learn the appropriate narrative structure. For example, studies of Alcoholics Anonymous have shown that the process by which AA works is a narrative induction: coming to learn to tell one's own story **as** the story of an alcoholic (Cain 1991; Holland 1998). Members learn how to frame stories of their pasts as stories of alcoholics, within the ideology of AA. Thus, a story about stealing one's child's piggy bank to buy booze would be a valued story of hitting bottom. In contrast, a story about having one glass of champagne at an anniversary party could be criticized or rejected because it shows that the speaker still clings to the unacceptable belief that it is possible for an alcoholic to drink moderately.

Danziger (1989) gives a specific example of how members of religious groups judge the sincerity of religious conversions by the appropriateness of the structure of their conversion story to a particular textual community. He describes a forum on "Returning to Judaism" in which two newly Orthodox Jews described their process of returning to Judaism. The first speaker was a young woman who had had a nonreligious upbringing, knowing only that her family was Jewish. She had moved directly from a period as a self-described Jesus freak to a return to Jewish Orthodoxy after an encounter over several days with a powerful and convincing speaker:

> In closing, she said, "I found Ha-Shem [Hebrew for "the Name, a reference to God] I was at peace, I felt great joy. I felt Ha-Shem was in me, that He loved me and cared for me. "Turning to the audience, she said, "You have to find Ha-Shem, to feel His love, to let Him come into your heart."
>
> Somehow this struck a false note with the audience of modernistic Orthodox ranging in age from fifteen to about fifty-five, with most in the thirty-five to forty-five age bracket. Most were professionals, both men and women. Those who were more involved and educated in Judaism were particularly skeptical of the young woman. They doubted that she would long remain Orthodox.
>
> The young man followed with a description of his return. He had become friendly with a neighbor who was Orthodox. His neighbor's practices intrigued him. He enjoyed the warmth and family life that accompanied the observance of the Sabbath and the holidays. Slowly he began some of these practices himself. His neighbor, while not affiliated with Lubavitch, admired the group's welcoming approach to other Jews and suggested that he contact Lubavitch to learn more about Orthodox Judaism. Through his neighbor and Lubavitcher tutors he has learned about Orthodoxy. He currently observes the laws of Shabbat and kashrut and continues to study with Lubavitch.
>
> This young man's talk was accepted by the audience as the story of someone who would probably remain Orthodox. Somehow his story was authentic while hers was inauthentic. Her story attaches her to Ha-Shem; his attaches him to the Jewish people, to community. Her story speaks of the sense of being loved by God; his speaks of study, of growing knowledge and awareness of Jewish law and practice. Her transformation was swift; his was slow. Finally, his story leaves him a beginner, one still learning from others. Her story places her in a position to proclaim a message to others, to be a leader.
>
> Both, of course, are telling their own stories as they knew them. Inquiry several years later revealed that both had remained Orthodox. But whereas her story was acceptable in Christianity, it was not acceptable in Judaism. The audience considered it false because it did not fit into the patterns of accepted motivation for Judaism. [Returnees] who tell such stories describing their motivation meet with incredulity. The repetition of such stories is discouraged, and a different account or biography of return is constructed, with neither the community nor the returnee aware of this process. (225–26)

This account is important because it gives a sketch of the kind of research we would need to make the link between narrative structure, acceptable ways of creating coherence, and social practices. To recast the author's analysis, the young man told a narrative whose structure, including what it picks out as events, its evaluations, and its coherence system was compatible with the ideology of the community to which he had converted, and with approved stories within it. The young woman told a narrative whose structure would have been appropriate for a Christian fundamentalist conversion, but it was felt to be inappropriate for a return to Judaism. On this basis, the audience made a judgment, which was in fact wrong, about the sincerity and likely duration of these people's conversion. Unfortunately, the author does not give full verbatim transcripts of these narratives. An extremely important direction for future research would be to gather such narratives and the social process of converts learning to tell narratives whose structure fits the ideology or religion to which they have been converted.

Although I have used the term "conversion stories" as if it were an obvious category, in fact, the term itself requires examination. In particular, it is important to determine whether "conversion story" is a category of the analyst or of the group being studied. For example, in a psychologically based examination of the nature of conversion, Stromberg (1993) takes the conversion story as a natural unit and proceeds to elicit such stories, attempting to keep the elicitation process as constant as possible across conversion stories from various religions. This method ignores differences in the form and use of conversion stories in different religious communities. His account also ignores the nature of the interaction between the interviewer and the addressee: while he considered that he was eliciting data, many of his interviewees considered that they were making an effort to convert him, as was their religious duty. In contrast, I would argue that one must attend to the work conversion narratives do within the practice of the particular religion, as well as within any given interaction. While Stromberg's assumptions about conversion stories are common, I would note that the classic work on the psychology of conversion, James (1987), avoids this error. Because James did not elicit accounts, but relied on published accounts of conversion, diaries, etc., the narratives he analyzes are written in the terms of, and for the use of, the particular religious group of the convert.

I would argue, therefore, that in examining conversion stories, it is particularly important to distinguish between religious groups in which conversion stories are **used** as part of the ongoing activities of the group and religious groups in which they are incidental, or even dispreferred. For example, a number of evangelical Christian groups include occasions for testimony: telling one's own story of becoming saved as an exemplary tale that, it is hoped, will serve to convince or convert others. Mormon services regularly include a segment in which a speaker describes coming to accept or to understand difficult tenets of church teachings, or exacting demands made on personal behavior (Kendall 1995). In contrast, many Zen and Tibetan Buddhist groups in the United States have grown entirely by conversion, but they do not officially include, and may even discourage, the exchange of stories about how one became a Buddhist. Buddhist views on the constructed and fictitious nature of ego suggest that the exchange of such stories is likely to support holding on to a "case history" of ego, rather than a lessening of the grip of this mischievous construct. It is those religious groups maintaining official occasions and purposes for telling conversion stories that are most likely to develop a preferred form for these stories that will be learned as part of the process of conversion.

Much Western, and particularly American, literature on conversion views it as a psychological issue, involving issues internal to the person, that is, as a decision made by an individual, for individual reasons. But in many social contexts, perhaps most in the history of the world, conversion involves the most serious possible issues of membership and social identity. Religious conversion may mean that an individual has removed him/herself from the support of family and community. Or, as Viswanathan (1998) argues in a study of religious conversion in colonial India, conversion is a political act, and one potentially subversive to dominant political ideology: "By undoing the concept of fixed, unalterable identities, conversion unsettles the boundaries by which selfhood, citizenship, nationhood, and community are defined, exposing these as permeable borders" (16). Or, as in the case of the mass conversions of many members of the Indian Untouchable caste to Buddhism in 1956, following their spokesman, Dr. Bhimrao Ramji Ambedkar, the conversion can represent an effort by an entire group to remove itself from a social definition imposed by the dominant religion by removing themselves from that religion (Jondhale and Belz 2004).

An American example of the political consequences of conversion comes from the Puritan church in colonial Massachusetts. Here, the preferred conversion story was a violent one—the convert went through a period of doubt approaching agony, leading to a final breaking of the unregenerate person and an influx of light. A gentler, more gradual conviction of the truth of the church was suspect as possibly not a real conversion at all. This was a serious matter, since an authenticated conversion was required for full Church membership, and Church membership was the necessary condition, for men, for citizenship until 1664 (Shea 1988).

In a detailed description of language use in a fundamentalist Christian group, Harding (2000) describes the experience of conversion as acquiring a specific religious language: both learning to respond to it appropriately and to use it oneself. She describes her own experience, which she understood as doing ethnography but which the people she was studying understood as an opportunity for her to hear their witnessing of the truth. As part of this experience she found that she was entering into this world of language use:

> Dusk had fallen by the time I left Jordan Baptist Church…I knew I was in some kind of a daze after my long talk with the Reverend Melvin Campbell. I usually am after an interview, and this one had been especially intense. Halfway across town, I stopped at a stop sign, then started into the intersection, and was very nearly smashed by a car that seemed to come upon me from nowhere very fast. I slammed on the brakes, sat stunned for a split second, and asked myself "What is God trying to tell me?" It was my voice but not my language. I had been inhabited by the fundamental Baptist tongue I was investigating. (33)

As she describes it, coming to become a member crucially involves learning to hear and tell stories appropriately. Believers and non-believers will differ in what they find credible. Even believers will have to weigh the evidence of each proffered miracle:

> A lifelong drunkard sobers up after receiving Jesus Christ into his heart, a believer's cancer goes into spontaneous remission, a ministry is spared certain destruction when a hurricane suddenly veers out of its path.

> Necessarily there is something incredible—in the simple sense of unbeliev-
> able—about a miracle, if only because the disbelief of outsiders is a precondition of
> miraculous action. (86)

But it is not enough to learn how to tell appropriate stories within a community. An additional and very important part of a person's induction into a community's narrative is to learn what parts of the model are *not* to be emulated. Christians may expect to have to take up their cross, but they understand that this will not include rising from death after the third day. Similarly, the Apostle Paul's life may serve as a model for narratives of sin and error, sudden realization, and repentance and conversion. But most Christian denominations encouraging converts to take Paul's story as a model for as their own would not then encourage them to expect to speak with apostolic authority.

Similarly, induction into MidWest as a textual community means not only knowing and accepting the founder's story as relevant, but also understanding which parts of it are to be used in guiding one's actions and which are not. So agents describe themselves as determined, highly principled entrepreneurs, just like the founder, Mr. McBee. But while they are business owners, they are not business founders. As we have seen, a dramatic turning point in Mr. McBee's life came when he complained about the insurance company he worked for and was told, "Well, T.D., if you don't like the way we run things, go start your own company." This determined him to do just that: found his own company run on the principles he felt were correct for an insurance company. This part of the story is frequently told as a praiseworthy indication of his character, but it is not presented as a model for action by the agents. Agents are not expected to start their own companies if they disagree with MidWest's policies. Similarly, agents cannot and are not expected to imitate the founder in developing new products or new pricing policies. A similar phenomenon in other types of business is discussed by Martin (1985) as "the founder's paradox."

Agents also describe themselves as holding values similar to Mr. McBee. However, unlike the tellers of most religious conversion stories, they do not describe themselves as deriving these values from the story and example of the founder. Rather they describe themselves as choosing to join MidWest because its values are similar to their preexisting values. For example, several managers and agents told us that they had chosen a career at MidWest because its values were consistent with the values of their churches. In fact, as already discussed, a number of them had been recruited into MidWest by a fellow church member. This phenomenon is generally known at MidWest. That is, we were told by managers that the process of successful recruitment requires identifying potential agents with the right values, because skills can be taught, but character cannot. Thus, unlike the claims of many business organizations, MidWest does not expect new members to be inducted into a new set of values. Rather, new recruits are to come to understand MidWest's values and the stories that present them as harmonious with the new member's own existing beliefs and values. Thus, the induction is not into a set of new values, but into the new set of texts maintained by the new textual community.

Intertextual relations between personal and institutional stories

Having discussed some of the issues in the establishment of a textual community, we may now turn to the question of how the stories told by agents and managers are related to the central, official texts maintained by MidWest as a textual community. In the following sections, I will discuss a variety of forms of intertextuality: different ways that speakers relate their own stories to the story of MidWest. These include: direct citation of the MidWest story, quotation of it, allusions to it, use of its values, critique of it, rejection of it, and irony about it. These are different ways for a speaker to position a personal story in relation to the body of stories maintained by the MidWest textual community. It is important to reiterate right at the beginning of the discussion of intertextual relations that the positioning of a speaker and the form of a story are shaped not only by their prior stories but by the present situation of speaking. Many of the examples I use come from situations in which an agent or manager is conversing with a member of our research team, a situation they know to be part of a study sponsored by upper management. (I note again that everyone we spoke with knew that we were doing a research project on agents' learning, knew that it was sponsored by management at headquarters, and knew who in particular had sponsored it.) Agents and managers frequently used these conversations with a researcher as an opportunity to make criticisms or suggestions they hoped we would convey to upper management. Often they explicitly asked us to tell management about particular problems or suggested solutions. In addition, much of the data was collected during a period when a new contract for agents was being awaited, announced, studied, and decided upon. This was an issue that aroused considerable uncertainty among agents about whether they should take the new contract or stay with the old one, and what each choice would mean both financially and politically for the agent. As a result, this was a time at which many agents were reflecting on both the past and the future of MidWest and their place within it. This gave rise to many conversations among the agents themselves as well as with the fieldworkers about whether MidWest's future could be relied upon to reward the same values as its past.

Direct citation of prior text

Direct citation of a prior text is the most explicit intertextual relation. Direct citation means an explicit mention of a privileged text: for example, "As the Bible tells us...." In the case of agents' and managers' stories, I count as direct citation an explicit account of the relation between the speaker's story and the story of MidWest, or of the founder. Such citations are rare, but they do exist. The most elaborate example comes from a district manager telling the interviewer his history as an agent and manager. As part of the account, he moves from his own history to a retelling of the history of MidWest (discussed in detail in chapter 5.) In one section, after describing the heroic response of agents to a crisis, he explicitly links this to his own history, arguing that his loyalty to MidWest was the same as theirs:

Manager: And then when the war was over well then the, uh—you know, everybody hits the road, they all have held back for years, vacationing and...and so, uh, in 1947 all of a sudden the statistics stuff start coming in. Come to find out, based on the number of losses we were paying and everything else, we were about, uh—we had twelve million dollars in assets. And we were losing money at the rate of a million dollars a month. So, in twelve months we (would be) broke. And they slammed on the brakes and, you know, did some drastic things....So, um, they literally canceled out, uh—well, first they canceled out the entire state of Minnesota because they were losing money like crazy.

Interviewer: Why was that?

Manager: Well, inadequate roads, people were sliding and slipping and—and driving too fast and, you know, number of accidents....Then he went out in the field to the agents and said, "We need your help, we've got to do this thing, we've got to re-underwrite, people have more than their share of accidents we need to cancel them, we need to get them off the books, we can't continue with (???)." So we've had some rough spots. (???) and, uh, **boy, if you said anything about MidWest, you know (???) to a MidWest agent them was fighting words. And I was the same way, still am.** [Author's emphasis]

The speaker here directly describes his own character as the same as that of the agents of the past who saved the company. Their heroism forms one of the key stories of the history of MidWest. He then goes on to offer a story about the founder (analyzed in chapter 6) showing how he too refused to allow criticism of MidWest or its agents.

Quotation

I distinguish between citation and quotation because they assume different amounts of knowledge in the addressee. Citation makes explicit the link between a particular story and a prior text, in the case above, between a personal story and the story of the founder. Citation therefore requires less knowledge on the part of the addressee about what the prior text is, although it still assumes that the addressee knows of the existence of the text cited and understands its importance. In contrast, quotation of a prior text is not marked as such. It thus requires that the addressee also knows the prior text in order to recognize the quotation.

One phrase from the biography of the founder we have heard quoted a number of times is "the moral character" of clients, or more briefly, "the moral factor." The founder insisted on "the moral factor" in choosing clients, feeling that policyholders of good moral character would be less likely to have automobile accidents and could therefore be charged lower rates. Initially, farmers were assumed to have a higher moral character than city dwellers, and people who owned their vehicles were more fiscally prudent (and perhaps more prudent drivers) than people who had to take out a loan to buy a car.

In one instance of a quotation of this phrase, the agent complained to a field-worker that the company has lost its standards for clients. In talking to a field-worker, he recalled canceling a woman's policy because of her "bad moral character: she was divorced and hung out in bars." When he called the woman to tell her he was canceling her policy, he said that he was honest with her: "You and I both know that people who hang out in bars do so for one reason..."

It might be argued that the use of this term is not a direct textual quotation but rather an independent formulation of the same idea as the founder's. This argument can not currently be disproved. But I would note that there are many other ways that management formulates this idea: "high risk client," "undesirable business," etc. The term for this general category within MidWest at the time of our fieldwork was "quality," or "quality business." During the period of our fieldwork, one of the major problems agents had with the new contract was that it would penalize them for writing policies that turned out to be unprofitable for MidWest, described as the issue of attracting "quality business." Thus, I argue that the use of the older term "the moral factor" or "moral character" represents a quotation, since it differs from the unmarked term in use in the present at MidWest, and it is also not a term in current usage within the larger business discourse. The use of the phrase "his guns fell silenced" discussed in the previous chapter is a similar example of quotation.

Parallel evaluations

Parallel evaluation is the most common form of intertextuality I have found in this body of data. By parallel evaluation I mean that agents and managers formulate their stories with evaluations that are the same as the evaluations contained in the biography of the founder.

Evaluation is a standard component of any narrative. Labov (1972) gives a now-standard taxonomy of the components of oral narrative, which include an optional abstract summarizing the main events or the relevance of the narrative, an orientation section establishing the characters, time, and place of the narrative, the narrative clauses, establishing the events, and an optional coda marking the ending. But most crucially, narratives also contain evaluations, which represent the means that the speaker uses to convey the point of the story, its meaning, or the reason that it is worth telling. Viewed interactionally, it is the evaluation of the narrative that conveys to its addressees how they are to understand the meaning of the sequence of events that is narrated, and what kind of response is desired. Evaluation is thus the part of the narrative conveying moral meaning: "I did this, and it was the right thing to do." "He did that, which was wrong." Or even, "I did this, which I thought was the right thing to do, but which I now see was wrong."

All narratives contain evaluations, because stories are not only about events, but about meanings, moral judgments about the way the world is, and the way it ought to be. A speaker frames a story in such a way as to present a particular view of how things ought to be. This view must be ratified by the addressees, by agreement, by gesture or eye gaze, or at least by absence of visible disagreement. If the addressee disagrees with the speaker's evaluation of the meaning of the events described, this usually leads to a process of negotiation about an evaluation of the events that all parties can agree to. It can also lead to a breakdown of communication, with one or more parties leaving the conversation. (See Polanyi (1989), Linde (1993), and Hunston and Thompson (2001) for in-depth discussions of evaluation, and Goodwin (1984; 1987) and Linde (1996) for a discussion of the social negotiation of evaluation.)

Intertextuality of evaluation occurs when speakers telling their own stories frame them in such a way that the evaluations of their personal stories are the same as the evaluations used in the prior texts in the textual field of their community, or in its weaker form, at least not in conflict with them. Obviously, this definition assumes that the tellers know the textual community's prior texts, either the original valued text, or other later texts consistent with that text. If I tell my story with evaluations consistent with some text I do not know directly or indirectly, that is a case of accident or parallel development, not intertextuality. Learning to tell one's story with values that are the same as or even refer to prior texts is one of the main ways that a person is inducted into a textual community. I now discuss the shared evaluations we heard most frequently: risk and intensity, entrepreneurialism, hard work, family, and shared values.

Risk and intensity

As I have already discussed in chapters 5 and 6, the story of the founder employs evaluations that stress integrity and family values, and agents and managers tell their own stories in a way that stresses these values. This may seem fairly banal: surely every U.S. business story pays at least lip service to family values. However, at present, it is common in business discourse to hear stories of success as a result of working eighteen- hour days and seven day weeks, wrecking health and families in the process. For Silicon Valley startup company stories, for example, such stories are proudly told. However, at MidWest, an agent could not boast about starting his own agency and destroying his family in the process. While such cases exist, we were told of them by others, in whispers. They were told as stories of failures, not as impressive proof of the protagonist's single-minded and admirable determination to succeed. Thus, in their stories of founding their agencies, MidWest agents may boast of their hard work, but may not prove it by accounts of divorces or heart attacks.

Agents also tell their stories as the story of relatively unbroken success: a trajectory that moves ever upwards. This matches to the official story of MidWest as an ongoing success. As I have already discussed, this is understandable, since the primary value for an insurance company is stability. Since insurance is primarily a promise to pay, there should never be a question raised about whether the company will actually be there if and when the time for payment comes. There is a necessary parallel between the business opportunity MidWest offers its agents and the way its agents represent MidWest to their clients. Agents sell insurance to clients as a way of minimizing or managing the client's risks. They sell the history, conservative money management strategies, and financial reserves of the company as a guarantee that the company itself can be trusted to manage the clients' risks, and to be able to pay any claims that come along. If the agents understood themselves to be taking serious risks in opening a MidWest agency, it would be that much harder for them to sell MidWest insurance to clients as safe way of to manage their own risks. This means that we do not find examples of agents telling stories about business turning points: points at which they were able to move their agency from impending failure to success. Yet turning point stories are a common type in other forms of business. At MidWest, the closest we have heard to this is either agents' stories about their decision to move their business to a new level of prosperity or, in one case, a reference to an agent overcoming an uncharacteristic depression and lassitude caused by management's curtailing the sale of new homeowners insurance.

Thus, the evidence for parallel evaluations is complex: it consists both of the evaluations speakers use and the possible evaluations they fail to use. As I have already mentioned, events that cannot be evaluated positively in the context of MidWest are divorce or other family problems caused by excessively long hours. Stories of taking extreme financial risk in starting or expanding one's business are also not told. The parallelism here is a complex matter. The founder, Mr. McBee, certainly took risks in starting a new insurance company, and the authorized biography credits him with courage as well as enterprise. However, the story of the growth of the company is a story of ever-expanding success, in which obviously good ideas about how to run an insurance company, and obviously virtuous values, led to continuous growth. While the company history contains examples of averted disasters, these potential disasters are presented as the result of unforeseeable external conditions, rather than the effects of business decisions by the founder or the management. Thus the return to the roads of too many dilapidated cars after World War II nearly caused the company to fold, but it was a problem caused by external events and solved by internal efforts. This is a strong contrast to stories of averted disasters in other corporations, where the potential disaster was caused by the company's business model and was averted by a change in business model.

The same evaluation of risk forms part of the paradigmatic narrative presented to prospective agents. Here, the evaluation is that founding one's own agency requires the risk of abandoning a fixed paycheck, but that success is nearly guaranteed if one works hard and does all the right things. As mentioned in chapter 7, this offer of success is a problematic issue. Upper management argues that agents have incorrectly taken this as a promise and an entitlement, while recruiters argue that they cannot recruit without this kind of promise. The point to be made here is that, again, the approach to risk remains consistent throughout all presentations of the company, its history, and its projected future.

Entrepreneurialism

Although risk taking is not part of the preferred story for MidWest agents, being an entrepreneur certainly is. As I have discussed previously, MidWest agents are independent contractors, which means that they do not receive a salary from MidWest, but rather depend on the commissions from their insurance sales. Many agents describe the attraction of a career with MidWest as an opportunity to be an entrepreneur, to depend not on a fixed salary but on what they can earn by their own efforts. A number of agents describe their move from employee status as operations staff to sales agent's independent contractor status in terms of their own desire for the entrepreneurial opportunity. These agents do not describe recruitment by a trusted manager or agent as prompting their decision; rather, it was their own recognition of the business opportunity and their desire for more control over their own destiny.

Thus one new agent, who had had a seven-year career in operations with MidWest, describes his own motives for moving into training for becoming an agent:

"Owning my own business, being an entrepreneur, in, in that I mean, you're ultimately responsible for my success and failure both financially, especially financially. And that...I think also for the time aspect, having control over your own schedule. Plus, it's kind of fun to not have to answer to anybody directly, other than yourself." This account is very much in harmony with the description of the founder, which stresses his enterprise and courage in starting a new business.

Another agent who also began in operations describes his desire for direct reward for his efforts, rather than a reward mediated by a potentially unfair bureaucratic system:

> Agent: Then what really became most appealing about it [moving into agency] was that you really could control your own destiny. Where you really can't when you're on the operations side of it.
> Interviewer: When you say, control your own destiny, what do you mean?
> Agent: I think mainly work-wise. I mean, you can work as hard as you want or you (?) as you want. And it's up to you. I mean, the more you work, the more you are going to get paid, the more perks are going to come your way. I'm a very hard-working type individual. I always have a strong work habit, and in operations, you didn't always see that being rewarded, you know. You saw a bunch of people that were managed, that you know all got paid the same, and their salaries were viewed the same, and you know, no matter what you did, you couldn't really, you know, hardly rise above that. So, in agency, if you work hard and do the right things, you're going to see that in your paycheck because it's going to reflect it. You're going to make more money, you're going to sell more things, you're going to have a little more control of what you do.

These examples cite the opportunity to be an entrepreneur, to control one's own destiny, as the deciding factor in choosing to become a MidWest agent. The following example, from someone in the agent training program who had been in operations for fifteen years, construes the opportunity somewhat differently, as a chance to become a professional who can help people:

> Ever since I went through MidWest, I wanted to be an agent. I have, um, my dad's a doctor, my brother's a doctor, my other brother's an attorney and they all play such an important role in people's lives, and I wanted a position like that...where I was really important in people's lives and in their family and stuff. And I didn't want to do all the schooling (laughs) though to become a doctor and this I think is the closest I can get to that. Um, also, um to be my own boss is really going to be nice. [In operations] we just really don't have any control over your life. You have to move every year or two and, um, that gets really old after a while (laughs).

Family

Family is a value stressed in many agents' account of their careers at MidWest, and it is also very highly valued in MidWest's account of its history and its current policies. There are three meanings of family as a value at MidWest, overlapping but distinguishable. The first is that working for MidWest tends to run in families, as I have already discussed. Many agents and managers had fathers who worked for Mid-West. Thus, from childhood, they knew MidWest, went to its picnics and Christmas parties, sang its jingles, etc. Two examples follow:

> When I was a little bitty girl, people would ask, "What are you going to be, little girl, when you grow up?" "I'm going to be a MidWest agent." You know, because that's what my daddy was.
>
> All I ever knew was MidWest. In fact, the very first song that I ever knew as a kid was, they had this little song, a little jingle.... That's my very first song that I ever learned.... My brother had this little car that had like a crank of the front of it. You know, old-timey cars. And as you turned the crank it would play that song. I used to play that song when I was a little kid. I grew up with it.

A similar example:

> I graduated from high school in 1967, and I was working [at a soft drink manufac-turer] and um decided to apply at MidWest, they were really the only big employer in [that] area at that time and my grandfather and my father, my whole family had always been in insurance, and I thought um I should give that place a whirl. Um so anyway, long story short, how I got hired, I finally did get hired, it took me several times in applying to get hired.

In this case, the speaker presents her employment at MidWest as a natural move, both because of family connections and geography, a move that did not require a great deal of analysis or decision.

The following is a more complex example, where a manager describes how his father worked in the insurance business, though not for MidWest. This example made him want to enter the insurance business:

> My dad is an agent, not with MidWest, but with another insurance company, and actually when I was fourteen that's when I decided I really wanted to be in this busi-ness. I got to observe him one day doing what he does and it just made me realize, he takes insurance, I don't know how much you know about insurance, but it's a very complicated product. And he takes it and he makes it so simple and so clear for these people. That I always thought, you know if I could, and I knew because of his association with a lot of different guys, I knew how well he did with those people. And I always thought you know if I could do something like that, take something that complicated and help other people. If I can inform you, you'll make the right decisions for you and your family. I just thought that was so neat. At that time I decided I wanted to do this.

This is a complex case. The speaker was attracted to the possibility of selling insur-ance by seeing the work his father did as an insurance agent. While having kin at MidWest is a strong value within the company, there are also many members who have kin in the insurance business but not with MidWest. Additionally, in MidWest's story the founder is presented as someone whose major skill was in relating to peo-ple. Although he did not master all the technicalities of the insurance business, his skill was in communication, both with customers and with the agents and employees of his company. In this example, the speaker cites his father as an inspiration, and he cites his father's ability to simplify complicated transactions, an ability also widely described as a virtue of the founder.

This kind of family lineage is common and respected at MidWest, as I have discussed in chapter 2. The children of agents and employees were considered promising recruits. We also found, not surprisingly, that in the training of new agents, those who had a family background with the company were assumed by the trainers to be somewhat more advanced in their knowledge than other trainees and, in our judgment, this was sometimes, though not always, true.

All of these are examples of stories told within MidWest, either at meetings or to an interviewer. It is rare for agents to describe their history with MidWest for clients, but there are some examples. These stories tend to be considerably shorter, with the agent's history referenced as an instance of the virtues of the company and the reasons why the client should buy insurance both from this company and this person. The following example is part of an agent's meeting with a new client for the first time. After a brief history of MidWest, the agent sketches her own history with the company: "As far as my own background with the company, it's long term since my father was an agent for MidWest, for thirty years down in [Town], so I grew up with MidWest. And that's given me a chance to really know the company, what their values are and how they perform. And they really follow through. They're just wonderful to work with." While this personal history is quite abbreviated, it is coherent with the main points of the founder's story and the company history. It includes the fact that the agent's father was an agent. This is used as a warrant to show that the agent has long-term knowledge of the company and that her claims about the virtues of the company are based on experience.

The second meaning of the value of family is the very common statement that "MidWest is a family." This statement includes the notion of family lineages within MidWest, but it also includes the belief that MidWest will take care of its agents and employees, that the bonds between people and the company are not merely the instrumental bonds of an employment or contractual relation but rather the human and moral bonds of blood relation.

For example, the following story comes from an agent who had spent a long career in operations. When her husband retired, he decided to return to his native state to become a farmer. The speaker describes the shock of losing her friends at MidWest, whom she felt to be part of her family:

> I kept in contact, all of my entire social life and everything had always revolved around MidWest. Every friend I had was a MidWest employee, um I mean I spend my entire adult life there you know. So I was just *destitute* when we moved to Kansas. It was, it was a culture—But anyway I kept in touch with everybody here because this was where my family was, this is where my friends were. And um my superintendent was [Name], really neat guy, he was the head of commercial and he was my boss. And about two or three times a year, I'd call him or he'd call me just to see what was up. One December, um snow's blowing, and I, I don't drive in the snow. I don't like driving in fair weather much less in the snow. So I'm housebound, going crazy, you know, I was making doll clothes, if you can imagine, I mean I got

into making Cabbage Patch clothes. I mean, I've got to have more to my life than this, it's driving me crazy. he calls one day, and in the conversation two of his supervisors had left or changed departments or something, he says "You wouldn't want your old job back would you?" And I said "Oh my gosh don't you dare make me an offer like that unless you mean it cause I'm like on the next plane." He said "I *mean* it" And I said "Well then I'm on the next plane." So I packed my little bag and came back to uh downtown California.

This example shows an agent describing the social ties that bind MidWest together as "family," even after leaving employment at MidWest. She kept in touch with her friends at MidWest, and they kept in touch with her. Further, her description of her eagerness to return makes clear the value she placed on such ties.

Another example, taken from upper management, comes in their description of attempts to avoid downsizing in the mid-1990s: They attempted to reduce the number of operations staff members by retirement and other forms of attrition, in order to avoid the need to fire anyone. (Although it must be noted that many operations centers were moved and consolidated in locations where existing operations staff could not or would not move.) This attempt to avoid firings was described in terms of family: "we do need to reduce the size of our staff, but you don't fire your family." This example is particularly striking because at the time, the general business climate was very much in favor of downsizing: it was viewed as prudent business decision.

The third meaning of family for MidWest agents and managers is that MidWest is a company that respects families, and it allows agents and managers time to spend with their families. For example, it was a general policy not to schedule meetings requiring travel on Mondays or Fridays, since it was considered illegitimate to ask managers or agents to travel on weekends when they should properly be spending time with their families.

As I discussed above, MidWest agents do not tell stories about how the hard work of setting up a business strained or destroyed their families. In the following example, an agent described being recruited by a MidWest manager at church, who stressed the issue of control over time for family as a major attraction at MidWest:

He said, you ought to think about MidWest if you're into sales because you can run your own business. You can travel and have a lot of time to do things that you think you should be doing with your family since you are running your business. So, all of a sudden it seemed like it could be a possibility because as I interviewed with corporate America the more and more successful you became the less and less control you had over your time, it appeared to me. Whether you were promoted to a regional vice president or whatever it might be, you spent a lot of time on the road having less control of your time. Whereas I saw these MidWest people, this particular individual being one who seemed to be able to be there for his kids. He was, you know, a teacher at church and still running a successful business.

These accounts are again in harmony with the story of MidWest's founder, as well as with continually repeated statements by upper management about MidWest's support for families. In the story of the founder, one important element is the fact that his wife's illness led him to leave his prosperous farm to seek first retirement in a climate that would be more beneficial for her health, and then to seek work less difficult for her than running a family farm.

Shared Values

Many agents and managers told us that they had joined MidWest because it was a company with values that accorded with their own values. As I have already discussed, a number of agents were recruited by members of their various churches. Often, it was a recruiting point that working for MidWest would allow the person being recruited to work for a company that would support rather than contradict their shared religious values.

To repeat a point from the example cited above, the agent describes being recruited into MidWest by a fellow church member, who seemed to be able to succeed at MidWest while still having enough time to engage in important church activities: "Whereas I saw these MidWest people—this particular individual being one who seemed to be able to be there for his kids. He was, you know, a teacher at church and still running a successful business. He actually taught [before-school classes] every morning at church which was an important school program for young people in our [Church] culture." This is exactly parallel with the story MidWest gives of its founder: he was a man of integrity and principle, who built his business in a way that reflected these principles. This may sound entirely banal: surely all U.S. business stories stress the principled nature of the founder. In fact, they do not. Depending on the business and the founder, the descriptions of their salient character traits vary widely. For example, stories about Howard Hughes or "Neutron Jack" Welch of General Electric cite ruthlessness. As already discussed, Bill Gates, the founder of Microsoft, is widely praised for his outstanding intelligence. While the accounts of him have become less uniformly laudatory after the 1999 federal antitrust lawsuit against Microsoft, it is intelligence that is still cited as his central virtue. The point is that business hagiography as a genre allows a wide variety of virtues for corporate founders and leaders. Therefore, there is information content in the particular virtues an institution chooses to ascribe to its founder and recommend to its members.

I would add one more odd note about values. For many agents and managers, the issue of values, quite understandably, is tied to their church membership, and MidWest is praised for practicing values aligned with their church's teachings. Yet this is one area in which the intertextuality between agents' and managers' stories and the story of the founder fails. The founder is not described as churchgoer. Although his biography lists the many civic organizations he belonged to, it includes no mention of any church. Yet if one were to try to read backwards from current MidWest stories, one would certainly expect to find that the founder was an ardent churchgoer. I believe that this represents the influence of wider American narratives about rural and family values, which include the importance of church membership.

Critique

Another possible relation of one text to a prior text is critique: criticism of the text itself or of the values it expresses. In our study of MidWest Insurance, we found many examples of critique, but they are cases in which speakers use the values of the company to criticize the present, arguing that current management is not living up to the values the company embodied in the past. These are thus examples of using the relevant and virtuous past to criticize the degenerating present, arguing that the company is losing or has lost its historical virtues. But there are no criticisms of MidWest as a bad company founded on bad values. Nor are there criticisms of the story of the founder or the history of the company as false, corny, or so outdated as to be irrelevant to present concerns. Some examples of critique of the present by the past follow.

In a meeting of the agents of one district, a panel of several retiring agents described their own careers in the company, relating it to the company's history and to the founder's vision. In particular the agents recalled previous hard times similar to MidWest's current situation and, in particular, a previous introduction of a new contract being offered to the agents. The effect was to gently satirize the managers' rhetoric of the present being a unique time of crisis. At the same time, the retiring agents assured their colleagues that just as they and the company had overcome previous hard times, so would they triumph again: "I've been with this company for over four decades. We've had the same damn problems, and we came out on the other end smiling."

One agent who gave his history was known in his district as someone who was particularly outspoken and willing to be critical, a rare trait among MidWest agents. In fact, he began his talk with a quote from the country music song "Take This Job and Shove It" as a reference to his upcoming retirement. He mentioned that he had come into the company just when the previous contract was being offered to agents. He drew the parallel to the new contract being offered, remembering that agents who did not take the new contract suffered. Thus, although he satirized the degree of crisis that management was claiming, he also affirmed that the company's past could be used to understand the present and to predict the future: the company could be relied on to change in a way that would preserve its essential identity and its concern for the welfare of its agents.

The following example is a complex one. Here, an agent who has had a long history with the company uses the past to criticize the present, arguing that the company has lost its compassion for its agents and customers. The use of the past to criticize the present is a common argument strategy in MidWest, since the past is so highly valued. What is particularly interesting about this example is that the agent shows the value of the past by citing the importance of the rural, midwestern origin of the company as a guarantee of its integrity. Yet this agent was born in a major metropolis and had worked for his entire career in California suburbs:

Agent: I don't believe the world of difference [between MidWest and other insurance companies] is so great, as great now as it was in 1969. I think that MidWest has lost their compassion for their agents and for their customers. They are more business oriented, they have that compassion towards their agent and their customer as long as, but in 1969 I could walk into any MidWest agents office and say "What do you think about MidWest?" And every one of them would say "This is the best thing in the world, I have never had anything better, it is wonderful." At that same time I could walk into any [competing company's] agent's office and probably get maybe thirty percent to tell me that it was the best thing they had ever done. The other seventy percent would tear the company down. Today I believe if you walk into fifty percent of the agents offices in MidWest, you would get fifty percent of them tearing MidWest down. And fifty percent of them saying it's the best. So it really has changed over those years.

Interviewer: Towards being more business like?

Agent: More Madison Avenue. MidWest started, was started by a farmer. And I think of farmers and country folk as very friendly, very down to earth. And I don't see MidWest as friendly and as down to earth as they were in the 90's as they were in the late 60's when I started.

This agent poses a contrast between the virtuous rural past and the degenerated urban "Madison Avenue" present of the company. This geographic assignment of virtue to the farm and dubious dealing to the city is common at MidWest. It is not, of course, exclusive to MidWest; it is a common evaluation in American discourse.

As discussed in chapter 2, there is an association of agents actively critical of MidWest policies. However, its strategy is to take the MidWest story as a valued text and use it to criticize the present, arguing that the company's current direction is not in line with the past, in which the company acted properly towards both agents and policy holders. Note that this is a very common strategy of critique for members of groups who want to see partial but not radical change, or for whom explicit critique is dangerous (Scott 1985).

The following is a very explicit example of using the past to criticize the present, taken from an interview with a manager who disliked the current direction he saw the company taking. It is particularly interesting in that it uses a quote from the grandfather of the current president to criticize the president's policies. This interview was done at the time of the contract change, although it is not clear from his criticism exactly what policies he objects to:

Manager: Frankly, MidWest the company has made it very clear to me that they are going to take care of the company. My job out here is to take care of the customer using MidWest products. MidWest's trying to, again, the company has got it backwards. One person's opinion. There was a president that said that "The day we serve the company first and not the customer."

Interviewer: Yeah, I've seen that on a plaque somewhere.

Manager: We'll go out of business." That's the father of the father. Too bad [the president] doesn't imprint it on his forehead so he sees it every day when he's shaving... And you can tell maybe you can tell that that really rubs me the wrong way because customer focus is critical.

This manager expresses no doubts about the virtues of previous upper management: he expresses a desire for the current company to be guided by the past, specifically by the grandfather of the current president.

One interview with a veteran agent shows an example of the agent boasting to the interviewer about a case (one of several) where he was willing to criticize a company policy to the president. It is also an example of his criticism of the president for being unwilling to take responsibility, contrasting it with his father's attitude of "the buck stops here." The agent said that he once wrote to the president about MidWest's regional sales conventions, complaining that they are often held at places, like Holiday Inn, whose rooms offer cable channels that show pornographic movies. Agents with "moral weaknesses" are especially susceptible when functions are held in such places. The agent recommended to the president that the company refrain from holding functions at places where such objectionable movies are shown. The president replied saying that such decisions are "regional and not company-wide" and were therefore out of his jurisdiction. The agent wrote to him again, saying that his father, the previous president, always accepted responsibility and would frequently say, "the buck stops here."

Note that it is a point of pride for agents that they are willing to write or call the president, or the senior vice president, of the agency with complaints and suggestions. When agents tell such a story, it functions for them as a claim about how bold, and how well-connected the agent is. I do not know whether they also intend it as a story about the company's being organized in a way that makes such contact possible. (For example, during national sales conventions, there are occasions on which the president and vice presidents stand in a ballroom under large hanging signs giving their names and functions so that agents can come up and speak to any of them.) For someone familiar with the rigid hierarchical structure of most large U.S. corporations, these stories are startling and certainly suggest that MidWest has unusually open and flexible communications channels. However, as most agents and managers have never worked for other large corporations, they may not know how unusual such open access is. Certainly, we never heard any agent or manager comment on this as a particular virtue of MidWest.

Irony

One possible stance a new text may take toward a highly valued prior text is irony. However, we have found no such examples in this data. As far as I can tell, MidWest is almost entirely an irony-free zone. That is, agents and managers do not engage in irony about MidWest either in the present or the past, and this means that the stories of MidWest's founder and its past are exempted from irony.

The only form of irony I have found is a case of an agent being ironic about MidWest's proof sources. Proof sources are brochures and other materials about specific insurance products furnished by MidWest for agents to give to their clients, either to explain the product or to show the financial stability of MidWest. In the case shown below, the agent explains how a whole life policy will grow because the dividends it pays can be used to buy more insurance. The rate of growth is not guaranteed; it depends on the success of MidWest's investment strategy. However, although MidWest does not guarantee the rate of return, its past track record has been excellent. The agent ironically notes that she has available

> a whole drawer of pieces of paper telling us how wonderful we are....OK, so, now, you've put in fifteen thousand four hundred and eighty, you've always had the twenty five thousand which is growing, now your death benefit is probably around thirty

two thousand, because the dividends buy more life insurance along the way... so each time, and we're ranked number one out of four hundred companies, for our giving people dividends, we're al- we've always been right on top, we've always been on the top five **there's a whole drawer full of pieces of paper telling us how wonderful we are.**

However, this piece of mild irony is immediately followed by a ratification of what an excellent product this type of insurance policy really is, whether it is used to allow the client's spouse or housemate to pay the mortgage on the occasion of her death, or whether she chooses to terminate the policy for its cash value:

> But anyway, so let's say that fifteen years from now you stop and your husband or your friend or whoever you're sharing the house with at that moment is is is either gone or has died, so you don't need this any more. You simply can take your money back, all along you've had that twenty five to thirty two thousand in case you died first.... So that's how it works. It's a wonderful product, works really really well.

We have seen similar cases of agents being ironic about proof sources showing home prices or college costs that may be accurate for a small town but are unrealistic for the California and Western cities where this data was collected. Here, agents are faced with the problem of working with materials that could make them appear to be naïve. They solve it by a strategy of distancing themselves from these materials by irony. However, they immediately follow this distancing by returning to a claim of how stable and reliable a company MidWest actually is. Proof sources are treated as ephemera, not very important representations of the company. In fact, many agents choose to draw their own diagrams and explanations rather than use prepared materials furnished by MidWest. A diagram drawn on a napkin is somehow more convincing than a four-color glossy brochure, since it gives the appearance of being produced specifically for the client's situation. MidWest's proof sources, glossy brochures and optimistic graphs, are very different from the central stories of the company. They can be ignored, disputed, or framed by the agents in ways very different from their apparent intention without in any way compromising the speaker's essential commitment to the value of the company and the product.

I have discussed the absence of irony in some detail because irony is currently a highly valued stance in academic discourse as well as in fashionable commercial art forms and advertising. Obviously, there are a multitude of relations of a text to a prior text, ranging from the ones discussed here to relations as bizarre as recasting it as a *manga*-style comic book or an epic in heroic couplets. I feel no obligation to discuss all imaginable absences, since the range of things that do not happen is infinite. It is necessary to consider only plausible or expectable events that turn out not to have happened. I note the absence of irony since, as I have said, the high value currently placed on irony requires that one ask about its presence in a field of intertextuality. The important point at MidWest is that the absence of irony does not mean an absence of either reflection or criticism. It reflects a style of speech in which irony is a dispreferred tone rather than suggesting the absence within MidWest of the ability to think critically.

Rejection

The most extreme form of critique of a prior text is an explicit rejection of it. Examples would be cases of texts that reject a prior text, such as a scriptural text, on the grounds that it is forged, morally incorrect, or irrelevant to the present. We find no examples at MidWest of such an explicit rejection of the history and biography of the founder. However, this absence is in fact ambiguous. We discovered that a very common form of critique for agents was silence. When, for example, they heard a presentation or speech with which they disagreed, their response was not to respond. If questioned, they would frequently reject it in its entirety by saying, "It was boring," or "It was repetitive," without responding to the content of the presentation. Determined probing would often reveal that the apparently bored audience member in fact had strong objections to the "boring" or "repetitive" speech.

We do have one example of a manager rejecting MidWest's style of constructing managers' and agents' life stories. She had come to MidWest from a prior career in banking and complained that the company placed no value on any prior experience. She argued that when she started work with MidWest, it was if she "had no past." She was profiled in one of MidWest's publications, and this article described where she came from (geographically) and her family, but it did not describe her prior work history. Her comment was: "It's weird, new people have no history but MidWest."

Perhaps the major rejection of prior narratives we saw actually came from upper management, rather than from district managers and agents. This was the rejection of the previous paradigmatic narrative (discussed in chapter 7). As the members of upper management came to believe that the career outlined in that narrative would no longer be possible under current and projected economic conditions, they found it necessary to reject that narrative and present a new model. However, the rejection was implicit or partial, rather than a full rejection of the possibility that the careers of successful agents of the present could be a guide for agents of the future. That is, no manager ever explicitly told agents to forget the old paradigmatic narrative of agents' success stories: "That was then, this is now, the future will be different, get over it." Rather, there were small acknowledgements that the future would be different from the past, without a major official rejection of the old narrative or proposal of a new narrative. As discussed above, I suspect that change in the industry may be too rapid to allow for a new narrative that could remain stable for a generation. If so, this situation would mean the abandonment of the possibility of developing a new narrative of a career trajectory within MidWest, a strong rejection indeed, though it would be a rejection at a metalevel rather than at the level of a specific example.

Who does not get inducted into the story?

Thus far, I have described the process of narrative induction primarily for agents. I have given some examples from agents and managers. Within MidWest, agents are the privileged group: nearly all managers enter as agents, and the company explicitly claims to give priority to the agents' interests and point of view. As independent contractors, they have a great deal of control over their actions, including their financial decisions, and are described by management as the foundation and primary asset of the company.

Because the topic of our research was agents' learning, we did not have the opportunity to study the operations staff: claims processors, underwriters, actuaries, etc. Incidental contact with people in these positions suggests that they are inducted into a belief in the values and possibly the history of MidWest as a part of being a member of the MidWest family. However, my suspicion is that the story of the founder, the master salesman, is aimed towards sales agents and is not well known or used by operations staff except those whose jobs require them to train agents or produce training materials for agents. Because of the limits on our fieldwork, I do not know whether they have a parallel history with its own heroes. However, there is a belief at MidWest, held both by agents and by operations staff, that the company is organized so that the agent is king, and all other functions exist, or should exist, to serve the agent.

The group that most clearly does **not** come to use the story of MidWest and its founder is the group of agents' staff members. Because of legal requirements on independent contractors, agents hire, train, and pay their own staff members as they choose. Their staff members are not selected or trained by MidWest, they are not formally employees of MidWest, nor is there currently a career track for them to move towards becoming agents. (In the past, some staff members were recruited to become agents.) While some agents' staff members speak of being a part of Mid-West, others orient only to their agent and that agent's office. And we have heard no staff members use the story of Mr. McBee as relevant to their own story, or cite the history of MidWest. This is not, I believe, an accidental omission. Institutionally, the story is not relevant to them, as they are only peripherally members of the institution.

In addition, not all agents choose to take on the story. After an initial probationary period, agents are independent contractors, and part of that independence includes a choice about to what degree they will participate in MidWest activities, semiotics, and culture. Thus, we have observed some agents taking on only parts of the story, or varying between using the MidWest story, a counterstory, or an entirely different story, depending on the occasion and the addressees. This, of course, is known to other members and forms part of their assessment of an agent. As already mentioned, we did, for example, hear some agents described as "very successful, but not really MidWest." This is a judgment that says that the particular agent has chosen to hold back from full participation in MidWest activities and symbolic forms and representations.

Conclusion

This chapter has covered a lot of ground. We began by introducing the related ideas of intertextuality and textual community. A textual community supports and organizes itself around a group of highly valued texts. Such texts are not isolated but are rather related to one another through various intertextual relations: citation, quotation, parallel evaluation, critique, irony, and rejection. In the case of MidWest agents and managers, new members are inducted not only into a new employment relation but also into a new textual community. Such induction requires them to learn the stories of the company and to learn to tell their own stories within the textual field of these prior texts. To show this process of narrative induction, the chapter discussed the issue of the relations between these individual stories and the prior texts maintained by the institution. We saw the relations of citation, quotation, parallel evaluation, and critique. Irony and rejection were not significantly present. Of the textual relations, the most frequent one was parallel evaluation: telling one's own story with evaluations that are coherent with the evaluations and moral meanings of the institution's stories.

As part of the description of MidWest's textual field, I drew comparisons between its use of valued texts and textual communities organized around such textual canons as scriptures or epics. This comparison may seem somewhat inflated. After all, how can one reasonably compare the story of the founding of an insurance company to the Bible or the *Iliad*? Surely these texts are different in kind.

However, both comparisons have important structural parallels in the way such texts are used. As Smith (1993) argues, if we look at scriptures across the world's religions, there is nothing in the form of these books that would lead one to group them as the same class of text. Rather, what makes them scriptures is that a community of believers treats them as scripture. Treating a text as scripture means that it is hyper-relevant, always relevant as a guide for the believer's understanding and action. In this sense, the biography of the founder is treated as a scripture at MidWest: despite enormous changes in the company, the insurance industry, and national economy, the founder's story is still relevant as a repository of values and a guide for action.

The parallel between MidWest's stories and the epic is more complex. It is in the study of epic traditions that we see the structural parallels to the textual field of MidWest's stories in the relations between older and new stories. The reason for this is that most scriptural traditions operate with a closed canon. The canon was established at a given time in the history of the religion, and most of the religions of the world do not expect or allow the introduction of new scriptural texts into the scriptural canon. (In an extreme simplification of a very complex set of relations, this argument applies only to the closed canon for specifically scriptural texts. It does not take account of the effect of scriptural texts on the literary form of other types of texts.) In contrast, many epic traditions are (or were) open canons. As discussed above, the Homeric epics gave rise to innumerable successors: the Greek, Hellenistic, and Roman epics of the later adventures of each of the surviving Greek and Trojan heroes and heroines, as well as Renaissance continuations and imitations of the classical epics. This tradition continues to this day. To cite just a few literary examples, there is Nikos Kazansakis's *The Odyssey: A Modern Sequel*, John Gardner's *Grendel*, a retelling of *Beowulf* from the viewpoint of the monster, and Marion Zimmer Bradley's *The Firebrand*, a retelling of the story of Cassandra from a feminist point of view.

Not only are the stories of the Greek epic told again and again, the ancient epics also shape many later epics, whose plot conventions, use of language, and values pay homage to their highly valued predecessors (Greene 1963).

Now back to the intertextual field of MidWest Insurance. I argue that the biography of MidWest's founder has this type of strong influence on the stories told about the lives of agents and managers in the company he founded. Although it may seem inflated to compare the high deeds of armed heroes and deities with the founding of an insurance company, the structural parallels are striking. Let us consider some of these parallels in detail, examining first the relations between epics and their historical and literary sources.

Epics always look to the past. For example, Homer composing some time between the eighth and the sixth centuries B.C., is at least 500 years later than the events of the Trojan War he describes. (The dates of both the Trojan War and the composition of the *Iliad* are the subject of much scholarly debate. The point that I want to make here is that there is a long period of time separating the war and the composition of the epic.) For another, more recent example, the eleventh-century *Song of Roland* is based on events in 777 and 778—an attack on Saragossa by the Emperor Charlemagne. Both Boiardo's *Orlando Innamorato*, composed during the 1480s, and Ariosto's *Orlando Furioso*, composed in 1516, use characters from the *Chanson de Roland* as well as a vast array of new characters, building complex ramified stories about their chivalric and amorous adventures before their heroic deaths (Ross 1989).

Similarly, MidWest in the 1990s looks to a valued and vanished past of the 1920s and 1930s, in the rural and small town environment of the U.S. Midwest, which is presented as a moral norm. Later versions draw upon earlier versions either to show that the present is worthy of its glorious past, or to criticize a degenerated present in order to exhort for a revitalized future based on the original values. As I have described, agents and managers who have lived their entire lives in large cities uncritically cite the rural origins and farm values of the company as a guarantee of the current virtue of the company.

A second parallel is that an epic is taken to be "the tale of our tribe." An epic describes who We are. I have described the individual life story as being "What you must know to know me" (Linde 1993). The epic is, for a group, "what we must know to know who we really are and where we come from." As we began our fieldwork at MidWest, many people showed us the biography of the founder and told us that we must read it if we wanted to understand MidWest fully.

Finally, within a given textual community its epic is pervasive, appearing in many forms. Among other implications, this means that no one ever comes to their epic for the first time. For example, no one comes to the Arthurian cycle by reading the earliest versions of Chrétien de Troyes, Geoffrey of Monmouth, or Thomas Malory. A child might see cartoons featuring characters from the King Arthur story, be told stories from that cycle, see one of the many movies made from the cycle, read T. H. White's *The Sword in the Stone*, or any one of many children's and adult's retellings before ever reading or even knowing that there is an earlier version of the story.[1] Many members of MidWest, particularly agents, will not read the entire authorized biography, or may never even see it. Even those managers who do read it cannot come to the book freshly, since they have been told stories from it from the beginnings of their induction into the MidWest community. It thus functions, just like an epic, as a matrix of stories, a source and inspiration for new stories.

This chapter has attempted to show the complex relations that exist between a given individual's story and the field of stories which a textual community maintains.

One's own story is not only one's own; it is shaped as a response to earlier stories one has heard and the appropriate values and actions those stories teach. The intertextuality of personal narrative is not just a formal matter of the structure of stories told within a given community. Rather, this intertextuality means that one's understanding of the events and meanings of one's life is not only individual but is strongly shaped by the stories of the communities of which one is a member.

9

Noisy Silences

Stories Not Told

Thus far, we have examined those narratives occasioned and used freely within an institution. We must also look at what stories are not told freely, both those that are never told and those that can be told only under very particular circumstances. Therefore, this chapter now turns the discussion to the question of official and unofficial silences, counterstories, erasures, and storytelling rights. Any institution exists within a larger ecology of institutions and persons. This means that stories about an institution may also exist outside the institution. Such stories may be oppositional, neutral, or favorable. However, they remain outside the control of the institution but must be dealt with by the institution, both officially and unofficially, as members of the institution come in contact with these stories. This chapter will concentrate on stories not told within the boundaries of an institution, but it will also glance at the work an institution must do to deal with stories outside its boundaries.

Both the terms "silence" and "absence" have been used by various authors to describe the phenomenon discussed in this chapter. I have chosen to use "silence" because it is more active: a silence may be the result of an act of silencing. Trouillot (1995) gives an excellent description of how this process works in the writing of history. In a description of multiple layers of silence about and within the account of the Haitian Revolution, he shows the historical mechanisms which produce silences:

> Thus the presences and absences embodied in sources (artifacts and bodies that turn an event into fact) or archives (facts collected, thematized, and processed as documents and monuments) are neither neutral nor natural. They are created. As such, they are not mere presences or absences, but mentions or silences of various kinds

and degrees. By silence, I mean an active and transitive process: one "silences" a fact or an individual as a silencer silences a gun. One engages in the practice of silencing. Mentions and silences are thus the active, dialectical counterparts of which history is the synthesis. (48)

I would add that the most interesting silences, in my data and probably elsewhere as well, are the noisy silences, silences in one situation about matters spoken loudly or in whispers in other situations. Except in an entirely totalitarian regime, complete and utter silences are silences about matters that are not of current concern. Noisy silences are matters of contested concern, matters that officially may not be spoken of but that must be discussed nonetheless. Obviously, this characterization of noisy silences fits for the situation I am describing, which is a relatively benign one, where authorities use persuasion rather than coercion. The situation is more complex under coercive regimes. It has always been the totalitarian political project to silence dissent and to control history completely. We know about the many failures of this project, sometimes at the time and, more often, in retrospect. The successes, by their nature, we cannot know.

How to find a silence

First, we must ask a methodological question: how is it possible to give an account of what is absent, what is not said? Obviously, there are an infinite number of things that are not said at any given time and place. However, what I am concerned with here is what is saliently unsaid, hearably unsaid, what could be said but is not. MidWest's stock of stories contains no account of the American Civil War or of the discovery of how to smelt aluminum economically. Yet we would hardly want to call these silences in the MidWest story. They have no relevance to MidWest's history or current business; there is no reason why they should be discussed. Even episodes from MidWest's history may be absent but not represent deliberate silences. For example, the stories told to and by agents contain few accounts of changes in actuarial practices over the years since the founding of the company. But I would not analyze this as a silence, since these are matters not relevant to agents. Management does not particularly need agents to know this history, but it would have no objection to having it as part of either the public or internal representation of the history of MidWest Insurance. These accounts simply do not make any point necessary to management's narrations to agents or agents' narrations to clients or to one another. In contrast to cases like these, what we want to find are the hearable silences: those stories saliently not present, those stories we could expect to find, and yet do not find in a particular circumstance.

Finding a silence is necessarily a work of comparison: comparison of one account with another account or with a counterstory, comparison of earlier and later accounts, comparison with other sequences of events of the same sort, comparison with another record, or comparison of the story with what one knows independently about how such matters usually work in the wider world.

The most technical study of hearable silences is offered by the field of Conversation Analysis, where silence or absence has been treated as part of the analysis of adjacency pairs. The basic idea is that certain types of conversational moves require a particular response, and therefore come in pairs. Thus, an utterance in conversation that can be recognized as a greeting normally requires its recipient to respond with another greeting. If the second greeting is not forthcoming, it is hearably absent, and the first speaker may allude to its absence, for example "I *said* ' Good morning.'" The technical definition, first offered by Harvey Sacks (1974), is "A basic rule of adjacency pair operation is: given the recognizable production of a first pair part, on its first possible completion its speaker should stop and a next speaker should start and produce a second pair part from the pair type of which the first is recognizably a member" (716).

This method for recognizing silences is admirably precise, but it requires a characterization of recognizable types of adjacency pairs. Within the discourse of institutions, it is possible to discover hearable silences, but the process is not as neatly delimited as the analysis of adjacency pairs, since the field of possible discourses is so much larger and less constrained, and takes place over a much greater time period than that required to produce two adjacent sentences. Nonetheless, there are ways to discover a silence within an institution. These all require comparisons:

How does one account compare to another?
What unofficial stories and counter-stories exist?
Who speaks for the institutions, and who does not?
Who is not present in the story?
What kinds of stories might we expect in such a situation?
What can be discovered by the investigation of the historical record outside the institution?

Most of these comparisons cannot be made a priori, or upon an initial acquaintance with an institution. It is necessary to be a member of the institution, or to be a long-term observer, before it is possible to recognize which stories are relevantly not told on any given occasion. I came to appreciate the amount of time it takes to develop this kind of insider knowledge in the course of our fieldwork. After about two years of intensive team fieldwork, I was beginning to believe that we had heard most of the stories of MidWest's story stock, and that there was little more to be discovered. That was the point at which an entire new stratum of unofficial stories began to be told to us. These were stories about management decisions about such crucial matters as how the succession to high positions was actually managed, which manager had been forcibly retired for unapproved behavior, and similar delicate matters. Initially, we were not sufficiently informed to be able to hear the silences about these matters on official occasions. It was only when we had come to be sufficiently trusted within the company that we were allowed to hear or overhear such stories told unofficially, or even to have such stories told to us directly.

Let us now turn to a discussion of the types of comparison which allow us to recognize silences.

Comparison of accounts

Perhaps the easiest way to find a silence is by a comparison of two or more different accounts of the same event or of the same time period. These can be comparisons of multiple official accounts or accounts by groups or individuals with opposed interests. In the case of MidWest, since an extensive field study was done, we have access not only to the official representations of memory but also to a broad range of unofficial conversations, meetings, interviews, etc. This allows us some considerable amount of information about what the institution does not publicly remember.

Chapter 5 offered a comparison of accounts and the differences between them. Each of these accounts is silent on certain issues present in one of the others. These silences come for different reasons: differences in audience, differences in relevancy, and, in some cases, disappearance of an event from the official historical account because it no longer makes a necessary point.

Thus, accounts of the building of the original and enlarged headquarters buildings are present in the written histories and in the speech by the headquarters trainer, but not in the interview with the local line manager. This is an understandable matter of audience and literal physical stance. The headquarters building is relevant to the people who work in it. It is unimportant as a physical structure to agents who have no regular reason to visit it—for them, the first meaning of the term "headquarters" is the nonphysical place from which policy emanates, the place where "they" live. It is the case that some favored agents and most local managers have visited the headquarters building on occasion: for training, to serve on a committee, etc. While we heard accounts of such visits, it was always about their purpose. We never heard any discussion of the building itself, although it is an architecturally interesting building with a number of unusual interior features designed to promote conversations and informal collaborations.

Similarly, the details of a new contract between the company and the agents are relevant at the time, and perhaps at the time of the next contract negotiation. Two contracts down the line, an old contract disappears from both public and private discourse as irrelevant to current concerns. This can be seen as another example of the notion of the "floating gap" described in Vansina (1985). A group or institution can maintain only so many generations of memory, the number, determined by its memory mechanisms. It will maintain memory of the first generation, and then N–1 generations of memory, counting back from the present. Anything in between will disappear into this floating gap.

Perhaps the most interestingly suspicious silence in the current account of the company's history is the initial error in the calculation of rates—and the disappearance of the secretary who is blamed for this error. (The secretary both left the company and disappeared from its history.) This is a story of interest, perhaps, to actuaries and underwriters, for whom changes in underwriting policy forms an important part of their history. For agents, an error in the form of calculation rectified more than a half century ago is ancient history indeed. Its only narrative value would be to make the point that the founder too was subject to making errors, either in insurance calculation or in choosing personnel. This is not a point anyone seems to need to make, officially or unofficially, and thus the story has become truly silent, even though it does appear in the official history. (As I will discuss later, there is a great need to believe that leaders are competent and know what they are doing. This need is all the greater in the case of a past founder who is presented as the source of the company's values.)

Counterstories

In addition to comparison of official and semiofficial accounts, another way to compare accounts is to look for counterstories. The term "counterstories" has a number of uses. It has been used in a broad sense to describe any narrative that differs from the society's master narrative on a particular topic. (See, for example, Andrews (2002), for a very extended definition of the term.) I use it more tightly to mean accounts explicitly oppositional to specific, and usually more official, accounts. There are a number of such types of oppositional stories. For example, the support staff of a company may pass along tales of their manager's incompetence. These may be of a radically critical nature: the guy is incompetent and should be fired. Or they may have a quality of carnival reversal, which does not serve to subvert the established order permanently. For example, a story told by the receptionist about how the boss tried to make a pot of coffee for a meeting and blew up the coffee machine and drenched his trousers is humorously critical, but it does not propose a radical reordering of relations. I heard such a story during a goodbye lunch for an employee at IRL, at which almost all the people present were members of the support staff. In what was apparently a common practice among the support staff, someone asked the person departing what his funniest work experience was. His response was the story of the manager and the coffee pot. This example is interesting because it suggests a type of occasion at which such humorously oppositional stories are regularly told. Similarly, in a software firm, software programmers and marketing staff may have very different accounts about how a particular product came to market, which can include strong opposition to and criticism of the other group. However, such stories do not project the possibility of a world without marketing staff or programmers.

There are also countermemories and counterhistories, which are explicitly critical of the official institutional memory. For example, Tulviste (1995), describes the relation between official and unofficial history in Estonia before the fall of the Soviet Union. They found the official history of the Soviet domination of Estonia to be coherent and well-organized. In contrast, individuals maintained an unofficial history carried by "isolated observations, reference to public individuals and events, stories about specific public episodes, and relatives' personal stories about their own or others' experiences (e.g., in Siberian camps)" (321). Because of its unofficial nature, this counterhistory was relatively unstructured, lacking a systematic all-encompassing narrative. To the extent it had a structure it was a counterstructure, a rebuttal of the official history, given its shape by the form of the official history.

Discussions within critical theory have focused on hegemonic discourse: the official accounts and narratives that function to naturalize the current state of affairs, to make current arrangements of power appear to be inalterable facts of nature (Mumby 1988). Completely successful naturalization would make counteraccounts impossible, since it would be impossible to fight for or even to imagine a different state of affairs. Yet ethnographic accounts of subordinated groups (for example, Scott (1985)) suggest that hegemonic discourse is rarely if ever fully successful. Subordinated groups are fully capable of acts of resistance such as grumbling, poaching, foot-dragging, pilfering, which clearly indicate that they do not accept without question the dominant account of their place in the world. (While there have been later critiques of Scott's theoretical framework of public and private discourses (Gal 1995), his observations of forms of covert resistance remain valuable.) Recent investigations of oppositional memory under state socialism in the former Soviet Union and the People's Republic of China show a range of ways in which unofficial and oppositional memory is represented, hidden, and maintained in the face of intense government repression (Watson 1994). Yurchak (2006) offers vivid examples from the Soviet Union of how the official Communist discourse could be subtly manipulated into a critique of itself. Wodak (1996) gives examples of professional discourses in which speakers in positions of power usually, but do not always, succeed in constructing what an encounter is and means, and in which in some circumstances critical reflection and change is possible.

Perhaps the most obvious way to look for such counterstories is to look for formal or organized groups within an institution that have, or may have, opposed interests, for example, an employer and a labor union. In this type of case, each group will have some pieces of the past it remembers and some it does not. Investigating the union's representation of the past is likely to provide stories upon which the employer's memory is silent, and vice versa.

For example, Pilcher (1972), in a study of Portland, Oregon, longshoremen, shows that memories and effects of a strike in 1934 were still important in the early 1970s.

> There are many waterfront legends and myths centered around the 1934 strike and especially around the exploits of the men who formed the riot squads. Some of these men have become truly legendary figures, and the tales of their exploits are told and retold, growing somewhat in the telling. Although all of the men who participated in the 1934 strike form a separate category among the longshoremen (the '34 men) and stand as examples of appropriate union conduct for the younger men, the fighting men of the riot squads offer living testimonial to the fact that battles were fought and won. The legends of the group center around these heroic figures, and, indeed, a special deference is shown to these now grizzled warriors. Although they have no official privileged status within the union, they are often excused for behavior that would bring heavy sanctions down upon any other member of the union. One of these men is now a notorious drunk, a condition with which the union grievance board is usually in little sympathy, and men who appear before this board charged with being drunk on the job or in the hiring hall are usually severely penalized. This individual, however, has been before the board on this charge many times, but no serious action has ever been taken against him, because, as one board member stated, "I couldn't forget what he did in '34." (47–48)

One reason that the memory of the strike is carried on by generations who did not participate in it is that there are memorial occasions, commemorating the killing of several longshoremen by the police during an attempt by employers to reopen the ports:

> The day on which [the violence] began was dubbed "Bloody Thursday" by the longshoremen, and large-scale memorial demonstrations for the men killed were held in all major West Coast ports. This memorial is still held up and down the Pacific

Coast and all ports are still closed on this day. Although no one was killed in Portland, the larger and most impressive memorial is held there. This memorial consists
of a two-mile parade and a memorial service held at the down-town seawall where
navy ships are normally docked on more festive occasions. It is a point of honor for
many of the veterans of the 1934 strike to attend this ritual, and it affords them an
opportunity to visit with old friends and to meet or be seen by many of the younger
longshoremen. (49)

It should be noted though, that this is a case in which union membership was the
only occupational membership of these men. They contracted for work by the day
with different shipping companies as the ships came into the harbor; they therefore
did not have any competing membership in a corporation as well as a union. It is
also important to note that this description was published in 1972. With the advent
of containerized shipping, fewer longshoremen are needed to load and unload ships.
Hence the strength of the union may well have diminished, and its memorial occasions become less important.

It would be desirable to have a full ethnographic study of the maintenance of a
counterhistory. As already discussed in chapter 2, there is an unofficial organization
of agents that takes an oppositional stance towards MidWest. However, for ethical
reasons, we were not able to study them in detail. We do know that while they are
strongly critical of management, their opposition is not one of values. Rather, it uses
the same account of MidWest's past to criticize current management decisions as not
consonant with the events and virtues of the past.

One of the few situated studies of the maintenance of a countertradition is
the account of the narratives of repair technicians, already discussed in chapter 3.
This study shows a contrast between the ways in which the official documentation
requires technicians to fix particular problems and the unofficial ways which actually
work (Orr 1996). More such studies are needed to provide a fuller understanding of
whether and how such discourses have a life within the institutions they criticize.
I suggest that posing the question in terms of institutional memory allows us to ask
questions not only about what the counterhegemonic discourses are, but how they
succeed or fail in creating an ongoing countermemory.

Who speaks for the institution and who does not

In previous chapters, I have attempted to specify who within the institution tells
which of the various kinds of stories in the institution's memory. This is extremely
important. It is not enough to consider en masse what narratives are occasioned and
used within an institution. Understanding narratives in institutions also requires
understanding of storytelling rights. Such rights include: who may speak for the
institution, whose account is taken up by others, whose account does not count as
part of the institutional memory. (See Shuman (1986) for a discussion of storytelling
rights in smaller informal groups.)

It is in the study of silences that it is most important to consider the position and
stance of the speaker. Position is the institutional position of the speaker; stance is

the attitude that a speaker takes toward the material spoken. Thus a speaker could be at a given occasion speaking as an official spokesman for the institution, could be speaking to convey sincerity, irony, distance, etc.

Part of the process of doing officially sponsored fieldwork within an institution means that one necessarily begins by hearing the official narratives of the institution from one's sponsors. As the fieldwork continues, one hears first the accounts of those who by virtue of their position have the right to speak for an institution, whether it be an executive vice president speaking for the company or an agent speaking for her own agency. That is, large institutions have levels, and all of these levels have their history and their official speakers of this history. It is important that in doing this project we were sponsored and introduced by the executive vice president in charge of agents: that is, one level from the top. Our initial task was to be introduced to managers at every level, as well as interested agents, in order to explain the project and get agreement about participation from people at each level. Thus we got to hear many versions of MidWest's story from people who had the right to speak for the institution at their level in the hierarchy.

In telling the institution's stories, in addition to the formal institutional hierarchy, there is also a narrative hierarchy of those present at the telling of the event: Usually the highest-ranked member of an institution present tells the story. (However, as Duranti has shown, this is not a cultural universal (1994). He gives the example of Polynesian designated storytellers, who are not as highly ranked as the chief, but whose job is to do the speaking at specified occasions.) In relatively stable institutions, the assumption is that the person in the highest position is also likely to be relatively senior, both in age and in tenure within the institution. This is usually the case at MidWest, which has a rate of job tenure unusually stable for U.S. industry in general, and insurance companies in particular. However, there are exceptions to this: for example, a junior member who is being groomed for promotion may be given the chance to speak in preference to a more senior member. Additionally, the low turnover rate means that there are many mid- and low-level employees who function as "oldest inhabitants" and who pass on a great deal of the institution's memory. As I have already mentioned, a number of these people refer to themselves, and are referred to, as "MidWest's unofficial historian." One issue for institutions concerned with preserving their institutional memory is to identify and support these unofficial history keepers. Academic readers may contemplate the role of department secretaries and administrative assistants in preserving a department's memories and the potential chaos when such a person leaves.

In chapter 4, I described a case in which the new director of IRL was required to describe the history of IRL after only a few weeks tenure in the job. The difficulty he had to manage was the discontinuity between his high position and his short tenure, exacerbated by the fact that there were people present who had been present since the beginning. Seniority won out over first-hand knowledge. The right to speak for the institution is contextually produced by the occasion and by the membership of those present, rather than determined absolutely by the fact of who present is known to have the greatest knowledge. In fact, I can demonstrate social consequentiality of these decisions by the effect of an infraction. At a similar meeting with potential clients at IRL, the wrong person told the founding story. The speaker was a newcomer to IRL, at that time a contractor rather than a permanent employee. Yet he jumped in to tell the story though there were people with more seniority present at the meeting. While there was no rebuke or rebellion at the time, the story of the incorrect telling of the story was told about this employee for several years thereafter as in indication of his impetuous character. The fact that this infraction could be remembered and discussed for so long shows the strength of these implicit conventions for determining the proper speaker at a given event.

The hierarchical nature of MidWest means that it is usually quite clear who has the best storytelling right in any given interaction. Within this hierarchy, there are also people who may be present but who will never have the right to speak for the institution. In the case of MidWest, the people in this position are sales agents' staff members. Because they are hired by the agent, not by MidWest, they are not legally employees of MidWest and do not represent MidWest. Accordingly, we never heard an agent's staff member telling the story of MidWest or of the founder, although they have certainly heard it many times at MidWest meetings.

Who isn't here

Another way to discover a silence is to ask, "Who is no longer here?" One kind of silence is the lack of stories about people who have left the institution. People who have left an institution, especially to go to another institution, rather than through retirement, tend to be erased, and their achievements attributed to others who remain. Thus, it is always important to ask, "Who is no longer here?" or "Who was never noticed as being here?" An extremely vivid example of the power of the question "Who isn't here?" is given by Plaskow (1990) in her discussion of the absence of women from the account of the entry of the Jewish people into the covenant with God:

> Entry into the covenant at Sinai is the root experience of Judaism, the central event that established the Jewish people. Given the importance of this event, there can be no verse in the Torah more disturbing to the feminist than Moses' warning to his people in Exodus 19:15, "Be ready for the third day; do not go near a woman." For here, at the very moment that the Jewish people stands at Sinai ready to receive the covenant—not now the covenant with individual patriarchs but with the people as a whole at the very moment when Israel stands trembling waiting for God's presence to descend upon the mountain, Moses addresses the community only as men. The specific issue at stake is ritual impurity: An emission of semen renders both a man and his female partner temporarily unfit to approach the sacred (Lev. 15:16 18). But Moses does not say "Men and women do not go near each other." At the central moment of Jewish history, women are invisible. Whether they too stood there trembling in fear and expectation, what they heard when the men heard these words of Moses, we do not know. It was not their experience that interested the chronicler or that informed and shaped the Torah. (25)

This example works because the author is able to answer the question "Who isn't here?" using the ordinary knowledge that a nation consists of both men and women. At some level of general or specific knowledge, the person asking such a question must know either the particular people or the types of people who might have been present but are not represented in the story.

Within corporate institutions, it is a common pattern that when an innovator leaves, the credit for his or her innovations become transferred narratively to people still within the institution or to the institution as a whole. Some familiar examples in U.S. business have to do with the relative disappearance of cofounders: Bill Gates is popularly credited with the founding of Microsoft, while Paul Allen has been backgrounded if not disappeared; Steve Jobs is popularly credited for Apple, while Steve Wozniak has similarly disappeared. (I speak here about general business discourse. People in Silicon Valley who care about the history of computing are vocal, indeed vociferous, about proper crediting of innovation. And I am not privy to the nature of the narratives within these two companies.) Still, the point is that key questions to ask about an institutional narrative are "Who isn't here? Who used to be here? and Has the credit for their accomplishments migrated to people still present?

Expectable stories

Another way to find a silence is to note the absence of any account about the kind of event that one would expect to find in the circumstances narrated. An institution containing no account of its founder or its founding would certainly rouse curiosity, since, as we have discussed, origin stories are the most frequently found item in institution's memories. The absence of other, more subtle types of events require for their discovery more detailed knowledge of what can be expected.

Let me give as an example the discovery of the existence of a succession crisis in the history of Waldorf education at the death of its founder. It is a rather abrupt move to go from a U.S. insurance company to a German educational and spiritual movement. I choose this example because I was personally involved in the discovery of this important silence.

Some years ago, my then student and now colleague, Ida Oberman, was compiling an oral history of Waldorf education (1999; 2008). In a conversation, she described to me the death of the founder, Rudolf Steiner, and the assumption of leadership by his widow. I mentioned that I was surprised by the smooth transition of leadership and the absence of succession crisis. As a result of this comment, Oberman went back to those people she had interviewed who remembered that episode, most now in their eighties, and discovered that there had indeed been a major succession crisis that came close to splitting the organization apart. As she describes it:

> Indeed, it turned out: when Steiner's body was still warm, fierce disagreements erupted on what the authentic continuation of Steiner's legacy was that reached deep into each Waldorf school's teacher community. Quarrels between his intimate associate and his wife were to result in a schism in the movement reaching as far north as Sweden and as far west as Manhattan's upper west side where Steiner followers were trying to set up the first school in the new world. Individuals generously gave me many an hour of their time to tell "their story." However, when I sent drafts of the study recording the matter, I was advised: don't report this, you do not do it justice.

[Note: Oberman's informants later changed their minds and gave her permission to publish their accounts.] (Oberman 1999)

The point I want to make about this episode is the reason that I originally asked her the question about the succession. As a member of a religious organization that suffered a wrenching succession crisis, I have become intensely aware of the issue of transfer of authority after the death of a charismatic founder (Weber 1947), and I have studied this issue as a way of trying to understand what I myself experienced. As thousands of years of history of religious movements suggest, the move from legitimacy based in the personal charisma of a founder to other forms of legitimate religious authority is almost always difficult, and frequently bloody, as it represents not only a change of leadership, but also a fundamental change from one type of authority to another. Hence, I had a background of expectation, both personal and scholarly, against which the apparent smoothness of the Waldorf succession seemed a startling exception to a rather general rule.

Looking for the absence of expectable stories is a move similar to looking for people or classes of people who are absent. One begins with a background of expectations of what is usually present, whether it is a class of people or a class of events. Such expectations can arise from personal experience, from knowledge of a particular institution, or from knowledge of how a particular type of event usually happens. With those expectations, one examines the situation in question to see whether those expectations are met, whether something entirely surprising has happened, or whether there is a silence waiting to be discovered.

External records

Thus far, I have discussed how to find a silence within the confines of information current within a single institution. However, there are always other records, particularly for a large corporation, which exists not in a vacuum but within an ecology of competitors, associated businesses, professional organizations, the press, and, of course, federal and state governmental bodies. Particularly with the advent of the Internet, the information boundaries between institutions have become yet more permeable.

Examination and comparison of different records is of course the bread and butter of the historian's method. However, in this study, I have not, in general, used external records, since my concern is not to verify the facts of what is told, but rather to establish the pattern of how narratives are used within MidWest's operations, which is a very different question. However, as will be seen below, I will use an examination of public legal records to understand the way in which MidWest handles its largest and most publicly accessible silence.

Silences and erasures

I have defined silences as salient absences—things that could have been said in a given situation, that might be expected, but are not found. I chose the term silence over absence because silence is more active: it suggests the possibility of silencing. The strongest form of silence is erasure.

It is possible to have silences with or without erasure. An institution may be silent about a given event, that is, have no official account of the event. Erasure is stronger. It is an attempt by an institution to eliminate all evidence of a past event that could suggest any account that differs from the official one or that could permit the reconstruction of such an event.

Striking visual examples of erasure are reported within the USSR during the rule of Stalin. As communist party officials fell out of favor with Stalin, they were also airbrushed out of re-issued or reused official photographs. And libraries and individuals owning the earlier versions were instructed to black out the faces and names of the disgraced. Text in encyclopedias and other official accounts similarly were replaced by new material pasted over the old. Thus, after the trial and execution of Lavrenti Beria, the head of the Soviet secret police (the NKVD [People's Commissariat of Internal Affairs and then the KGB [Committee for State Security], under Stalin, his biography in the *Great Soviet Encyclopedia* was replaced by an article containing "new information" about the Bering sea and photographs of whalers harpooning their catch, sent to subscribers to paste over the previous adulatory biography of Beria. (King 1997, 181). One wonders what the effect of this activity was on those who airbrushed the photographs or pasted in the innocuous new articles. Clearly their activities and responses could not be discussed in public. But what did they think? What did they say in private?

Trouillot (1995) also discusses erasures, but in a slightly different way. He is considering the representation of the Haitian past within the community of professional historians:

> The treatment of the Haitian Revolution in written history outside of Haiti reveals two families of tropes that are identical, informal (rhetorical) terms, to figures of discourse of the late eighteenth century. The first kind of trope are formulas that tend to erase directly the fact of a revolution. I call them, for short, formulas of erasure. The second kind tends to empty a number of singular events of their revolutionary context, so that the entire string of facts, gnawed from all sides, becomes trivialized. I call them formulas of banalization. The first kind of tropes characterizes mainly the generalist and the popularizers—textbook authors, for example. The second are the favorite tropes of the specialists. The first type recalls the general silence on [black slaves' movements of] resistance in eighteenth century Europe and North America. The second recalls the explanations of the specialists of the times, overseers and administrators in Saint-Domingue, or politicians in Paris. Both are formulas of silence.
>
>   The literature on slavery in the Americas and on the Holocaust suggests that there may be structural similarities in global silences or, at the very least, that erasure and banalization are not unique to the Haitian Revolution. At the level of generalities, some narratives cancel what happened through direct erasure of facts or their relevance. "It" did not *really* happen; it was not that bad, or that important. Frontal challenges to the fact of the Holocaust or to the relevance of Afro-American slavery belong to this type: The Germans did not really build gas chambers; slavery also happened to non-blacks. On a seemingly different plane, other narratives sweeten

the horror or banalize the uniqueness of a situation by focusing on details: each convoy to Auschwitz can be explained on its own terms; some U.S. slaves were better fed than British workers; some Jews did survive. The joint effect of these two types of formulas is a powerful silencing: whatever has not been cancelled out in the generalities dies in the cumulative irrelevance of a heap of details. This is certainly the case for the Haitian Revolution.

The general silence that Western historiography has produced around the Haitian Revolution originally stemmed from the incapacity to express the unthinkable [that black slaves could organize, revolt and conquer a government of Europeans]. (96–97)

Erasures do happen, for a variety of reasons, and by a variety of means. Thus, in discussing institutional accounts, we must look for both silences and erasures—absences of an account of salient events, for whatever reason, and also attempts to eradicate the evidence of such events.

Silences at MidWest

Having discussed the nature of silences within a history, let us now turn to the question of what silences exist in MidWest's official narratives, and the relation of these official silences to what is told or represented privately or nonofficially.

Antidiscrimination lawsuit: A silence of fact

At MidWest, we have one central case of an official silence within the living memory of most members of the company. In the 1980s, a lawsuit was brought against the company charging that the company discriminated against women in its hiring of agents. In the early 1990s, the company settled the suit out of court and began an extensive program of recruiting women and minorities. These facts are known. They are available in the public press and are, of course, known to agents and employees of the company who have lived through these years. Yet they are rarely if ever mentioned in the company's official statements and form no part of the company's official representation of its past.

We may begin by asking where we should look in the representations of the official institutional memory to determine whether there exists an official representation of this important event. The official history of the company was published in 1955, so of course it has no account of this event. Given the attitudes and practices of the entire nation at the time, it is not surprising that this official history assumes that the typical MidWest agent is a white male. However, there is a more promising place to investigate. As we have already discussed, in 1992 the official monthly magazine of the company printed a series of twelve articles on company history, including highlights of each decade of that history. The highlights for the 1980s and 1990s included items about changes in the leadership of the company, growth of number of policies, record sales, record losses, unveiling of a portrait of the president, and the induction of the founder into the U.S. Business Hall of Fame. But no mention was made of the lawsuit and its consequences, although it caused perhaps the largest change in corporate policy of those decades. This silence raises a question about what kind of corporate history these newsletters represent. They are by no means intended as a complete story: they are never used to discuss problems or difficult issues. They do announce changes in products offered or of company policy, but they are not the main communication channel for substantive news. That is communicated by managers to agents: another example of the personalistic rather than bureaucratic organization of MidWest. Primarily, these newsletters are used to chronicle the idealized ordinary. Much of the space is given over to profiles of exemplary agents, stories of how alert agents can prevent fraud, and occasional celebration of corporate triumphs or obstacles averted. Their tone is a familiar one: they are like airline magazines, intended to be interesting but never alarming.

The absence of official discussion of the antidiscrimination lawsuit represents a silence in the official institutional memory, but it is not a full erasure. That is, while the lawsuit and its consequences are not officially discussed, they are unofficially discussible and discussed, and there have been no efforts to erase all indication of the changes. The following is an unusual phenomenon: an example of a potential erasure that was not made. As part of regional sales conventions, a yearbook of agents in the region was customarily distributed. This yearbook contains pictures of the agents, their names, and the length of their tenure with the company, arranged first by half decade, and within that, alphabetically. The book begins with agents of forty-five or more years of service, then forty years or more, and so on. What is striking about this arrangement is that at ten-plus and particularly five-plus years, the number of pictures of faces of women and minorities begin to approach their numerical representation in the general population. Anyone flipping through this book, knowing nothing of the company's history, could guess that a major change of policy in recruiting and hiring policy happened in the early 1990s. The nature of the yearbook is not so fixed a form that it could not have been changed to erase the shift in policy. If MidWest had wished to erase indications of the changed hiring policy, it could have organized the book not temporally but purely alphabetically, thus blurring the representation of this major change, making it much more difficult to notice or at least to date.

Why didn't MidWest work to blur or eliminate the representation of the change? Why was there no erasure? This question cannot be answered definitively, but there are two reasons that can be suggested. One is the obvious one: the change in policy could not be erased since it forms a part of so many people's memories. Yet this argument is not sufficient in itself. There are all too many historical examples of totalitarian regimes erasing and denying events that may be remembered by millions of survivors. Of course, in such circumstances, physical survival often requires at least a pretence of forgetting. MidWest neither has nor would want such powerful control of its members' lives. The power relations involved are very different from those that exist between a totalitarian government and its subjects.

In addition to the fact that the company does not have the power to demand silence, there is also a reason based in the culture of MidWest, and of MidWest's agents' construction of their identity. For agents, tenure within the company is a key building block of people's identities. It is one of the first ways people in the company characterize themselves, identify their peers, and keep in touch with their training classmates. An alphabetical arrangement would wipe out this very salient characterization and probably make the yearbook less appealing to and usable by the agents. Had MidWest wanted to accomplish a complete erasure, it would have done better to eliminate the yearbook entirely. However, the yearbook served a function in the present that was important to agents and managers, while the embarrassment of the lawsuit was receding into the past and was not so salient that it required current erasure of all its traces.

Although there is no official, public account of the lawsuit, the story is known by virtually all members of the company. Thus, we find an odd situation in which there is a speakable refutation of a story never officially told. This refutation is told indirectly and implicitly by the institution and quite explicitly by members when they speak in unofficial situations. The argument of the refutation is that the lawsuit was overly demanding, and MidWest's settlement of the case was unnecessarily generous, because MidWest had hired (at least some) women and minorities from its founding. This claim is not made overtly, but it is represented indirectly. For example, as discussed above, in the newsletter series on the history of MidWest by decade, women and minority agents are profiled in greater numbers than their actual representation in the company in that period. Such inclusions suggest, without explicitly arguing, that MidWest's hiring practices were never as discriminatory as the lawsuit claimed, because MidWest always hired women and minorities.

In conversation with the fieldwork team and with one another, agents and managers were quite frank about the lawsuit. There was no attempt to hide its existence. They do, however, offer an explanation for the company's prior behavior: the company was no different than the rest of the society in its treatment of women. The only difference was that when change became necessary, the company changed quickly and effectively.

As an example of this stance, in the district manager's account of MidWest's history, described in chapter 5, there is a reference to the change in policy but not to the lawsuit. In his account of how he recruited agents, he explicitly discusses the changed policy:

> Yeah, and oftentimes they'd say, well, you know, I've got a guy you ought to talk to. And then we started hiring women. I'd do the same thing, I'd do the same thing.... The agents would know, uh, women. A lot of agents would have sisters that were maybe teachers and, uh, so we—we did a darn good job. And they're doing a good job.
> And [the regional vice president] said, "You know, I don't know what it is with you guys wanting to hire men." He said, "Every woman we bring in, you know, she just blows them away." (Laughter)

This account mentions not only the changed policy: "then we started hiring women." It also claims that "we did a darned good job" of recruiting women. However, it still omits the lawsuit as the reason for the change. Thus, in effect, the speaker indicates that the company made an appropriate remedy for an error that is never mentioned. He also eliminates any suspicion of his own guilt by recounting that when he was in a position to do hiring, he personally recruited women. Finally, by implication, he suggests that the initial policy barring women agents was wrong: once women agents were hired, they "blew the men away."

As discussed in chapter 5, this interview with the district manager stands at the border between an official and an unofficial account, as he gives a chronological account of the history of MidWest. In addition to his account, we heard a number of purely unofficial narratives that either recount the suit and its consequences, or assume it as background knowledge. In the ecology of unofficial stories about the company, there is neither silence nor erasure about the lawsuit. All agents who were appointed after the lawsuit have some relation to the suit and its aftermath. While we did not hear an agent or manager specifically explain the lawsuit, many of them told us stories that assume we already know about it.

The following example is an older white male agent explicitly criticizing Mid-West's handling of the suit. The interviewer did not elicit this story; the agent brought it up himself as one example of his claim that MidWest's current policies were inferior to the past:

> Yes, I mean some of the things we had to go through and [a senior manager] brings it out, I had forgotten all about it, we had a lawsuit back in the '80s with female discrimination. And I mean MidWest really went through, they went through terrible times trying to be, trying to justify. But also the times were different, they made mistakes in the '70s that they had to pay for in the '80s or in the '90s. Which I felt wasn't right. I mean yes they discriminated against women. But if you discriminated against somebody in 1974 because that was the way it was supposed to, I mean that's just the way business was done, then when you discover that. You know when somebody says "You've been doing wring." It's what you do from that point, it's not what you did. Because if you didn't know it was wrong, how could you, you can't change the past. You can only change from where you are today. And this [lawsuit], and they had to hire so many, they had to appoint so many women and so many minorities. And they bypassed so many good white guys that it wasn't right. If they had started at that point and said "We will hire the best women and the best minority and the best person. We don't care what their blood line is." That would have been much better. But that [lawsuit], they couldn't, and they paid dearly for that.

This is a complex (though familiar) argument about affirmative action. In effect, this agent argues that the company went too far in its reparations. MidWest should not have been asked, nor should its management have chosen to make amends retroactively for a policy shared by the entire society. Rather, when societal beliefs changed, management should have brought current hiring policies in line with the change. But they should not have been forced to make retroactive changes. The argument also blurs the issue of who should be blamed: MidWest or the society at large.

I heard a much more accepting mention of the lawsuit from a younger white male agent telling the story of how he came to be admitted as an agent. He started his career as a salesman for an auto repair chain and came to know MidWest agents as he solicited them for business. Several agents were impressed by his sales style and suggested that he try to become a MidWest agent. As a result of this encouragement, he spoke with several MidWest managers and went with "the first one who had a slot for a white male." As he recounted this event in the longer story, his tone was very matter of fact, with no special intonational marking or evaluative comment about the gender and race issue. He told it as one not very remarkable background condition in the story of his becoming an agent and founding his agency.

A more dramatic and negatively evaluated account of the initial discriminatory policy and its change was given by a female agent who had a long history with the company. Her father was "agent of the year" in the fifties and she had a long work history as an employee of MidWest. As she told us, when she expressed her desire to become an agent, a vice president who was a friend of her father discouraged her saying, "But you're a girl!" Several years later she packed her bags and headed west, hearing it was more "progressive." Her car broke down in Montana and she stayed. She sold cosmetics door to door for a while and her mother encouraged her to try MidWest again. Her story continues: "The company was looking to hire women and minorities, that's the only reason I got hired." Here, the speaker reveals some bitterness about past policies but the discussion was embedded within an account of her loyalty to the company and her belief in its fundamental values.

The next example is yet more complex. It is the story of an Asian-American woman, a recent graduate of an elite women's college. She started with a general prejudice against a career in insurance, perhaps a social class issue. She was also distressed by the small number of women in general in the company, and by the very few women from her college in the company. However, on talking to a MidWest employee who was an alumna of her college, she was reassured that change was happening:

> And then I have role models. I mean people who mentored me, people that I looked up to and there was one woman in particular. And she graduated I think in the early 80's and I talked to her, I said "God Sarah, what do you know about MidWest and what can you share with me about this company? Because as I look at the directory from our college, there is only like one or two, I don't, there was only like one person. They weren't even listed. I only learned later that there was one. I said "Does that say anything about this industry and this company if there aren't any women [from our college]? Because we are known for being pretty vocal and pretty opinionated and where we like to have an environment where we can thrive. You know, not having anything like where you have to alter so much of who you are. And she said "Well you have to look at the industry. That industry as a whole, it is very very conservative. And your company is very conservative." I have to tell you that MidWest, because they were sued, they had a humungous law suit a couple years earlier. Yeah, so Sarah said "you know, looking at the company now, it is conservative. But I think it is trying to make changes. And it has to." It is mandated by the courts and just by society at large. They can't no longer ignore that women are very much part of the work force and that they have to make room for women. And so she said "if I were you, I think that would be a good call for you. I know that on the whole, the company is a little bit conservative, but I think that there will be a lot of opportunities for women." And so when she put it that way, I said okay.

This example is interesting because of the frankness with which the speaker discusses her initial prejudice against insurance as a business and against MidWest for its apparent conservatism. It also shows an example of a very explicit admission that MidWest did indeed discriminate against women, because they were (and still are) very conservative. But the speaker's fellow alumna does indicate her belief that MidWest's efforts to make changes are real and form a good business opportunity for a woman newly entering the company. Note also that discrimination against women is explicitly discussed. Concern about whether someone with her particular college background (which she values very highly) is also mentioned. Race or ethnicity, which we will consider next, is not mentioned at all.

The discussions above have focused on gender discrimination, a difficult enough issue. The following examples show how agents deal with the issue of racial discrimination, which was also part of the lawsuit. Racial and ethnic issues are notoriously difficult to discuss within current discourse norms in the United States. The following examples show some of the ways in which members of MidWest attempt to speak this difficult subject.

In a discussion sitting on a lawn during a break in a meeting, a recently hired African-American manager mentioned to me that it was very important to him that he was hired and promoted on his own merits, not because of racial quotas. This conversation was perhaps made more possible by the fact that the manager who had promoted him, who was also the person who was the supervisor of IRL's contract, was an African-American woman with a long tenure in the company and very highly respected by her peers. And still, this was a conversation on a lawn, not in an office or a conference room. The matter could be discussed, but I did not hear it discussed in any official situation. Similarly, I heard a group of long-term, Anglo-American agents and managers complaining about unqualified affirmative action promotions as they drove to a meeting, but the complaints were voiced in the van, not in the meeting.

In a direct discussion with a field-worker, a Hispanic agent explains why he did not accept the first offer he was given to train as an agent:

> They were looking for an agent to be placed in an inner city location in [City] but they were looking for someone that was either, had to be at least twenty five years old and **uh, of certain racial makeup, and of which I qualified**. They only problem was that I was new. I was about to be married and had no money, so there was no way I was going to go and do it.

While there is some awkwardness and disfluency in the way that this normally fluent speaker specifies that there was a desired racial identity, there are two points to be made. First, the issue is speakable, at least to the extent that American discourse generally allows for discussion of race as an issue across racial or ethnic boundaries (the interviewer is Anglo-American). Secondly, the main topic is the explanation of why the speaker did not at this time accept an offer he later was glad to accept. Indeed, when asked if his current location in an inner-city location is a challenge, his argument is that it is just the opposite:

> I think this area here is ideal for me. I am probably one of the luckiest guys around. Because the people that are here are of, at the, you know, they're of the ethnic makeup that works for us. You know there's a lot of Hispanics. We have Filipinos. Uh, Samoans. Uh, African Americans um, so and then a lot of folks that speak Spanish. And so they feel very comfortable when they speak to me in their native tongue.

Thus, the agent is able to construct his ethnicity as a business advantage and to praise MidWest for having located him in an ideal neighborhood.

These stories are tellable, without apparent embarrassment or anger, to relative outsiders, which suggests that the official silence apparently does not require a corresponding oppositional stance in an unofficial breaking of the silence. This is a noisy silence—it speaks out, apparently, everywhere but in conference rooms.

Comparison to the public record

Let us continue the exploration of the question of how one can learn to hear a silence. During the entire course of our ethnographic study of MidWest, I relied on internal accounts of the lawsuit to understand the pattern of silence and speakability on the subject. Only after considerable time working on this internal analysis did I consult the public record on the lawsuit. In doing so, I was surprised to find a number of major points that did not appear in any internal version of the lawsuit.

The first of these was the time the suit took: more than a decade passed between the initial suit and its final settlement. Even for a major class action suit, this is a markedly long time. The second point was that MidWest initially attempted to settle each claim individually, which led to further delay and litigation. Only after a long period did it agree to a class settlement.

Elimination of these two points from the story of the lawsuit within MidWest leads to a sanitized story, from which wrongdoing is eliminated. Piecing together the story as I heard it within MidWest, it appears as if once the problem was brought to MidWest's attention by the lawsuit, management saw that times had changed, and so their hiring policies must change with them. Therefore, they settled the lawsuit immediately and without contesting it. The more complex facts in the legal record suggest that MidWest continued to battle the issue until it became obvious that further contestation would have a high cost both financially and to the company's reputation. Thus, the internal story eliminates any suggestion that the company was forced into proper behavior; it rather suggests an immediate willingness to change once they realized that their policies were now wrong.

As a methodological issue, this example shows the limits of restricting the analysis to the internal narratives. While the focus of this investigation is on the ecology of stories within an institution, those boundaries can only be properly understood by comparison with external records as well. There is also an issue of what constitutes the external record. At the time this study began, finding out the details of the lawsuit would have required extensive library research or fee-based access to specialized databases such as the legal database LexisNexis. With advances in Internet search engine technology, such research is immeasurably easier. However, it still requires some initial knowledge and some reason to do the search.

Is silence about wrongdoing inevitable?

We might also ask whether it is reasonable to expect that MidWest would speak publicly about an event in which tacitly, if not legally, they admitted past wrongdoing, by agreeing to change its hiring and promotion policies. It might be argued that it is impossible for an institution to represent events in the past that put it in a bad light. That is, institutional silence about its own wrongdoing in the past is inevitable. However, there are certainly examples, many of them recent, in which the representatives of institutions do just that, acknowledging past wrongdoing and presenting apologies for it. A few of many political examples include F. W. de Klerk's apology for apartheid, Jacques Chirac's apology for the French people's persecution of the Jews during the German occupation of France, and Bill Clinton's apology for the United States' history of slavery. Religious examples include Pope John Paul II's apology for the errors of the Catholic Church over its 2000 year history, the Southern Baptist Convention's apology for its past defense of slavery. (See Power (2000).)

What has recently been called a "culture of apology" has led to a great deal of debate about what constitutes a sincere apology: whether it requires an attempt at reparation in the case of past offenses, and who may give, and who may choose to accept, an apology. However, this recent spate of historical apologies certainly demonstrates how previously hidden misdeeds may come to be publicly speakable.

In the case of MidWest's lawsuit, the fact that it was settled out of court means that the company agreed to change its business practices, while legally not admitting guilt. Ironically, the fact that there was no formal court finding of guilt may make the official silence deeper: since the company admitted no wrong at the time, it cannot officially admit it later. Thus, apologies are not possible. And yet, because of the changes in policy, unofficial discussions are inevitable.

Oppositional agents' association: A silence about existence

In addition to the affirmative action suit, another notable silence in MidWest's official memory is any mention of the existence of an organization of disaffected agents, described in an article in the outside business press as "a would be union" of discontented agents, who consider that the company is "run for the benefit of its management and nobody else." The fieldwork team heard the organization mentioned and even discussed by agents and managers and was shown copies of the newsletter distributed by the organization to all agents. Agents and managers were quick to express publicly their distance from the organization and their disgust with its lack of loyalty to the company, even those agents who showed us these publications.

As I have already discussed, although we were not able to study the organization in detail, we did have the chance to read some of their newsletters. It is clear from these writings that the organization maintains a counterstory of the history of MidWest in which the current executives have strayed from the original values of MidWest, while the members of the organization attempt by critique to maintain these values. MidWest maintains an official silence about its existence. Its existence is never mentioned on public occasions, and its arguments are never mentioned, even to counter them. When I asked about this, one former manager explained the reason for this silence: "We try to avoid a pissin' match with a skunk."

The existence of this association is widely, perhaps universally, known throughout MidWest. When the fieldwork team came to find out about it, we were able to discuss it without difficulty with the members of management with whom we worked. However, it did not appear to be a polite question (either for us, or for agents) to ask any agent whether he or she was a member. Agents either volunteered that they were members, mentioned their disdain for the association, or did not bring the subject up. As an example of how membership was mentioned, a senior agent did tell us that he was a member of the Association as part of discussion of what kinds of information he finds useful in making business decisions:

> Agent: I literally toss the National Magazines, the National Life Insurance Magazines. The National Association of MidWest Agents, I'm a member, and the reason I am a member is because I want to know. I want to be fed information, and MidWest isn't feeding me enough. They don't give me enough information in their publications. They seldom admit, they are like politicians. Politicians never say "I made a mistake."
>
> Interviewer: Yeah, so what information do you get from the Association?
>
> Agent: Well I'm, right now I am particularly interested in retirement. And so their most recent articles in their national publication and to do, hang on here. Have to do all with what happens when you retire. And they talk a lot more about what really, I think the real world in here then early retirement, questions and answers that they've got. I can't tell you that every thing they say is the gospel or is true. But I get to see another side. I look at the MidWest magazines. And I really don't, I can show you this magazine, which is their January 1997 and I can show you January 96, I can show you 1979, I can show you 1970, I can show you, cause they are all right up there. All the [Name] magazines and this basically says the same thing. All they do is change the cover.

I should note here that the issue of information about retirement was particularly salient at the time of this interview. As previously discussed, MidWest was instituting a new contract, allowing veteran agents to choose the new contract, stay with the old contract, or move slowly from one to the other. For older agents, the main issue in choice of contract was the difference in their retirement provisions, and it was not clear to anyone in advance exactly how the various options would play out for each individual. Thus, agents were hungry for impartial and even critical analyses of the contracts in order to make a good decision in a situation of great uncertainty. The newsletter of the association provided a great deal of analysis and argument about this issue. The analysis was a natural consequence of the association's main premise: that MidWest was eroding the position of the sales agents and was thus turning its back on its most core value.

"Monarchy": A silence of interpretation

The silences on the issues of the lawsuit, and the existence and critiques of the association, are silences of fact: these facts are not spoken in particular contexts by particular people, although they are, as we have seen, quite speakable in less official circumstances. We now turn to a more complex silence: one in which the facts are known and are centrally part of the official story of MidWest. One plausible interpretation of these events and their relation to other company policies are matters of official silence—and uneasy unofficial talk.

The issue here is the nature of the succession to power at the highest levels of the company. The company has had five presidents in its more than seventy-year history, and these presidents have come from two families. This fact is a central part of the official story of the company. However, a detailed discussion of the nature of succession under such circumstances is an uneasy matter. There is a tension between pride that the business, however large, has remained in some sense a family business, and the general American belief that fairness and democracy require equal opportunities for all to rise to power: the level playing field. Yet the company is *not* a family business: its stock is not held privately by the founding family, but by a mutual company. The tension around succession to high office is exacerbated by the fact that the current president assumed that office at an exceptionally young age, which raises potential questions about whether he was the best choice for the job. Under such circumstances, if he does not prove himself to be exceptionally able, his appointment is easy to see as nepotism.

When speakers within MidWest are discussing the company as embodying family values, the fact that the succession has been held in only two families in over seventy years is mentioned as a point of pride: an example of family values at the highest level of the corporation. However, when the speaker is expressing doubt about the competence of the president or the fairness of the process, the same facts can bear a very different evaluation.

Within MidWest, as with most large U.S. companies, there is no detailed public account of the process of succession, or the grounds for the choice; officially the president is chosen by the board of directors, and that is the basis of the legitimacy of the succession. The criteria used by the board are not discussed in the official account. Insider gossip among long-term managers contains accounts of struggles for control between powerful families on the board, but this gossip is not necessarily known to all agents.

This lack of transparency about the grounds for the choice of leadership might be attributed to the fact that MidWest is a privately held corporation and thus not responsible to an independent board of directors, stockholders, and Wall Street analysts in the same way that publicly held companies are. However, Khurana (2004) has argued that even for publicly held companies, the process of selecting the president or chief executive officer, particularly one from outside the organization, is not driven by what would be analyzed as rational market forces and optimal use of available information. Rather, succession is decided by boards of directors who act on a quasi-religious belief that some few candidates inherently possess charisma and that charisma is essential for a CEO. Thus, the board members act on a set of habits of mind that restricts the number of apparently plausible candidates to an extremely small pool.

These are difficult matters to discuss within any institution. Most members of most institutions have little or no say in who their leadership is, and yet the success or failure of their leaders makes a major difference in their lives. Under such circumstances, people would prefer to believe that these leaders have been legitimately and appropriately chosen, and that they know what they are doing and can be trusted. While people may make minor criticisms of leadership, they tend to try to protect the top man (almost always the man) from criticism, because it would cause almost unbearable anxiety to doubt him without being able to influence him. However, we did observe some rather uneasy discussion of the nature of the president's succession by agents and managers. The issues were both the fairness of the succession procedure and the question of whether this president was actually the best man for the job.

To give one example of such discussion, I turn to my observation of a program for training new staff members for agents. In this session, a first-level manager has been leading the introduction to MidWest's history. She showed a video from headquarters about the company's history, which included the lineage of presidents, and she then led a discussion about the video. She herself raised the issue of the presidency, noting that it was "interesting" that there had been a couple of sons and fathers as presidents: "Can you believe, in more than seventy years of this company, the leaders have only come from two families."

One of the trainees objected: "I don't know if that's always good. It's like a kingdomship [sic], a dictatorship. A single family becomes more and more powerful." This is an understandable objection, framed in the most basic terms of the founding American political ideology: the rejection of monarchy. (However, this ideology, of course, does not discuss the existence of American political dynasties, whether at the presidential level or other levels of politics.)

It is also worth noting that the objection contains the interesting neologism "kingdomship." I believe that the use of such a constructed term is an indication of how difficult it is for people to discuss such issues. As supporting evidence of this linguistic point, I would mention that as a part of a different project, I had I had the opportunity to talk with a relatively low-level employee of a privately held corporation about the issue of family succession to the highest positions. At dinner (that is, very unofficially) he made a similar complaint about the "monarchism" of his employer. I find it notable that both of these discussions involved neologisms: "kingdomship" and "monarchism." I suspect that the issue of the legitimacy of inherited authority is so rarely discussed, and so difficult and painful for the speakers, that it gives rise to neologism: speakers need to reach for words that are not available to them, and hence to invent them. This lack of available terms suggests that American discourse contains few occasions and little vocabulary for analysis of the nature of power.

In the initial example of "kingdomship," we see an objection raised by someone who is not yet a member of MidWest, who either does not know, or who can take advantage of his position to appear not to know that this is a sensitive issue. The trainer's response was a smooth one, blending large-scale company issues and her own personal evolution of feeling about this issue. She began by citing the net worth of the company as one of the highest in the country and used that to argue that therefore, "someone must be doing something right." This is a standard response to a critique of the legitimacy of leadership. But then she went on to discuss the issue more personally, admitting that she had had the same doubts herself: "I asked that question: 'You just have to marry into the family?' But the sons were so good, they got the chance. There's a sense of family and closeness. These core values having leadership have kept us number one. It's not because you have the last name, it's because they were very good."

This is a complex and skillful response to the problem posed by the student. The trainer has validated the student's objection by admitting that she has asked the same question. Indeed, her formation of the question shows that her validation is not just a momentary pedagogical trick. Rather, she has considered the issue in light of the question of how she herself will rise in the company. Since she was not born into an important family within MidWest, does she have to marry into one in order to rise? She manages to turn the succession by birth back into succession by merit: the sons deserved the chance they were given. Given that the sons' own worth made them deserving of their office, the nature of the succession within two families is actually a good thing, because it strengthens the family values that are so important to Mid-West. When I later discussed this issue with her privately, she told me previously that this issue used to bother her, but she became convinced that all the presidents were very competent, so it was really not wrong to keep the succession within the family. Which means, essentially, that she told me that she really believed what she had said to the group of trainees.

We find a similar argument made in the headquarters trainer's speech to new managers, discussed earlier in chapter 5. This speaker reflects on the succession of presidents, naming them all and their relation to one another. This means that he explicitly lays out the familial nature of the succession. He never raises the issue of whether this might be problematic: by the time trainee managers have reached the point of this talk, they must already know the sequence of the succession and have accepted it as just, or at least acceptable. This speaker concludes with the same reflection as the young local trainer: this means of succession is a good one, because all the presidents have been excellent: "So here you have the five presidents from the three families over. And we are so lucky or blessed, sometimes in the family, the second generation is sometimes weaker than the first, and the third certainly than the second. And we seem to just get better and better as the years go along."

As discussed above, it is difficult and painful for a member of any institution to raise doubt about the legitimacy and competence of one's management. This low-level local manager has no ability to affect who holds upper management positions. Given that she is stuck with her management, it is much more tolerable to believe that they are competent, that they know what they are doing, that they should hold the positions that they do. If she comes to believe that they are not competent or legitimate, her only choices are to remain in a state of fear and opposition, or leave to find another job. While she is relatively new in the company and could find other work, employees and agents with longer tenure have a great deal of time, money, and emotional investment in the company—leaving would mean a major change in their lives. Rather than living in doubt, it is easier to come to persuade themselves that they can trust their management. (I would note that living with doubts about management is perhaps easiest for the oldest generation of agents and employees, who can feel that the company's prosperity is likely to last till their own retirement, even if they bemoan current problems or problems that they see coming up on the horizon for others.)

Thus far, I have been discussing the issue of succession for upper management and how it affects lower-level employees, including other managers. As I have suggested, this is an official silence, but it is discussable unofficially. However, there is a connection between this issue and another, which is considerably more immediate, and is hotly discussed unofficially. That has to do with the fact that the powerful managerial families in the company have been able to pass on management positions to their children, while agents are not permitted pass on their businesses to their children.

Agents, as I have already explained, are independent contractors to MidWest. This means that they own or lease their offices, furniture, and equipment. However, they do not own their book of business: the insurance policies of the clients whom they insure. When an agent retires, he may want to pass his business to his son (or more recently, daughter). Under the terms of the agents' contract, this is not possible. The book of business belongs to MidWest. While MidWest unofficially gives preferential treatment to the children of agents and employees, there is no guarantee that a child will be certified as an agent even if they undergo the training. There is certainly no guarantee that an agent's child will be allowed to inherit a parent's book of business. Such inheritance is rather rare and happens at the discretion of the manager in charge of allocating the accounts of a retiring agent to other agents. We were told stories of this happening in the past. We were also told that it was becoming much less possible, under the new management system, for a district manager to pass on a book of business in this way. In general, the new management system was less personalistic and more bureaucratic than the previous relation between agents and managers. Thus, the newer managers were not as strongly tied to their agents economically or relationally. They had less reason to bend the rules to allow this kind of succession.

Agents whose children are themselves interested in becoming agents are quite bitter in their discussion of the fact that their children may not inherit their business (as they could with any other type of small business). Yet this problem is rarely if ever directly discussed as an unjust contrast to the apparent inheritability of the presidency and other high management positions. Why this silence? First, like the presidential succession within the company, there is little or nothing that the agents can do about this issue. It is a fundamental part of every contract that MidWest has ever written with agents, and there is no likelihood that it will be changed. Second, as I discussed above, the available discourse for agents contains little or no resource for political analysis of the nature of power. An issue which can not be changed, and which can not be intelligently discussed, is likely not to be discussed at all.

Conclusion: The loudness of silence

This chapter on silences has been loud with the sound of stories. Silences within institutions are not absolute. They are utterly contextual—what is unspeakable from the podium of a formal meeting is endlessly speakable in the bar after the meeting is over. It is very hard to keep silences within an institution—something always leaks. At the same time, it is difficult for people to speak about issues when they do not have an analytic or moral vocabulary for such issues. There is a difference between a grumble that something is wrong, and an analysis of why it is wrong, and how it might be different.

The rustle of silences that I have described at MidWest is by no means confined to that institution: these noisy silences are everywhere. Just listen for them.

10

Working the Past

Identity and Memory

At the beginning of this book, I promised to tell a story about stories, and that is what this book has been. I have presented an ethnography of the structure and the use of stories within an institution, taking both the story and the institution as the primary units of analysis. There are many ways to study institutions and institutional remembering, just as there are many ways to study the work of representing the past. So why stories? I study stories in this way because stories are where the action is, both literally and figuratively. Narrative is the discourse unit that presents both what happened, that is, events in the past, and what they mean, that is, the evaluation or moral significance of these events. Taken together, this presentation of the past and its meaning make stories one of the primary means for proposing and negotiating identity, both individual and collective identities. There are many ways of constructing who I am, and who We are. The answers that are crafted for this central question of identity are important for any group that acts like a We, whether We are a family, an insurance company, or a nation. The answers shape how the members act; how they think they should act; how they try to predict the results of their actions; how they or others decide whether someone is or is not really one of Us; how they use, change or contest that past in order to understand the institution as a whole as well as their place in it. This book has focused on narrative as a central tool in the work of representing the past. Stories are perhaps the most pervasive, and certainly the most easily examined, method for doing this work of creating and maintaining identity. Stories certainly do other work as well, but this book has been primarily concerned with issues of the identity of an institution and the identities of individuals within an institution.

Any analysis of identity is also an examination of memory. Identity, whether individual or collective, is identity though time. The very idea of identity requires at least some degree of continuity through time. An identity of this moment, not related to the past and not remembered in the future, hardly counts as an identity at all. Memory is thus central to the concept of identity. In this book, I have treated memory as a verb and as a task: the acts of remembering, the practices of remembering, the ways in which people learn to remember as part of their own identity events they did not themselves experience. Identity and memory are acts of construction. The past is not inert, not written in stone as we used to say before the digital age. The past or, more accurately, various representations of various past events are brought into the present to shape the future by continuous work, large-scale work, and intimate work, by collectivities and individuals. While this work of bringing the past into the present also includes file cabinets, databases, laws, regulations, practices, etc., this book has concentrated on the way that stories are used by individuals and institutions. There have been many excellent studies of the large-scale resources for collective memory, but very few examinations of how these collections are actually used. This work has therefore examined not only the repertoire of stories within an institution, but also the ways in which people come to learn these stories, the occasions on which they are told, and the different ways different people tell them. It has examined the relations between stories in an institution, the ways that a narrator of a story changes previous tellings and shapes them for a time, an audience and an occasion. It also looks at the ways in which members of an institution link their own stories to the salient institutional stories, and in this way, come to be heard as members.

One of the important discoveries of this study is that in order to work the past, one central resource is the institutional existence of occasions for doing so, first discussed in chapter 3. A story not having a proper occasion on which it can or must be told exists in an archive if it exists at all. An institution not having a range of occasions for telling stories is not likely to be working its past very hard. If there is any place where the process of institutional remembering can be deliberately altered, it is the creation, maintenance, or abandonment of narrative occasions.

Occasions for narration are usually occasions for renarration. As discussed in chapter 4, it is the stories that are retold within an institution that are central to the work of institutional remembering. These retold stories are important because they are a direct way that an institution can continue to bring a particular account of the past into the future. If a story can acquire new tellers, it can break free of the lifetime of its participants and witnesses and develop what is potentially an indefinitely long lifetime. Having established the retold story as a key piece in institutional remembering, the argument then turned to the examination of the stories told within MidWest Insurance, showing how these stories live within an institution. This analysis moved along a scale of scope and intimacy from the highest level of stories known to every member to the details of how particular people tell their own stories of life as members of MidWest.

First, in chapter 5, it looked at the core stock of stories: the stories known to members of an institution. The important point of this part of the analysis is that stories in an institution are not a random, unordered collection, where it is impossible to predict which story any member may know. Rather, there are central stories everyone can be expected to know, as well as other rarer stories known mainly by people with particular concern for the topic, or by "history buffs" with a particular interest in the past of the institution. I have defined this collection of stories at MidWest Insurance as forming an open canon. That is, there is currently a collection of stories everyone can be expected to know. While the institution continues, we can expect that new stories of averted disasters, triumphs, and changes of direction will be added. It is even possible that a new hero will join the founder in the narrative pantheon.

The very rich data of this study has allowed for a number of different kinds of narrative comparisons. The comparison of five different tellings of a temporally complete account of MidWest's history allowed for the development of a description of the contents of the core stock of stories. It also allowed for a study of the importance of positioning: the ways narrators use their position within MidWest as well as the nature of the occasion of a telling to shape the ways they tell a particular story at a particular time to a particular audience.

Chapter 6 presented a comparison of three different versions of the same story of the founder. This comparison analyzed in detail the ways in which the microstructure of a story is shaped by its teller and its occasion for telling: the particular details of what events are narrated and what meaning is given to them. The positioning a speaker assumes is important to the form the narrative. In this example, a story about an adventure of Mr. McBee with a hostile newspaper editor is told either as an account by management of Mr. McBee's management skills, or as an account for agents of Mr. McBee's care for his agents, and the admirable skills and character traits his agents still share with him. This comparison also demonstrated the complex relation between written and oral narrative within an institution: in particular, the continuous movement of a narrative from oral form to written form back to oral form, which continues without a necessary ending point at which the process is complete. This part of the study points to a promising area of investigation in other research sites: the continued existence of a rich and unexpected oral culture and the social mechanisms that support it within modern corporate life.

Moving from the central stories of MidWest, I then examined, in chapter 7, the paradigmatic narrative: the narrative of an agent's ideal career at MidWest, told variously through stories of different agents at different times in their careers. This part of the study shows some of the mundane work of using individual pasts of members as a way to demonstrate to a potential agent or new agent what being a member could mean. It is proposed within the institution as the story of Everyman and, as such, uses parts of different people's stories to form the whole narrative. This analysis provides one case study for how an identity is proposed to a prospective member. This is the on-the-ground work of how a representative of an institution suggests to a new or prospective agent: "You see the kind of career Bob has had? You could do that too, you could be like him." This discovery of the paradigmatic narrative offers another promising area for research. Do other types of institutions have paradigmatic narratives? What kinds of institution are most likely to create and maintain them? How do they differ across institutions?

Chapter 8 then moved the analysis to individual members' stories: the ways in which members tell their own stories within the textual field of the stories of the institution. This examination of how an individual's past is told within an institutional past produced an initial taxonomy of the possible forms of relation between individual stories and these highly valued institutional stories. These relations include citation and quotation of institutional stories, use of the same moral values, critique, irony, and rejection. All of these are possible ways members can frame their own stories in relation to the institution's stories. One's own story is not only one's own. It is always told and heard against a background of others' stories. This part of the book showed the details of how that happens within an institution. Again, this is an examination of one piece of the small-scale daily work of identity formation. People shape their own identities (or their narrative representation of their identities) at least partially through the influence of other stories within the institutions of which they are members. Learning the valued stories of the past, learning how to tell one's own story as a member, is part of the intimate work of the creation of identity.

Finally, in chapter 9, the study considered silences within institutions. Not telling a story, or making it difficult for a particular story to be told, takes another kind of work. Every institution has something it is not talking about, whether the topic of that silence is relatively benign or appalling. The study of silence at MidWest has shown that silence is profoundly contextual. What is unspeakable in a public situation may be endlessly spoken in private.

So this has been a story about the adventures of stories in groups of people and the adventures of people in groups of stories. Maintaining a useable past takes work. It is as much work as maintaining a useable building, though very different work, using very different tools. The work of this book has been to demonstrate the existence and the nature of this work—mundane, daily, and utterly essential to any group that considers that it has an identity. This is the work that keeps us Us, whoever We may be.

NOTES

Chapter 3

1. The designer of the exhibit, whose main job was special promotional programs and awards, told me that he developed it from materials which had been stored rather haphazardly. They required considerable restoration to make them exhibitable. He emphasized how much fun it had been to develop it.

Chapter 4

1. The implicational hierarchy is a common concept in the study of linguistic universals. (See Greenberg (1963), Comrie (1989), and Croft (1990.) The basic idea is that certain types of linguistic properties are related, and therefore can be used to predict which of them a given language will have. For a set of related properties A B C D, if a language has property D, it will also have C, B, and A; if it has C, it will also have B and C, and if it has B, it will also have A. On the other hand, the presence of property A does not predict whether or not any of the other properties are present.

Chapter 5

1. Interestingly, two of the tellings, the newsletter articles and the speech by the head-quarters trainer, have a variant version of the slogan: "A million or more in spite of the war." I have never heard this variant used in any other telling.

2. Harricane Katrina in 2005, probably is an even stronger boundary for MidWest. It happened, however, after the period of the fieldwork, and so I do not have the necessary evidence to discuss it.

Chapter 6

1. As a methodological note I would add that this kind of on-the-fly interview is a particularly valuable technique for this kind of fieldwork. While a formal interview is usually conducted between strangers, the shadowing process allows the two participants to develop some kind of relationship. It also prevents the interview from being an imposition in an already busy schedule. Finally, and most important, it allows the interviewee to link the conversation to the context of the ongoing work activity, which gives it a much higher degree of both relevance and authenticity.

Chapter 7

1. During the period of our fieldwork, one major concern of upper management was the proposed repeal of the Glass-Steagal Act. This was a law which separated banking and investment activities and, among other provisions, forbade the sale of insurance by banks. In 1999, this law was indeed repealed by Congress, opening the way for an entire new class of competitor in the area of insurance sales.

2. I am grateful to my colleague and teammate Charline Poirier for forcing me to see the difference between a paradigmatic narrative and a myth, and thus saving me from the scorn of folklorists, and the potential misunderstanding of the managers at MidWest who would have heard "myth" as meaning "a story that is not true."

3. I thank my colleague and teammate Nancy Lawrence for her analysis of the notion of "contentment" as an alternate analysis for the negatively charged notion of "plateauing."

4. In a discussion of police work, Van Maanan (1998) has argued that consistency of character across many situations and relationships is the trait that police officers value most highly in their colleagues. More generally, he argues that any occupation requiring a high degree of trust will *not* easily support a postmodern, fragmented self.

5. I am indebted to my colleague and teammate Christopher Darrouzet for this analysis of the homologous nature of the relations of MidWest to its agents, the agents to their clients.

Chapter 8

1. I owe this observation to Dr. Robin Kornman. He argues that this is a common feature of all epics: that they are so pervasive in the culture that they are known to members of that culture before they are encountered in their full form.

REFERENCES

Agha, Asif. 2005. "Voice, Footing, Enregisterment." *Journal of Linguistic Anthropology* 15 (1): 38–59.

Aikehnvald, Alexandra Y. 2004. *Evidentiality*. New York: Oxford University Press.

Allen, Graham. 2000. *Intertextuality*. New York: Routledge.

Andrews, Molly. 2002. "Introduction: Counter-narratives and the Power to Oppose." *Narrative Inquiry: Special Issue on Counter-narrative* 12 (1): 1–6.

Argyris, C., and D. A. Schon. 1978. *Organisational Learning: A Theory of Action Perspective*. Reading, Mass.: Addison-Wesley.

Basso, Keith H. 1996. *Wisdom Sits in Places: Landscape and Language Among the Western Apache*. Albuquerque: University of New Mexico Press.

Bauman, Richard. 1992. "Performance." In *Folklore, Cultural Performances and Popular Entertainments: A Communications Centered Handbook*, edited by R. Bauman. Oxford: Oxford University Press.

Berger, Peter L., and Thomas Luckmann. 1967. *The Social Construction of Reality*. Berkeley: University of California Press.

Berman, Laine. 1998. *Speaking through the Silence: Narratives, Social Conventions, and Power in Java*. Edited by W. Bright, *Oxford Studies in Anthropological Linguistics*. New York: Oxford University Press.

Berube, E. M. 1966. "Mentoring is One Approach to Agent Retention Issue." *Best's Review: Life-Health Edition* 96 (82).

Biggart, Nicole Woolsey. 1989. *Charismatic Capitalism: Direct Selling Organizations in America*. Chicago: University of Chicago Press.

Bishop, Libby, and Lucy Suchman. 2000. "Problematizing 'Innovation' as a Critical Project." *Technology Analysis and Strategic Management* 12(3): 327–333.

Bonanno, Bill. 1998. *Bound by Honor: A Mafioso's Story*. New York: St. Martin's Press.

Borofsky, Robert, Frederick Barth, Richard A. Shweder, Lars Rodseth, and Nomi Maya Stolzenberg. 2001. "WHEN: A Conversation about Culture." *American Anthropologist* 103 (2): 432–446.

Bowker, Geoffrey. 1993. *Science on the Run: Information Management and Industrial Geophysics at Schlumberger, 1920–1940*. Cambridge, Mass.: MIT Press.

Bowker, Geoffrey, and Susan Leigh Star. 2000. *Sorting Things Out: Classification and Its Consequences*. Cambridge, Mass.: MIT Press.

Brown, John Seeley, and Paul Duguid. 2000. *The Social Life of Information*. Boston: Harvard Business School Press.

Cain, Carole. 1991. "Personal Stories: Identity Acquisition and Self-understanding in Alcoholics Anonymous." *Ethos* 19 (2): 210–253.

Cappelli, Peter. 1999. *The New Deal at Work: Managing the Market-Driven Workforce*. Boston: Harvard Business School Press.

Chafe, Wallace, and Johanna Nichols. 1986. *Evidentiality: The Linguistic Coding of Epistemology*. Stamford, Conn.: Ablex.

Comrie, Bernard. 1989. *Language Universals and Linguistic Typology*. Oxford: Blackwell.

Croft, William. 1990. *Typology and Universals*. Cambridge: Cambridge University Press.

Crosby, Alfred W. 1997. *The Measure of Reality: Quantification and Western Society, 1250–1600*. Cambridge: Cambridge University Press.

Danziger, Murray Herbert. 1989. *Returning to Tradition: The Contemporary Revival of Orthodox Judaism*. New Haven: Yale University Press.

Davies, Bronwyn, and Rom Harré. 1990. "Positioning: The Discursive Production of Selves." *Journal for the Theory of Social Behavior* 20 (1): 43–63.

DeLong, David W. 2004. *Lost Knowledge: Confronting the Threat of an Aging Workforce*. New York: Oxford University Press.

Dorsey, David. 1994. *The Force*. New York: Random House.

Du Bois, John. 1986. "Self-evidence and Ritual Speech." In *Evidentiality: The Linguistic Coding of Epistemology*, edited by Wallace Chafe and Johanna Nichols. Norwood, N.J.: Ablex.

Duranti, Alessandro. 1994. *From Grammar to Politics: Linguistic Anthropology in a Western Samoan Village*: Berkeley: University of California Press.

Enhong, Yang. 1999. "Min Jian Shi Shen, Ge Sa Er Wang Chang Ren Yan Zhou, (Popular Divine Poets: Study on the singing tradition of 'King Gesar')." *IIAS Newsletter* 18.

Etorre, Barbara. 1994. "The Contingency Workforce Moves Mainstream." *Management Review* 83 (February): 10–16.

Fairclough, Norman. 1992. *Discourse and Social Change*. Cambridge: Polity Press.

Feenberg, Andrew. 1999. "Distance Learning: Promise or Threat? My Adventures in Distance Learning." Winter:http://www-rohan.sdsu.edu/faculty/feenberg/TELE3.HTM#Distance Learning: Promise or Threat.

Fentress, James and Chris Wickham. 1992. *Social Memory*. Oxford: Blackwell.

Fernandez, James. 1986. "The Argument of Images and the Experience of Returning to the Whole." In *The Anthropology of Experience*, edited by V. W. Turner and E. M. Bruner. Urbana: University of Illinois Press.

Finnegan, Ruth. 1988. *Literacy and Orality: Studies in the Technology of Communication*. New York: Blackwell.

Foley, John Miles. 1995. *The Singer of Tales in Performance*. Bloomington: Indiana University Press.

Frankel, Barbara, and M. G. Trend. 1991. "Principles, Pressures and Paychecks: The Anthropologist as Employee." In *Ethics and the Profession of Anthropology: Dialogue for a New Era*, edited by C. Fluehr-Lobban. Philadelphia: University of Pennsylvania Press.

Gal, Susan. 1995. "Language and the 'Arts of Resistance.'" *Cultural Anthropology* 10 (3): 407–424.

Galbraith, J. R. 1977. *Organizational Design.* Reading, Mass.: Addison-Wesley.

Goffman, Erving. 1981. "Footing." In *Forms of Talk*, edited by E. Goffman. Philadelphia: University of Pennsylvania Press.

Goodwin, Charles. 1984. "Notes on Story Structure and the Organization of Participation." In *In Structures of Social Action*, edited by J. M. Atkinson and John Heritage. Cambridge: Cambridge University Press.

Goodwin, Charles, and Marjorie H. Goodwin. 1987. "Concurrent Operations on Talk: Notes on the Interactive Organization of Assessments." *IPRA Papers in Pragmatics* 11:1–54.

Goodwin, Majorie H. 1990. *He-Said-She-Said: Talk as Social Organization Among Black Children.* Bloomington: Indiana University Press.

Goody, Jack, and Ian Watt. 1969. "The Consequences of Literacy." In *Literacy in Traditional Societies*, edited by J. Goody. Cambridge: Cambridge University Press.

Greenberg, Joseph H. 1963. "Some Universals of Grammar with Particular Reference to the order of Meaningful Elements." In *Universals of Language*, edited by J. H. Greenberg. Cambridge, Mass.: MIT Press.

Greene, Thomas. 1963. *The Descent from Heaven: A Study in Epic Continuity.* New Haven: Yale University Press.

Hakken, David. 1991. "Anthropological Ethics in the 1990s: A Positive Approach." In *Ethics and the Profession of Anthropology: Dialogue for a New Era*, edited by C. Fluehr-Lobban. Philadelphia: University of Pennsylvania Press.

Hambrick, D. C., and P. A. Mason. 1984. "Upper Echelons: The Organization as a Reflection of Its Top Managers." *Academy of Management Review* 8:193–206.

Harding, Susan Friend. 2000. *The Book of Jerry Falwell: Fundamentalist Language and Politics.* Princeton, N.J.: Princeton University Press.

Harré, Rom, and Luk van Langenhove. 1991. "Varieties of Positioning." *Journal for the Theory of Social Behavior* 21 (4): 393–407.

Heckscher, Charles. 1995. *White-Collar Blues: Management Loyalties in an Age of Corporate Restructuring.* New York: Basic Books.

Hill, Jane H., and Judith T. Irvine, eds. 1992. *Responsibility and Evidence in Oral Discourse.* Cambridge: Cambridge University Press.

——. 1992. "Introduction." In *Responsibility and Evidence in Oral Discourse*, edited by Jane H. Hill and Judith T. Irvine. Cambridge: Cambridge University Press.

Hirsch, Marianne. 1997. *Family Frames: Photography, Narrative and Postmemory.* Cambridge, Mass.: Harvard University Press.

Hobsbawm, Eric. 1985. *Workers: Worlds of Labor.* New York: Pantheon.

Holland, Dorothy, William Lachicotte, Jr., Debra Skinner, and Carole Cain. 1998. *Identity and Agency in Cultural Worlds.* Cambridge, Mass.: Harvard University Press.

Hunston, Susan, and Geoff Thompson, eds. 2001. *Evaluation in Text: Authorial Stance and the Construction of Discourse.* New York: Oxford University Press.

Ikeda, Keiko. 1998. *A Room Full of Mirrors: High School Reunions in Middle America.* Stanford, Calif.: Stanford University Press.

James, William. 1987. "Varieties of Religious Experience: A Study in Human Nature. Being the Gifford Lectures on Natural Religion Delivered at Edinburgh in 1901–1902." In *William James: Writings 1902–1910*, edited by B. Kuclick. New York: The Library of America.

Jondhale, Surendra, and Johannes Belz. 2004. *Reconstructing the World: B. R. Ambedkar and Buddhism in India.* New York: Oxford University Press.

Judah, Tim. 1997. *The Serbs: History, Myth, and the Destruction of Yugoslavia*. New Haven, Conn.: Yale University Press.

Karmay, Samten Gyaltsen. 1998. *The Arrow and the Spindle: Studies in History, Myths, Rituals and Beliefs in Tibet*. Kathmandu: Mandala Book Point.

Kendall, Shari. 1995. "Language Authority and Belief Systems in Religious Testimony." Paper presented at Georgetown Linguistics Society, Washington D.C.

Khurana. 2004. *Searching for a Corporate Savior: The Irrational Quest for Charismatic CEOs*. Princeton, N.J.: Princeton University Press.

Kiesler, S., and L. Sproull. 1982. "Managerial Response to Changing Environments: Perspectives on Problem Sensing from Social Cognition." *Administrative Science Quarterly* 27:548–570.

King, David. 1997. *The Commissar Vanishes: The Falsification of Photographs and Art in Stalin's Russia*. New York: Metropolitan Books.

Kornman, Robin. 1997. "Gesar of Ling." In *Religions of Tibet in Practice*, edited by D. Lopez, Jr. Princeton, N.J.: Princeton University Press.

Kristeva, Julia. 1984. "Word, Dialogue and the Novel." In *The Kristeva Reader*, edited by T. Moi. Oxford: Blackwell.

Labov, William. 1972. "The Transformation of Experience in Narrative Syntax." In *Language in the Inner City: Studies in the Black English Vernacular*. Philadelphia: University of Pennsylvania Press.

Law, John. 1994. *Organizing Modernity*. Oxford: Blackwell.

Leidner, Robin. 1993. *Fast Food Fast Talk: Service Work and the Routinization of Everyday Life*. Berkeley: University of California Press.

Levi, Carlo. 1963. *Christ Stopped at Eboli: The Story of a Year*. Edited by F. Frenaya. New York: Farrar, Straus and Company.

Linde, Charlotte. 1993. *Life Stories: The Creation of Coherence*. New York: Oxford University Press.

———. 1996. "Evaluation as Linguistic Structure and Social Practice." In *The Construction of Professional Discourse*, edited by B.-L. Gunnarsson, P. Linnell, and B. Nordberg. New York: Longman House.

———. 1998. "Other People's Stories: Person and Evidentiality in Individual and Group Memory." In *Papers from Berkeley Linguistics Society 1997*. Berkeley: BLS Press.

———. 2000. "The Acquisition of a Speaker by a Story: How History Becomes Memory and Identity." *Ethos* 28 (4): 608–632.

———. 2001. "Narrative and Tacit Knowledge Exchange." *Journal of Knowledge Management* 5 (2): 160–170.

———. 2001. "Narrative in Institutions." In *Handbook of Discourse Analysis*, edited by H. Hamilton, D. Schiffrin, and D. Tannen. New York: Blackwell.

Loftus, G. R., and E. F. Loftus. 1976. *Human Memory: The Processing of Information*. Hillsdale, N.J.: Erlbaum.

Lopes, Sal. 1987. *The Wall: Images and Offerings from the Vietnam Veterans Memorial*. New York: Collins Publishers.

Lord, Albert. 1965. *The Singer of Tales*. New York: Atheneum.

———. 1986. "The Merging of the Two Worlds: Oral and Written Poetry as Carriers of Ancient Values." In *Oral Tradition in Literature: Interpretation in Context*, edited by J. M. Foley. Columbia: University of Missouri Press.

Lowenthal, David. 1998. *The Heritage Crusade and the Spoils of History*. Cambridge: Cambridge University Press.

Lyotard, Jean-Francois. 1985. *The Post-Modern Condition: A Report on Knowledge*. Translated by B. Massumi. Minneapolis: University of Minnesota.

Martin, Joanne, Martha S. Feldman, Mary Jo Hatch, and Sim Sitkin. 1983. "The Uniqueness Paradox in Organizational Stories." *Administrative Science Quarterly* 28:438–453.

Martin, Joanne, Sim Sitkin, and Michael Boehm. 1985. "Founders and the Elusiveness of a Cultural Legacy." In *Organizational Culture*, edited by P. J. Frost, Larry F. Moore, Meryl Reis, Craig C. Lundberg, and Joanne Martin. Beverly Hills, Calif.: Sage Publications.

McCrea, Brian. 1990. *Addison and Steele Are Dead: The English Department, Its Canon, and the Professionalization of Literary Criticism.* Newark: University of Delaware Press.

Miller, Peggy. 1994. "Narrative Practices: Their Role in Socialization and Self-construction." In *The Remembering Self: Construction and Accuracy in the Self-Narrative*, edited by U. Neisser and R. Fivush. Cambridge: Cambridge University Press.

Mumby, Dennis. 1988. *Communication and Power in Organizations: Discourse, Ideology and Domination.* Norwood, N.J.: Ablex.

Munk, Nina. 2000. "The Price of Freedom." *New York Times Magazine* March 5.

Mushin, Hana. 1998. "Evidentiality and Epistemological Stance in Macedonian, English and Japanese Narrative." Ph.D. diss., State University of New York, Buffalo.

Nalanda Translation Committee. 1989. *The Rain of Wisdom: The Essence of the Ocean of True Meaning: Bringing the Rain of Wisdom, The Spontaneous Self-Liberation, The Blazing Great Bliss, The Quick Path to Realization of the Supreme Siddhi, The Vajra Songs of the Kagyu Gurus.* Boston: Shambhala Publications.

Newton, Judith Jowder. 1989. "Feminism and the New Historicism." In *The New Historicism*, edited by H. A. Veeser. New York: Routledge.

Nora, Pierre. 1989. "Between Memory and History: Les Lieux de Mémoire." *Representations* 26 (4): 7–25.

Noyes, Dorothy, and Roger D. Abrahams. 1999. "From Calendar Custom to National Memory: European Commonplaces." In *Cultural Memory and the Construction of Identity*, edited by D. Ben-Amos and L. Weissberg. Detroit: Wayne State University Press.

O'Reilly, C. A. 1983. "The Use of Information in Organizational Decision Making: A Model and Some Propositions." In *Research in Orgnizational Behavior*, edited by L. L. Cummings and B. M. Staw. Greenwich, Conn.: JAI Press.

Oberman, Ida. 1998. "Fidelity and Flexibility in Waldorf Education." Ph.D., diss. Stanford University.

——. 1999. "Institutional Memory in an Alternative Education Movement: Strategies of Textual Reproduction and Challenge." Paper presented at American Anthropological Association, Chicago, IL.

——. 2008. *1919-2006: A Century of Fidelity and Flexibility in Waldorf Education.* Lewiston, N.Y.: Edwin Mellen Press.

Ochs, Elinor, and Lisa Capps. 2001. *Living Narrative: Creating Lives in Everyday Storytelling.* Cambridge, Mass.: Harvard University Press.

Ong, Walter. 1982. *Literacy and Orality: The Technologizing of the Word.* New York: Methuen.

Orr, Julian. 1990. "Sharing Knowledge, Celebrating Identity: Community Memory in a Service Culture." In *Collective Remembering*, edited by D. Middleton and Derek Edwards. Thousand Oaks, Calif.: Sage Publications.

——. 1996. *Talking about Machines.* Ithaca, N.Y.: ILR Press.

Palmer, Laura. 1987. *Shrapnel in the Heart: Letters and Remembrances from the Vietnam Veterans Memorial.* New York: Random House.

Peters, Tom. 1997. "The Brand Called You." *Fast Company* (10): 83ff. (http:www.fastcompany.com/magazine/10/brandyou.html)

Pilcher, William W. 1972. *The Portland Longshoremen: A Dispersed Urban Community.* Edited by George and Louise Spindler, *Case Studies in Cultural Anthropology.* New York: Holt, Rinehart and Winston.

Pink, Daniel H. 1997. "Free Agent Nation." *Fast Company* (12):131–145.

Plaskow, Judith. 1990. *Standing Again at Sinai: Judaism from a Feminist Perspective*. New York: Harper and Row.

Polanyi, Livia. 1989. *The American Story*. Cambridge, Mass.: MIT Press.

Portelli, Alessandro. 1990. *The Death of Luigi Trastulli and Other Stories: Form and Meaning in Oral History*, (SUNY Series in Oral and Public History). Albany: SUNY Press.

Power, Mary, R. 2000. "Reconciliation, Restoration and Guilt: The Politics of Apologies." *Media International Australia* 95:192–94.

Prost, Antoine. 1997. "Monuments to the Dead." In *Realms of Memory: The Construction of the French Past*, edited by P. Nora. New York: Columbia University Press.

Quinn, Naomi. 2005. "How to Reconstruct Schemas People Share, From What They Say." In *Finding Culture in Talk: A Collection of Methods*, edited by N. Quinn. New York: Palgrave MacMillan.

Riddy, Felicity. 1991. "Reading for England: Arthurian Literature and National Consciousness." *Bibliographical Bulletin of the International Arthurian Society* 43:314–332.

Ross, Charles Stanley. 1989. "Translator's Introduction." In *Orlando Innamorato* by Matteo Maria Boiardo. Berkeley: University of California Press.

Sacks, Harvey. 1992. *Lectures on Conversation*. Edited by G. Jefferson. Oxford: Blackwell.

Sacks, Harvey, Emanuel Schegloff, and Gail Jefferson. 1974. "A Simplest Systematics of the Organization of Turn-taking in Conversation." In Language 50 (4): 696–735.

Samuel, Raphael. 1994. *Theatres of Memory*. Vol.1: Past and Present in Contemporary Culture. London: Verso.

Sandelans, L. E., and R. E. Stablein. 1987. "The Concept of Organizational Mind." In *Research in the Sociology of Organizations*, edited by S. Bachrach and N. DiTomaso. Greenwich, Conn.: JAI Press.

Schwartz, David G. 2005. *Encyclopedia of Knowledge Management*. Hershey, Pa.: Idea Group Publishing.

Scott, James. 1985. *Weapons of the Weak: Everyday Forms of Peasant Resistance*. New Haven, Conn.: Yale University Press.

Shea, Daniel B. 1988. *Spiritual Autobiography in Early America*. Madison: University of Wisconsin Press.

Shuman, Amy. 1986. *Storytelling Rights: The Uses of Oral and Written Texts by Urban Adolescents*, *(Cambridge Studies in Oral and Literature Culture, No 11)*. Cambridge: Cambridge University Press.

Sims, H. P., and D. A. Gioia. 1986. *The Thinking Organization: Dynamics of Organizational Social Cognition*. San Francisco: Jossey-Bass.

Smith, Douglas K. 1988. *Fumbling the Future: How Xerox Invented, Then Ignored, the First Personal Computer*. New York: Morrow.

Smith, Wilfred Cantwell. 1993. *What Is Scripture?* Minneapolis, Minn.: Fortress Press.

Stock, Brian. 1983. *The Implications of Literacy: Written Language and Models of Interpretation in the Eleventh and Twelfth Centuries*. Princeton, N.J.: Princeton University Press.

Stone, Elizabeth. 1988. *Black Sheep and Kissing Cousins: How Our Family Stories Shape Us*. New York: Times Books.

Strauss, Claudia. 1997. "Partly Fragmented, Partly Integrated: An Anthopological Examination of 'Postmodern Fragmented Subjects.' " *Cultural Anthropology* 12 (3): 362–404.

Street, Brian. 1995. "Towards a Critical Framework: A Critical look at Walter Ong and the 'Great Divide.' " In *Social Literacies: Critical Approaches to Literacy in Development, Ethnography and Education*, edited by B. Street. London: Longman.

Stromberg, Peter G. 1993. *Language and Self-Transformation: A Study of the Christian Conversion Narrative*. Cambridge: Cambridge University Press.

Sturken, Marita. 1997. *Tangled Memories: The Vietnam War, the AIDs Epidemic, and the Politics of Remembering*. Berkeley: University of California Press.

Traweek, Sharon. 1992. *Beamtimes and Lifetimes: The World of High Energy Physicists*. Cambridge, Mass.: Harvard University Press.

Trouillot, Michel-Rolph. 1995. *Silencing the Past: Power and the Production of History*. Boston: Beacon Press.

Tulviste, Peeter, and James V. Wetsch. 1995. "Official and Unofficial History: The Case of Estonia. *Journal of Narrative and Life History* 4 (4): 311–331.

Tyson, Eric. 1994. *Personal Finance for Dummies: A Reference for the Rest of Us*. San Mateo, Calif.: IDG Books.

Ungson, G. R., D. N. Braunstein, and P. D. Hall. 1981. "Managerial Information Processing: A Research Review. *Administrative Science Quarterly* 26:116–134.

Vansina, Jan. 1985. *Oral Tradition as History*. Madison: University of Wisconsin Press.

Vinitzky-Seroussi, Vered. 1998. *After Pomp and Circumstance: High School Reunion as an Autobiographical Occasion*. Chicago: University of Chicago Press.

Viswanathan, Gauri. 1998. *Outside the Fold: Conversion, Modernity and Belief*. Princeton, N.J.: Princeton University Press.

Wallulis, Jerald. 1998. *The New Insecurity: The End of the Standard Job and Family*, (SUNY Series in Social and Political Thought). Albany: SUNY Press.

Walsh, James P., and Gerardo Rivera Ungson. 1991. "Organizational Memory." *Academy of Management Review* 16 (1): 57–91.

Watson, Rubie. 1994. *Memory, History and Opposition Under State Socialism*. Santa Fe, N.Mex.: School of American Research Press.

Weber, Max. 1947. *The Theory of Social and Economic Organization*. Translated by A. M. Henderson and Talcott Parsons. New York: The Free Press.

White, Geoffrey M. 1997. "Museum/Memorial/Shrine: National Narrative in National Spaces." *Museum Anthropology* 21 (1): 8–27.

Witten, Marsha. 1993. "Narrative and the Culture of Obedience at the Workplace." In *Narrative and Social Control: Critical Perspectives*, edited by D. Mumby. Thousand Oaks, Calif.: Sage Publications.

Wodak, Ruth. 1996. *Disorders of Discourse, Real Language Series*. New York: Longman.

Wolfson, Nessa. 1976. "Speech Events and Natural Speech: Some Implications for Sociolinguistic Methodology." *Language and Society* 5:189–209.

Yates, JoAnne. 1989. *Control through Communication: The Rise of System in American Management*. Baltimore: Johns Hopkins Press.

Yerushalmi, Yosef Hayim. 1989. *Zakhor: Jewish History and Jewish Memory*. New York: Schocken Books.

Yurchak, Alexei. 2006. *Everything Was Forever, Till It Was No More: The Last Soviet Generation*. Princeton, N.J.: Princeton University Press.

Zeliser, Viviana A. Rotman. 1979. *Morals and Markets: The Development of Life Insurance in the United States*. New York: Columbia University Press.

Zussman, Robert. 1996. Autobiographical Occasions. *Contemporary Sociology* 25 (2): 143–48.

INDEX

academics, paradigmatic narratives and, 142–44
adults
  induction into textual communities of, 172
  second-person narratives for, 76
Agent of the Millennium, 32, 51
agents. *See also* MidWest agents
  clients and, 20, 25, 28–29
  employee *vs.* free, 160–62
  entrepreneurship and, 23
  as independent contractors, 22–24, 25, 163
  management and, 17–18, 19, 23, 25, 27, 28
  mentors and, 27
  nature/image of, 24–28
  relations with insurance companies, 22–24
Agha, Asif, 171
Allen, Graham, 168–69
anthropology
  contract, 41
  ethics of field work, 37–39
  linguistics and, 46
  research, 38
  taxonomy and, 46
Apache place names, 65–67
Apple Computer employment relation, 162–63
artifacts
  institutional, 68–71
  memorial, 67–71
  spatial occasions *vs.,* 67
artifacts as occasions for remembering
  designed, 67–70
  used, 67, 70–71, 71*n*1
artifacts designed as occasions for remembering
  institutions and, 68–70
  MidWest and, 68–70
  photo albums as, 67–68
artifacts used as occasions for remembering, 67
  MidWest and, 70–71, 71*n*1
automobile insurance, MidWest, 17–18, 19
averted disaster stories, 82, 83, 84

bard, 56, 137
Basso, Keith H., 65–67

Biggart, Nicole Woolsey, 23
Bonanno, Bill, 51–52
brigand wars, 64–65
business/management studies
    institutional remembering and, 10
    the past and, 10
business stories
    in institutional retold tales, 82–83, 85, 86
    of MidWest, 85–86
    origin stories and, 85
    risk in, 85
    success stories and, 85, 86

canon
    literary, 87
    open vs. closed, 87–88, 223
    oral, 87
    religious, 87, 88
    textual, 87
Cappelli, Peter, 162
careers, paradigmatic narratives and, 159–66
causes, as lieux de mémoire, 59
change stories
    in institutional retold tales, 83
    of MidWest, 83–84, 108, 109–10
children
    induction into textual communities of,
        172
    second-person narratives for, 75–76
choice
    narratives and, 7
    personal identity and employment, 7
citation
    in intertextuality, 178–79
    intertextuality and direct, 177–78
    quotation vs., 177–78
clients. See also MidWest clients
    agents and, 20, 25, 28–29
coherence
    in individual's life story, 4–5
    as property of texts, 4–5
collective memory. See group memory
community, 170. See also textual
    communities
comparison of accounts
    counterstories and, 200
    MidWest stories and, 199
    silences and, 198–99
competition, MidWest management
    fostering of, 31–32

complete tellings. See MidWest history
    complete tellings
confidentiality, ethical issues and, 39–41
consultants, 36. See also corporate fieldwork
continuity, MidWest and, 9–10
contract. See independent contractors;
    MidWest agents new contract
convention, sales, 49–50
conversation analysis, 167
    silences and, 197–98
conversations
    institutions and, 45
    narratives in, 45
conversion
    politics and, 175
    religion and, 172–74, 175–76
conversion stories
    induction into textual communities and,
        172–74, 175–76
    religion and, 172–74, 175–76
core institutional memory
    MidWest history versions and, 94, 95
core story stock
    institutional identity and institutional, 110
    institutional retold tales and, 89, 122
    of institutions, 89, 110, 122, 222–23
    MidWest history versions and MidWest,
        223
corporate fieldwork
    epistemological issues in, 35, 36–37
    ethical issues in, 35, 38–39, 40
    at MidWest, 35–43
    MidWest agents and, 39, 41
    MidWest management and, 39, 41
    MidWest managers and, 39
    narrative collection in, 35–36
    practical issues in, 35
    privacy in, 41
counterstories
    comparison of accounts and, 200
    institutions and, 201–2
    about MidWest, 202
    politics and, 200–201
    silences and, 197, 200–202
critique
    in intertextuality, 186–89
    in MidWest agents stories, 187–88, 189
    in MidWest managers stories, 188
    rejection and, 191
cultural memory, 13

current teller's stories, prior texts and, 169
current texts
    intertextuality and, 169
    MidWest agents stories as, 169
    MidWest managers stories as, 169

Danziger, Murray Herbert, 173
databases
    institutional remembering and, 12
    narrative, 12
disability insurance, MidWest, 17
discourse unit, paradigmatic narratives as,
    148–49
district managers. See MidWest district
    managers

economics, of MidWest agent/manager
    personal relations, 29–30
employee, free agent vs., 160–62
employment, membership and, 7
entrepreneurship
    agents and, 23
    MidWest agents stories of, 181–82
epics
    MidWest stories and, 193
    textual communities and, 193–94, 194n1
epistemological issues, in corporate
    fieldwork, 35, 36–37
erasure
    politics and, 207–8
    silences and, 206–8
ethical issues
    confidentiality and, 39–41
    in corporate fieldwork, 35, 38–39, 40
    IRL and, 42
    publishing study findings as, 41
ethnographic fieldwork. See also corporate
    fieldwork
    at MidWest, 36–39, 41
ethnographic methodology, for MidWest,
    15–16
evaluation. See also parallel evaluations;
    present evaluations
    intertextuality of, 179–80
    of MidWest founder's story, 180
    narrative and, 179
    similarities of MidWest history versions,
    96
    working the past and past/present
    comparison, 3

events. See historical events; seasonal
    recurring events
Everyman. See also paradigmatic narratives
    exemplary narratives of, 141
    paradigmatic narratives and, 141, 223
evolutionary narratives, heroic narratives
    vs., 83
exemplary narratives. See also paradigmatic
    narratives
    of Everyman, 141
    paradigmatic narratives and, 141, 142
exemplary triumph stories
    in institutional retold tales, 84
    of MidWest, 84
experience. See personal experience

family. See also MidWest as family
    memory, 13
    MidWest agents stories and, 180,
    182–86
    values, 180
Fernandez, James, 55
fictive kin ties
    in MidWest agent/manager personal
    relations, 30
fieldwork. See corporate fieldwork
first-person
    narrative of personal experience, 74–75
    plural, 74
    plural "we" in retold tales, 79
    story narrator vs. protagonist, 74
floating gap, 80
folklore, 46
founder stories. See also MidWest founder's
    story
    founder's paradox in institutional retold
    tales, 81–82, 85
    of universities, 81–82
framing
    of retold tales, 78
    story, 89
Frankel, Barbara, 41
free agent, employee vs., 160–62
Full-Time Agent concept, 83
    in MidWest history versions, 105–6

Gesar epic, 138–139
grammatical person, 74
Great Divide theory, 136–37
group life story, 5

group memory
    narrative function in, 6
    in past representations, 13–14
    social science and, 9
group stories
    groups of people and, 224
    membership in, 7

Haitian Revolution, 207–8
Harding, Susan Friend, 175
health insurance, 16
    MidWest, 17
heritage, history *vs.,* 63–64
heroic narratives
    evolutionary narratives *vs.,* 83
    of MidWest, 83
high school reunions
    past remembering at, 53–55
    present evaluations at, 55
historical events, 47, 48
    detemporalization of, 49
historical museums, 60
history. *See also* oral history
    heritage *vs.,* 63–64
    institutional memory and, 45
    Jewish, 48–49
    memory and, 8–9, 59–60
    oral history and, 9, 45
    past and, 8–9
    referencing as temporally irregular event
        used for remembering, 58
    silences in, 196–97, 207–8
    subjectivity of, 8–9
    victors writing of, 8–9
    written, 45
home insurance, MidWest, 17–18, 19

IBM, 81
identity
    institutional memory and, 111
    of institutions, 221
    membership types and, 6
    memory and, 221–24
    MidWest agents, 164–65
    MidWest core memory and, 110
    narratives and, 3–4, 224
    personal, 7, 221, 224
    stories and, 221
    working the past and stable narrative
        of, 3

implicational hierarchy, of retold tales, 81,
    81*n*1, 88
independent contractors, agents as, 22–24,
    25, 163
individual life story, 6, 72, 90
    coherence in, 4–5
    as individual construction, 5
    interviews and, 5
    MidWest history complete tellings and, 90
    narratives and, 72
    property of, 4–5
    as social construction, 5
individual memory, 13
    in institutional remembering, 11
individual stories
    institutional narratives and, 90, 224
    within institutions, 14
    intertextuality of, 195
    in textual communities, 194–95, 223–24
induction, as occasions for remembering,
    51–53
Institute for Research on Learning (IRL), 6
    ethical issues and, 42
    MidWest and, 15
    retold tales, 78–79
    unusual terms at, 57–58
institution(s). *See also* specific institution
        topics
    artifacts designed as occasions for
        remembering and, 68–70
    conversations and, 45
    core story stock of, 89, 110, 122, 222–23
    counterstories and, 201–2
    identity of, 221
    individual stories within, 14
    institutional narratives from outside, 90
    meanings of, 7–8
    memory and, 10–11, 73
    narrative remembering and, 3, 4
    narratives and, 3–4, 44, 45, 46, 72, 123,
        172, 196
    occasions for narrative remembering and,
        53–55, 71
    organization *vs.,* 7–8
    repeated narratives and, 72
    silences in, 198–206, 207, 224
    stories and, 72, 73, 110–11, 221
    storytelling in, 45, 202–3
    working the past in, 3, 14, 72
institutional artifacts, 68–71

institutional identity
  institutional core story stock and, 110
  narratives and, 110
  personal identity and, 221
institutional memory, 14. *See also*
    institutional remembering; MidWest
    core memory
  active/working, 73
  core, 94, 95
  history and, 45
  identity and, 111
  institutional retold tales and, 80, 84
  in insurance companies, 84
  narratives used in, 202
  organizational memory *vs.,* 8
  single *vs.* multiple, 90
  stories and, 111
  third-person narratives and, 77
institutional narratives. *See also* institutional
    retold tales
  evolutionary, 83
  heroic, 83
  individual stories and, 90, 224
  not told, 196
  from outside institutions, 90
  outside its boundaries, 196
  personal identity and, 224
  retold, 72–73
institutional past representations, 13, 45, 46
  story teller position towards, 89, 90
institutional remembering. *See also*
    institutional memory
  appropriate, 8
  business/management studies and, 10
  choice of term, 7–8
  databases and, 12
  individual memory in, 11
  institutional retold tales and, 89, 222
  mandated policies/procedures in, 13
  modes of, 11–12
  narratives and, 4, 8, 44
  occasions for telling stories and, 44, 222
  repeated narratives and, 72
  stories and occasions for, 72
  working the past and, 72
  written records and, 12
institutional retold tales, 73
  averted disaster stories in, 82, 83, 84
  business stories in, 82–83, 85, 86
  change stories in, 83–84

  choosing, 79–85
  core story stock and, 89, 122
  differences between institutions in, 79–80
  exemplary triumph stories in, 84
  founder's story in, 81–82, 85
  implicational hierarchy of, 81, 81*n*1, 88
  institutional memory and, 80, 84
  institutional remembering and, 89, 222
  insurance companies and, 80–81, 84
  master narratives and, 86
  McBee/editor story versions and, 135–40
  of MidWest, 80, 82, 83–84, 85–86, 87,
    88, 89
  narrative patterns in, 85–86
  oral canon and, 87
  origin stories in, 81, 84, 85
  risk in, 85
  story teller position towards, 89
  success stories in, 85, 86
  technology companies and, 80–81
  turning point stories in, 81, 82
  types/ordering of, 81, 81*n*1, 82, 84
institutional stories. *See* institutional narratives
institutional work, stories and, 110–12
insurance. *See* specific insurance topics
  stories and, 112–13
  types/comparisons of, 17–18
insurance business
  MidWest founder and, 98–99
  MidWest history versions and, 98–99,
    121–22
insurance companies, 15
  agents relations with, 22–24
  institutional memory in, 84
  institutional retold tales and, 80–81, 84
  MidWest as multiline, 17–19, 20–21
  multiline, 17–19, 20–21, 26, 83
  risk and, 85
  technology companies *vs.,* 80–81
insurance industry, 15, 16
interdiscursivity, 168
Internet
  narratives, 45
  past representations and, 45
intertextuality. *See also* specific text or
    textual topics
  citation in, 178–79
  critique in, 186–89
  current texts and, 169
  direct citation and, 177–78

intertextuality (*continued*)
  of evaluation, 179–80
  of individual stories, 195
  interdiscursivity and, 168
  irony in, 189–90
  literary studies and, 168, 177
  meaning of, 168
  of MidWest agents stories, 177–78,
    179–92
  MidWest founder's story and, 179
  of MidWest managers stories, 177–78,
    179, 186
  of MidWest stories, 176–94
  of MidWest textual community, 177,
    192–93
  originality and, 168
  parallel evaluations in, 179–80, 181
  prior texts and, 169, 170, 177–78
  quotation in, 178–79
  rejection in, 191
  textual communities and, 167, 169–70,
    192
interviews, individual life story and, 5
IRL. *See* Institute for Research on
    Learning
irony
  in intertextuality, 189–90
  in MidWest agents stories, 189–90

Jewish history, 48–49

Kornman, Robin, vii, 138–39
Kristeva, Julia, 168

Labov, William, 75, 179
Levi, Carlo, 64–65
lieux de mémoire, 59
life insurance
  MidWest history versions and, 121–22
  moral issues in, 19–22, 29
  permanent, 18, 21–22
  term, 18, 21–22
life insurance, MidWest, 17, 18–19, 20–21,
    22
  MidWest agent/manager personal
    relations and, 29–30
life story. *See* group life story; individual
    life story
linguistics
  anthropology and, 46

differences between McBee/editor story
    versions, 129–33
  narratives and, 45
  oral narratives and, 167
  taxonomy and, 46
  universals, 81n1
Lin, Maya, 60
literary canon textual communities, 170–71
literary studies, intertextuality and, 168
Lord, Albert, 56
Lowenthal, David, 63

Mafia induction narrative, 51–53
management. *See also* MidWest
    management
  agents and, 17–18, 19, 23, 25, 27, 28
marketing partnership, 23
master narratives
  institutional retold tales and, 86
  and MidWest, 86
McBee/editor story version(s), 123, 125–26
  argument structure differences in, 133
  common features of, 127–28
  comparison of, 127–35, 223
  evaluative structure differences in, 133–35
  evidential markers in, 129–32
  institutional retold tales and, 135–40
  linguistic differences between, 129–33
  oral *vs.* written narratives and, 135–40
  positioning differences of, 128–29
  textual history of, 124
  word choice/syntax differences in, 132
McBee/editor story version 1, memoir, 123,
    124–25
McBee/editor story version 2, newsletter,
    123, 125–26
McBee/editor story version 3, oral, 123,
    126–27
McBee, George, 82, 84. *See also* specific
    McBee or MidWest founder topics
  MidWest history versions about, 97–101,
    107
medical insurance. *See* health insurance
membership
  employment and, 7
  in group stories, 7
  of MidWest, 7
  secondary socialization and, 7
  types and identity, 6
  voluntary *vs.* involuntary, 6–7

memorial artifacts, 67–71
memorials, 67
  as places designed as occasions for
    remembering, 60–63
  Vietnam Veterans Memorial Wall, 60–61
  World Trade Center site and, 61–62
  World War I veterans antiwar ceremonies
    at war, 61–62
memory. *See also* specific types of memory
  active/working, 73
  history and, 8–9, 59–60
  identity and, 221–24
  institutions and, 10–11, 73
  past representations and active, 44
mentors, agents and, 27
MidWest. *See* MidWest Insurance Company
MidWest agent(s), 22–23, 24, 27–28. *See
    also* agents; specific MidWest agent
    topics
  1990s natural disasters and, 114–15
  change stories involving, 83–84, 108,
    109–10
  competition of, 25–26
  corporate fieldwork and, 39, 41
  identity and, 164–65
  MidWest clients and, 28–29, 178–79
  MidWest management and, 23, 26, 27, 28,
    31, 33, 163–64, 165
  MidWest managers and, 29–32, 33
  MidWest textual community and, 171,
    172, 176, 177
  paradigmatic narratives and, 142, 143,
    144–59, 163–65
  World War II difficulties/company saving
    and, 114
MidWest agent/client personal relations,
    28–29
MidWest agent/manager personal relations,
    29
  economics of, 29–30
  fictive kin ties in, 30
  MidWest life insurance and, 29–30
MidWest agents new contract
  economics of, 32–33
  MidWest management and, 32–33
  MidWest managers and, 33–34
  past remembering and, 34
  present evaluations and, 34, 35
  reaction to, 34–35
MidWest agents stories

critique in, 187–88, 189
as current texts, 169
of entrepreneurship, 181–82
family and, 180, 182–86
of induction into MidWest textual
  community, 186, 191–92, 193
intertextuality of, 177–78, 179–92
irony in, 189–90
MidWest as family and, 184–85
MidWest founder's story and, 169, 179
MidWest textual community and, 177,
  186
risk in, 180–81
values in, 186
MidWest antidiscrimination lawsuit
  comparison to public record, 214
  silences and, 208–15, 216
MidWest as family, 85–86, 180
  MidWest agents stories and, 184–85
  MidWest history versions of, 106–7
MidWest clients. *See also* clients; MidWest
    agent/client personal relations
  MidWest agents and, 28–29, 178–79
MidWest core memory, 90. *See also* specific
    MidWest history version topics
  1990s internal changes and, 109–10
  1990s natural disasters and, 108
  identity and, 110
  of MidWest founder, 97–101
  MidWest history versions and, 91,
    97–110
  MidWest recent stories and, 108
  MidWest stories and, 115
  story teller positions and, 115
MidWest core story stock, 89, 113
  MidWest history versions and, 122
  positioning and, 122
  story teller positions and, 122
MidWest district managers, 29–30
  external recruitment by, 31
MidWest founder. *See also* specific McBee
    or MidWest founder topics
  insurance business and, 98–99
  MidWest core memory of, 97–101
  MidWest history versions about, 97–101,
    107
  MidWest stories and, 113
MidWest founder's story, 82, 85. *See also*
    founder stories
  evaluations of, 180

MidWest founder's story (*continued*)
  induction into MidWest textual
    community, 176
  intertextuality and, 179
  MidWest agents stories and, 169, 179
  MidWest managers stories and, 169, 179
  as prior texts, 169
MidWest history. *See also* MidWest history
    version topics
  multiple versions of, 89, 90
MidWest history complete tellings. *See also*
    MidWest history version(s)
  individual life story and, 90
MidWest history version(s), 90, 223. *See
    also* MidWest core memory; specific
    MidWest history version topics
  MidWest authorized history/founder bio,
    91
  MidWest private founder memoir, 92
  MidWest newsletter articles, 92–93
  MidWest headquarters trainer's speech,
    93–94
  MidWest district manager interview,
    93–94
  1990s internal changes and, 109–10
  1990s natural disasters and, 108–9
  comparison method of, 94–97
  core institutional memory and, 94, 95
  differences between, 96
  evaluation similarities of, 96
  of Full-Time Agent concept, 105–6
  historical verifiability of, 95
  insurance business and, 98–99, 121–22
  life insurance and, 121–22
  main headquarters building in, 102
  of MidWest as family, 106–7
  MidWest core memory and, 91, 97–110
  MidWest core story stock and, 122, 223
  MidWest expansion to other states in,
    102
  about MidWest founder, 97–101, 107
  MidWest ruling dynasties entry in, 101
  million auto policies goal in, 102–3
  point-of-view issues in, 96–97
  positioning of, 116–22
  prior texts and, 169, 193
  recent stories and, 108–10
  story teller positions and, 91, 116–22
  World War II difficulties/company saving
    in, 103–5

MidWest history, authorized history/founder
    bio, 91
  of Full-Time Agent concept, 105
  MidWest founder in, 99, 100
  positioning of, 116–17
  World War II difficulties/company saving
    in, 103
MidWest history, private founder memoir, 92
  MidWest founder in, 99, 100–101
  positioning of, 117
MidWest history, newsletter articles, 92–93
  of Full-Time Agent concept, 105
  MidWest founder in, 99
  positioning of, 117–18
MidWest history, headquarters trainer's
    speech, 93
  1990s natural disasters and, 108–9
  of Full-Time Agent concept, 105–6
  MidWest founder in, 100
  positioning of, 118
  World War II difficulties/company saving
    in, 103–4
MidWest history, district manager interview,
    93–94
  of Full-Time Agent concept, 105–6
  MidWest founder in, 100
  positioning of, 119
  World War II difficulties/company saving
    in, 103–4
MidWest Insurance Company (MidWest),
    6–7. *See also* specific MidWest topics
  artifacts designed as occasions for
    remembering and, 68–70
  artifacts used as occasions for
    remembering and, 70–71, 71n1
  business stories of, 85–86
  change stories of, 83–84, 108, 109–10
  continuity and, 9–10
  conventions as regular occasions for
    narration at, 49–50
  corporate fieldwork at, 35–43
  counterstories about, 202
  ethnographic fieldwork at, 36–39, 41
  ethnographic study methodology for,
    15–16
  exemplary triumph stories of, 84
  heroic narratives of, 83
  institutional past representations of, 90
  institutional retold tales of, 80, 82, 83–84,
    85–86, 87, 88, 89

IRL and, 15
master narratives and, 86
membership of, 7
MidWest founder's story of, 82, 85
as multiline insurance company, 17–19,
    20–21, 83
narrative use of, 9–10
oral canon of, 87–88
organization of, 16–17
origin stories of, 85
paradigmatic narratives and, 141, 142,
    143, 144–59, 163–66
places designed as occasions for
    remembering and, 63–64
risk at, 85, 180–81
story teller positions within, 90
success story of, 86
temporally irregular events used for
    remembering at, 57, 58
at time of change, 28–35, 43, 108, 109–10
training programs at, 51
unusual terms at, 57
women at, 208–20
MidWest management. *See also*
    management
of agents in district, 31
changes in, 29–32, 109–10
competition/rewards fostering in, 31–32
corporate fieldwork and, 39, 41
internal recruitment by regional, 31
MidWest agents and, 23, 26, 27, 28, 31,
    33, 163–64, 165
MidWest agents new contract and, 32–33
paradigmatic narratives and, 142, 144–53,
    156, 159
single district manager, 31, 32
three-person, 31, 32
MidWest managers, 29. *See also* MidWest
    management
corporate fieldwork and, 39
MidWest agents and, 29–32, 33
MidWest agents new contract and, 33–34
MidWest management and single district,
    31, 32
paradigmatic narratives and, 142, 144–53
MidWest managers stories
critique in, 188
as current texts, 169
of induction into MidWest textual
    community, 186, 191, 193

intertextuality of, 177–78, 179, 186
MidWest founder's story and, 169, 179
MidWest textual community and, 177,
    186
rejection in, 191
values in, 186
MidWest management succession, silences
    and, 216–20
MidWest narratives. *See* MidWest stories
MidWest oppositional agents association,
    215–16
MidWest past representations
complete story in, 90
single event, 90
story teller positions in, 90
two basic forms of, 90
MidWest stories, 186–87. *See also* MidWest
    agents stories; MidWest founder's
    story; MidWest managers stories
comparisons of accounts and, 199
critique in, 186–87
epics and, 193
intertextuality of, 176–94
MidWest core memory and, 115
MidWest founder and, 113
scriptures and, 193
silences and, 197, 198, 199, 202, 204,
    208–20, 224
silences and official, 208–20
values in, 186, 187
work of MidWest and, 112–13
MidWest textual community
intertextuality of, 177
MidWest agents and, 171, 172, 176,
    177, 186
MidWest agents stories and, 177, 186
MidWest managers stories and, 177, 186
MidWest textual community, induction into
MidWest agents stories of, 186, 191–92,
    193
MidWest employees not participating in,
    191–92
MidWest founder's story and, 176
MidWest managers stories of, 186, 191,
    193
religion and, 186
values and, 186
MidWest, work of, MidWest stories and,
    112–13
Miller, Peggy, 75–76

moral issues
  in life insurance, 19–22, 29
  places used as occasions for remembering
    and, 65–67
multiple versions. *See also* MidWest history
    versions
  of MidWest history, 89, 90

narrative(s). *See also* retold tales; specific
    narrative topics
  basic challenge of, 3
  choice and, 7
  collection in corporate fieldwork, 35–36
  in conversations, 45
  databases and, 12
  ephemeral, 72–73
  evaluation and, 179
  first-person, 74–75
  founding, 81
  function in group memory, 6
  identity and, 3–4, 224
  as individual construction, 5
  individual life story and, 72
  institutional identity and, 110
  institutional remembering and, 4, 8, 44
  institutions and, 3–4, 44, 45, 46, 72, 123,
    172, 196
  Internet, 45
  linguistic, 45
  MidWest use of, 9–10
  occasions for, 45
  past representations and, 4, 221
  patterns in institutional retold tales, 85–86
  person, grammatical, of a, 74
  positioning and shaping of, 123
  second-person, 75
  as social construction, 5
  third-person, 74, 75
  used in institutional memory, 202
  visual, 45
narrative induction, 172–73, 191, 193
narrative remembering. *See also* occasions
    for narrative remembering; taxonomy
    of types of occasions for narrative
    remembering
  institutions and, 3, 4
narrative structure, induction into textual
    communities and, 173–74
narrator
  oral narratives and, 74

protagonist *vs.* first-person story, 74
national memory, 13
new teller
  of retold tales, 73–74
  of stories, 73–74
Nora, Pierre, 59–60

Oberman, Ida, 205–6
occasions
  artifacts *vs.* spatial, 67
  for narratives, 45
  for storytelling, 45
occasions for institutional remembering,
    stories and, 72
occasions for narrative remembering, 46.
    See also narrative remembering;
    taxonomy of types of occasions for
    narrative remembering
  induction as, 51–53
  institutions and, 53–55, 71
occasions for telling stories
  institutional remembering and, 44, 222
  as occasions for renarration, 222
  working the past and, 222
offshoring, 161
oppositional agents association, 41, 215–16
oral canon
  institutional retold tales and, 87
  of MidWest, 87–88
oral epics. *See* epics
oral history, history and, 9, 45
oral narratives
  linguistics and, 167
  narrator and, 74
  personal experience and, 75
  taxonomy of, 179
  written narratives and, 44–45, 124
  vs. written narratives and McBee/editor
    story versions, 135–40
orality and literacy, 135–41
organization
  institution *vs.,* 7–8
  meanings of, 7–8
  of MidWest, 16–17
organizational memory
  institutional memory *vs.,* 8
  opinions about, 11
origin stories, 80
  business stories and, 85
  in institutional retold tales, 81, 84, 85

of MidWest, 85
Orr, Julian, 111

paradigmatic narrative(s)
    academics and, 142–44
    careers and, 159–66
    creation of terminology of, 145–47
    discourse unit and, 148–49
    Everyman and, 141, 223
    exemplary narratives and, 141, 142
    of ideal agent's career, 169, 223
    inappropriateness of, 159–63
    meaning of, 141, 142
    MidWest agents and, 142, 143, 144–59,
        163–65
    MidWest and, 141, 142, 143, 144–59,
        163–66
    MidWest management and, 142, 144–53,
        156, 159
    MidWest managers and, 142, 144–53
    rejection of, 191
    risk and, 181
    of The Story of Bob, 151–59, 223
paradigmatic narrative elements, 149
    evaluations of, 150–51
    events in, 150
    MidWest promotion/reward structure as,
        151
    relevance scope of, 150
    story teller as, 150
    storytelling occasions in, 151
parallel evaluations, intertextuality and,
    179–80, 181
the past. *See also* working the past; specific
        past topics
    business/management studies and, 10
    history and, 8–9
    storytelling and, 11
past appropriations, 78
past remembering
    at high school reunions, 53–55
    MidWest agents new contract and, 34
    present evaluations and, 55
past representations. *See also* institutional
        past representations; MidWest past
        representations
    active memory and, 44
    in group memory, 13–14
    Internet and, 45
    narratives and, 4, 221

social/linguistic mechanisms of, 13
    taxonomy of, 46
person
    first, 74
    grammatical, 74
    third, 74
personal experience
    first-person narrative of, 74–75
    oral narratives and, 75
personal identity
    employment choice and, 7
    institutional identity and, 221
    institutional narratives and, 224
Peters, Tom, 160–61
photo albums, 67–68
Pilcher, William W., 201
Pink, Daniel H., 160
places
    sites as, 59
    use of term, 59, 60
places as occasions for remembering, 59
    designed, 59, 60–64
    used, 59, 64–67
places designed as occasions for
        remembering, 59
    memorials/historical museums as, 60–63
    MidWest and, 63–64
    symbolic reproductions/recreations of, 63
places used as occasions for remembering,
    59
    moral issues and, 65–67
    salient, 67
    sites of notable events as, 64–67
Plaskow, Judith, 204
point-of-view
    character/speaker and protagonist, 75
    issues in MidWest history versions, 96–97
Polangi, Livia, 179
policies, institutional remembering and
        mandated, 13
politics
    conversion and, 175
    counterstories and, 200–201
    erasure and, 207–8
    silences and, 200–201, 207–8
position, stance *vs.*, 202–3
positioning. *See also* story teller positions
    differences of McBee/editor story
        versions, 128–29
    event choosing for narration and, 119–21

positioning (*continued*)
  MidWest core story stock and, 122
  of MidWest history versions, 116–22
  rendition and, 115–16
  shaping of narratives and, 123
practical issues, in corporate fieldwork, 35
present evaluations
  at high school reunions, 55
  MidWest agents new contract and,
    34, 35
  past remembering and, 55
prior texts
  current teller's stories and, 169
  earlier prior texts and, 169
  ideal agent's career paradigmatic narrative
    as, 169
  intertextuality and, 169, 170, 177–78
  MidWest founder's story as, 169
  MidWest history versions and, 169, 193
privacy, in corporate fieldwork, 41
Prost, Antoine, 61
protagonist
  first-person story narrator *vs.,* 74
  point-of-view character/speaker and, 75
publishing study findings, as ethical issue,
  41

quotation
  citation *vs.,* 177–78
  in intertextuality, 178–79
quoted speech, in retold tales, 79

record keeping
  advances in, 12–13
  written records and, 12
recruitment, MidWest
  changes in, 31, 32, 110
  district manager external, 31
  diversity lack in, 30–31
  fictive kin ties in, 30
  regional management internal, 31
rejection
  critique and, 191
  in intertextuality, 191
  in MidWest managers stories, 191
  of paradigmatic narrative, 191
religion
  canon of, 87, 88
  conversion and, 172–74, 175–76
  conversion stories and, 172–74, 175–76

  induction into MidWest textual
    communities, 186
  silences and, 204, 206
  textual communities and, 171, 172–74, 186
remembering. *See* specific remembering
  topics
rendition, positioning and, 115–16
repeated narratives. *See also* retold tales
  institutional remembering and, 72
  institutions and, 72
  by nonparticipants, 73
  stories as, 72
retirements, 51
retold tales. *See also* institutional retold
  tales; repeated narratives; stories
  description of action/feelings/character
    motives in, 79
  exploration of characters point-of-view
    in, 79
  first-person plural "we" in, 79
  framing of, 78
  identifying, 73
  IRL, 78–79
  meaning of, 72, 74, 77–78
  new teller/nonparticipant of, 73–74
  quoted speech in, 79
  relevance of past to present in, 79
reward structure, 151
Riddy, Felicity, 170
risk
  in business stories, 85
  in institutional retold tales, 85
  insurance companies and, 85
  at MidWest, 85, 180–81
  in MidWest agents stories, 180–81
  paradigmatic narratives and, 181

sales agents. *See* agents
scriptures, MidWest stories and, 193
seasonal recurring events, 47, 48
second-person narratives
  for adults, 76
  for children, 75–76
  meaning of, 75
Shakespeare, William, 77
silences
  about wrongdoing, 214–15
  adjacency pairs and, 198
  comparison of accounts and, 198–99
  conversation analysis and, 197–98

counterstories and, 197, 200–202
erasure and, 206–8
expectable stories and, 205–6
external records and, 206
hearable, 197–98
in history, 196–97, 207–8
in institutions, 198–206, 207, 224
MidWest antidiscrimination lawsuit and,
    208–15, 216
MidWest managerial succession and,
    216–20
MidWest official stories and, 208–20
MidWest oppositional agents association
    and, 215–16
MidWest stories and, 197, 198, 199, 202,
    204, 208–20, 224
noisy, 197
people leaving institutions and, 204–5
politics and, 200–201, 207–8
recognizing, 197–206
religion and, 204, 206
terminology of, 196
unofficial stories and, 197, 198
as work of comparisons, 197
sites, as places, 59
sites of notable events
    Apaches and, 65–67
    Italian brigand wars and, 64–65
socialization
    as induction into textual communities, 172
    membership and secondary, 7
social science, group memory and, 9
speaker, point-of-view character/protagonist
    and, 75
stance. *See also* positioning; story teller
    positions
    position *vs.,* 202–3
Stanford, Jane Lathrop, 81
Star Trek, 170
Steiner, Rudolph, 205–6
Stock, Brian, 170
story(ies). *See also* institutional retold tales;
    retold tales; silences; specific story
    topics
    ephemeral, 73
    expectable, 205–6
    first-person, 74
    framing, 89
    identity and, 221
    institutional memory and, 111

and institutional work, 110–12
institutions and, 72, 73, 110–11, 221
insurance and, 112–13
nonparticipant/new teller/appropriated,
    73–74
not told, 196
occasions for institutional remembering
    and, 72
as repeated narratives, 72
story teller choice of, 89
unofficial, 197, 198
work and, 110–12
The Story of Bob. *See also* paradigmatic
    narrative, 151–59
    as hungry agent, 152
    future inappropriateness of, 159–63
    as mature agent, 153
    paradigmatic narrative of, 151–59, 223
    recruitment in, 152
    as senior agent, 153
story teller
    as paradigmatic narrative element, 150
    story choice of, 89
story teller positions, 89. *See also*
    positioning
    external, 89–90
    towards institutional past representations,
        89, 90
    towards institutional retold tales, 89
    internal, 90
    MidWest core memory and, 115
    MidWest core story stock and, 122
    MidWest history versions and, 91, 116–22
    in MidWest past representations, 90
    official, 89, 90
    semiofficial/personal, 89
    unofficial/oppositional, 89, 90
storytelling. *See also* occasions for telling
    stories
    conventions of, 75
    in institutions, 45, 202–3
    occasions for, 45
    occasions in paradigmatic narrative
        elements, 151
    the past and, 11
structuralism, 46
success stories
    business stories and, 85, 86
    in institutional retold tales, 85, 86
    of MidWest, 86

taxonomy
  anthropology and, 46
  cultural embeddedness and, 46
  linguistics and, 46
  of oral narratives, 179
  of past representations, 46
  as speaker's knowledge, 46
taxonomy of types of occasions for narrative
    remembering, 46, 47 t. *See also*
    narrative remembering; occasions
    for narrative remembering
  artifacts as occasions for remembering in,
    67–71
  design intention axis of, 47
  modality axis of, 46–47
  places as occasions for remembering in,
    59–67
  temporally irregular events in, 50–58
  temporally marked occasions in, 47–50
technological determinism, 13
technology companies
  institutional retold tales and, 80–81
  insurance companies *vs.,* 80–81
teller. *See* new teller; story teller
temporally irregular events, 50
  creating the institution by remembering
    it in, 53–55
  designed for remembering, 51–53
  used for remembering, 55–58
temporally irregular events used for
    remembering, 55
  at MidWest, 57, 58
  traveling bards as, 56
  unusual terms as, 56–58
temporally marked occasions
  designed for remembering, 47–49
  temporally regular events used for
    remembering in, 49–50
temporally regular textual rituals, 48
texts. *See also* intertextuality; specific text or
    textual topics
  coherence as property of, 4–5
textual communities, 48
  epics and, 193–94, 194n1
  individual stories in, 194–95, 223–24
  intertextuality and, 167, 169–70, 192
  literary canon, 170–71
  meaning of, 170–71
  religion and, 171, 172–73, 186
  strong, 170–71

weak, 170, 171
textual communities, induction into, 167
  of adults, 172
  of children, 172
  conversion stories and, 172–74, 175–76
  means of, 171–72
  narrative structure and, 173–74
  religion and, 172–74
  as socialization, 172
third-person
  plural, 74
  singular, 74
third-person narratives, 74, 75, 78
  institutional memory and, 77
  nature of knowledge in, 77
  types of, 77
training programs, at MidWest, 51
traveling minstrels, 56
Traweek, Sharon, 143–44
Trend, M. G., 41
Trouillot, Michel-Rolph, 196, 207–8
turning point stories, in institutional retold
    tales, 81, 82
Tyson, Eric, 21–22

Ungson, Gerardo Rivera, 11
universities
  changes in, 161–62
  founder stories of, 81–82
unusual terms, 56
  at IRL, 57–58
  at MidWest, 57
U.S. corporations, 49
USSR, 207

values
  family, 180
  induction into MidWest textual
    communities and shared, 186
  in MidWest stories, 186, 187
Vansina, Jan, 9, 79
Vietnam Veterans Memorial Wall, 60–61
Vinitzky-Seroussi, Vered, 53–54, 55

Waldorf Education, 6, 205–6
Walsh, James P., 11
women, MidWest antidiscrimination lawsuit
    by, 208–15, 216
work
  stories and, 110–12

stories and institutional, 110–12
working the past
  to establish stable narrative of identity, 3
  indicating history's divine purpose in, 3
  institutional remembering and, 72
  in institutions, 3, 14, 72
  legitimacy of authority establishment in, 3
  meaning of, 3, 72
  occasions for telling stories and, 222
  ownership claiming in, 3
  past/present comparison evaluation in, 3
  political/intellectual priority claiming
    in, 3
  stability establishment in, 3
World Trade Center site, 61–62

World War I veterans, 61–62
written history, 45
written narratives
  oral narratives and, 44–45, 124
  vs. oral narratives and McBee/editor story
    versions, 135–40
written records
  institutional remembering and, 12
  record keeping and, 12

Xerox Corporation, 82–83

Yerushalmi, Yosef Hayim, 48–49

Zeliser, Viviana A. Rotman, 20